Writing and Defending Your Expert Report
The Step-by-Step Guide with Models

Steven Babitsky, Esq.
James J. Mangraviti, Jr., Esq.

SEAK, Inc.
Legal and Medical Information Systems

Falmouth, Massachusetts

Writing and Defending Your Expert Report: The Step-by-Step Guide with Models
Copyright © 2002 by SEAK, Inc.
ISBN: 1-892904-21-7

CONTENTS

Acknowledgments

The authors wish to acknowledge the following persons whose assistance in the production of this book was invaluable: Robert Allen, PhD; Terrance L. Baker, MD; Christopher R. Brigham, MD; Richard Carman; Mary Cataudella, Esq.; Donald Clark, PE; Nancy Coffone; Eugene A. Cook, Esq.; Malin Dollinger, MD, FACP; Paul Dorf, APD; Beatrice Engstrand, MD; Sheri Estes, RN; Vince Gallagher; Richard S. Goodman, MD; Andrew E. Greenberg, Esq.; Tom Gutheil, MD; Captain John Hardin; William G. Hime; Keith Kasper, Esq.; H. Boulter Kelsey, Jr., PE; Robert L. Klein; Kathy Lamson; William C. Lanham, Esq.; William Lewis, MD, PC; Kenneth MacKenzie, MCBA; James Marsh; Daniel Pacheco, PE; Lloyd J. Patton; Robert W. Powitz, PhD, MPH, RS, DLAAS, ACD, DABFET; Martha Sorensen, PhD; Leslie D. Star, PhD; Johann Szautner, PE; Christopher J. Todd, JD; and David C. Toppino, MA.

Related Products by SEAK, Inc.

TEXTS
The Independent Medical Examination Report
How to Excel During Cross-Examination
The Comprehensive IME System
The Successful Physician Negotiator
How to Excel During Depositions
The Comprehensive Forensic Services Manual

SEMINARS
Testifying Skills Workshop
How to Be an Effective Medical Witness
SEAK Law School for Physicians™
Malpractice Survival Training for Physicians
How to Be a Successful Independent Medical Examiner
SEAK Negotiating Skills for Physicians™
SEAK Business School for Physicians™
National Expert Witness and Litigation Seminar

AUDIOTAPE PROGRAMS
Achieving Success as a Medical Witness
How to Be a Successful Independent Medical Examiner
Marketing Your Forensic Practice
Law School for Experts

VIDEOTAPES
The Expert Deposition: How to Be an Effective and Ethical Witness
Winning Over the Jury: Techniques for Experts That Work
Symptom Magnification, Malingering, and Deception
Cross-Examination of the Expert
The Most Difficult Questions for Experts: With Answers

DIRECTORIES
SEAK, Inc. National Directory of Independent Medical Examiners
 (www.imenet.com)
SEAK, Inc. National Directory of Medical Experts™
 (www.seakmedexperts.com)

For more information call SEAK at 508/457-1111. Inquiries may also be addressed to SEAK, Inc. at P.O. Box 729, Falmouth, MA 02541. Fax 508/540-8304; e-mail address: seakinc@aol.com; Internet address: http://www.seak.com

About the Authors

Steven Babitsky, JD, is the President of SEAK, Inc. He was a personal injury trial attorney for twenty years and is the former managing partner of the firm Kistin, Babitsky, Latimer & Beitman. Mr. Babitsky is the co-author of the texts *How to Excel During Cross-Examination: Techniques for Experts That Work, The Comprehensive Forensic Services Manual: The Essential Resources for All Experts,* and *How to Excel During Depositions: Techniques for Experts That Work.* Attorney Babitsky is the co-developer and trainer for the "How to Be an Effective Medical Witness" seminar, the seminar leader for the National Expert Witness and Litigation Seminar, and the scriptwriter for the videos "How to Be an Effective Medical Witness" and "The Expert Medical Deposition: How to Be an Effective and Ethical Witness." Mr. Babitsky trains hundreds of experts every year.

James J. Mangraviti, Jr., JD, has trained hundreds of expert witnesses across the United States and Canada. He is a former trial lawyer with experience in defense and plaintiff personal injury law and insurance law. He currently serves as Vice President and General Counsel of SEAK, Inc. Mr. Mangraviti received his BA degree in mathematics *summa cum laude* from Boston College and his JD degree *cum laude* from Boston College Law School. His publications include the texts *SEAK Law School for Physicians, Law School for the Safety and Health Professional, The Independent Medical Examination Report: A Step-by-Step Guide with Models, The Successful Physician Negotiator: How to Get What You Deserve, How to Excel During Cross-Examination: Techniques for Experts That Work, How to Excel During Depositions: Techniques for Experts That Work,* and *The Comprehensive Forensic Services Manual: The Essential Resources for All Experts.*

Preface

Over the past several years we have traveled across the United States and trained thousands of professionals in testifying skills and in how to be more effective, ethical expert witnesses. We try to make our training as realistic as possible. One technique we use to do this involves cross-examining experts on actual reports used in closed cases.

We have, unfortunately, found far too many poorly written expert reports. These reports needlessly open up the expert to devastating cross-examination. Our clients have requested a comprehensive text to assist them in writing high-quality and defensible expert reports. This work is the text that they have requested.

There are innumerable ways to draft high-quality, defensible expert reports. Perhaps the best place to start is by looking at some other well-written reports. Appendix B provides examples of some of the better reports we have come across. The reader can get good ideas on formatting, style, and content from these reports. A highly defensible report can then be drafted by following the advice contained in the chapters of this work, which are summarized in chapter 1.

As in our previous works, we get directly to the point, use numerous examples, and make this an easy-to-use reference text. The examples show why the language was effective or why it was problematic, the consequences thereof, and how the language could have been improved easily. We have also listened to our clients and, for the first time, have dedicated an entire chapter to how to defeat the cross-examining attorney's tactics. Your feedback is always welcome.

Steven Babitsky, Esq.
James J. Mangraviti, Jr., Esq.

SEAK, Inc.
P.O. Box 729
Falmouth, MA 02541
Phone: (508) 457-1111
Fax: (508) 540-8304
www.seak.com

Chapter 1 Introduction

1.1 Why Counsel May Want a Written Report

There are many reasons counsel may want an expert to draft a written report. These include the following.

- A written report may be required by the court or forum where the litigation is pending. For example, written reports are required in all civil cases in federal court under Federal Rule of Civil Procedure 26(2)(B), unless otherwise stipulated or directed by the court.
- Counsel may want a written report to assist in settlement negotiations. A well-written and soundly reasoned report will improve the settlement value of a case.
- A well-written expert report, in the form of an affidavit signed under the pains and penalties of perjury, may be needed in support of or in opposition to a motion for summary judgment.
- In some arbitration proceedings or bench trials, experts may be required to present their direct testimony via a written report signed under the pains and penalties of perjury.
- Expert reports that are marked and introduced into evidence as exhibits may go to the jury room. Jurors normally are permitted to take into the jury room for their deliberation all exhibits in evidence.[1]

1.2 The Importance of a Well-written Report

The expert's report will become a crucially important document in any contested legal proceeding. **The expert report will also become a permanent part of the expert's "record."** A poorly written report can and will be used to impeach the credibility of the expert for years to come. Conversely, a well-written report may lead to future referrals. It is, therefore, very important that reports are drafted carefully. Experts need to take whatever time is necessary to do this.

1.3 The Golden Rule of Expert Report Writing

The law of the discoverability of expert reports is discussed in detail in chapter 2. It provides some protections from discovery for certain expert reports. However, experts need to assume that anything they write will be discoverable and will end up in front of the jury. This assumption leads us to the golden rule of expert report writing: **Experts should never, under any**

---

[1] *Kuta v. Newberg,* 600 N.W.2d. 280 (1999).

circumstances, create any written reports unless specifically instructed to do so by retaining counsel.

1.4 Legal Requirements

Chapter 3 discusses in detail the legal requirements concerning the format and content of expert reports. Experts should coordinate with counsel to ensure that their reports comply with all applicable legal standards. Rule 26 reports must contain the following:

- a complete statement of all opinions to be expressed,
- the basis and reasons for the opinions,
- the data or other information considered,
- any exhibits to be used in summary of the opinions,
- any exhibits to be used as support for the opinions,
- the qualifications of the witness,
- a list of all publications authored by the witness in the preceding ten years,
- the compensation to be paid for the study and testimony, and
- a listing of any other cases in which the witness has testified as an expert at trial or by deposition within the preceding four years.[2]

Reports prepared to support or oppose motions for summary judgment must meet the following requirements:

- the report needs to properly address the key factual issues in dispute in the case upon which the motion for summary judgment will be decided by the court (for example, causation or breach of standard of care),
- the report needs to be signed by the expert under the pains and penalties of perjury, and
- the report needs to be prepared and signed within the applicable time deadlines.

1.5 Working with Counsel

If opposing counsel can show that retaining counsel improperly influenced the expert's report, the expert will lose credibility and the report will be discredited. This is easily done where the expert circulates a draft report and retaining counsel suggests "improvements" or "corrections" to the report. Draft reports are discoverable. **It is, therefore, the best practice for the expert to avoid producing any draft written reports and to refuse to let**

---

[2] Fed. R. Civ. Pro. 26(2)(B).

counsel influence the fundamental substance of the expert's findings, conclusions, and reasoning.

A conference with counsel, either on the telephone or, preferably, in person, should be the expert's first step prior to preparing any reports. At this initial conference with counsel, the expert will want to determine:

- if a report is being requested,
- the type of report sought by counsel,
- the issues to be covered in the report,
- how the report is to be formatted,
- the factual assumptions to be relied upon,
- the opinions the expert will offer,
- the proposed language of the opinions, and
- any questions the expert might have.

The format of the final report can be covered during this "expert conference." Each expert should come to the meeting with an outline of how the report is to be formatted, including detailing the separate sections and findings of fact and opinions. The attorney must take this opportunity to act as advisor and counselor.[3]

Experts are also well advised not to write any reports until they have confidence in their conclusions.

> Experts must be cautioned to not reduce any of their work to a written report until they are sufficiently comfortable with their preliminary conclusions and they have been specifically instructed to do so by counsel. Nothing looks worse at an expert's deposition than conflicting reports. Usually, the conflict is the result of preparing an earlier report based more on speculation than fact. Even though the later report is more accurate, the expert will spend a very long day trying to explain why the earlier report is wrong.[4]

For detailed information on the problems that can arise when counsel assists the expert in preparing the report, please see chapter 4.

1.6 Formatting and Proofing
The value of an expert report is related directly to the report's ability to persuade the lay audience to whom it is directed. The report will be more likely to persuade the reader if it is easy to read and looks professional.

---

[3]Burke, "The Use of Experts in Environmental Litigation, a Practitioner's Guide," 25 N.K6.L. Rev.111 (1997) 136.
[4]Fisher, "Selection, Use and Management of Experts in Environmental Legal Practice," 33 Tulsa L.J. 1003 (1998) 1015.

Proper formatting helps considerably in this regard. The authors recommend the following regarding formatting.

- Use a cover page.
- Use a 12-point font that is easy to read, especially if the report is likely to be faxed.
- Use topic headings to break up the report.
- Use short, concise paragraphs and avoid run-on paragraphs.
- Use 1 ½ lines of space.
- Number the pages in the following way: 1 of 5, 2 of 5, 3 of 5, etc.
- Use an executive summary at the beginning of the report.
- Make sure that summary judgment reports are in the form of an affidavit (i.e., "signed under the pains and penalties of perjury").

Experts need to carefully proof their reports for mistakes. Each mistake made in a report will lessen the expert's credibility. Opposing counsel will argue that if the expert could make one mistake in his report he may have made other mistakes and his entire report may be suspect. Common mistakes to correct in the proofreading process include:

- substantive mistakes,
- bad grammar,
- typographical errors, and
- misspelled words.

Chapter 5 discusses formatting in much greater detail and chapter 15 examines the importance of proofreading.

1.7 Disclosure of Documents Reviewed
All expert reports should explicitly and precisely describe all of the documents, reports, photos, tangible evidence, and depositions that have been reviewed prior to the preparation of the report. The authors recommend the following regarding properly disclosing documents reviewed prior to drafting the report.

- The list should be numbered.
- The documents may be listed alphabetically, chronologically, or according to some natural, logical grouping (for example, all medical reports, all depositions).[5]

---

[5] Thomas G. Gutheil, *The Psychiatrist as Expert Witness* (Washington, DC: American Psychiatric Press, 1998) 104-105.

INTRODUCTION

- All key documents should be reviewed and this review should be documented.
- The following descriptives should be avoided: "including," "including but not limited to," "relevant portions of," and "various."
- Each document should be described precisely, including, where appropriate, date, length, author, and other descriptive information.
- Experts need not make opposing counsel's job easier by explicitly listing documents that were not available for review.

Chapter 6 provides detailed information regarding properly disclosing the precise documents reviewed.

1.8 Qualifications of the Expert

Many expert reports contain a description of the expert's qualifications. Federal Rule of Civil Procedure Rule 26(a)(2)(B) requires Rule 26 expert reports to contain "the qualifications of the witness, including a list of all publications authored by the witness in the preceding ten years." Reports that fail to do so may result in the expert being precluded from testifying.

Many experts attach their qualifications or CV to the end of their reports as addenda. This is perhaps the easiest way to incorporate a description of the expert's qualifications into the expert report.

Qualifications should not be over- or understated. This sounds simple, but can sometimes be quite challenging. The authors recommend the following.

- An expert should make sure to include a copy of her qualifications in the report if this is a legal requirement in the case at hand.
- The statement of qualifications must be 100% accurate.
- Experts should state qualifications objectively and avoid subjective, self-serving statements and characterizations.
- One should not claim as a qualification a degree or designation that sounds like it was earned but, in reality, was bought.
- An expert should be careful when claiming knowledge of the current literature in her field.

Chapter 7 discusses stating the expert's qualifications accurately and objectively.

1.9 Expressing Factual Assumptions

An expert's opinion is only as good as the factual assumptions upon which the expert's opinion is based. These factual assumptions form the foundation of the expert's opinion and should be expressed in the expert report. The authors recommend the following.

- One should describe factual assumptions in a detailed and specific way, not vaguely.
- The report should provide a precise citation to the source of the factual assumptions made. For example, it should include a cite to a specific page in a deposition transcript.
- Experts should not guess regarding factual assumptions. They should avoid terms such as "supposedly," "it has been reported," "is said," "as I understand the facts," and "presumably" in describing factual assumptions.
- The expert should verify as many factual assumptions as possible.
- One should expect counsel to focus on any dates expressed in the report.
- A wise expert bases factual assumptions on reliable information.
- Experts should not rely on unverified information provided by retaining counsel.

Chapter 8 discusses expressing and documenting detailed and specific factual assumptions.

1.10 The Importance of Staying within the Expert's True Area of Expertise

Experts may be tempted to, and often do, opine in areas that are beyond their true areas of expertise. Experts who do this open up themselves and their reports to easy challenge on cross-examination. The authors recommend the following.

- Expert reports should only express opinions that are within the expert's true area of expertise.
- Experts should only use terms for which they know the definition.
- Experts (other than legal experts such as judges and lawyers) should avoid the use of legal terms in reports.
- Experts (other than legal experts such as judges and lawyers) should avoid expressing legal opinions in their reports.
- Unless they are qualified to do so, experts should not opine on cost estimates.

Chapter 9 discusses in detail the importance of staying within the expert's true area of expertise and the consequences of what happens when this advice is not followed.

1.11 Stating Opinions

The main reason an expert is involved in a case is to state his opinion. The only reason an expert writes a report is to communicate his opinion. The opinion should be communicated effectively and expressed in a defensible manner. The authors recommend the following.

- Experts should state all opinions clearly, explicitly, and with confidence.
- One should use the magic words "based upon a reasonable degree of (medical, engineering, legal, accounting, jewelry appraisal, or other field) certainty" or "based on a reasonable degree of (medical, engineering, legal, accounting, jewelry appraisal, or other field) probability" when expressing an opinion in the report.
- It is best to avoid hedge words, such as "it seems," "I think," and "I believe," when expressing opinions in the expert report.
- One should state the reasons that justify the opinion in a concise, bullet-point format.
- Experts should avoid expressing net opinions, that is, bare conclusions without supporting justification.
- It is best to state all of the opinions the expert expects to express at trial.
- The report should document a detailed and reliable methodology so that it will not be challenged under *Daubert.*

Chapter 10 discusses how to properly state an expert's opinions and conclusions in a defensible manner.

1.12 The Importance of Research

Citations to authority that support an expert's opinions will bolster the credibility of the report. Such citations will also greatly increase the chances that the expert's report and opinion will survive a challenge under the *Daubert* line of cases. The authors recommend the following.

- The citations should be detailed and precise. They should include title, author, edition, publisher, and year published.
- A pinpoint cite should be used if specific pages are referenced.
- The expert should be prepared to be cross-examined on any authority cited in the report.

- When an expert fails to search the literature and authority in his report, the testimony may be excluded.
- An expert report is less credible and more vulnerable to cross-examination if it does not cite the supporting literature.
- General statements that the expert's conclusion is supported by the "weight of the literature" or "studies" should be avoided.
- Experts should attempt to use authority that is as recent as possible and avoid the use of dated authority.
- Quoting authority may bolster the report's credibility, but the expert should expect to be questioned closely about the quoted passage.
- Experts should be cautious in describing any authority as being authoritative.

Chapter 11 examines how to use citations to texts, guidelines, codes, articles, and other authority to bolster a report's credibility.

1.13 The Well-written Expert Report
There are numerous techniques that can be utilized to make an expert report well written. The authors recommend the following. One should

- state things clearly and directly,
- not speculate or guess,
- be especially careful about speculating as to future costs or monetary values,
- not use boilerplate language,
- avoid the use of absolute words, such as "always" and "never,"
- make sure the report is not vague, equivocal, or uncertain,
- avoid the use of emphatic language, exclamation points, boldface, italics, and capital letters to emphasize findings or conclusions,
- use the active voice,
- use precise language,
- use confident language that avoids hedge words, such as "it seems," "could," "apparently," and "I believe,"
- define all technical terms and technical jargon,
- use objective language and avoid subjective characterizations to describe the investigation, findings, and conclusions,
- explain explicitly the meaning of any abbreviations,
- avoid argumentative language,
- beware of commenting on the credibility of witnesses,

- make sure the report is internally consistent and consistent with any previous reports in the case or other similar cases in which the expert was involved, and
- avoid any evidence of bias in the report.

Chapter 12 examines how to make an expert report powerful, persuasive, and understandable.

1.14 What Not to Include in an Expert Report

The only language that should appear in expert reports is language that objectively states or objectively supports an expert's findings and conclusions. All other information is superfluous and should not be included in the report.

Including superfluous language in a report is one of the most common mistakes experts make. This mistake can cost the expert's credibility dearly. Superfluous language often provides fertile grounds for cross-examination that can damage the expert's credibility. The authors recommend the following.

- Avoiding "friendly" language to counsel that thanks them for the assignment, invites comments or questions, or includes personal salutations.
- Not including speeches in the expert report that expose the expert's beliefs.
- Making sure letterhead does not include references to being an "expert witness."
- Cover letters accompanying reports should be short and formal. One sentence is ideal.
- Not documenting discussions with retaining counsel in the expert report unless they are relevant.
- Experts should self-edit their reports aggressively to remove all superfluous language.

Certain words will raise red flags with an attorney whose job it is to undermine an expert, her credibility, and her opinions. These words should be avoided. Some of the most commonly used words to avoid are discussed in chapters 13 and 14. They include the following.

- "Authoritative" to describe a text. This term has special legal significance that may allow a cross-examining attorney to question the expert about everything in the text.
- "Legal" or "legally." What is and is not legal is usually outside of the area of expertise of most experts.

- "Draft." This term alerts counsel to the existence of prior or subsequent reports that are usually extremely fertile grounds for cross-examination.
- "Work product," "confidential," or "privileged." These terms make it appear as though the expert is trying to hide something.
- "Probable" and "possible." Experts should avoid these ambiguous words.
- "Substantially." One should avoid this ambiguous word.
- "Obviously" and "clearly." These words can be used to make the expert appear patronizing or presumptive.
- "Appears," "presumably," "supposedly," "is said," and "evidently." These words imply uncertainty.
- "He," "she," "it," "they," and other pronouns. Pronouns are uncertain. It is better to use a proper noun.
- Royal "we." This can be used to make the expert look silly, pompous, or even dishonest.
- "It seems," "could," "apparently," "I believe," and other hedge words. It is always better to use confident language.
- "Complete," "thorough," "meticulous," "exhaustive," and other such words. These self-serving words will hold the expert and the report to an extremely high standard.

Chapters 13 and 14 describe what to leave out of a report.

1.15 Defending the Expert Report
Counsel will use many tactics in an attempt to destroy the expert, her report, and her credibility. The best way to defeat these tactics is to write a strong, carefully worded report as described in this text. Chapter 16 provides detailed and specific advice to defeat 40 tactics used by cross-examining attorneys.

1.16 Help from Colleagues
Much in the way of writing a defensible expert report can be learned from your colleagues. Unfiltered advice on expert report writing from experts across the country is provided in appendix A. Model reports from different experts across the country are provided in appendix B. These reports have been annotated by the authors in an attempt to make them more useful to the reader. They should give the reader many good ideas for writing excellent expert reports.

Chapter 2 Discoverability of Expert Reports and Related Material

2.1 Executive Summary
The law regarding the discoverability of expert reports is somewhat unsettled. A survey of this law, with examples, is provided below. The authors recommend the following.

- Experts should assume that anything they write will be discoverable.
- Experts should not include anything in a report or any other document that they wouldn't want a jury to see.
- Experts should not create any written reports unless specifically instructed to do so by retaining counsel.
- Experts should never hide or destroy reports with the purpose of preventing the discovery of those reports.

2.2 Attorney-client Privilege
The attorney-client privilege protects confidential communications between a client and an attorney and the attorney's agents, made for the purpose of obtaining legal services or advice from that attorney. **Because an expert is not the attorney's client, the attorney-client privilege generally *does not* protect communications between the expert and the retaining attorney.** Therefore, experts should *assume* that any oral or written report they make to or for their retaining attorney will be discoverable and can and will be used against them.

2.3 Work Product Protection
Rule 26 of the Federal Rules of Civil Procedure provides in part:

> (3) *Trial Preparation: Materials.* Subject to the provisions of subdivision (b)(4) of this rule, a party may obtain discovery of documents and tangible things otherwise discoverable under subdivision (b)(1) of this rule and prepared in anticipation of litigation or for trial by or for another party or by or for that other party's representative (including the other party's attorney, consultant, surety, indemnitor, insurer, or agent) only upon a showing that the party seeking discovery has substantial need of the materials in the preparation of the party's case and that the party is unable without undue hardship to obtain the substantial equivalent of the materials by other means. In ordering discovery of such materials when the required showing has been made, the court shall protect against disclosure of the mental

impressions, conclusions, opinions, or legal theories of an attorney or other representative of a party concerning the litigation..."[1]

(4) *Trial Preparation: Experts.*

(A) A party may depose any person who has been identified as an expert whose opinions may be presented at trial. If a report from the expert is required under subdivision (a)(2)(B), the deposition shall not be conducted until after the report is provided.

(B) A party may, through interrogatories or by deposition, discover facts known or opinions held by an expert who has been retained or specially employed by another party in anticipation of litigation or preparation for trial and who is not expected to be called as a witness at trial only as provided in Rule 35(b) or upon a showing of exceptional circumstances under which it is impracticable for the party seeking discovery to obtain facts or opinions on the same subject by other means.

(C) Unless manifest injustice would result, (i) the court shall require that the party seeking discovery pay the expert a reasonable fee for time spent in responding to discovery under this subdivision; and (ii) with respect to discovery obtained under subdivision (b)(4)(B) of this rule the court shall require the party seeking discovery to pay the other party a fair portion of the fees and expenses reasonably incurred by the latter party in obtaining facts and opinions from the expert.[2]

The work product privilege protects documents and tangible things prepared in anticipation of litigation. *Core,* or *opinion, work product* refers to analysis, while *fact,* or *ordinary, work product* refers simply to factual information underlying an analysis. The work product privilege held by the attorney attaches to materials prepared by counsel or counsel's representatives in anticipation of litigation and allows them to be discovered only upon a showing of need. The need that the discovering party must show varies and depends upon whether the materials sought are fact or opinion work product. The privilege is waivable. Disclosure of work product to a testifying expert can result in a waiver of the work product immunity. In *Johnson v. Gmeinder,*[3] the court found that disclosure of fact work product to an expert and his consideration of the materials resulted in the waiver of work product immunity. Nontestifying experts are given far greater protection than testifying experts.

The discovery rules say that the "things" that an expert considers when forming an opinion are discoverable. However, the discovery rules contain explicit protections for the mental impressions, conclusions, opinions, or legal theories of an attorney. This is a conflict that the courts have resolved inconsistently. These inconsistencies make it difficult to present a clear picture of the discovery rules as they relate to work product.

---

[1] 26(b)(3).

[2] 26(B)(4).

[3] 191F.R.D. 638 (D.Kan. 2000).

They make it more difficult still to answer the expert's ultimate question here: what is discoverable? An overview of the general rules appears below.

2.4 Nontestifying Experts

Documents reviewed by or produced by nontestifying experts receive more protection than those reviewed by or produced by testifying experts. Under Rule 26(b)(4)(B), facts known or opinions held by an expert who has been specially employed in anticipation of litigation or preparation for trial—but who is not expected to be called as a witness—may be discoverable only upon a showing of exceptional circumstances under which it is impracticable for the party seeking discovery to obtain facts or opinions on the same subject by other means. Please consider the following examples.

Example 2.41: Circumstances not exceptional

Hartford Fire Ins. Co. v. Pure Air on the Lake Ltd., 154 F.R.D. 202 (N.D. Ind. 1993)

In this litigation arising out of a subsurface collapse that resulted in extensive property damage to a construction site at a generating plant, the defendant sought to discover the reports of the plaintiff's nontestifying engineer expert. The reports contained information on the cause of the cave-in and attendant property damage. The court found that the subject of discovery was the cause of the collapsed pipes and that the defendant had ample opportunity to investigate and evaluate these pipes during the excavation process and, in fact, did undertake an investigation. Thus, the defendant made no showing that it could not discover equivalent information regarding the cause of the pipes' collapse.

Example 2.42: Circumstances exceptional

Delcastor, Inc. v. Vail Assoc., Inc., 108 F.R.D. 405 (D. Colo. 1985)

In this case, a mudslide destroyed a construction site. The next day, the defendant's consulting expert was at the site and subsequently prepared a report. The plaintiff's expert was unable to inspect the site until five days later, when the conditions had changed considerably. The conditions of the site immediately after the mudslide could not be reconstructed. The court found exceptional circumstances and ordered the nontestifying expert's report disclosed.

Example 2.43: Expected to be called at trial

Re Commitment of Rachel v. Rachel, 591 N.W.2d 920 (Wis.App. 999)

The issue in this case was whether the expert was expected to be called at trial. The court stated:

> Next, we must determine whether Rachel's expert's report is discoverable, given that § 804.01(2)(d), stats., applies. That section provides that a party may "discover facts known or opinions held by an expert … who is not expected to be called as a witness at trial only upon … showing that exceptional circumstances exist." Section 804.01(2)(d)2. Furthermore, Wisconsin case law holds that an expert's pretrial examinations are part of an attorney's work product, and thus protected from discovery....

Only once the expert is a "person who has been identified as an expert whose opinions may be presented at trial" do his or her reports and opinions become discoverable....

Here, there is no support in the record for a finding that Rachel expected to call this expert as a witness at trial. Rather, the trial court appeared to base its decision on the appointment statute's language that an expert be appointed "to perform an examination and *participate in the trial*." Section 980.03(4), stats. (emphasis added). The trial court seemed to interpret the statute to mean that, as a matter of legislative fact, a person requesting an expert under the statute has already decided to use that expert as a witness at trial. We do not agree. The statute mandates appointment of an expert to aid in the proceedings "on behalf of an indigent person." *Id.* Thus, the expert may be requested for a variety of services, including assessment of the respondent and a determination whether he or she has a disorder, critique of the State's expert and testing methods, and exploration of placement and treatment programs available. Yes, the expert may also be called at trial. But the respondent, like any other civil litigant, has the right to decide, after reviewing the expert's findings, whether to call the expert at trial.[4]

2.5 Testifying Experts

The courts agree that factual information provided by an attorney to a testifying expert (fact work product) is subject to discovery. [See, for example, *Bogosian v. Gulf Oil Corp.*, 738 F.2d 587, 595 (3d Cir.1984) and *Baise v. Alewel's Inc.*, 99 F.R.D. 95, 97 (W.D.Mo.1983).] Similarly, there is ample authority indicating that information and opinions provided by a testifying expert are not protected by the work product doctrine. [See *Abruzzo v. United States*, 21 Cl.Ct. 351 (1990).] However, a split exists among federal courts as to the discoverability of "opinion" work product (for example, the mental impressions, conclusions, opinions, or legal theories of an attorney), often known as "core work product," provided to a testifying expert. On one side of the spectrum are protection-oriented cases, such as *Bogosian v. Gulf Oil Corp,*[5] which have held that work product materials provided to testifying experts are not discoverable. At the polar opposite are discovery-oriented cases, such as *Intermedics, Inc. v. Ventritex, Inc.*,[6] which have held that "written and oral communications from a lawyer to an expert that are related to matters about which the expert will offer testimony are discoverable, even when those communications otherwise would be deemed opinion work product."[7] Somewhere in the middle is a third line of jurisprudence that holds that work product provided to an expert is discoverable only where the "impeachment value in the particular case would significantly outweigh the chill on development of legitimate work product that would admittedly accompany disclosure."[8]

---

[4] At 921-922.

[5] 738 F.2d 587.

[6] 139 F.R.D. 384 (N.D.Cal.1991).

[7] 139 F.R.D. at 387.

[8] *Bogosian,* 738 F.2d at 598 (Becker, J., dissenting).

2.6 Oral and Draft Reports

Oral and draft reports are generally discoverable. Experts may be tempted or encouraged by counsel to hide, destroy, or deny the existence of oral or draft reports in an attempt to prevent their discovery. This is a serious mistake and may result in a devastating and permanent loss of the expert's credibility. The best way to prevent the discovery of draft reports is to not create draft reports in the first place. If draft reports are prepared, these should only be discarded as a usual and regular business[9] practice and not in an attempt to hide them from discovery.

Example 2.61: Cross-examination on oral and draft reports
Cross-examination:
Q. Attorney Smith has certified that there are no other expert reports prepared by you. Is that correct?
A. Yes.
Q. You did discuss your preliminary findings with Attorney Smith, did you not?
A. Yes.
Q. This was an oral report, was it not?
A. It was a discussion of my findings.
Q. Did you have notes before you when you discussed the case with Attorney Smith?
A. Yes.
Q. You did have a preliminary or draft report, did you not?
A. Yes, I did.
Q. Where is the draft report now?
A. I no longer have it.
Q. Did you misplace it?
A. No.
Q. What happened to it?
A. I destroyed it.
Q. So that you would not have to produce it?
A. No,…as a…course of business.
Q. Would that preliminary report still be available on your computer?
A. I am not sure.
Q. When did you destroy your draft report?
A. Right after I talked to Attorney Smith.

Comment: When an expert composes a written draft report or a preliminary oral report and shares this report with counsel, it is easy for opposing counsel to show that retaining counsel may have improperly influenced the expert. The most persuasive reports are those that have not been influenced by retaining counsel. Draft reports should be avoided.

---

[9] Many experts commonly do this.

Example 2.62: Draft reports destroyed prior to deposition

W.R. Grace and Co.-Conn. V. Zotos International, Inc., 2000 WL 1843258
(W.D.N.Y. 2000)

The court dealt with a discovery battle that the expert was drawn into after retaining counsel instructed the expert to destroy draft reports prior to deposition. The court stated:

> During the deposition, Barber confirmed the existence of documents in his file which were not produced to Plaintiff, including Defendant's Request for Proposals, the final contract between Plaintiff and Barber for his services, a diary containing notes of Barber's meetings with defense counsel, phone calls, and other work Barber performed on the case, and correspondence and memoranda between Barber and defense counsel after October 1, 1999. Hogan Affidavit, ¶ 5. Additionally, Barber testified that prior drafts of his final report, including written comments to him on the drafts received from Defendant's attorneys had been destroyed two weeks prior to the deposition upon instructions from defense counsel. *Id.* Specifically, Barber testified he had been instructed to discard the drafts in order "not…to confuse things."[10]

Not only was the expert eventually forced to produce his diary entries, but the integrity of his work product was called into question.

> The materials provided for *in camera* review include copies of Barber's draft reports transmitted to Defendant's attorneys via facsimile, on September 28 and 30, 1999, together with Barber's request for the attorneys' comments. On each page of the typewritten texts appear hand written notations, presumably written by one of Defendant's attorneys to whom the drafts were sent for review and comments. Defendant states that only the notes of counsel on the September 30, 1999 draft report were communicated to Barber. Defendant's Memorandum at 20. Defendant also represents that three documents, constituting redrafts of Barber's draft reports, were transmitted from defense counsel to Barber, *id.*, thereby implying they were prepared by counsel to assist Barber in formulating his final report.
>
> The court's review of the documents shows that although some of the revisions suggested and as redrafted by counsel appear to represent matters of form, others are plainly directed to matters of substance. For example, in the September 30th draft report, the section of the document addressing selection of remedial alternatives was then blank with an "In progress" notation only. However, in the September 30th and October 1st drafts, transmitted from Defendant's attorneys to Barber, the section includes two full paragraphs of text discussing the draft's conclusion that the remedy selected by Plaintiff was not consistent with the National Contingency Plan. Thus, the exchange of documents between counsel and Barber raises an issue of the extent to which Barber's final report represents Barber's own product or that of Defendant's attorneys.[11]

In the end, the court ordered all of the material in question and supporting documents to be produced.

---

[10] At 3.

[11] At 5.

Example 2.63: Buried draft report surfaces

The *Pennsylvania Law Weekly* recently reported on a similar, if not more serious, case. The article[12] deals with an alleged attempt to change a report and then bury the first version. Counsel was alleged to have failed to turn over the first draft of a doctor's report that was unfavorable. He then allegedly had the doctor change his opinion. The draft report came to light when it was inadvertently faxed to defense counsel. The deposition transcript reported in the article reveals the following.

> On direct, Michael M. Badowski, of Margolis Edelstein, questioned Boal about what he believed was the cause of Johnson's injury. "I do not believe [Johnson's low back pain] was related to the car accident but was related to what we call degenerative disc disease of the lumbar spine," he answered. The doctor called this—as well as Johnson's failure to promptly complain of back pain—"the crux of this case."
>
> On his cross of Boal, Brandes asked, "Any drafts of your report, or you just wrote your report and gave it to defense counsel?"
>
> "Just wrote it and gave it to him" Boal answered.
>
> "You wrote in your report on the last page that no one can say that the back injury and the surgery are directly related to the motor vehicle accident due to that few week gap between the date of the accident and her first complaint of pain. … But it's really not true, there are people who can say it's directly related, right?" asked Brandes. It was then, over objection by Badowski, that Brandes confronted Boal with the earlier report the doctor had written. "You said previously the draft you're telling this jury about was the one and only draft. Doctor, isn't this the first draft of your report you sent to defense counsel, Mr. Kronthal?"
>
> Boal said he did not recall whether he sent the draft to Kronthal, nor did he recall whether he discussed the first draft with Kronthal but said, "I'm sure [Kronthal] pointed out things that would make me think there was something different than my opinion, which would have necessitated writing a second draft."
>
> The Judge was quite upset with counsel due to the fact that the second report had a completely different opinion on causation from the first. The Judge warned counsel as follows:
>
> "That's why we're going through this rather extraordinary proceeding here this morning. You could be criminally prosecuted, given a certain set of facts, for subornation of perjury, criminal conspiracy to be involved in perjury, and perjury as an accomplice. Those are all felonies for which you can spend a substantial portion of your life in a penitentiary."
>
> Counsel's explanation left something to be desired.
>
> "Judge, if there was any intent to bury this report from the beginning…the fact of the matter is it wouldn't have been in our file in the first place. We would have thrown it away," said Banko. "What we've had at all turns in this case, unfortunately, Judge…is really a comedy of errors."
>
> "Oh, this is no comedy," said Clark.
>
> "The allegations are serious, Judge."
>
> "Serious is an understatement…so serious you can be disbarred for this."

Comment: It is reasonable to assume that the expert in this case had his credibility seriously and irreparably ruined. Obviously, this expert should not

---

[12] "Harrisburg Attorney under Fire over Expert Report," *Pennsylvania Law Weekly,* 8/7/2000.

have allowed himself to have been improperly influenced by counsel, and should not have been dishonest about the existence of a prior draft report.

Example 2.64: Draft report and cover letter discoverable
Krisa v. Equitable Life Insurance Society, 196 F.R.D. 254 (M.D.Pa. 2000)
The court held:

> Relevant precedent holds that materials prepared by a party's expert are not covered by the attorney work product privilege. Because the conclusion that draft expert reports and other documents prepared by testifying expert witnesses are discoverable is consistent with the policy considerations underlying the attorney work product privilege, Equitable will be required to produce the draft reports and other documents prepared by its experts. Cover letters that do not contain the mental impressions, opinions or conclusions of Equitable's counsel are not covered by the attorney work-product doctrine. Because the cover letters are relevant to an evaluation of what documents were considered by Equitable's experts, Equitable will be required to produce them.[13]

---

[13] At 261.

Chapter 3 Legal Requirements: Rule 26 Reports, Reports Used in Summary Motions, and Magic Words

3.1 Executive Summary

Expert reports need to be written so that they comply with all applicable legal standards. Failure to comply with applicable legal standards could result in the expert being prohibited from testifying or in a negative disposition of a claim by summary judgment. Experts need to coordinate with counsel to make sure that their reports comply with all applicable legal requirements.

3.2 Rule 26

Expert reports in all civil actions in federal court must comply with Fed.R.Civ.P. Rule 26. Reports that fail to satisfy the requirements of Fed.R.Civ.P. 26(a)(2)(B) are stricken with regularity. Fed.R.Civ.P. 26(a)(2)(B) provides:

> (B) Except as otherwise stipulated or directed by the court, this disclosure shall, with respect to a witness who is retained or specially employed to provide expert testimony in the case or whose duties as an employee of the party regularly involve giving expert testimony, be accompanied by a written report prepared and signed by the witness. The report shall contain a complete statement of all opinions to be expressed and the basis and reasons therefor; the data or other information considered by the witness in forming the opinions; any exhibits to be used as a summary of or support for the opinions; the qualifications of the witness, including a list of all publications authored by the witness within the preceding ten years; the compensation to be paid for the study and testimony; and a listing of any other cases in which the witness has testified as an expert at trial or by deposition within the preceding four years.

The following are the nine requirements of Rule 26 in easy-to-read format.

1. Written report,
2. signed by the expert,
3. complete statement of all the expert's opinions,
4. complete statement of the basis and reasons for all the expert's opinions,
5. any exhibits to be used as support for or a summary of the opinions,
6. the qualifications of the expert,
7. all publications offered by the expert in the past 10 years,
8. the expert's compensation for his review and testimony, and

9. a list of all other cases in which the expert has testified at trial or
    at deposition in the past four years.

The courts have interpreted the Rule to mean that:

Each expert report must be in writing and signed by the expert, and must
contain: a complete statement of all the expert's opinions and the basis and
reasons therefore; the data and information considered by the expert; any
exhibits to be used as support for or a summary of the opinions; the
qualifications of the expert and all publications authored by the expert in the
past 10 years; the expert's compensation for his review and testimony; and
a list of all other cases in which the expert has testified at trial or at
deposition in the past 4 years. The report itself should contain all the
required information with considerable detail, and may not satisfy Rule
26(a)(2)(B) by incorporating interrogatory answers.[1]

When a court finds that the requirements of Fed.R.Civ.P. 26(a)(2)(B)
are not met by a proffered report, the court can strike the expert designation
and prohibit the expert from testifying. The designation and testimony will
not be stricken if the court considers the resulting prejudice to be harmless.

Example 3.21: Expert report inadequate under Rule 26
Campbell v. McMillin, 83 F.Supp.2d 761 (S.D.Miss. 2000)
The court dealt with a Sec. 1983 action and an expert report of John Murray,
MD. The court's analysis of the numerous inadequacies of the expert's report is
instructive.

In the case *sub judice*, the Rule 26 requirement of a "detailed and complete" report
is not met. The brief four-paragraph report of Murray consists of conclusory
unsupported allegations. The opening paragraph of Murray's report states "[t]he
following is a *summary* of my *initial conclusions* regarding this case." *See*
Plaintiff's Response to Defendant Estes' Motion for Summary Judgment, Exhibit
"F." (emphasis added). The following paragraph states "[t]he abrupt
discontinuation of any of these medications *could* result in severe life threatening
consequences." *Id.* (emphasis added). The conclusion of the third paragraph of
Murray's report reads "[t]here were numerous clinical findings as well as laboratory
results described in the records *suggesting* worsening of these [heart] problems
(although I do not feel that I have been provided with all the laboratory results).
Any or all *could have* contributed to Mr. Campbell's death." *Id.* (emphasis added).
No basis or reasoning for Murray's opinions are stated in the expert's report.
Furthermore, Murray provides no summary of the data upon which he allegedly
relied in forming his unclear opinions.
The second requirement of an expert's report under Rule 26(a)(2)(B) is
that the data or information considered by the expert in forming the opinions must
be included in the report. To the extent that Murray states that his opinion is based
on a review of Campbell's medical records, this requirement is met. However, no
data and information regarding the conclusions drawn from Murray's review of the

---

[1] Baicken-McKee, *Federal Civil Rules Handbook* (West Group, 2001) 494.

records is included in the report. Murray merely states conclusory allegations without providing the basis for his opinions. Overall, the Court finds that the expert's report fails to meet the second requirement of Rule 26(a)(2)(B).

The third Rule 26(a)(2)(B) requirement, the production of any exhibits to be used as a summary of or support for the opinions, is not met. No summaries or exhibits were provided to the Defendants. The fourth requirement mandates the expert to provide a list of his qualifications, including a list of all publications authored by the expert within the preceding ten years. This requirement was not met. Fifth, Rule 26(a)(2)(B) requires the disclosure of compensation paid to the expert for his services. This requirement was not met. Sixth and finally, the expert must provide a listing of cases in which he has testified as an expert at trial or by deposition within the past four years. This requirement was not met.

Based on an analysis of both Federal Rule of Civil Procedure 26 and applicable case law, this Court finds that the expert designation and disclosure of the expert's report were deficient. Therefore, unless the Plaintiffs can come forward with an excusable reason for the inadequacies, the use of Murray as an expert witness at trial should be barred. *See* Fed.R.Civ.P. 37(c)(1).[2]

Example 3.22: Sketchy and vague report not "detailed and complete," inadequate under Rule 26

Sierra Club, Lone Star Chapter v. Cedar Point Oil Company, Inc., 73 F.3rd 546 (5th Cir. 1996)

Counsel attempted to get by with sketchy and vague information with disastrous results.

The district court's discovery order required that the parties' *initial* expert disclosures "include a *complete* statement of *all* opinions to be expressed and the basis and reasons therefor" and "the data or other information relied upon in forming such opinions." The Advisory Committee Notes to Rule 26 of the Federal Rules of Civil Procedure state that such reports must be "detailed and complete." Fed.R.Civ.P. 26 advisory committee's note. These Notes also explain that the purpose of the reports is to avoid the disclosure of "sketchy and vague" expert information as was the practice under the former rule.

The district court's finding that Cedar Point's initial expert disclosures did not meet this standard does not constitute an abuse of discretion. A review of the disclosures bears out this assessment. Don Harper's statement of opinions and reasons was a one-and-a-half page outline listing his "points of testimony." Carl Oppenheimer offered two one-paragraph descriptions of his opinions. Stanley Pier and John McGowan also provided only one-paragraph statements relating to their opinions. Finally, Joe Haney's statement included no substantive opinions, but only declared what subjects he intended to research and to discuss at trial. Although Cedar Point later reinforced these statements with rebuttal and supplementary disclosures, the discovery order and Rule 26(a) clearly require that the *initial* disclosures be complete and detailed. The purpose of rebuttal and supplementary disclosures is just that--to rebut and to supplement. These disclosures are not intended to provide an extension of the deadline by which a party must deliver the lion's share of its expert information. Therefore, we hold that the district court did not abuse its discretion in finding that Cedar Point failed to comply with the expert disclosure provisions of its accelerated discovery order."

"When a district court strikes a party's designation of expert witnesses and excludes their testimony as a sanction for violation of a discovery order, we

---

[2] At 764,765.

determine whether the court's action is an abuse of discretion by examining four factors:

(1) the importance of the witnesses' testimony;

(2) the prejudice to the opposing party of allowing the witnesses to testify;

(3) the possibility of curing such prejudice by granting a continuance; and

(4) the explanation, if any, for the party's failure to comply with the discovery order. *See Bradley v. United States*, 866 F.2d 120, 125 (5th Cir.1989) (citing *Murphy*, 639 F.2d at 235).[3]

Example 3.23: Harmless error, insufficiencies of report do not result in stricken expert testimony

Sherrod v. Lingle, 223 F.3rd 605 (7th Cir. 2000)

When the court finds that failure to comply with a discovery order requiring disclosure of an expert's reports is harmless, it will not exclude the testimony of the expert. The court in this case utilized a liberal construction of Rule 37 and stated:

> However, on the facts of this case, we find the imposition of this drastic sanction unjustified considering the harmless nature of the plaintiff's failure to comply with the discovery order. The expert witness discovery rules are designed to aid the court in its fact-finding mission by allowing both sides to prepare their cases adequately and efficiently and to prevent the tactic of surprise from affecting the outcome of the case. *See* Fed.R.Civ.P. 26(a)(2) advisory committee's note (stating that expert disclosure rule intended to give opposing parties "reasonable opportunity to prepare for effective cross examination and perhaps arrange for expert testimony from other witnesses."); *Gorby v. Schneider Tank Lines, Inc.,* 741 F.2d 1015, 1018 (7th Cir.1984); *see also Klonoski v. Mahlab*, 156 F.3d 255, 271 (1st Cir.1998). In this instance, Sherrod disclosed the names of both retained experts and their initial reports well before the deadline, thus preventing the chance that unfair surprise would hamper the defendants' preparation of the case. The trial still appeared a long way off, and the defendants had plenty of time to prepare their examinations of Sherrod's experts. Furthermore, because both sides were at fault for the difficulties in scheduling depositions, which pushed discovery up to the December deadline, the delay in finishing the experts' reports was partially justified. While in most cases, a district court would be fully within its discretion in strictly applying the rules and excluding reports that were incomplete or submitted a day late, *see e.g., Salgado,* 150 F.3d at 742, in this instance we can see no harm that came from Sherrod's failure to meet the December 30 deadline. Because Rule 37 does not require sanctions against a non-disclosing party if that party's violation was harmless, the district court abused its discretion by excluding Sherrod's experts without any indication that the defendants had been harmed by his discovery violation.[4]

Example 3.24: Failure to provide lists of cases deposed in

Palmer v. Rhodes Machinery, 187 F.R.D. 653 (N.D.Okla. 1999)

Plaintiff requested that the defendant produce a list of cases in which defendant's expert witness, Dr. Sami Framjee, had testified. Defendant asked to be excused from the requirements saying it would be too difficult and expensive to produce and instead pointed the plaintiff to a site on the internet which covers

---

[3] At 571, 572.

[4] At 613.

a 3-year period and lists 169 cases in which Dr. Framjee had testified. The court was not impressed and stated:

> The Court finds that the cost or difficulty of compiling the list is insufficient for the purpose of meeting the "substantial justification" requirement. The Rule has been in existence since 1993. Dr. Framjee is deposed, according to Defendant, an average of three to five times each week. If Defendant's expert plans to continue to offer his services in federal court, he must comply with the federal rules. The initial cost and trouble of compiling the list, since Defendant's expert apparently does not maintain one, may be expensive. The expense is a one-time cost, and the list can then be used in subsequent litigation. Maintenance of the list should be comparatively easy. Furthermore, counsel for Plaintiff and Defendant suggested that Dr. Framjee's yearly income from depositions was approximately $90,000. [FN2] Defendant provides no estimates of the actual cost of compiling the list. Given Dr. Framjee's income from expert testimony, requiring the expenditure of funds to compile a list which is mandated by the federal rules is not a draconian measure.[5]

When asked for a second chance, the court was not in the least sympathetic.

> Defendant suggests that Dr. Framjee be given "one warning." Defendant is uncertain whether Dr. Framjee has ever testified in federal court, [FN3] but assumes, based on the size of his practice, that he has. Defendant states that Dr. Framjee has never been requested to comply with the federal rule, and that he did not know about the federal rule. Defendant notes that, for the purposes of future testimony in federal court, because Dr. Framjee now knows of the federal rule which requires such disclosures, he be required to comply with it. Defendant requests that the Court make an exception in this case due to Dr. Framjee's lack of knowledge, the difficulty of compiling the list, and the impending trial date.
>   A "one warning" exception to the rule is not contemplated by the rule. Such an exception in this case would be to the disadvantage of this Plaintiff. The federal rule has been in existence since 1993. Assuming Dr. Framjee did not know of the requirements of the rule, certainly defense counsel knew of the rule prior to employing Dr. Framjee. A simple inquiry by defense counsel prior to his retention would have averted this situation.[6]

3.3 Supplemental Rule 26 Reports

Rule 26(e)(1) states that a party is under a duty to supplement its pretrial disclosures "at appropriate intervals" if it learns that in some material respect the information provided is incomplete, inaccurate, and if the additional or corrective information has not otherwise been made known to the other parties during the discovery process. The commentary to this rule states that supplementation "need not be made as each new item of information is learned but should be made at appropriate intervals during the discovery period, and with special promptness as the trial date approaches."[7] When counsel and the expert he has retained fail to file a timely supplemental

---

[5] At 656.
[6] At 656, 657.
[7] Fed.R.Civ.P. 26 advisory committee's note.

expert report, the proposed report and associated testimony may be stricken. Please consider the following examples.

Example 3.31: Failure to file supplemental report, expert testimony limited to original report

NutraSweet Company v. X-L Engineering Company, 227 F. 3rd 776 (7th Cir. 2000)
The defendant and his expert failed to file a supplemental expert report. The court limited the expert's testimony to his initial report and stated:

> Because X-L did not file a supplemental expert witness report on the site work at X-L's property, the district court excluded Shepherd from testifying about this work and limited his testimony to his initial expert witness report. X-L attempts to explain its failure to file a supplemental expert report by complaining that NutraSweet used a new expert (Dr. Ball) in its supplemental report and changed (more accurately, supplemented) its theory of the case. Assuming NutraSweet did so (on that, more later), X-L still fails to explain why this justified its failure to file a supplemental expert report. The site work occurred in early October 1997; NutraSweet filed its test results by the March 4, 1998 deadline (X-L did not); and NutraSweet filed its supplemental expert witness report of Dr. Ball ahead of schedule on March 20, 1998. Even though Ball's report contained new theories, X-L does not explain why it could not file its supplemental expert report by the April 10, 1998 *extended* deadline it requested and received. Nor does it explain why it could not meet its proposed, revised May 5 *super-extended* deadline. By the time of these deadlines, X-L had had Ball's report for three weeks and five and one-half weeks, respectively. Even if Ball's report was not sufficiently specific (an argument X-L made below but not here), it should have at least filed a preliminary supplemental report or told the court of its concerns with Ball's report by the April 10 deadline (or certainly by its proposed May 5 deadline). There was no reason for it to just sit by for six weeks after the April 10 deadline and do nothing while the trial date was fast approaching. There appears to be no justification for X-L's failure to file some sort of a supplemental report that would have enabled Shepherd to expand his testimony. *See Salgado*, 150 F.3d at 741 ("Salgado never offered--indeed, does not offer to this date--a satisfactory explanation for its failure to comply with the directive of the district court").[8]

The court went on to find that the failure to file the supplemental report was not harmless.

Example 3.32: Supplemental report filed four months prior to trial acceptable where facts and circumstances do not indicate that counsel "sat" on report and delayed supplementation

Tucker v. Ohtsu Tire and Rubber Co, Ltd., 49 F.Supp.2d 456 (D.Md. 2000)
The court found exclusion of a supplemental expert witness report was not warranted when it was made four months prior to trial.

> The March 12, 1999 supplementation of Mr. Grogan's Rule 26(a)(2)(B) disclosure was both technically timely, and sufficiently in advance of trial that it cannot fairly be characterized as "ambush tactics." Defendants previously had been made aware

---

[8] At 785.

during Mr. Grogan's deposition in September, 1998 that he had reached the conclusion that there had been improper adhesion between the steel cords and the rubber components of the tire, based upon his examination of the brass coated steel cord removed from the tire just before his deposition. The RAPRA report reflected the results of testing which confirmed Mr. Grogan's conclusion, and was dated February 24, 1999, sixteen days before the supplementation. This does not suggest that plaintiff's counsel "sat" on the results of the report before supplementing Mr. Grogan's disclosure.[9]

3.4 Reports Used to Support or Oppose Motions for Summary Judgment

Expert reports are commonly used as evidence to support or oppose motions for summary judgment. There are three major legal requirements for these reports. First, the report needs to properly address the key factual disputes upon which the motion for summary judgment will be decided by the judge. Second, the report needs to be signed by the expert under the pains and penalties of perjury. This requirement is discussed in greater detail in chapter 5 on formatting. Finally, the report needs to be prepared and signed in a timely fashion. This requirement also applies to Rule 26 reports and is discussed below.

In terms of the first requirement, the judge will decide if the report properly addresses the key factual disputes upon which the motion for summary judgment has been brought. The expert will need to find out from counsel the issues the expert needs to address. For example, let's say that a plaintiff is claiming that chemical X causes cancer. The defendant moves for summary judgment on the basis that the plaintiff will not be able to prove at trial that chemical X indeed causes cancer. To avoid this motion for summary judgment being granted in favor of the defendant, the plaintiff will have to submit sworn expert testimony establishing the causal relationship between chemical X and cancer. This sworn testimony may be in the form of an expert report signed under the pains and penalties of perjury (that is, in the form of an affidavit). The wording of the plaintiff's sworn expert report will be subject to review from the court. Imprecise wording or wording that does not address the issue of causation could result in summary judgment being granted against the plaintiff. Please consider the following examples.

Example 3.41: The breach of standard of care not established by report, summary judgment granted against plaintiff
Romans v. Lusin, 997 P.2d 114 (Mont. 2000)
The court dealt with an action against a physical therapist for an alleged negligently administered FCE (functional capacity evaluation). The court found the plaintiff's expert report inadequate to avoid a motion for summary judgment and stated:

---

[9] At 461.

The entirety of Dr. Nelson's report, advanced by Romans as sufficient expert testimony to establish the applicable standard of care and Lusin's breach of that standard, is as follows:

Reviewing Kester Romans [sic] status initial injury to ankle with tarsal tunnel decompression. Following that with physical therapy which exacerbate [sic] pain in L-5 area and onset of jerking and movement revealed of the foot and leg. No surgical lesions of L-5 has [sic] been found but revealed conjoined nerve root as S-1, S-2, on left, facet hypertrophy and pain of a referred pain origin is not due to nerve root pain carrying from discal root facet or other support structures.

I would like to see discography done to tell us if discal referred pain is present as per Dr. John Moseley suggested [sic].

His movement disorder of the lower extremity is responding possitively [sic] to Depakene and Baclofen, but it still persists.

Peripheral traumatic injury may have superimposed itself on myoclonic disorder emanating from basal ganglia. Further studies would be necessary, i.e., discography and I recommend magnetic resonance spectography or a pet scan to deliniate [sic] brain level source of the movement disorder.

Dr. Nelson's report addresses Romans' medical history and recommends additional studies necessary for a medical diagnosis. However, it does not address or establish the standard of care applicable to a physical therapist conducting an FCE or a breach of that standard by Lusin; indeed, Dr. Nelson's report does not even mention the FCE. We hold, therefore, that Romans' Rule 26(b)(4), M.R.Civ.P., disclosure does not satisfy his burden for purposes of avoiding summary judgment.[10]

Example 3.42: Causation not established in expert report, summary judgment granted against plaintiff

Samarah v. Danek Medical, Inc., 70 F.Supp.2d 1196 (D.Kan. 1999)
The court dealt with a pedicle screw products liability case. The court granted summary judgment due to the weakness of the plaintiff's expert reports on the issue of causation. The court stated:

As additional support for his causation argument, plaintiff offers a one and one-half page expert report from Dr. Dubinsky. In that report, Dr. Dubinsky outlines his understanding of plaintiff's history of back problems as gleaned from his review of plaintiff's medical records, and offers the following conclusion on the issue of causation: It is probable that the continuation of his right leg pain in 1994 was due to the pedicle screws and the psuedoarthosis [sic] of L5 and S1. It is also probable that the arachnoiditis is the result of retained Pantopaque (R) from myelograms performed while the patient was living in Syria.

The court finds Dr. Dubinsky's report wholly inadequate to establish the element of causation. First, Dr. Dubinsky's conclusion is completely unsupported by any specific facts. Indeed, the majority of Dr. Dubinsky's report merely recounts the undisputed facts of plaintiff's medical history, and identifies no justification for his conclusion that plaintiff's injuries were caused by the TSRH device. Moreover, Dr. Dubinsky states that plaintiff's treatment while in Syria constitutes an additional probable cause of plaintiff's recurrent back pain. Dr. Dubinsky's report fails to differentiate or otherwise analyze which of the two possible causes stated therein is more likely to have caused plaintiff's pain. Instead, it appears that Dr. Dubinsky considers both the TSRH construct and plaintiff's previous spinal treatment equally likely causes of plaintiff's recurrent back problems. Thus, in addition to being

---

[10] At 119.

conclusory and completely unsupported by specific facts, Dr. Dubinsky's report does nothing more than establish the mere possibility that plaintiff's injuries are causally related to defendants' product. Without a more detailed analysis, or at least some type of comparison between the two probable causes identified by Dr. Dubinsky, the court concludes that no reasonable fact finder could infer the existence of a causal connection between the TSRH construct and plaintiff's injuries from Dr. Dubinsky's report.

As a final attempt to avoid summary judgment on the issue of causation, plaintiff refers the court to Dr. Alexander's generic expert testimony report regarding the use of pedicle fixation devices. Dr. Alexander's report speaks in generalities, detailing the possible risks associated with the use of pedicle screw systems in spinal fusion surgery, but identifies no specific defects attributable to defendants' product. As detailed above, the court finds Dr. Alexander's report insufficient to create a material fact issue with respect to whether defendants' product is defective. To establish causation, plaintiff must adduce evidence tending to show a causal connection between the allegedly defective product and plaintiff's specific injuries. Dr. Alexander's report is insufficient in this regard for two reasons: first, Dr. Alexander's testimony relates to pedicle screw systems as a whole, and not to the specific TSRH device at issue here. More importantly, however, because Dr. Alexander is a "generic" expert, his opinion is not case-specific, and fails, therefore, to establish a causal connection between defendants' product and Mr. Samarah's particular injuries. As such, the opinions set forth in Dr. Alexander's report are insufficient to establish causation in the case at bar.[11]

What is required is that the expert's report be legally sufficient to support the elements of the case that must be proven by expert testimony.[12] When an expert report fails to use the magic words to make the report legally sufficient (e.g., "more probable than not"), it is likely to come under attack. Experts need to closely coordinate with counsel to make sure reports filed to support or oppose summary judgment motions are properly worded. Of course, this coordination should never include allowing counsel to improperly influence the substance of the expert's opinions. Please consider the following examples.

Example 3.43: Provided justification for opinion sufficient for avoidance of summary judgment
Vollment v. Wisconsin Department of Transportation, 197 F.3d 293 (7th Cir.1999)
The court found that the opinion expressed in the expert's report was not a type of "naked conclusion" because the expert connected the facts with his conclusions.

In demanding a "roadmap" the Department would require an expert to not only provide the justification for the opinion, but also to give a primer on why the facts allow the expert to reach that conclusion. That requires too much of the plaintiff to

---

[11] At 1206, 1207.

[12] For example, let's say the issue at hand on summary judgment is causation and the expert's report reasonably and justifiably concludes that it is more likely than not that there is causation in the case at hand. The expert need not state his opinion beyond a reasonable doubt or to a moral certainty.

avoid summary judgment. It is akin to requiring a radiologist not just to present the X-Ray and her diagnosis, but to explain why the X-Ray allows her to arrive at that conclusion. The X-Ray itself provides the basis for her conclusion, and that is sufficient to entitle the diagnosis to weight. A person seeking to challenge it can easily do so by having another radiologist read the X-Ray. Similarly, Schutz presented the evidence underlying his conclusion, and explained how he deemed that evidence relevant to his conclusion. An expert need not conclusively establish a fact and need not answer all potential challenges to the opinion in order for his opinion to be given weight in a summary judgment proceeding. A contrary holding would require an expert to provide the analysis, not just the basis, for an opinion.[13]

Example 3.44: Failure to use magic words, report fails, summary judgment granted
Samos Imex Corporation v. Nextel Communications, 194 F.3d 301 (1st Cir. 1999)
The expert was Carota, a structural engineer.

> Prior to the suit being filed, John Carota, a structural engineering expert, gave Samos Imex a report evaluating the condition of the building, recommending repairs, and identifying "the probable cause" of the damage to the building and the freight elevator. The probable cause section of the report began by concluding that "[t]he probable cause of the recent movement and racking [*i.e.,* shifting] [of] this three story brick building ... can be directly attributed to the building responding to the effects of constructing the monopole project." The report then identified various "aspects" of the antenna project that "either singularly or in combination could have caused the failed elevator and cracked building support columns and walls.[14]

As a result of the language used by the expert, the case was dismissed on summary judgment. Counsel saved the case by his offer of proof explaining what the expert meant and what he would testify to if permitted.

> In all events, counsel for the plaintiff made an immediate proffer that the expert would testify that the monopole was more likely than not the cause of the injury and that was what he had intended by use of the phrase "probable cause" in the report. If there were any doubt, it would be easy enough to conduct a brief deposition of the witness. It is one thing to allow counsel to contradict by proffer something the expert said in the report or to supply a manifest omission; in that event, case management and discovery concerns would be legitimate objections. But it is hard to justify dismissal of a case on summary judgment, based on what is at worst ambiguous language, in the face of an explicit proffer by counsel that the witness meant just what many readers would expect the witness to have intended.[15]

3.5 Timeliness
Expert reports need to be filed on time. When an expert witness report is not filed in a timely fashion, counsel runs the risk of having the report stricken, the case dismissed, or having a motion for summary judgment granted

---

[13] At 300, 301.
[14] At 302, 303.
[15] At 304.

against his client. Filing an expert witness report even a few hours late can be fatal. Please consider the following examples.

Example 3.51: Expert report filed 3 hours and 25 minutes late, summary judgment granted

Skidmore v. Initial DSI Transport, Inc., 757 So.2d 107 (La.App. 5 Cir. 2000)
An expert witness report was filed 3 hours and 25 minutes too late.

> The record indicates that a report from the plaintiffs' expert dated April 12, 1999 was filed into the record on April 12, 1999 at 12:25 p.m. This report was unaccompanied by any other documents. The minutes in the record indicate the Motion for Summary Judgment was granted on 4/12/99 at 9:00 a.m. Clearly, the report by plaintiffs' expert was filed after the Motion for Summary Judgment had been granted. Additionally, we note this report was not sworn. As such it did not meet the requirements for documents to oppose a Motion for Summary Judgment.[16]

Example 3.52: Failure to file within court-imposed deadline

Firefighter's Institute for Racial Equality ex rel. Anderson v. City of St. Louis, 220 F.3d 898 (8th Cir. 2000)
The court held:

> FIRE contends the district court erred when it granted a motion to strike FIRE's expert for failing to meet the deadline for filing expert reports. There is no question, however, that the expert's report was untimely. The district court set a deadline of December 28, 1998, for disclosure of FIRE's expert and the expert report. FIRE named an expert on that date, but did not provide a report. FIRE assured the court that the report would be completed the first week of January, but failed to fulfill that promise as well. When the district court held a hearing on the motion to strike on February 19, 1999, the report still had not been filed.
>
> Federal Rule of Civil Procedure 16 permits the district court to set deadlines for the disclosure of evidence and to impose sanctions on a party for failing to meet a deadline. *See Trost v. Trek Bicycle Corp.*, 162 F.3d 1004, 1008 (8th Cir.1998). Unless the failure to meet a deadline was either harmless or substantially justified, the court may sanction a party by excluding its evidence.[17]

3.6 Requirements under State Law

State law may provide certain requirements for expert reports. The requirements of all 50 states are beyond the scope of this book. Experts should check with counsel prior to issuing their written report to make sure that the report will comply with any applicable standards or requirements under state law. Please consider the following examples.

Example 3.61: Texas malpractice suit

Palacious v. American Transactional Care Centers of Texas, Inc., 4 S.W.3d 857 (Tex.App.-Hous. [1 Dist.] 1999)
The Texas court dealt with a medical malpractice case. Under Texas law, "An 'expert report' must provide a 'fair summary' of the expert's opinions 'as of the

---

[16] At 109.
[17] At 902.

date of the report,' describing the standards of care, how the defendant failed to meet them, and the harm caused by that failure."[18] The court gave the plaintiff's expert the benefit of the doubt and stated:

> But the controlling issue is not whether the report provided the requisite "fair summary." Rather, the controlling issue is stated in section 13.01(1): whether Dr. Bontke's report "does not represent *a good faith effort to comply* with the definition of an expert report in subsection (r)(6) of this section." § 13.01(1) (emphasis added).
>
> Section 13.01(1) favors the plaintiff. It means that, before a report is deemed inadequate, it must do more than fail to constitute a "fair summary." Rather, it must fail even to "represent a good faith effort to comply" with the requirement of a "fair summary." Many reports that may arguably fail to provide a fair summary will nonetheless comply with section 13.01(1) by constituting a good faith effort to do so. This is such a case.[19]

Example 3.62: Criminal insanity defense

Ballard v. State, 768 So.2d 924 (Miss.App. 2000)

The court found that a clinical psychologist should have been permitted to testify regarding an insanity defense despite the fact that his report did not contain the *M'Naghten* test's magic words. The court urged a pragmatic approach to the case and report and stated:

> The record clearly shows that Ballard's intent to utilize this report as the basis of his insanity defense came as no surprise to the State, for it was the State that brought the issue to the attention of the Court out of the presence of the jury and prior to Dr. Morris's having been called as a witness. Although it is evident that the report did not use the magic words for the *M'Naghten* test as adopted in *Laney,* 421 So.2d at 1218, it clearly notified to the State that it was Ballard's basis for his insanity defense. In addition, the State was fully prepared and presented its own expert witness who extensively discussed *M'Naghten* and testified unequivocally that Ballard knew right from wrong at the time of the incident and did not qualify under the test. With regard to a *M'Naghten* defense rebuttal, the State would not have been unfairly prejudiced by the excluded testimony.[20]

---

[18] At 860.
[19] At 862, 863.
[20] At 928.

Chapter 4 Preparation of Reports and the Assistance of Counsel

4.1 Executive Summary

Experts are commonly given some level of assistance by retaining counsel when drafting their expert reports. The level of assistance is an extremely slippery slope. At one end of the spectrum is counsel correcting a grammatical or typographical error in a draft report. The other end of the spectrum could have counsel completely changing the expert's opinions and asking the expert to sign off on these changes.

The more assistance counsel provides, the more vulnerable the expert's report will be on cross-examination to a line of questioning suggesting that the expert merely wrote what counsel asked her to write. At some point, the expert's report may even be stricken for being in essence written by retaining counsel, and not by the expert. Experts are well advised to avoid producing any draft written reports and to refuse to let counsel influence the fundamental substance of the experts' findings, conclusions, and opinions.

4.2 Vulnerability on Cross-examination

Attorneys walk a fine line between assisting the experts in the preparation of their reports and actually being responsible for writing them. The closer counsel and the expert get to the line, the more vulnerable the expert becomes during cross-examination at trial. Experts thus should not permit counsel to write, significantly alter, or dictate the opinions expressed in their reports.

> Trial attorneys face significant risks when they alter draft expert reports. The first risk is obvious: trial counsel for the other side will ask for all drafts of the report, will focus upon any differences in the text, and will ask why those changes were made. When the testimony is elicited that the attorney was responsible for the change in the document, this will seriously affect the credibility of the expert witness, and his/her independent opinion concerning technical matter.[1]

Experts should have in mind how they will be cross-examined when preparing their reports. Here is advice given to counsel for deposing an expert witness:

> ...Determine whether the witness was asked to prepare a report.
>   a. Inquire about reports prepared under Fed.R.Civ.P.26 as well as other reports.

---

[1] Burke, "The Use of Experts in Environmental Litigation, a Practitioner's Guide," 25 N.K6.L. Rev.111 (1997) 136.

    b. If a report was prepared, inquire about drafts of the report and instructions that were given as to how to prepare the report.

    c. Find out if opposing counsel participated in the preparation and editing of the report.

    d. Consider examining the witness about any differences among the contents of her report(s), her answers to any expert interrogatories and her testimony at the deposition. However, you might want to postpone all or part of this inquiry until cross-examination at trial.[2]

Please consider the following sample cross-examination on the issue of assistance by counsel in preparing the expert report. Notice how vulnerable the expert and his credibility become when the expert allows retaining counsel to influence his report.

Example 4.21: Expert conclusions verbatim from complaint, including typos

Cross-examination:

Q. Is your report dated April 2, 2001 your final report in this case?

A. Yes it is.

Q. Did you issue a preliminary or draft report in this case?

A. No.

Q. Is this your opinion expressed on page 4 of your report?

A. Yes.

Q. What input, if any, did Attorney Duff have in formulating the opinion expressed on page 4 of the report?

A. Very little.

Q. Attorney Duff retained you and discussed your role as an expert, correct?

A. That's correct.

Q. She told you what issues you were to express an opinion on?

A. Correct.

Q. Attorney Duff also told you what issues not to express an opinion on, correct?

A. That's true.

Q. The complaint in this suit was filed on January 2, 2001, correct?

A. Correct.

Q. On page 4 of your report under the opinion section you stated:

> The Defendant did cause too exist on its premises an unreasonably dangerous and defective condition, i.e., the improperly constructed floor hole covering;
>
> The Defendant did, by failure to reasonably inspect its premises, suffir or permit the unreasonably dangerous and defective condition to remain on its premises;
>
> The Defendant failed to provide adequate warnings or other safeguards to prevent injury to persons such as Plaintiff from the unreasonably dangerous and defective condition on its property; and

---

[2] Zweifach, *Deposing the Expert Witness,* 19 PLI/NY 85 (Practice Law Institute: 1998) 117.

The Defendant failed to take responsible action to correct the dangerous and defective condition existing on its property.
Correct?

A. Yes.

Q. This language is the same as page 3 of the complaint, is it not?

A. It is similar.

Q. Sir, is it not exactly the same including the two typos made in the complaint and repeated in your report?

A. Which two typos, counselor?

Q. "Did cause *too* exist…inspect its premises," *"suffir…."*

A. Yes, they are the same.

Q. Did you prepare the report or was that done by counsel?

A. I did it myself.

Q. Can you explain how you happened to have the same exact language as the complaint, including the typographical errors?

A. No, I cannot.

Q. Did you have conversations with counsel about not issuing a preliminary report?

A. Yes.

Q. Counsel told you not to issue a preliminary report and you didn't issue one, correct?

A. I did as I was instructed.

Q. The opinion in your report is exactly the same as Mr. Todd's reports, who was also retained by Attorney Duff in this case, correct?

A. Well…it is sim…correct.

Q. Is that another coincidence or could you favor us with an explanation?

A. I have an explanation.

Q. How many phone calls did you have with Attorney Duff prior to issuing your report?

A. Three or four. I am not sure.

Q. Referring to your invoice, you had phone calls on January 4, 2001, January 17, 2001, February 4, 2001, February 17, 2001, February 19, 2001, March 7, 2001, March 8, 2001, April 1, 2001, and April 4, 2001, correct?

A. Yes, but they were not all about my report.

Q. Which ones were, sir?

A. I can't recall.

Q. Do you recall by whom and where this report was typed?

A. By someone at Attorney Duff's office.

Q. What did her staff type it from?

A. My handwritten notes.

Q. Were these notes typed verbatim as you sent them to her?

A. Yes.

Q. I show you a copy of your handwritten notes and ask you to compare them to your final report of April 2, 2001. Can you explain the changes in your opinion?

A. Well, Attorney Duff called me and we discussed some problems with the report and they were corrected.

Q. You did as instructed, didn't you, sir?

A. Yes.

Q. Do you still maintain that Attorney Duff had very little to do with the opinion you expressed?
A. I would like to take a break.

Comment: When experts allow counsel too much influence over their reports they are vulnerable to devastating cross-examination as in this example. Experts need to maintain the independence of their reports and must not let counsel directly or indirectly draft reports for them.

4.3 Legal Requirements of Rule 26

Experts who are retained to provide testimony in federal court are required to "prepare and sign" a report under F.R.C.P.26 (2)(B). The issue of how much "help" counsel can and should be in the preparation process is a contentious one.

> Another less-known requirement of Rule 26(a)(2) is that the expert must "prepare" his or her own written report, and cannot allow counsel or the party who hired the expert to prepare it for him. But some uncertainty remains as to acceptable level of involvement that counsel may have in the preparation of the expert report. The Advisory Committee Notes to Rule 26(a)(2)(B) offer some guidance:

>> Rule 26(a)(2)(B) does not preclude counsel from providing assistance to experts in preparing the reports, and indeed, with experts such as automobile mechanics, this assistance may be needed. Nevertheless, the report, which is intended to set forth the substance of the direct examination, should be written in a manner that reflects the testimony to be given by the witness and it must be signed by the witness.[3]

> Please consider the following cases.

Example 4.31: Counsel types draft report, resulting in potential disciplinary action against counsel

Occulto v. Adaman of New Jersey, 125 F.R.D. 611 (D.N.J. 1989)
This was a simple slip and fall case that perfectly illustrates the potential hazards to experts when counsel provides too much "assistance."

> The videotaped deposition of Dr. Demko went forward on January 12, 1989, and Mr. Goldenziel concluded the direct examination and Mr. Riordan, on behalf of defendant, had almost completed cross-examination when something quite remarkable occurred. Mr. Riordan discovered that Dr. Demko did not write his own Report. Instead, Dr. Demko's file contained a draft letter, not on Demko's letterhead, also dated December 20, 1988 [hereinafter "Draft Report"] which was verbatim the same as the Demko Report with one important exception. The Draft Report bore the typewritten legend across the top:

---

[3] Feldman, ALI-ABA Course of Study: "Expert Witnesses in Insurance Class Actions and Individual Cases Defense Perspective" (SF50 ALI-ABA 239: 2000) 281.

PLEASE HAVE RE-TYPED ON YOUR OWN STATIONERY.
THANK YOU.[4]

Dr. Demko testified that he did not know who typed the Draft Report (Dep. Tr. 44, lines 23-25) and that he did not even know who wrote it...

This entire colloquy must be set forth, beginning with the cross examination questioning of Mr. Riordan [Tr. 45, line 1 to 46, line 19]:

Q. What does it say at the top of that report that's in the...

A. "Please have retyped on your own stationery. Thank you."

Q. Do you know who put that language on the report?

A. No I don't.

BY MR. RIORDAN:

Q. So, Doctor, that the language of that letter was prepared by someone other than you and sent to you for review and approval?

A. This is my synopsis of the case.

Thus, Mr. Goldenziel explicitly denied knowledge of the Draft Report, saying, "I've never seen that document before." This denial was false, and Mr. Goldenziel's subsequent lines of questioning were likewise calculated to create the false impression that he did not prepare the report, such as his re-direct examination [Tr. at 59, lines 13-20]:

Q. [by Mr. Goldenziel]. And, Doctor, to your personal knowledge did my office write the letter, you know, which you referred to which counsel marked in evidence?

A. To my personal knowledge?

Q. Yes.

A. No. I mean, I don't know. To my personal knowledge, no.

His denial of knowledge and his own questioning confused even his own expert witness.[5]

The court was highly suspicious of what occurred and was displeased with counsel's explanation that his writing of a medical expert's report was "an innocent practice, and in fact his normal procedure."[6]

The court admonished counsel and, implicitly, the expert. The court found the draft report and transmittal cover letter not protected as work product under Rule 26(b)(3), Fed.R.Civ.P. The court stated:

Finally, we turn to Ex. P-1, Mr. Goldenziel's December 20, 1988 cover letter to Dr. Demko. This letter falls directly into the same subject matter as Mr. Goldenziel's instruction to his expert on Ex. D-1, above, to retype the report on the expert's own stationery. Ex. P-1 has not previously been disclosed to defense counsel, but the defendants' showing supporting disclosure is just as compelling as with respect to Ex. D-1, above.

We are concerned not just with the discoverability of a few documents but with the integrity of the truth-finding process. The work-product protection, as noted above, shields disclosure of the attorney's preparations because higher values are to be served in protecting the thought processes of counsel. But what "higher value" can possibly be served by suppressing the Goldenziel cover letter which contains, in my view, such dramatic confirmation of attorney misconduct undermining the integrity of this process?

In this case, Mr. Goldenziel, [FN2] an attorney at law, admitted to practice before this court in this case *pro hac vice*, has made a false exculpatory statement

---

[4] At 613.

[5] At 613, 614.

[6] At 614.

concerning his conduct upon the record of a trial testimony deposition, stating that "I've never seen that document before," and interfering with the orderly cross-examination of his own expert witness, and conducting the misleading re-direct examination described above. In fact, these documents demonstrate the opposite. This conduct cannot be tolerated; whether disciplinary action is warranted is not considered in this discovery motion.[7]

Example 4.32: Court highly critical of report that matches language in complaint
Manning v. Crockett, 1999 WL 342715 (N.D.Ill. 1999)
The court expressed its opinion on an expert's report written by counsel.

In contrast, preparing the expert's opinion from whole cloth and then asking the expert to sign it if he or she wishes to adopt it conflicts with Rule 26(a)(2)(B)'s requirement that the expert "prepare" the report. Preparation implies involvement other than perusing a report drafted by someone else and signing one's name at the bottom to signify agreement. In other words, the assistance of counsel contemplated by Rule 26(a)(2)(B) is not synonymous with ghost-writing. The court thus disagrees with the Manning's belief that "no rule…prohibits an expert from adopting the precise language alleged in a complaint" in his report. Rule 26(a)(2)(B)'s inclusion of the phrase "prepared and signed by the witness" does just this. Allowing an expert to sign a report drafted entirely by counsel without prior substantive input from an expert would read the word "prepared" completely out of the rule. With these principles in mind, the court turns to Dr. Ostrov's reports.

Dr. Ostrov's report is essentially a nullity as it does not provide any detail as to the substance of his testimony. The court finds that the second report is virtually identical to the Mannings' complaint and that the third report is largely similar to the complaint. The court will focus on the third report because it has previously found that the first two reports were inadequate."[8]

Example 4.33: Changes made to draft report after conference with attorney-counsel sanctioned
Marek v. Moore, 171 F.R.D. 298 (D.Kan. 1997)
This case dealt with the following factual background.

Mr. Brazeal prepared and submitted to the attorney for plaintiffs a report dated September 3, 1996. It set forth his expert opinions, as required by Rule 26(a)(2). Later that day Mr. Brazeal and the attorney discussed the report by telephone. During that discussion the witness authorized a number of changes to his report. Anticipating the deadline of September 6, 1996, for the disclosure, counsel for plaintiffs then caused the report to be retyped by his own staff, ostensibly on the letterhead of the witness. Counsel then sent to the defense attorney this unsigned revision, also dated September 3, 1996. It incorporated the changes authorized by the expert.[9]

---

[7] At 617.
[8] At 4.
[9] At 299.

The court imposed sanctions against counsel but did not strike the report. The court carefully reviewed the "changes" in the report:

> Does the involvement of the attorney in its preparation preclude it from qualifying as a report "prepared... by the witness," within the meaning of Rule 26(a)(2)(B), and particularly when the witness has testified he himself did not "prepare" it. In determining this question, the court has compared the two versions of the report. A number of the differences are simply grammatical or stylistic: the insertion and deletion of commas, quotation marks, or a preposition; the addition of the first name of the decedent; and inclusion of a professional title of the witness under a space for his signature. These changes do not alter the substance of the report.
>
> Other changes require closer scrutiny: The second version of the report includes additional description of material reviewed by the expert, such as "voluminous portions of the discovery record," depositions of three identified persons, personnel files, and "numerous exhibits." The first version expresses the opinion that defendant applied a choke hold and excessive weight to the decedent. The second version revises the opinion to state defendant applied either or both. The first version states that anyone trained in unarmed defense should recognize when someone is unconscious from lack of oxygen. The second version adds the duty to recognize when someone "is not resisting force in a manner to cause imminent harm." The first version says that the conduct of Moore "may have" led to the physical confrontation in question. The second says his conduct "probably" led to it. The first version expresses the concern of the expert if the testimonies of "some of the witnesses" are accurate. The second conditions his concern upon the testimonies of "the students and/or McGinnis."[10]

The court went on to admonish the parties as to their ethical responsibilities.

> Notwithstanding its findings in this instance, the court also emphasizes that in no way does it suggest that attorneys have license to change the opinions and reports of expert witnesses. Any changes in the preparation of a report must be what the expert himself has freely authorized and adopted as his own and not merely for appeasement or because of intimidation or some undue influence by the party or counsel who has retained him. Absent some showing to the contrary, however, the court will assume that an attorney ethically abides by his responsibility as its officer and that a witness, expert or otherwise, will abide by his oath to tell the truth.[11]

---

[10] At 300.
[11] At 302.

Chapter 5 Formatting

5.1 Executive Summary

It is important to use formatting that makes the expert report easy to read and look professional. The authors recommended the following.

- A cover page,
- twelve-point font that is easy to read, especially if the report is faxed,
- topic headings to break up the report,
- short, concise paragraphs,
- avoiding run-on paragraphs,
- 1 ½-line spacing,
- pages numbered 1 of 5, 2 of 5, 3 of 5, etc.,
- an executive summary at the beginning of the report, and
- summary judgment reports in the form of an affidavit (that is, signed under the pains and penalties of perjury).

5.2 Cover Page

Some experts construct a cover to their expert report. A well-drafted cover may indicate to the reader that the expert is a methodical person. This will help to bolster the expert's credibility. Consider the following example.

Example 5.21: Well-drafted cover page
Report States:

INVESTIGATION OF ENGINEERING PLANS

CHARMING HILLS SUBDIVISION NO. 2, PHASE 2
SUNNY CITY
COUNTY OF LINCOLN, OHIO

SUBMITTED TO: SUSAN E. JONES, ESQ.
JONES AND LARSEN CO., L.P.A.
900 WEST MAIN ST., SUITE A
SUNNY CITY, OHIO 40004

PERTAINING TO: CHARMING ESTATES
VS.
THOMS & ASSOCIATES
CASE NO. 123456
COURT OF COMMON PLEAS OF LINCOLN COUNTY

JULY 1, 2001

ATTORNEY WORK PRODUCT

PREPARED BY: CATLIN SALLEY, P.E., P.L.S.
MARSHALL ASSOCIATES, INC.
1001 W. ELM ST.
CARSONVILLE, PA 18000
TELEPHONE (215) 555-0000

Comment: A well-drafted cover page as in the above example makes an expert report look as if it were carefully drafted. This will serve to bolster the expert's credibility and increase the value of her opinion.

5.3 Font

It is wise for the expert to use a 12-point font in reports. Smaller fonts can be very difficult to read. This is especially true if the report is faxed one or more times. Some experts may be tempted to use a smaller font when presenting tables, graphs, or appendices because the smaller font may help get more information onto a page.

Example 5.31: Font too small
The following example shows a report with text in an eight-point font. It is difficult to read and takes away from the effectiveness of the report.

Report States:
These complaints are symptoms or problems the patient states she did not experience prior to the accident or are obvious exacerbations of symptoms the patient reports she experienced prior to the accident. Ms. X XX states she currently experiences the following symptoms:
1.   Occasional stiffness in the neck. This is worse in the morning. "I can't sleep well due to my neck pain. Sometimes this gets worse than at other times. It has gotten some better with treatment but it still bothers me every day. My neck hurts a lot more when I have to read or study a lot for my nursing exam." The patient rates this pain level as 2-4.
2.   Frequent soreness and dull aching in the spinal column area of the low back and on the muscles on right side and on the left side. A reduction of the normal ability to bend and twist at the waist is reported. She states that moving from a seated position to a standing position and back again is difficult now. The pain is reportedly increased by minimal physical activity that involves the use of this area. The patient rates this pain level as 4-5. "This is my worst pain. I can't stand for long without a lot of pain."
3.   A sensation of numbness in the posterior...

Comment: The expert would have been better served by using the following larger, easier-to-read font.

These complaints are symptoms or problems the patient states she did not experience prior to the accident or are obvious exacerbations of symptoms the patient reports she experienced prior to the accident. Ms. X XX states she currently experiences the following symptoms:

1.　　　Occasional stiffness in the neck. This is worse in the morning. "I can't sleep well due to my neck pain. Sometimes this gets worse than at other times. It has gotten some better with treatment but it still bothers me every day. My neck hurts a lot more when I have to read or study a lot for my nursing exam." The patient rates this pain level as 2-4.

2.　　　Frequent soreness and dull aching in the spinal column area of the low back and on the muscles on right side and on the left side. A reduction of the normal ability to bend and twist at the waist is reported. She states that moving from a seated position to a standing position and back again is difficult now. The pain is reportedly increased by minimal physical activity that involves the use of this area. The patient rates this pain level as 4-5. "This is my worst pain. I can't stand for long without a lot of pain."

3.　　　A sensation of numbness in the posterior...

5.4 Topic Headings

Topic headings break things up. They make the report easy to read and make it easy to find what one is looking for in the report. This can be particularly useful to the expert who is using her report while testifying. If an expert fails to use topic headings, people will not want to read her report.

Example 5.41: Failure to use topic headings
The following report has not been broken down into topic headings.

Report States:

At the request of Ms. Mary Miller, senior claims representative of ABC Insurance Company, I did review the extensive medical file that had been sent to me. This file consisted of the office notes (not complete) of Dr. Stevens, Healthy Orthopedic Group, cardiology notes of Dr. Riley of Browning University as well as extensive physical therapy notes and in-hospital records and numerous test results.

Mr. Hall sustained injuries to his neck, upper back, and lower back when in the course of his employment on 4/25/95, he attempted to break up a fight between the students at the school where he is a vocational teacher. Mr. Hall was initially seen at the Best Medical Center by Dr. Stanton, who after evaluation, prescribed medication and a course of physical therapy. The patient did begin a course of physical therapy but was unable to complete this due to increase in pain.

Mr. Hall was then referred for evaluation and treatment to Dr. Stevens, an orthopedic surgeon in Cary, CT. Dr. Stevens's initial evaluation has not been available to me but Dr. Stevens's appears to have an extensive course of physical therapy. Dr. Stevens refers repeatedly to "muscular ligamentitis sprain strain syndrome."

Some time in June or July of 1995, Mr. Hall sustained a massive anterior myocardial infarction involving the anterior wall of the heart. He was treated for this by Dr. Andersen of the Browning Cardiology Department. Dr. Stevens did see Mr. Hall again on 9/11/95 following his myocardial infarction and did continue to recommend physical therapy.

One note throughout the multiple evaluations by Dr. Stevens that there was not any focal neurologic signs—either objective sensory losses or reflex abnormalities. Evidently the x-rays of the entire spine were eventually taken and these are reported as being negative.

Mr. Hall continued with neck, upper and lower back pain and was unable to return to work throughout the Fall of 1995. One notices a marked lack of any objective findings with respect to his neck, upper and lower back. An MRI of the lumbar spine was obtained (? location) on 12/21/95 and was consistent with "mild changes" of degenerative disease at L1-2, L4-5, and L5-S1. There is no evidence of disc herniation. An MRI of the thoracic spine was obtained on 3/11/96 (? location) and was interpreted as "within normal limits." An MRI of the cervical spine was performed on 12/29/95 (? location) and interpreted as:

1. Multilevel changes of bulging degenerative intervertebral discs;
2. Mild central disc protrusion at C3-C4;
3. Acquired canal and foraminal stenosis at C5-6 "greater on the left."

It is further noted throughout that the patient never presented with any localizing signs or specific neurologic signs.

On January 10, 1996, Dr. Stevens allowed Mr. Hall to attempt to return to work on "about 2 hours per day" basis which was all that Mr. Hall could tolerate due to the pain.

On 2/26/96, Mr. Hall was reported by Dr. Stevens as "having undergone open heart surgery a couple of weeks ago". "His complaint is a persistent pain in his back which has always been his major complaint". Once again there was a lack of any objective findings.

It is inconceivable to me that without any more objective findings than the minimal ones that are present (cervical spine-MRI which may be a normal variant) that the event of 4/25/95 may be a factor in Mr. Hall's inability to work and continued complaints of back pain.

It is obvious that this patient's severe cardiac status coupled with his myocardial infarction and open heart surgery are the major factors in prohibiting his return to work and his ongoing problems.

It appears that Mr. Hall's problems particularly with his upper and lower back are related to a chronic weakness of the musculature coupled with what appears to be some sort of fibromylasia syndrome. The patient has had more than an extensive course of physical therapy and he must accept his present condition and be assured that symptoms should improve, if honestly reported, with time.

Once again I stress the lack of orthopedic findings within this entire case.

It is impossible to state at the present time what Mr. Hall's work capacity is as I have not had the advantage of examining myself.

Once again, it is to be noted that the patient's problems are due in only the most minimal manner to the events of 4/25/95 and are due to his cardiac problems with the deconditioning of the muscles following all of his cardiac problems as well as the minimal degenerative changes present throughout his entire spine present prior to the event of 4/25/95.

Comment: The same report can be made much more valuable with a little rewriting, some careful proofreading, and the addition of topic headings.

FORMATTING

Documents Reviewed
At the request of Ms. Mary Miller, senior claims representative of ABC Insurance Company, I reviewed the extensive medical file that had been sent to me. This file consisted of the office notes (not complete) of Dr. Stevens, Healthy Orthopedic Group, cardiology notes of Dr. Riley of Browning University as well as extensive physical therapy notes and in-hospital records and numerous test results.

History of Injury
Mr. Hall sustained injuries to his neck, upper back, and lower back when in the course of his employment on 4/25/95, he attempted to break up a fight between the students at the ACES school where he is a vocational teacher.

Initial Treatment
Mr. Hall was initially seen at the Best Medical Center by Dr. Stanton, who after evaluation, prescribed medication and a course of physical therapy. The patient began a course of physical therapy but was unable to complete this due to increase in pain.

Physical Therapy
Mr. Hall was then referred for evaluation and treatment to Dr. Stevens, an orthopedic surgeon in Cary, CT. Dr. Stevens's initial evaluation has not been available to me but Dr. Stevens's appears to have an extensive course of physical therapy. Dr. Stevens refers repeatedly to "muscular ligamentitis sprain strain syndrome."

Subsequent Myocardial Infarction
Some time in June or July of 1995, Mr. Hall sustained a massive anterior myocardial infarction involving the anterior wall of the heart. He was treated for this by Dr. Andersen of the Browning Cardiology Department. Dr. Stevens saw Mr. Hall again on 9/11/95 following his myocardial infarction and continued to recommend physical therapy.

Lack of Objective Findings
One note throughout the multiple evaluations by Dr. Stevens was that there was not any focal neurologic signs of either objective sensory losses or reflex abnormalities. Evidently the x-rays of the entire spine were eventually taken and these are reported as being negative.

Mr. Hall continued with neck, upper and lower back pain and was unable to return to work throughout the Fall of 1995. There was a marked lack of any objective findings with respect to his neck, upper and lower back. An MRI of the lumbar spine was obtained (? location) on 12/21/95 and was consistent with "mild changes" of degenerative disease at L1-2, L4-5, and L5-S1. There is no evidence of disc herniation. An MRI of the thoracic spine was obtained on 3/11/96 (? location) and was interpreted as "within normal limits." An MRI of the cervical spine was performed on 12/29/95 (? location) and interpreted as:

1. Multilevel changes of bulging degenerative intervertebral discs;

2. Mild central disc protrusion at C3-C4; and
3. Acquired canal and foraminal stenosis at C5-6 "greater on the left."

It is further noted throughout that the patient never presented with any localizing signs or specific neurologic signs.

Return to Work
On January 10, 1996, Dr. Stevens allowed Mr. Hall to attempt to return to work on "about 2 hours per day" basis which was all that Mr. Hall could tolerate due to the pain.

Continued Lack of Objective Findings
On 2/26/96, Mr. Hall was reported by Dr. Stevens as "having undergone open heart surgery a couple of weeks ago." "His complaint is a persistent pain in his back which has always been his major complaint." Once again there was a lack of any objective findings.

Conclusions
In my opinion, based on a reasonable degree of medical certainty the event of 4/25/95 is not a factor in Mr. Hall's inability to work and continued complaints of back pain. This is based on the lack of objective findings other than the minimal ones that are present (cervical spine-MRI which may be a normal variant).

In my opinion, based on a reasonable degree of medical certainty, this patient's severe cardiac status coupled with his myocardial infarction and open heart surgery are the major factors in prohibiting his return to work and his ongoing problems.

In my opinion, based on a reasonable degree of medical certainty, Mr. Hall's problems, particularly with his upper and lower back, are related to a chronic weakness of the musculature coupled with a fibromylalgia syndrome.

It is impossible to state at the present time what Mr. Hall's work capacity is as I have not had the advantage of examining him myself. The patient's problems are due in only the most minimal manner to the events of 4/25/95 and are due to his cardiac problems with the deconditioning of the muscles following all of his cardiac problems as well as the minimal degenerative changes present throughout his entire spine present prior to the event of 4/25/95.

5.5 Short, Concise Paragraphs
Short, concise paragraphs are easy to read and understand. Thus, they are valuable to the reader. Long, run-on paragraphs tend to come about when the expert dictates portions of the report. In this situation, the expert is well advised to either include "new paragraph" directions in his dictation or edit the report post-transcription to eliminate any lengthy, run-on paragraphs.

FORMATTING

Example 5.51: Run-on "history" paragraph

The history section of the following report is a single run-on paragraph. This is difficult to read, torturously boring, and not at all valuable to the end-user.

Report States:

History

The examinee is a right hand dominant 51-year-old male who is here for evaluation of a neck injury sustained in a motor vehicle accident on 01/14/1997. Prior to that time he never had any significant neck problems. On the date of injury, the examinee was on the way to a doctor's appointment for follow-up of a gastrointestinal condition (see Past Medical History). The examinee was driving a 1991 full-size pickup truck. As he was going through an intersection, he was hit broadside on the driver's side of his vehicle. He says he never saw the other vehicle coming. There were stop signs at the intersection for the cross traffic, but not for the examinee. He was wearing his seat belt with shoulder harness. The vehicle that hit him was a compact car and its front end went under the back end of the examinee's pickup truck, lifting up the back end of the truck such that the back wheels of the pickup truck went over the front of the compact car. The impact caused the examinee's pickup truck to spin around about 270 degrees, landing against the opposite curve. The bolts of the pickup truck's left rear tire were sheared off from the impact. The examinee recalls being thrown forcefully forward and to the right against his shoulder strap. This resulted in a large bruise across his left chest wall. The examinee was stunned after the impact. He dialed 911 on his cell phone, and remained in the pickup truck for about five or six minutes. Then he got out of the pickup truck around the same time emergency assistance arrived. The examinee recalls being "numb and stunned by the whole thing." He was interviewed by emergency personnel and was determined to be medically stable. He called his wife and she came to pick him up. She took him to the medical clinic where he was heading towards originally for his doctor's appointment. At the medical clinic they took some x-rays of his right shoulder, as he was complaining of immediate pain in the right shoulder and right upper extremity. A suspicious finding of a fracture in the shoulder blade was noted, and he was placed in a right arm sling for the next couple of weeks. Since that time, he continued to suffer from the effects of this motor vehicle accident. Within a day or two after the accident, he started to experience numbness and tingling in his right hand. He also began to experience neck pain. Because of these symptoms, he decided to go to a chiropractor. He had never been to one before, and decided to try one. The chiropractor took x-rays and told him he had a whiplash injury of the neck. He proceeded to adjust the examinee about six or seven times, but the examinee notes that he really wasn't making much improvement. He notes that because of his lack of response to chiropractic treatment he stopped going to the chiropractor and just hoped it would get better on its own. However, it did not and he continued to have symptoms of persistent neck pain, and in particular numbness and difficulty using his right hand, especially in performing fine manipulation. He subsequently again sought medical treatment with his physician because of his persistent symptoms,

45

particularly in the neck and right hand, and his doctor referred him to an orthopedic specialist at the University of Maine. Carpal Tunnel Syndrome was suspected. He was treated conservatively with wrist braces and anti-inflammatory medication, but his condition never improved. In fact, he says it got worse. By this time, he was not only having the numbness in the right hand, but also a dull aching pain extending down the inside of his right upper extremity. EMGs revealed a problem with a pinched nerve in the neck. He was referred to a spinal specialist at the UM Spine Clinic. An MRI scan of the cervical spine was performed showing problems with 2 disks in the neck. He was diagnosed with a cervical radiculopathy of the right upper extremity caused by abnormalities with the discs in the neck. He was treated conservatively with physical therapy and traction devices, and has continued a daily home exercise program. This has helped his condition somewhat in that he has increased range of motion in his neck. However, he remains with persistent numbness, tingling, and difficulty using the right hand. He has been told that should his condition deteriorate or become intolerable, the next step would be surgery. Currently, he is functionally limited in use of his right hand. He does work with power tools such as table saws, and he has to take special amounts of caution because of the lack of sensation and inability to finely manipulate the right hand. He has trouble sleeping at night because he frequently wakes up with numbness in his entire right upper extremity. He says last night's sleep was a good example of what he suffers with: he work up every hour or so with his right upper extremity feeling numb. He experiences daily chronic pain in the right upper extremity which is treated with Vioxx, making it more tolerable. He used to be an avid fisherman, but has not fished since this condition developed because he has difficulty feeling the line or the hook. He used to enjoy golf, but no longer is able to play because he has no control of his swing. Performing any work activity at shoulder or above height is particularly difficult for him. He avoids this type of work activity whenever he can. Driving the car for prolonged periods of time causes an exacerbation of symptoms. Simple things like buttoning his shirt buttons with his right hand are difficult to perform because he has trouble feeling and manipulating the buttons with his right hand. Any physical activities such as pushing a lawnmower or shoveling snow exacerbate the pain in his neck and the numbness, tingling, and pain in the right upper extremity. Prior to the accident he lived in a house that required a lot of these activities. After the accident, he decided to sell the house and move to a condo in order to avoid these types of activities. One of the hobbies he used to enjoy was woodworking. He continues to do woodworking to the best extent that he is able. However, simple activities he formerly was able to perform are now much more difficult, and this is a source of frustration for him. For example, several weeks ago he was building a crib for the anticipated arrival of his new grandchild. It was extremely frustrating for him to perform such simple activities as inserting slats into a small groove to make the crib railing. Even brushing his teeth is done with some difficulty since the accident. Every morning he awakens with his neck extremely stiff and he requires a long, hot shower to loosen it up. He also does daily physical therapy exercises and uses a home traction unit.

Comment: Breaking up this run-on paragraph makes the report easier to read and much more interesting and valuable to the reader. Adding a few subheadings improves the report even more.

History

The examinee is a right-hand dominant 51-year-old male who is here for evaluation of a neck injury sustained in a motor vehicle accident on 01/14/1997. Prior to that time he never had any significant neck problems.

Motor Vehicle Accident of 01/14/1997
On the date of injury, the examinee was on the way to a doctor's appointment for follow-up of a gastrointestinal condition (see Past Medical History). The examinee was driving a 1991 full-size pickup truck. As he was going through an intersection, he was hit broadside on the driver's side of his vehicle. He says he never saw the other vehicle coming. There were stop signs at the intersection for the cross traffic, but not for the examinee. He was wearing his seat belt with shoulder harness. The vehicle that hit him was a compact car and its front end went under the back end of the examinee's pickup truck, lifting up the back end of the truck such that the back wheels of the pickup truck went over the front of the compact car.

The impact caused the examinee's pickup truck to spin around about 270 degrees, landing against the opposite curve. The bolts of the pickup truck's left rear tire were sheared off from the impact. The examinee recalls being thrown forcefully forward and to the right against his shoulder strap. This resulted in a large bruise across his left chest wall.

The examinee was stunned after the impact. He dialed 911 on his cell phone, and remained in the pickup truck for about five or six minutes. Then he got out of the pickup truck around the same time emergency assistance arrived. The examinee recalls being "numb and stunned by the whole thing." He was interviewed by emergency personnel and was determined to be medically stable. He called his wife and she came to pick him up.

His wife took him to the medical clinic where he was heading towards originally for his doctor's appointment. At the medical clinic they took some x-rays of his right shoulder, as he was complaining of immediate pain in the right shoulder and right upper extremity. A suspicious finding of a fracture in the shoulder blade was noted, and he was placed in a right arm sling for the next couple of weeks.

Post-Accident Treatment
He continued to suffer from the effects of this motor vehicle accident. Within a day or two after the accident, he started to experience numbness and tingling in his right hand. He also began to experience neck pain.

Because of these symptoms, he decided to go to a chiropractor. He had never been to one before, and decided to try one. The chiropractor took x-rays and told him he had a whiplash injury of the neck. He proceeded to adjust the examinee about six or seven times, but the examinee notes that he really wasn't making much improvement. He notes that because of his lack of response to chiropractic treatment he stopped going to the chiropractor and just hoped it would get better on its own. However, it did not and he continued to have symptoms of persistent neck pain, and in particular numbness and difficulty using his right hand, especially in performing fine manipulation.

He subsequently again sought medical treatment with his physician because of his persistent symptoms, particularly in the neck and right hand, and his doctor referred him to an orthopedic specialist at the University of Maine. Carpal Tunnel Syndrome was suspected. He was treated conservatively with wrist braces and anti-inflammatory medication, but his condition never improved. In fact, he says it got worse.

By this time, he was not only having the numbness in the right hand, but also a dull aching pain extending down the inside of his right upper extremity. EMGs revealed a problem with a pinched nerve in the neck. He was referred to a spinal specialist at the UM Spine Clinic. An MRI scan of the cervical spine was performed showing problems with 2 disks in the neck. He was diagnosed with a cervical radiculopathy of the right upper extremity caused by abnormalities with the discs in the neck.

He was treated conservatively with physical therapy and traction devices, and has continued a daily home exercise program. This has helped his condition somewhat in that he has increased range of motion in his neck. However, he remains with persistent numbness, tingling, and difficulty using the right hand.

He has been told that should his condition deteriorate or become intolerable, the next step would be surgery. Currently, he is functionally limited in use of his right hand. He does work with power tools such as table saws, and he has to take special amounts of caution because of the lack of sensation and inability to finely manipulate the right hand. He has trouble sleeping at night because he frequently wakes up with numbness in his entire right upper extremity. He says last night's sleep was a good example of what he suffers with: he work up every hour or so with his right upper extremity feeling numb. He experiences daily chronic pain in the right upper extremity which is treated with Vioxx, making it more tolerable.

Effects of Conditions on Daily Activities
He used to be an avid fisherman, but has not fished since this condition developed because he has difficulty feeling the line or the hook. He used to enjoy golf, but no longer is able to play because he has no control of his swing. Performing any work activity at shoulder or above height is

particularly difficult for him. He avoids this type of work activity whenever he can. Driving the car for prolonged periods of time causes an exacerbation of symptoms. Simple things like buttoning his shirt buttons with his right hand are difficult to perform because he has trouble feeling and manipulating the buttons with his right hand. Any physical activities such as pushing a lawnmower or shoveling snow exacerbate the pain in his neck and the numbness, tingling, and pain in the right upper extremity.

Prior to the accident he lived in a house that required a lot of these activities. After the accident, he decided to sell the house and move to a condo in order to avoid these types of activities. One of the hobbies he used to enjoy was woodworking. He continues to do woodworking to the best extent that he is able. However, simple activities he formerly was able to perform are now much more difficult, and this is a source of frustration for him. For example, several weeks ago he was building a crib for the anticipated arrival of his new grandchild. It was extremely frustrating for him to perform such simple activities as inserting slats into a small groove to make the crib railing. Even brushing his teeth is done with some difficulty since the accident. Every morning he awakens with his neck extremely stiff and he requires a long, hot shower to loosen it up. He also does daily physical therapy exercises and uses a home traction unit.

5.6 Spacing

Ideally, a report will have 1 ½ lines of space between lines. This makes the report easy to read and easy for the reader to make notes on. Using 1 ½ lines of space can also help in making concise reports seem longer and more impressive.

Example 5.61: 1 ½ lines of space
The following report is presented in single-space format.

Report States:
In order to be considered complete and appropriate, a patient's treatment record must clearly and legibly include: adequate and appropriate patient identification information; all relevant historical information that may influence the delivery or outcome of dental care; notations that substantiates adequate diagnosis of existing dental and orofacial conditions; documentation of the patient's dental, periodontal and oral health condition; and progress notes descriptive of the course of the treatment *(ADA Council of Dental Practice, 1994)*. Documentation in the Castle Dental Centers of Texas treatment record regarding the plaintiff's presenting periodontal condition is lacking. Individuals of all ages are susceptible to periodontal disease to varying degrees. Therefore, the dental records of all patients with remaining teeth must contain routine periodontal evaluation data including, but not limited to: periodontal probing depths; clinically apparent tissue conditions; bleeding on probing; tooth mobility; furcation involvement; overriding occlusal concerns; presence or absence of periodontal bone loss; adequate and up-to-date radiographic evaluation; and assessment of the patient's oral hygiene status *(Palat, 1990)*. With regard to periodontal

diagnosis and documentation of a patient's periodontal status during clinical evaluation, the following is true:

Step one...in fulfilling the standard of care to diagnose periodontal disease is recognition of clinical signs and symptoms of the disease. It is necessary to be aware of the many factors related to periodontal disease and to record them, since our interest is in the patient who has the disease, not simply the disease itself *(Palat, 1989).*

Thus, the standard of care that first must be exercised by the practitioner is the recognition of...periodontal clinical signs and the gathering of the clinical data in order to make a diagnosis. Part two of this standard must be the duty to document the clinical signs and symptoms that are necessary both in the treatment of the patient and in the defense against allegations of failure to diagnose periodontal disease *(Palat, 1989).*

There appears no evidence that standard *(Palat, 1990),* pre-treatment, periodontal evaluation was performed or documented in the Castle Dental Centers of Texas treatment record. The absence of evidence that reasonable diagnostic examination and documentation of the plaintiff's existing periodontal conditions was accomplished by the defendants constitutes dental therapy below the acceptable standard of care *(Palat, 1989).*

Comment: The report is easier to read in the following 1 ½-line spacing format.

In order to be considered complete and appropriate, a patient's treatment record must clearly and legibly include: adequate and appropriate patient identification information; all relevant historical information that may influence the delivery or outcome of dental care; notations that substantiates adequate diagnosis of existing dental and orofacial conditions; documentation of the patient's dental, periodontal and oral health condition; and progress notes descriptive of the course of the treatment *(ADA Council of Dental Practice, 1994).*

Documentation in the Castle Dental Centers of Texas treatment record regarding the plaintiff's presenting periodontal condition is lacking. Individuals of all ages are susceptible to periodontal disease to varying degrees. Therefore, the dental records of all patients with remaining teeth must contain routine periodontal evaluation data including, but not limited to: periodontal probing depths; clinically apparent tissue conditions; bleeding on probing; tooth mobility; furcation involvement; overriding occlusal concerns; presence or absence of periodontal bone loss; adequate and up-to-date radiographic evaluation; and assessment of the patient's oral hygiene status *(Palat, 1990)*. With regard to periodontal diagnosis and documentation of a patient's periodontal status during clinical evaluation, the following is true:

Step one...in fulfilling the standard of care to diagnose periodontal disease is recognition of clinical signs and symptoms of the disease. It is necessary to be aware of the many factors related to periodontal disease and to <u>record</u> them, since our interest is in the patient who has the disease, not simply the disease itself *(Palat, 1989)*.

Thus, the standard of care that first must be exercised by the practitioner is the recognition of...periodontal clinical signs and the gathering of the clinical data in order to make a diagnosis. Part two of this standard must be the duty to document the clinical signs and symptoms that are necessary both in the treatment of the patient and in the defense against allegations of failure to diagnose periodontal disease *(Palat, 1989)*.

There appears no evidence that standard *(Palat, 1990)*, pre-treatment, periodontal evaluation was performed or documented in the Castle Dental Centers of Texas treatment record. The absence of evidence that reasonable diagnostic examination and documentation of the plaintiff's existing periodontal conditions was accomplished by the defendants constitutes dental therapy below the acceptable standard of care *(Palat, 1989)*.

5.7 Page Numbering
One must number the pages of a report. A good format to follow will list the page number and total number of pages (e.g., page 7 of 15). Failure to number the pages makes the report appear unprofessional and sloppy.

Example 5.71: Failure to number pages
The following cross-examination regarding page numbers is an example of the way an expert can needlessly lose credibility by preparing a sloppy report without page numbers.

Cross-examination:
Q. I am looking at what appears to be page six of your report. You didn't number the pages, sir?
A. Let me see, I guess not.
Q. Was that done intentionally?

A. No. My secretary probably forgot.
Q. Did you write this report or did your secretary?
A. I did.
Q. Did you read the report carefully before you signed it?
A. Of course.
Q. You didn't notice that there were no page numbers?
A. Is there a point to this?
Q. Did you carefully prepare and read over this report?
A. Page numbers were not and are not important. It's a little detail. My report is my report and I stand by it.
Q. What other little details that you didn't think were important did you omit from your report?

Comment: The expert would have avoided this needless distraction by proofing the report carefully and making sure page numbers were included.

5.8 Include an Executive Summary

Wise experts include an executive summary, especially when reports are lengthy. The executive summary should consist of a brief summary of one's conclusions with supporting rationale. An executive summary to a lengthy report is more likely to be read and understood by mediators, judges, opposing counsel, retaining counsel, jurors, and other persons with whom the report is designed to communicate.

The following example contains a good executive summary. It is followed by a very detailed and lengthy (5,000+ words) custody evaluation. The executive summary helps make sure that the expert's conclusions are read.

> **Example 5.81: Executive summary**
> *Report States:*
> EXECUTIVE SUMMARY
> Both parents love A and are able to provide a proper home environment. A is not, however, a good candidate for joint custody because his parents are unable to work with one another in a civil, businesslike manner. By design, necessity or choice, Mrs. X has been A's primary care provider since birth. Therefore, this examiner respectfully recommends to the Court that Mrs. X be considered as the sole custodian and primary residential parent of the minor child, A.

Comment: A get-to-the point executive summary similar to the above can help ensure that the expert's opinions are communicated to the reader and do not become lost in a detailed and lengthy report.

Consider a second example of a well-written executive summary.

Example 5.82: Executive summary
Report States:

EXECUTIVE SUMMARY

I have reviewed the videotape deposition of Mr. Robert, which includes his testimony as to how this incident occurred and a demonstration on the videotape of his actions at the time of the injury while utilizing the miter saw in question. I have also reviewed all of Mr. Robert's pertinent medical records to date pertaining to the injury to his hand, including the x-rays and operative report of his surgeon. Finally, I have personally examined the miter saw in question, and conducted a physical examination of Mr. Robert and his injuries.

Based upon my review and examinations, it is my opinion at this time that:

(1) The injuries to Mr. Robert's left hand were caused by his hand being pulled into the rotating miter saw blade during a kickback, as opposed to being caused by his bringing the rotating blade down on his hand. This opinion is based upon the pattern of injury, the type of injuries to his digits and thumb, the nature of the amputation reflected on x-ray and examination, and the rotation of the hand required to cause these injuries.

(2) It is further my opinion that had the miter saw in question included a wraparound blade guard, or a more complete blade guard, that would have prevented exposure to the rotating blade.

Comment: A well-written and concise executive summary is part of a well-written report.

5.9 Summary Judgment Reports in the Form of Affidavits
Expert reports offered in support of or in opposition to a motion for summary judgment should be sworn to under the pains and penalties of perjury. Failure to do so may mean that the court will not consider the report. Please consider the following examples.

Example 5.91: Unsworn report not competent evidence for summary judgment
Encalade v. United Insurance Company of America, 735 So.2d 954 (La.App. 4 Cir. 1999)
The court rejected a group of experts' accident reconstruction report. The report was attached to a motion for summary judgment. The court found that:

> To their motion for summary judgment, defendants attached the report of a group of experts in the area of accident reconstruction. In considering a motion for summary judgment, courts should consider "the pleadings, depositions, answers to interrogatories, and admissions on file, together with the affidavits, if any." LSA-C.C.P. art. 966(B). Defendants rely on facts contained in this report and the records, including the police report, attached to this report in both their arguments to this court and their arguments to the trial court. However, defendants did not accompany this report with any affidavits or depositions. Such evidence, without accompanying affidavits or depositions, is not considered as competent evidence.[1]

---

[1] At 956.

Example 5.92: Unsworn letter from safety expert not sufficient
Carr v. Wal-Mart Stores, Inc., 772 So.2d 865 (La.App. 5 Cir. 2000)
In this case, a letter from a safety expert was not in the form of a sworn affidavit. The unsworn letter was rejected by the court in a motion for summary judgment.

Example 5.93: Unsworn report rejected
Rainforest Café, Inc. v. Amazon, Inc., 86 F.Supp.2d 886 (D.Minn. 1999)
A signed report was rejected in a motion for summary judgment because the report was unsworn, unverified, and had not been stated to be true and correct and declared under the penalty of perjury.

The purpose of the expert report is to persuade and educate. Making the report easy to read through proper formatting will help ensure that it is read.

Chapter 6 Properly Disclosing Precise Documents Reviewed

6.1 Executive Summary

It is essential that the expert organize, explicitly list, and precisely describe all of the documents, reports, photos, depositions, tangible evidence, and other materials he has reviewed in his reports. This serves several purposes:

- it forces the expert to account for all the material he has reviewed,
- it removes any ambiguity about what was and was not reviewed by the expert, and
- it permits the expert to consult his report quickly and testify to what was and was not reviewed.

In terms of presentation of the list of documents reviewed, the authors recommend the following.

- The list should be numbered.
- The documents may be listed alphabetically, chronologically, or according to some natural, logical grouping (for example, all medical reports, all depositions).[1]
- All key documents should be reviewed and this review should be documented.
- The following descriptives should be avoided: "including," "including but not limited to," "relevant portions of," and "various."
- Each document should be precisely described, including where appropriate, date, length, author, and other descriptive information.
- Experts should not make opposing counsel's job easier by explicitly listing documents that were not available for review.

6.2 Thoroughness

The more thorough the expert's investigation, the more credible the expert's conclusions will be. The thoroughness of the expert's investigation is directly related to the documents the expert reviewed. Failure to review key

---

[1] Thomas G. Gutheil, *The Psychiatrist as Expert Witness* (Washington, DC: American Psychiatric Press, 1998) 104-105.

documents can result in the expert's report and opinion being given reduced weight or being stricken entirely.

Example 6.21: Failure to review depositions, report stricken
United Phosphorus Ltd. V. Midland Fumigant, Inc., 173 F.R.D. 675 (D.Kan. 1997)
In this case the court rejected the report of Dr. Richard Hoyt, explaining:

> The court determines, based on the foregoing, that Hoyt violated a fundamental principle of economics when he failed to consider in his report the actions of Midland in estimating a value for the Quick-Phos trade name. Hoyt did not read any of the depositions (notably of Fox, Lynn, or Estes) before he rendered his report. Consequently, he was required to evaluate the Quick-Phos trademark with little knowledge about the facts of the case, and no knowledge about the underlying admissions from Midland's president and sales managers. The court finds that such ignorance of undisputed facts violates *Daubert's* requirement that an expert report and opinions must be based on "scientific knowledge."

6.3 Numbering Lists
The authors recommend that the list be numbered. This is visually pleasing and makes the report appear carefully and precisely drafted.

Example 6.31 Numbering the list of documents reviewed
Report States:
I have reviewed the following documents:

1. Complaint dated 1/1/01
2. Answer and counterclaim dates 1/19/01
3. Medical Center Emergency Room Records, 27 pages, Visit of 4/7/98
4. Autopsy Report, 5 pages, dated 4/9/98
5. Deposition of Joe Brown, DO, defendant, 67 pages, taken 5/14/01
6. Deposition of Jim Kale, EMT, 21 pages, taken 5/18/01
7. Deposition of Shelley Stone, daughter of victim, 21 pages, taken 5/21/01...

Comment: This is an effective listing. The documents reviewed are numbered and precisely described. This suggests that the documents were carefully reviewed. The expert report appears to have been carefully drafted, which will bolster the expert's credibility and value.

6.4 "Including" and "Including, but Not Limited to"
The word "including" in front of the list of documents should be avoided. This word implies that other documents were reviewed but not listed. This could be spun by opposing counsel as either an intentional omission or laziness. Either way, the expert will lose credibility.

Example 6.41: "These include"
Report States:

> I have reviewed the records of Jane Doe. These include the following:....

Resulting Cross-examination:

Q. On page one of your report you state that the documents you reviewed prior to forming your opinion include a history and then you list several documents. Is that correct?

A. Yes, that's what I stated.

Q. What documents did you review prior to forming your opinion that you did not include in the listing on page one of your report?

A. I don't know if there were any.

Q. Are you sure?

A. No, I am not. I'd have to check my file.

Comment: Use of the word "include" has given counsel an opportunity to make the expert unsure of herself.

Example 6.42: "Including, but not limited to"
Report States:

> In preparing this preliminary report, I have reviewed documents including, but not limited to, the following:....

Comment: The use of "including, but not limited to" should be avoided. The expert should list all of the documents reviewed.

> Prior to preparing this initial report I have reviewed the following documents:....

6.5 "Relevant Portions of"

Another red flag for attorneys is using the descriptive "relevant portions of" prior to the documents reviewed. Including the descriptive term "relevant portions of" prior to a list of documents is a serious error. How is the expert to know what is not relevant unless he reviews the document in its entirety? Was the expert rushing and not reviewing everything? Perhaps, worst of all, did retaining counsel screen out the "irrelevant" portions of the documents?

Example 6.51: "Relevant portions of"
Report States:

> Documents reviewed:
> Relevant portions of deposition transcripts of John Jones and Peter Peters.

Resulting Cross-examination:

Q. Your report states that prior to forming your opinion you reviewed the relevant portions of the Jones and Peters deposition, is that correct?

A. Yes.

Q. You would agree, wouldn't you, that it is important that you do in fact review all relevant information?

A. Yes, that was done in this case.

Q. I see. But the irrelevant portions of those depositions you didn't review?

A. Correct.

Q. I was wondering if you could help me with something. In regards to the Jones and Peters depositions, how can you possibly have determined which portions of the depositions were relevant if you didn't review the entire depositions?

A. I can't. Retaining counsel sent me the relevant portions.

Q. You reviewed what counsel wanted you to review, correct?

A. Yes.

Q. And you didn't see the portions of the depositions counsel didn't want you to see?

A. Correct.

Q. Did you ever ask counsel to provide you with the entire depositions?

A. No, it wasn't relevant.

Q. Do you know what was contained in the portions of the depositions that counsel didn't send you?

A. No.

Q. That's because you never reviewed them, correct?

A. Correct.

Comment: Experts should review all of the available documents and explicitly list the documents that were reviewed. "Relevant portions of" language in reports should be avoided.

6.6 "Various"

The word "various" in an expert's list of documents reviewed communicates the idea that the expert is not thorough and precise. It is best avoided. Documents reviewed should be listed precisely.

Example 6.61 "Various"
Report States:

I have reviewed the following documents:
1. Various photos of the accident scene...

Comment: A better way to list the photos would be to say:

I have reviewed the following documents:
1. 27 4 x 6 photos of the accident scene, taken June 4, 2001 by me.
These photos are copied and attached to this report as exhibits #1 through #27...

Example 6.62: "Various"
Report States:

I have reviewed the following documents:
1. Various documents from residents and City of Philadelphia officials.

Comment: It is better practice to list and describe explicitly each document reviewed.

6.7 Missing Records and Documents Not Reviewed

An expert's opinion can easily be called into question if the expert did not have access to or did not review all of the documentary records in the case. Some experts state explicitly in their reports which records they did not have access to. This makes cross-examination easy. It may be better practice to simply list all documents that were reviewed and let opposing counsel figure out for herself what the expert did not review. The best practice of all is to demand and then review all relevant documents. If all relevant documents are not made available to the expert, the expert should strongly consider refusing to offer an opinion in the case.

Experts should expect and, when necessary, demand all the pleadings, documents, and relevant information in the case before formulating their opinions.

> Experts must be furnished with sufficient information to become familiar with the facts of the case in order to form a valid opinion. Experts cannot be expected to function effectively if they lack an adequate legal and factual foundation. To this end, counsel should provide experts with all pleadings, briefs, copies of witness' depositions and all relevant documentary evidence. Experts should review the information provided to them by counsel and communicate any data gaps. Although many experts are knowledgeable about litigation matters, it is also useful to provide experts with an oral outline of the procedural history of the case and its current procedural posture.[2]

Consider the following examples.

Example 6.71: Failure to review complete transcripts

Cross-examination:

Q. You relied on the deposition transcripts of Ted Taylor and Jack Jacobs in formulating your opinion, correct?

A. In part.

Q. When you say "in part," do you mean your opinion is based in part on the deposition, or did you rely only on part of the depositions?

A. Both, counsel. My opinion was based in part on relevant portions of the deposition transcripts.

Q. What percentage of the Taylor deposition transcript did you find relevant?

A. I had approximately 50 pages.

Q. What percentage is that of the entire transcript?

A. I don't know.

---

[2] Fisher, "Selection, Use, and Management of Experts in Environmental Legal Practice," 33 Tulsa L.J. 1003 (1998) 1013.

Q. That's because counsel only furnished you with 50 pages of the 473-page transcript, correct?
A. I was provided with 50 pages by counsel.
Q. Do you know how many pages the Jacobs deposition transcript was?
A. No.
Q. How many pages did counsel provide you with?
A. 27 pages.
Q. 27 pages out of a 325-page transcript is less than 10% of the transcript?
A. If that's a question, the answer is yes, it is.
Q. It is fair to say that some statements, facts, or admissions contained in the missing hundreds of deposition transcript pages could be important?
A. They might be.
Q. But you have no way of knowing that because you don't know what's in those pages?
A. That's correct.
Q. Would you have liked to have seen the entire transcripts to see if anything contained there would have changed your findings or opinion?
A. In the ideal world, yes.
Q. Did you request counsel to send you the entire transcripts?
A. No…I mean…yes, I did.
Q. How many times did you request them?
A. 2 to 3.
Q. Did you become the slightest bit curious or suspicious when counsel would not send you the complete transcripts?
A. Well…let's just say…I would have preferred to have them.

Comment: This expert should have insisted on reviewing the entire deposition transcripts. He could have refused to write his report until he was provided with complete documentation.

Example 6.72: "No records have been made available to me"
Report States:
> Dr. Z. performed some sort of surgical procedure on the back of her neck in late 1998. No records have been made available to me by Dr. Z. or of any operative notes. This procedure appears to have been some sort of a surgical procedure on the occipital nerve.

Resulting Cross-examination:
Q. You don't know what surgery Dr. Z. performed on the patient, do you?
A. That's correct.
Q. That's because the records were not provided to you before you reached your conclusions and formed your opinions?
A. True.
Q. Would you have liked to have had the op. notes and medical records?
A. Yes.
Q. Would they have changed your opinion in this case?
A. I don't know.
Q. So, your opinion may be incorrect?

A. I did the best I could with what I had.

Q. Could you have refused to reach a conclusion and form an opinion until the records were provided to you?

Comment: Any expert who bases her opinion on incomplete records places that opinion in question.

Example 6.73: Many key records missing

Report States:

> I did not have school records or records from the psychologist who treated Ms. X after the alleged sexual harassment. Dr. Jones's monthly handwritten notes were illegible. I did not have any previous medical or employment records.

Resulting Cross-examination:

Q. When you start treating patients you like to see their past medical and other records, don't you?

A. Yes.

Q. That is because they are part of the puzzle you are looking into?

A. Yes.

Q. Here there were crucial parts to the puzzle missing, correct?

A. Records were missing.

Q. Are the school records important?

A. They could be.

Q. No way of knowing without looking at them?

A. That's right.

Q. The same for the psychologist records?

A. Yes.

Q. The same for Dr. Jones's records?

A. No, I have them.

Q. But you say you can't read them, correct?

A. True.

Q. So they are of no help?

A. Correct.

Q. The prior medical records are important to establish a baseline, correct?

A. Yes.

Q. But you didn't have them so you could not establish a baseline?

A. True.

Q. The same for the employment records?

A. Correct.

Q. So you have five crucial parts to this puzzle that are missing?

A. Yes.

Q. Did you ever consider holding off forming an opinion until counsel provided you with these crucial missing records?

Comment: This expert's opinion can be easily questioned because she did not have access to key documentation. In a situation like this the expert may have been better off to list all the records she did review and not red flag the missing records for opposing counsel.

6.8 Additional Examples

Consider the following examples. The listings which are most detailed indicate that the expert was thorough and help bolster credibility and increase the value of the expert's assistance. The listings which are vague can be used to show that the expert was not thorough and may have failed to consider key information.

Example 6.81 Imprecise description of documents
Report States:

Documents reviewed:
Autopsy Report

Resulting Cross-Examination:
Q. Which autopsy report did you review?
A. The one in my file.
Q. Who drafted the autopsy report?
A. I don't know.
Q. When was the autopsy report drafted?
A. I can't remember.
Q. How long was the report?
A. I'd have to check my file on that.

Comment: Precise descriptions of the documents reviewed will help experts prepare for trial and avoid having to answer a seemingly endless series of questions about what was reviewed with "I don't know" or "I can't recall."

Example 6.82: Vague description of documents
Report States:

Coroner's investigation, including interviews with firemen, EMS, highway patrolmen and family members

Resulting Cross-examination:
Q. Your final report of 8/12/01 indicates that the investigation included interviews with firemen, EMS, highway patrolmen, and family members?
A. That's correct.
Q. Did you rely in whole, or in part, on the results of this investigation in forming your opinion on the cause of the fire?
A. Yes, I did.
Q. What were the names of the firemen interviewed?
A. I don't know.
Q. Which family members were interviewed?
A. The records don't indicate that.
Q. Who were the highway patrolmen interviewed?
A. I don't know.
Q. How many interviews were there in total?
A. I am not sure.
Q. Where were they done?
A. I don't have that information.

Q. When were they done?
A. I don't know.
Q. Do you know if they were done at the scene of the fire or six months later?
A. I do not know that.
Q. Would that be important to know?
A. It could be.
Q. If you were conducting a fire investigation and did interviews, would you indicate in your report the names of the persons questioned, and when and where the interviews took place?
A. Yes.
Q. Why is that?
A. For accuracy and completeness.
Q. Do you normally rely on undated, anonymous interviews in forming your opinion for your report?
A. No.
Q. But you did so in this case, didn't you?
A. Yes.

Comment: This expert report would have been far better had it listed precisely who had been interviewed by the coroner.

1. Coroner's interview with Bill Williams, fireman, 2 pages, 4/15/01
2. Coroner's interview with Lucas Young, fireman, 3 pages, 4/15/01
3. Coroner's interview with Al Barnes, Highway Patrolman, 3 pages, 4/16/01
4. Coroner's interview with James Conroy, Highway Patrolman, 1 page, 4/16/01
5. Coroner's interview with Tim Esposito, EMS, 2 pages, 4/17/01
6. Coroner's interview with Sherry Feng, EMS, 1 page, 4/17/01
7. Coroner's interview with Maria Van Dorn, spouse, 1 page, 4/17/01
8. Coroner's interview with Paul Stobbs, brother, 1 page, 4/17/01

Example 6.83 Imprecise description of documents
Report States:
  I have reviewed the following documents:
  1. OSHA Citation to Acme Construction Company
  2. Contract between Acme Construction and Builder Co, Inc.

Comment: A precise description makes the report and the expert appear more credible.

  I have reviewed the following documents:
  1. OSHA Citation #01-1234 to Acme Construction Company, dated 3/6/01.
  2. Contract between Acme Construction and Builder Co, Inc., 25 pages, dated 8/7/00.

Example 6.84: "I did review"

Report States:

I did review the MRI study from 1999 with her and she had plain films that I have seen from the chiropractor which are unremarkable.

Resulting Cross-examination:

Q. In your report you note and I quote, "I did review the MRI study from 1999." Am I reading that correctly?

A. Yes.

Q. You found it noteworthy to document in your report that you did in fact review the MRI?

A. Yes.

Q. What records didn't you review?

A. I can't recall. I believe I reviewed them all.

Q. Apparently not, Doctor. You said you "did" review the MRI. That implies that there are other records that you "did not" review, does it not?

A. I guess it does.

Comment: This needless loss of credibility occurred because of the expert's use of the seemingly innocuous "I did review" preface. The expert would have been better served with a straightforward list of what was reviewed.

MRI report, 1 page, dated 7/6/01, signed by M. Jones, MD

Chapter 7   Stating the Expert's Qualifications Accurately and Objectively

7.1 Executive Summary
Expert reports often contain a description of the expert's qualifications. Federal Rule of Civil Procedure Rule 26(a)(2)(B) requires Rule 26 expert reports to contain "the qualifications of the witness, including a list of all publications authored by the witness in the preceding ten years." Reports that fail to do so may result in the expert being precluded from testifying.

Many experts attach their qualifications or CV to the end of their reports as an addendum. This is perhaps the easiest way to incorporate a description of the expert's qualifications into the expert report.

Qualifications should not be exaggerated nor should they be understated. This sounds simple, but can sometimes be quite challenging. The authors recommend the following.

- Experts should include a copy of their qualifications in their reports if this is a legal requirement in the case at hand.
- The statement of qualifications must be 100% accurate.
- One should be objective when stating qualifications and avoid subjective, self-serving statements and characterizations.
- An expert should not claim as a qualification a degree or designation that sounds like it was earned but was, in reality, bought.
- Wise experts are careful when claiming knowledge of the current literature in their respective fields.

7.2 Legal Requirements
An expert who fails to provide his curriculum vitae (CV) as required by applicable discovery rules or court orders can jeopardize not only the admissibility of his testimony but, in some instances, the case itself. Consider the following examples.

Example 7.21: Failure to provide CV prior to testifying
Seivewright v. State, 7 P.3d 24 (Wyoming 2000)
In this criminal case, the expert, Dr. Huben, failed to provide his CV before he testified. The court pointed out the importance of the CV, which is relevant to qualifications and credibility. "In the case of an expert witness, in which qualifications go to both admissibility and weight, a vitae is material information by which the opposing party's counsel can challenge the expert's qualifications and credibility."

The Wyoming Supreme Court found that the trial court committed reversible error by allowing the expert to testify without producing his CV and report. The court stated:

> In accordance with W.R.Cr.P. 26.2, if a party elects not to comply with an order to deliver a statement, the district court has three options for sanctioning that behavior. The rule requires that the trial court "*shall* order" (1) that the witness not be permitted to testify; or (2) that the testimony of the witness be stricken from the record; or (3) if the attorney for the State elects not to comply, the court *shall* declare a mistrial if required in the interest of justice. W.R.Cr.P. 26.2(e). The rule is mandatory in all respects; it does not allow the district court any discretion to refuse to act in the face of uncontradicted allegations of discovery violations in a criminal prosecution. Allowing Seivewright to object to "particular questions" at trial is not one of the sanctions mandated by the rule. Thus, it cannot be argued that the district court's ruling was within the parameters of the rule despite its failure to determine if the discovery order has been violated.
>
> When Seivewright alleged the State failed to comply with W.R.Cr.P. 26.2, the district court should have ordered the State to submit the document for *in camera* inspection or held a hearing to determine whether the report and the curriculum vitae fell within the purview of the rule or the pretrial discovery order. Failure to take any action at all violated the rule and was reversible error.

Example 7.22: Rule 26 report, qualifications not provided
Elswick v. Nichols, 144 F.Supp.2d 758 (W.D. Kentucky 2001)
This was a medical malpractice case. Plaintiff's expert nurse was not permitted to testify in part because her Rule 26 report did not include a list of her qualifications. The court stated:

> The plaintiff's counsel submitted a copy of this report to the defense counsel. However, the defendants were never provided with Craig's qualifications, a list of her publications, any information regarding previous testimony by her, or a list of items that she reviewed in this case. Finally, there is no written report expressing Craig's opinions about the causation of Plaintiff Elswick's injury [FN4]. Discovery in this case is now closed. Clearly, these omissions indicate a substantial violation of Fed.R.Civ.P. 26(a). Therefore, Craig is unable to testify in this case as an expert witness because disclosures on this matter are clearly inadequate with respect to Rule 26(a).[1]

Example 7.23: Qualifications not provided in report, testimony barred
Campbell v. McMillan, 83 F.Supp.2d 761 (S.D. Mississippi 2000)
The court found the designated expert's report inadequate and precluded the expert from testifying. The court stated:

> The fourth requirement mandates the expert to provide a list of his qualifications, including a list of all publications authored by the expert within the preceding ten years. This requirement was not met...
>
> Based on an analysis of both Federal Rule of Civil Procedure 26 and applicable case law, this Court finds that the expert designation and disclosure of the expert's report were deficient. Therefore, unless the Plaintiffs can come forward

---

[1] At 765.

with an excusable reason for the inadequacies, the use of Murray as an expert witness at trial should be barred. *See* Fed.R.Civ.P. 37(c)(1).[2]

Example 7.24: Report without qualifications insufficient, expert must supplement or will be barred from testifying
Nguyen v IBP, Inc., 162 F.R.D. 675 (D. Kansas 1995)
This case also involved an insufficient Rule 26 report. The court stated:

> The disclosures served by plaintiff clearly and indisputably do not comply with Fed.R.Civ.P. 26(a)(2)(B). The only document signed by the expert witness was a letter addressing the expert's opinions and the basis therefor, the data considered by the expert, and exhibits to be used as a summary of or support for the opinions. While a curriculum vitae was provided, it was not signed by the witness and did not include publications authored by the witness within the past 10 years. Although plaintiff, by interrogatory answer, provided the compensation agreement, this agreement was not a part of the report signed by the witness. Plaintiff's counsel supplied a list of 137 patients about whom the witness had apparently testified during the 34 month period prior to October 28, 1994, and the dates of the deposition testimony. No identification of the "cases" in which these depositions were given is provided. The court or administrative agency in which the depositions were taken is not provided. Although an attorney's name is provided as to most of the patients, in many instances the first or last name of the attorney is missing. The telephone numbers are not supplied for the attorneys for 55 patients. The list is not signed by the witness. It includes entries for less than three years rather than for four years as required by the rule.[3]
>
> Plaintiff's failure to provide a report including a statement of the expert's compensation agreement, the expert's qualifications, or an identity of the publications authored by the expert during the past 10 years, in light of the lack of any such publications, is harmless since the facts were otherwise supplied and the failure may be cured by simply having the witness sign a disclosure to these facts. As noted above, the failure to provide the listing of cases is not harmless. The court will allow the plaintiff to provide a supplemental disclosure which corrects the deficiencies identified herein within 40 days from the date of the filing of this order, otherwise, Dr. Shechter will not be permitted to testify at the trial of the action.[4]

7.3 Accuracy
The statement of qualifications should be 100% accurate. Even honest mistakes in stating an expert's qualifications can have a devastating effect on the expert's credibility. Consider the following example.

Example 7.31: Incorrect use of "diplomate" instead of "board certified by"
Report States:
Diplomate, American Board of Independent Medical Examiners

---

[2] At 765.
[3] At 679.
[4] At 682.

Resulting Cross-examination:

Q. Doctor, your report indicates on page 3, second paragraph, that you are a Diplomate of the American Board of Independent Medical Examiners or ABIME, correct?

A. Yes, that's right.

Q. For how long have you been a Diplomate of ABIME?

A. Two years.

Q. During that time, how many expert reports have you issued?

A. I am not sure.

Q. Approximately, Doctor.

A. 100 or more.

Q. Did you list your ABIME Diplomate status on these reports?

A. Yes.

Q. Doctor, you carefully check your report for mistakes or errors, do you not?

A. Yes, as best I can within my time constraints.

Q. What do you think of doctors who claim credentials they do not possess?

A. That's not right.

Q. What about their credibility?

A. They would have none as far as I am concerned.

Q. Doctor, I show you a letter from the American Board of Independent Medical Examiners and ask you if you would read the highlighted portion.

A. "I am the Executive Director of ABIME and state that the American Board of Independent Medical Examiners has no current, nor has ever had any Diplomates." There must be some mistake.

Q. Apparently so, Doctor. Are you going to continue to use this Diplomate status of ABIME in the future?

A. Absolutely not.

Q. Do you intend to correct the 100+ reports in which you previously claimed these credentials?

A. Huh? I am not sure. I think I need to consult with counsel.

Comment: The doctor in question was in fact board certified by ABIME. He mistakenly—and innocently—claimed to be a diplomate. This simple error destroyed the expert's qualifications. The expert should have verified that the qualifications stated in his report were 100% accurate. He should have stated:

> Board Certified as an Independent Medical Examiner by the American Board of Independent Medical Examiners

7.4 Objectivity

Subjective, self-serving statements and characterizations should be left out of reports. Such subjective characterizations of an expert's qualifications will almost invariably lead to trouble on the witness stand.

Example 7.41: "Internationally recognized expert"
Report States:

> I am an internationally recognized expert on futures and option sales and am frequently interviewed and quoted in *Securities Weekly*.

Resulting Cross-examination:

Q. You state in your report that you are an internationally recognized expert on futures and option sales and are frequently interviewed and quoted in *Securities Weekly.*

A. That's correct.

Q. When you say "internationally recognized," what percentage of the world's four billion people do you think would recognize your name?

A. Counsel, obviously I meant by my peers.

Q. How many people read and would recognize your name from *Securities Weekly?*

A. At least 5,000 to 10,000.

Q. So you consider yourself internationally recognized because 5,000 to 10,000 members of the world's population have heard of your name?

Comment: Statements to the effect that the expert is "nationally recognized" or a "leading authority" are fairly common in expert reports. Such statements should be avoided. As can be seen in this example, counsel will use such statements to make the expert appear to be exaggerating her own qualifications and importance. This will result in a loss of credibility. This particular expert would have been better served by including the following *objective* evidence of her qualifications.

Journal and Press Quotations
"Hedging your bets," *Wall Street Journal,* September 28, 2001
"New paradigm in futures trading," *Securities Weekly,* March 6, 2000

Awards
1999 Annual Award for Excellence, International Futures and Options Trading Society

7.5 Unearned Designations or Degrees

It is unwise to claim as a qualification a degree or designation that sounds like it was earned but was, in reality, bought. One should not claim such status unless one has truly earned it; for example, by passing a serious examination and having appropriate and qualifying experience. Listing a bought-and-paid-for designation or degree from a "diploma mill" will lessen an expert's credibility, not increase it.

Example 7.51: Bought and paid for designation
Report States:

Board Certified, International Board of Forensic Science and Services
Diplomate, International Board of Forensic Science and Services

Resulting Cross-examination:

Q. You state in your report, do you not, that you are Board Certified by the International Board of Forensic Science and Services?

A. That's correct.

Q. You also state, do you not, that you are Diplomate of the International Board of Forensic Science and Services?

A. Yes.

Q. You never took a written examination to earn your board certification, did you?

A. It wasn't required.

Q. You never took an oral examination to earn your board certification, did you?

A. No, it wasn't required.

Q. You never took a written examination to earn your diplomate status, did you?

A. No.

Q. You never took an oral examination to earn your diplomate status, did you?

A. No.

Q. You did apply for the diplomate status and the board certification and the diplomate status, did you not?

A. Yes, I did.

Q. And when you sent in your applications, there was an application fee?

A. Yes.

Q. Isn't it a fact that the "application" fee was $1,250 for the board certification and $1,500 for the diplomate status?

A. Yes.

Q. You sent them the money and they gave you the designations, that about sums it up, doesn't it?

A. I met all their requirements, sir.

Q. What requirements were there beyond sending the money?

Comment: Unearned, "bought" certifications should not be included in a CV. They are not relevant to an expert's qualifications and can be used to lessen an expert's credibility.

7.6 Knowledge of Literature

Wise experts are careful when claiming knowledge of the current literature in their field. There is a *lot* of literature out there, especially in the medical field. It is easy for counsel to use a statement that an expert is current with the literature against the expert.

Example 7.61: "Current with the literature"
Report States:
> I keep current with the literature in this field.

Resulting Cross-examination:

Q. You state in your report that you keep current with the literature in "this field," meaning shoulder dystocia, is that correct?

A. Yes.

Q. Did you read the article entitled "What is shoulder dystocia" in the February 2001 issue of the *Journal of Reproductive Medicine?*

A. I can't recall.

Q. Did you read the article entitled "Shoulder dystocia: The event that wraps a midwife's heart in cold terror" in the Autumn 2000 issue of *Midwifery Today?*

A. No.

Q. Did you read the article entitled "Shoulder dystocia" in the December 2000 issue of the *Journal of Reproduction Medicine?*

A. Yes.

Q. Could you please summarize the conclusions of that article?

A. I can't recall.

Q. Did you read the article entitled "Shoulder dystocia: lessons from the past and emerging concepts" in the June 2000 issue of *Clinical and Obstetrical Gynecology?*

A. I can't recall.

Comment: If an expert claims in her report to keep current with the literature, she can expect a cross-examination similar to that provided above. It would be extremely difficult for even the most brilliant expert to do well in this type of a cross-examination. This expert report would have been better had it not included the statement regarding keeping current with the literature in the expert's field.

Chapter 8 How to Best Express and Document Detailed and Specific Factual Assumptions

8.1 Executive Summary
An expert's opinion is only as good as the factual assumptions upon which the expert's opinion is based. These factual assumptions form the foundation of the expert's opinion and should be expressed in the expert report. The authors recommend the following.

- Describing factual assumptions in a detailed and specific way, not in a vague fashion.
- Providing a precise citation to the source of the factual assumptions; for example, a specific page in a deposition transcript.
- Not guessing about factual assumptions and avoiding terms such as "supposedly," "it has been reported," "is said," "as I understand the facts," and "presumably" in describing factual assumptions.
- Verifying the veracity of factual assumptions.
- Expecting counsel to focus on dates expressed in the report.
- Basing factual assumptions on reliable information.
- Not relying on unverified information provided by retaining counsel.

8.2 Provide Detailed and Specific Information
A well-written expert report contains detailed and specific factual information. Vague statements of factual assumptions should be avoided because they will damage the expert's credibility.

Example 8.21: Vague facts
Report States:
> He stated that he was on a USA Airlines Flight #1235 when someone opened up a luggage bin and some material fell and struck him on the back of the head and neck.

Resulting Cross-examination:
Q. You state in your report that "he was on a USA Air Flight #1235 when someone opened up a luggage bin and some material fell and struck him on the back of the head and neck," is that correct?
A. Yes.
Q. Who was it that opened up the bin?
A. I don't know.

Q. What was the date of the flight?
A. I'm not sure.
Q. At the time of the accident, was the plane flying or on the ground?
A. I don't know.
Q. Was the plane moving?
A. I don't know.
Q. Specifically, what fell on him?
A. I assume it was luggage.
Q. What kind of luggage?
A. I don't know.
Q. How heavy was the luggage that fell on him?
A. I don't know.

Comment: This is the type of vague factual assumption that should be avoided in expert reports. It suggests that either the expert didn't know what all the facts were, didn't care to know what all the facts were, or that he intentionally omitted certain facts from his report. This statement would have been better had it been more precise and detailed and read:

> The plaintiff was on USA Airlines Flight 1235 from Boston to Raleigh/Durham on December 23, 2001. (Gore deposition at 7.) The plane had just parked at the gate at Raleigh/Durham and the captain had just turned off the seatbelt sign. (Gore deposition at 7.) The plaintiff then stood up to stretch out. (Gore deposition at 7.) When another passenger seated behind the plaintiff went to retrieve his carry-on luggage from the overhead bin, a large, heavy, carry-on suitcase with wheels fell out of the bin and struck the plaintiff on the back of the head and neck. (Gore deposition at 8.)

8.3 Citations to Information Source

The specific source of the information that gave rise to factual assumptions should be cited. Citing the source of factual assumptions serves two important purposes. First, the citations show that the report was carefully researched and written. Second, the citations can help the expert prepare to testify by serving as a reminder of the source of the information gathered. Citing the source of factual assumptions will help bolster the expert's credibility. The more precise the citation, for example, by including the page number (a pinpoint cite), the more the expert's credibility will be bolstered.

Example 8.31: Failure to cite source of factual information
Report States:
> During this initial assessment Mrs. Perry denied chest pain, back pain or shortness of breath to the nursing staff and Dr. K.

Resulting Cross-examination:

Q. You state in your report that during the initial assessment Mrs. Perry denied chest pain, back pain or shortness of breath to the nursing staff and Dr. K, is that correct?
A. Yes.
Q. On what do you base this assumption?
A. It's in the records.
Q. Which records?
A. The hospital records, I would assume.

Comment: The above report segment is written well in that it avoids pronouns and uses objective language. However, it fails to cite the source or sources of the expert's assumptions. On the stand, the expert was unable to remember all of the sources of information on which she based her assumptions, thus suffering a needless loss of credibility. This statement would have been better had it read:

> During the initial 6/4/01 assessment Mrs. Perry denied chest pain, back pain or shortness of breath to the nursing staff and Dr. K. (Perry deposition at 7, Hospital Records dated 6/4/01)

Example 8.32: Failure to use pinpoint citation
Report States:
> As testified by Dr. Su, her family physician, Mrs. Elderly was not in a dying condition at the time of his examination.

Comment: This statement is helpful in that it generally states the source of the expert's factual assumption. This statement would have been much better, however, had it more precisely cited the source of information upon which the expert based his factual assumption through the use of a pinpoint cite.

> Dr. Su testified that Mrs. Elderly was not in a dying condition at the time of his examination. (Su deposition at 27)

8.4 Do Not Guess about the Facts
Certain words and phrases such as "supposedly," "it has been reported," "is said," "as I understand the facts," and "presumably" suggest that the expert is at best uncertain as to what the actual facts are. Such words and phrases should be avoided in an expert report because they will lessen an expert's credibility.

Example 8.41: "As we understand the facts"
Report States:
> As we understand the facts, a fire occurred at the Long residence on February 12, 2001, at approximately 8:00 P.M.

Resulting Cross-examination:
Q. Are the facts of this case clear-cut?
A. Yes.
Q. That's not what you wrote in your report, is it?

A. I'm not sure what you mean.

Q. You are testifying here today that the facts of this case are clear-cut, but did you not write in your report that, "As we understand the facts, a fire occurred at the Long residence on February 12, 2001, at approximately 8:00 P.M.?"

A. Yes. I wrote that.

Q. Which is it, sir, are the facts clear-cut or do you need to somehow understand them?

A. They are clear. There was a fire on February 12 at the Long residence.

Q. But that's not what you wrote in your report, is it?

Comment: The "as we understand the facts" language in the above statement should have been avoided. This statement suggests that the expert believes that there are different possible reasonable understandings of the facts. Because an expert's opinions are only as good as the facts upon which they are based, experts should avoid such language. This statement would have been better had it read:

> A fire occurred at the Long residence on February 12, 2001, at approximately 8:00 P.M. (Milton Fire Department Report 2/13/2001).

Example 8.42: "It has been reported"
Report States:
> It has been reported that the water discharged from the fractured pipe for approximately 45 minutes.

Resulting Cross-examination:

Q. In forming your opinion, did you assume that the length of time that the water discharged from the fractured pipe was 45 minutes?

A. Yes.

Q. You don't know how long it was actually discharging water?

A. No.

Q. It actually could have been 40 minutes?

A. Yes.

Q. It actually could have been 30 minutes?

A. Correct.

Q. You weren't there at the time and you have no way of knowing, do you?

A. No.

Q. When you say in your report that "it has been reported that the water discharged from the fractured pipe for approximately 45 minutes," where was that reported, what I mean is, what document was it in?

A. I can't recall.

Q. I show you here a letter to you from attorney Van Buren dated 3/6/01 in which he states to you, and I quote, "the water discharged from the fractured pipe for approximately 45 minutes." Is that the basis of your assumption?

A. That's possible, yes.

Comment: "It has been reported" will be pounced on by opposing counsel since it sounds as though the expert is basing his opinion on unreliable information.

The expert's report and opinion are only as good as the factual information upon which they are based. If the facts are shown to be unreliable, it is easy to show that the opinion is unreliable. This expert's factual assumption would have been on more solid ground had it cited a reliable basis for the assumption.

> A loud bang was heard by the security guard at 9:23 P.M. (Gordon Depo at 11) On the guard's rounds at 9:00 P.M. he had noticed that all was well in the room with the pipe in question. (Gordon Depo at 10) According to the police log, the police were called at 9:24 P.M. The fire department records state that the water was shut off shortly after 10:00 P.M.

Example 8.43: "Is said"
Report States:
> The system is said to be 50 years old.

Resulting Cross-examination:
Q. Your report states that "the system is said to be 50 years old." Is that what you wrote?
A. Yes.
Q. Who said that?
A. I believe that's what one of the employees stated.
Q. Which employee?
A. I don't remember.
Q. How long had the employee been working there?
A. I'm not sure.
Q. Was it more than 50 years?
A. I don't think so.
Q. How did this employee know how old the system was?
A. I think it was his impression that that was the age. Somebody told him that at one point while he was working there.
Q. So in other words, you based your assumption on how old the system is on a statement of an unknown employee who got it from another unknown employee?
A. Yes.

Comment: Factual assumptions based on rumors and unreliable hearsay should be avoided because they will damage an expert's credibility. Factual assumptions should be based on objective and reliable information.

> The exact age of the system in question is unknown. However, according to the manufacturer, this particular system was manufactured from 1946 through 1954. It is therefore between 46 and 54 years old.

8.5 Incorrect Factual Assumptions
An expert's opinion that is based on incorrect assumptions is not credible. Consider the following example.

Example 8.51: Incorrect factual assumption
Culley v. Trak Microwave Corp., 117 F.Supp.2d 1317, (M.D.Fla. 2000)
In this case, the expert in question incorrectly assumed that one half of the subject company's workforce was below the age of 40 and one half was above the age of 40. The court found that due to this incorrect assumption the expert's resulting conclusion was "fundamentally flawed" and "entitled to no probative value." The court stated:

> Culley's statistics consist of a report prepared by Dr. Chris P. Tsokos, a professor of statistics at the University of South Florida. Dr. Tsokos' "Expert Opinion and Report" (Doc.51) considers 112 Trak Microwave employees "who were terminated (either by termination [f]or cause, resignation or permanent lay-off during the period of January 1991 through December 1996)." *See* Affidavit of Chris P. Tsokos, Ph.D., at ¶ 1 (Doc.51). Dr. Tsokos found that 64.29% of the terminated employees were forty years of age or older at the time of their terminations and 35.71% of the terminated employees were thirty-nine years of age or younger. *Id.* at ¶ 3. These figures, of course, tend neither to prove nor to disprove whether Trak discriminated against employees on the basis of age unless the percentages are statistically significant when compared to the age of Trak's workforce as a whole. In his report, Dr. Tsokos failed to compare Trak's termination rates to the age of Trak's workforce, even though Trak provided the ages of all the company's employees to the plaintiff in discovery. Instead, the only age comparison Dr. Tsokos performed was to assume that 50% of Trak's employees were forty or older and 50% thirty-nine or younger. No basis in the record exists for this assumption, and the record establishes that the assumption is incorrect.
>
> .....
>
> From his incorrect "50/50" assumption and the datum that 64.29% of the 112 terminated employees were forty years of age or older, Dr. Tsokos reasoned: "Thus, we can conclude that there is a much higher chance that the 40 year old or older individual would be laid off with a high degree of assurance." Affidavit (Doc. 51) at ¶ 11. This conclusion is fundamentally flawed and entitled to no probative value.

8.6 Dates

When counsel prepares his or her cross-examination he will carefully look at any dates contained in the report. Counsel may ask themselves the following questions.

- Was the report drafted and inspection or examination conducted long after the accident such that things might have changed?
- Was the report drafted well before trial such that things may have changed between the time the report was drafted and the time of the trial?
- Are there any inconsistencies in the dates? For example, was the report drafted before certain documents could have been available to the expert?
- Was the report drafted promptly after the examination or inspection?

Experts can do a few things to insulate themselves from counsel's questions regarding dates. Inspections and examinations should be performed as soon as possible to minimize the likelihood of changes in the condition of what is to be inspected or examined. Follow-up inspections or examinations should be made immediately prior to trial and reports should be dictated promptly after the examination. Consider the following examples.

Example 8.61: Date of accident two years before date of report
Report States:
    D.O.A. 9/28/98 Report Date November 15, 2001

Resulting Cross-examination:
Q. When was the accident?
A. September 28, 1998.
Q. When did you visit the scene?
A. October 28, 2001.
Q. More than three years after the accident?
A. Yes.
Q. Is it best to visit the scene as soon as possible after an accident?
A. Yes.
Q. Why?
A. Because things are the same and there is less chance of modifications or alterations on the scene.
Q. Would it have been better for you to visit the scene in September 1998 or October 1998?
A. Yes.
Q. Why did you wait three years?
A. I didn't. I was hired October 25, 2001.
Q. So you did the best you could do three years later?
A. Yes.
Q. What were the changes to the scene in the intervening three years?

Comment: Experts should expect this line of questioning whenever their inspection is made long after the date of accident.

Example 8.62: Independent medical exam performed and report issued 3 years prior to trial
Report States:
    Date of Examination August 1, 1998. "Examinee is totally disabled."

Resulting Cross-examination:
Q. You haven't examined this examinee for three years, correct?
A. Yes.
Q. Three years ago you found him to be totally disabled?
A. Yes.
Q. You don't know from your personal knowledge if he got better in 1998, 1999, or 2000, do you?
A. Correct.

Comment: To insulate himself from this line of questioning, the expert should request a follow-up examination immediately prior to testifying at trial.

Example 8.63: Report drafted 3 months after inspection
Report States:
> Inspection conducted May 1st, report issued August 1st.

Resulting Cross-examination:
Q. You inspected the building site on May 1, correct?
A. Yes.
Q. You found a dangerous defect that was potentially hazardous?
A. Yes.
Q. You stated in your report it should be corrected immediately?
A. Yes.
Q. But you waited three months before you issued your report?

Comment: Experts should not procrastinate. They should issue their reports as soon as possible after inspection and evaluation.

8.7 Reliability of Data and Information
An expert's opinion is only as reliable as the information and data upon which it is based. Experts should be prepared to be cross-examined closely on any areas of their reports relying on shaky, ambiguous, or unreliable data. The cross-examining attorney understands that "garbage in" means "garbage out." Please consider the following examples.

Example 8.71: Relying upon unreliable witness (inmate)
Report States:
> We were told by an inmate in that area that although everyone has the opportunity to get their clothes cleaned, it is necessary to pay a gratuity to the inmate workers to assure the safe return of one's clothing.

Resulting Cross-examination:
Q. Part of your job is to assess the quality of information provided to you, correct?
A. Yes.
Q. And the veracity of the person providing it?
A. Yes.
Q. The inmate you talked to, did you happen to get his name or number?
A. No.
Q. Can you tell us if this felon who you relied on for information was a convicted murderer, child rapist, or perjurer?
A. No, I can't.

Comment: For an expert report to be persuasive, it must be based upon reliable information. Experts should expect counsel to zero-in on the source of any underlying factual information that may be suspect.

Example 8.72: Missing information
Report States:

An MRI of the lumbar spine was obtained (? Location) on 12/21/95 and was consistent with "mild changes" of degenerative disease at L1-2, L4-5, and L5-S1. There is no evidence of disc herniation. An MRI of the thoracic spine was obtained on 3/11/96 (? Location) and was interpreted as "within normal limits."

Resulting Cross-examination:

Q. The location of these MRIs was significant enough for you to question it in your report?
A. Yes.
Q. Where was the 12/21/95 MRI performed?
A. I don't know.
Q. Where was the 3/11/96 MRI performed?
A. I don't know.
Q. Were they both done at the same location?
A. I don't know.
Q. If these MRIs were done on a family member or loved one, would you have made an attempt to find out where they were done?

Comment: For an expert to be as credible as possible, her report should be based upon complete information. Failure to do so will make the expert's report suspect.

An MRI of the lumbar spine was obtained from NE Radiological on 12/21/95 and was consistent with "mild changes" of degenerative disease at L1-2, L4-5, and L5-S1. There is no evidence of disc herniation. An MRI of the thoracic spine was obtained from NE Radiological on 3/11/96 and was interpreted as "within normal limits."

Example 8.73: Expert's interpretation of events
Report States:

My interpretation of the events leading to the amputation of Mr. B's right leg is as follows:....

Resulting Cross-examination:

Q. Your report sets forth your interpretation of the events leading to the amputation, correct?
A. Yes.
Q. You based your conclusion and opinion on your interpretation of the events?
A. Yes.
Q. Another expert might have interpreted them differently, correct?
A. Yes.
Q. Her conclusions and opinion would also then be different?
A. Possibly.
Q. If you interpreted the events incorrectly, your opinion would most likely be incorrect?

A. That's possible.
Q. You do make mistakes, don't you?

Comment: As counsel rightly points out, an expert's opinion is only as strong as the facts and assumptions upon which it is based. Experts should be extremely careful when making factual assumptions and interpretations.

8.8 Illegible Records

Relying on illegible records can also be problematic. Consider the following example.

Example 8.81: "If this is the whole entry and I read it correctly"
Report States:
> There is a comment in the nursing notes from the Post-Anesthesia Care Unit (PACU) at 8 AM on 8/12/99 regarding "DP" or (?) PT Doppler." I totally reject this assessment (if this is the whole entry and I read it correctly), as it should be disregarded by anyone who had knowledge of the catheter placement in this patient and understands the time requirements of urokinase therapy.

Resulting Cross-examination:
Q. You are not sure what the nursing note says, correct?
A. It's hard to read.
Q. But you are willing, despite your inability to read it, to tell others to disregard it, reject it yourself, and offer your opinion about it under oath?

Comment: Expert opinions that are based on illegible records will be questioned closely.

8.9 Information Supplied by Retaining Counsel

The source of the facts and data relied upon by the expert can make those facts and data suspect. This is especially true where the facts and data are provided by someone with a vested interest in the outcome of the litigation, for example, a party to the case or retaining attorney. Wherever possible, experts should avoid exclusively relying upon facts and data provided by a party or retaining attorney that cannot be independently verified. If the expert does rely upon information from an interested party, she can expect to be questioned closely. Experts who rely on information, data, calculations, etc. given to them by counsel and blindly incorporate that information into their reports run the risk of being discredited. Please consider the following examples.

Example 8.91: Information provided by attorney and plaintiff
Report States:
> My opinions are based on the records, materials, and other information made available to me by plaintiff's counsel and information gathered during my clinical dental examination of the plaintiff.

Resulting Cross-examination:
Q. Plaintiff's counsel provided you with the records upon which you based your opinion, correct?
A. In part, yes.
Q. Did she provide you with all of the records or just the ones favorable to her position?
A. As far as I know, all of the records.
Q. Were you provided with the 7/19/99 ER record?
A. No.
Q. What about the 8/19/97–8/19/99 orthodontic records?
A. No.
Q. What about the prosthetic records?
A. No.
Q. The implant records?
A. No.
Q. The prior oral surgery records?
A. No.
Q. Would you agree that counsel did not provide you with "all the records"?
A. Yes.
Q. Do you know why that was done?
A. No.

Comment: This expert's report would have been better if he had simply listed the records that he had reviewed. There was no need to telegraph to the reader that all of the records reviewed were obtained from counsel.

Example 8.92: Opinion based on discussion with plaintiff's counsel
Report States:
> Our opinion is based upon an inspection of the loss premises, an inspection of the ruptured sprinkler, and a discussion with plaintiff's counsel.

Resulting Cross-examination:
Q. You based your opinion on what plaintiff's counsel told you?
A. Yes, in part.
Q. He is an advocate trying to win this case for his client, correct?
A. Yes. I assume so.
Q. You are supposed to be an impartial, unbiased expert, correct?
A. Yes.
Q. Isn't it the job of counsel to put the best spin possible on the facts?
A. I suppose so.
Q. Were you unable to form your own opinion without the help of counsel?
A. No.

Q. You did so because it was easier and he was the one who retained you, correct?
A. No. It was just an additional source of information.
Q. Could you tell us the so-called facts provided to you by counsel and how you independently verified each one?

Comment: It is common and quite appropriate for the expert to have discussions with retaining counsel. However, close communication between counsel and the expert can almost always be made to look suspicious in front of the jury. Because the retaining counsel is an advocate, basing an expert opinion in part on a conversation with retaining counsel does not make the expert report more persuasive. It is therefore best practice not to document in a forensic report the conversations between the expert and retaining counsel. Documenting these conversations merely makes the cross-examining attorney's job that much easier.

> Our opinion is based upon an inspection of the loss premises and an inspection of the ruptured sprinkler.

Example 8.93: Counsel present during inspection
Report States:
> Counsel accompanied me throughout this inspection.

Resulting Cross-examination:
Q. Counsel assisted you with your independent inspection, correct?
A. He accompanied me.
Q. Did he talk to you during the inspection?
A. Yes.
Q. Did he point certain things out?
A. Yes.
Q. Did he voice his opinion on the significance of certain items?
A. Yes.
Q. Did he downplay the importance of other items?
A. No, not in so many words.
Q. Would you have rather done the inspection alone?
A. Yes.
Q. Why?

Comment: There is nothing wrong per se with counsel being present at the time of the inspection. That being said, counsel's presence at the inspection will usually undermine the expert's credibility. The perception will be that counsel improperly influenced the expert's work. If counsel is present at the inspection, there is usually no reason that this needs to be documented in the report. Doing so does not make the report more persuasive, it merely makes opposing counsel's job that much easier.

Example 8.94: Deposition transcript summary prepared by counsel
Report States:
   I have reviewed...deposition summary and deposition transcript of John K. Smith, M.D.

Resulting Cross-examination:
Q. You relied on the deposition of Dr. Smith in forming your opinion, correct?
A. In part, yes.
Q. How many pages was the deposition transcript summary of Dr. Smith that you reviewed?
A. Approximately ten.
Q. How many pages was the complete transcript?
A. I don't know.
Q. Here is the complete transcript. How many pages is it?
A. It appears to have 174 pages.
Q. You were not able to review 164 pages of the transcript because they were not provided to you?
A. Correct.
Q. Was there crucial information on those 164 pages?
A. I don't know.
Q. Because you didn't review them?
A. That's right.
Q. Could the material contained in the 164 pages have impacted your analysis, conclusion, and opinion?
A. It's possible.
Q. Who wrote and provided you the sanitized ten-page summary?
A. Attorney Will.
Q. Did you ask for the entire transcript to review?
A. Yes.
Q. Do you know why he did not provide it to you?
A. No, I don't know.
Q. Did you become suspicious when the entire transcript was not provided to you?

Comment: Deposition transcript summaries prepared by counsel should not be relied upon. The summaries are counsel's take on what is important from the deposition. It is much better practice to read, review, and rely upon the actual deposition transcript, which has not been filtered through counsel.

Example 8.95: Rejection of testimony for failure to verify figures given by retaining counsel
United States Equal Employment Opportunity Commission v. Rockwell International Corporation, 60 F.Supp.2d 791 (N.D.Ill. 1999)
The court rejected an ADA report by a vocational counselor due to his failure to follow traditional methodology and also due to his inclusion of information and language supplied by counsel that the expert failed to independently verify. The court stated:

   Nor does it explain Brethauer's failure to verify figures given to him by attorney Waldron, or his inclusion in his report of information he did not think was relevant but was in fact insisted upon by Waldron. It is very clear from Waldron's statements at the June 26, 1999, hearing, and from Brethauer's own testimony, that Brethauer included in his report anything that Waldron requested, relied on reports prepared by Waldron, and even included specific wording supplied by Waldron…

…

Finally, he incorporated language drafted by Waldron. It is one thing for lawyers to make authorized revisions to an expert's prepared report. *See Marke v. Moore*, 171 F.R.D. 298 (D.Kan.1997). It is quite another for an expert to include calculations upon which he did not rely and he would not rely on simply to appease his client's attorney. A proffered expert must "bring to the jury more than the lawyers can offer in argument." *Salas v. Carpenter*, 980 F.2d 299, 305 (5th Cir.1992). In short, Brethauer's own admissions demonstrate that he failed to employ the same level of intellectual rigor that characterizes the practice of experts in his field, or even his own normal practice.[1]

Example 8.96: Sample cross-examination, reliance on information supplied by counsel

Cross-examination:

Q. Is it important for a vocational expert to know the medical history of the individual about whom he is testifying?

A. Well…yes in most cases.

Q. Did you review the plaintiff's medical history in this case before you authored your report?

A. No.

Q. Did you review the plaintiff's deposition before you wrote your report?

A. Portions of it.

Q. These are excerpts you selected?

A. No, they were provided by counsel.

Q. Did you determine what educational courses were taken by the plaintiff before you wrote your report?

A. No, I just had a summary provided by counsel.

Q. Did counsel tell you to say in your report you saw Dr. Fen's ergonomic report when in fact you had not?

A. No. That was my mistake.

Q. On page 10 of your report is a chart, correct?

A. Yes.

Q. Can you tell us where the data came from for the chart and how the calculations were done?

A. No, I can't.

Q. You blindly accepted and incorporated all the material provided to you by counsel in your report, correct?

A. No. I utilized some of the information provided.

Q. Did you include your references to your own depositions in your report?

A. Yes.

Q. You in fact have never even read your transcript, correct?

A. Correct.

Q. These references were supplied by counsel and incorporated in your report, correct?

---

[1] At 797.

A. Yes.

Q. Could you point to any information, data, or language that was supplied to you by counsel which did not find its way into your report?

A. No.

Q. On your oath, would it be fair to say that your sole source of information about the plaintiff in this case comes from summaries provided to you by counsel?

A. Yes.

Comment: This expert's report would have been much more credible if it had been based upon information that was not filtered through retaining counsel.

Chapter 9 The Importance of Staying within One's True Area of Expertise

9.1 Executive Summary
The authors recommend that an expert stay within her true area of expertise. Advice for achieving this follows.

- Expert reports should only express opinions that are within the expert's true area of expertise.
- Experts should only use terms for which they know the definitions.
- Experts (other than legal experts, such as judges and lawyers) should avoid the use of legal terms in reports.
- Experts (other than legal experts, such as judges and lawyers) should avoid expressing legal opinions in their reports.
- Experts should not opine on cost estimates unless they are qualified to do so.

9.2 Beyond Area of Expertise
Expert reports should only express opinions that are within the expert's true area of expertise. Experts should also only use terms for which they know the definition. Experts all too often express multiple opinions in their reports, some of which are beyond their true area of expertise. This should be avoided.

When an expert expresses an opinion that is beyond her true area of expertise, she can expect that opinion to be legally challenged.[1] Even if the expert is permitted to express the opinion, she can expect to be closely questioned about opinions that may be beyond the expert's true area of expertise. When conducting such questioning, counsel will attempt to leave the jury with the impression that the expert was beyond her true area of expertise when she expressed one or more of the opinions in her report. If counsel succeeds in this regard, he can then argue to the jury that the expert

---

[1] See, e.g., *Brodersen v. Sioux Valley Memorial Hospital,* 902 F.Supp. 931 (N. D. Iowa 1995) (orthopedic surgeon not qualified to testify regarding chiropractic malpractice); *Williams v. Rene,* 72 F.3d 1096 (3rd Cir. 1995) (actuary not permitted to testify that victim's gross earnings would triple in 17 years); *Walker v. The Bluffs Apartments,* 477 S.E.2d 472 (S.C. App. 1996) (builder not qualified to testify on architect's standard of care); *Talle v. Nebraska Dept. of Social Serv.,* 541 N.W.2d 30 (Neb. 1995) (economist not permitted to testify on enjoyment of life); *Chase v. Mary Hitchcock Memorial Hosp.,* 668 A.2d 50 (N.H. 1995) (general practitioner not qualified to testify on failed induced delivery); *Tucker v. Nike, Inc.,* 919 F.Supp. 1192 (1995) (podiatrist not permitted to testify on defect in basketball shoe).

would say anything and opine on any topic to help the party that is paying her bill. Consider the following examples.

Example 9.21: Mechanical engineer opining on injury
Report States:

> Based on my education and experience as a mechanical engineer…It is most likely that prior to being injured, Mr. Robert released the trigger switch that controls power to the saw's motor. Had the saw been equipped with an automatic blade brake which is actuated by releasing the trigger switch, the blade would have stopped or slowed prior to Mr. Robert's contacting the blade. Brown and Drecker made miter saws with such an automatic brake as early as 1976. These would stop a saw blade in typically less than two seconds. As the time between releasing the trigger switch and contacting the blade is not known, the speed of the saw blade at the moment of hand contact cannot be determined but any decrease in blade speed would have resulted in a less serious accident.

Resulting Cross-examination:

Q. When you say that "any decrease" in blade speed would have resulted in a less serious accident, that's not what you really mean, is it sir?
A. Yes it is.
Q. Is it your testimony under the pains and penalties of perjury that you can say with a reasonable degree of engineering certainty that if the blade speed was reduced by .5% it would have resulted in a less serious accident?
A. Well, it would have to be a significant decrease in blade speed.
Q. That's not what you said in your report is it?
A. That's right, that's not what I said.
Q. Would you like to express an opinion on what you would consider to be a significant decrease in blade speed in this case?
A. Not unless I have to.

Comment: It is common sense that a mechanical engineer is generally not an expert on the nature and extent of injuries. By expressing an opinion beyond his true area of expertise, this expert has undermined the value of *all* his opinions. This expert would have been better served not addressing the issue of injury at all.

> Based on my education and experience as a mechanical engineer…It is my opinion, based on a reasonable degree of engineering certainty, that prior to being injured Mr. Robert released the trigger switch that controls power to the saw's motor. Had the saw been equipped with an automatic blade brake which is actuated by releasing the trigger switch, the blade would have stopped or slowed prior to Mr. Robert's contacting the blade. Brown and Drecker made miter saws with such an automatic brake as early as 1976. These would stop a saw blade in typically less than two seconds. As the time between releasing the trigger switch and contacting the blade is not known, the speed of the saw blade at the moment of hand contact cannot be precisely determined.

Example 9.22: Forensic pathologist on saw blade
Report States:

It is further my opinion that had the miter saw in question included a wraparound blade guard, or a more complete guard that would have prevented exposure to the rotating blade in a kickback incident, Mr. Garcia would have received no injuries. (Written by forensic pathologist.)

Resulting Cross-examination:
Q. You are a medical doctor by training, correct?
A. Yes.
Q. You are not a mechanical engineer or a safety engineer, correct?
A. That's correct.
Q. Have you ever actually designed or helped to design guards on power tools?
A. No.
Q. Despite your lack of formal training and practical experience, you are willing to offer an "expert" opinion on what kind of safety guard was appropriate and would have prevented this accident?

Comment: As the above cross-examination shows, an expert is extremely vulnerable to cross-examination when he opines in areas beyond his true area of expertise. This expert would have been far better off had he not addressed the issue of the design of the saw at all and left that issue to other qualified experts.

Example 9.23: Mechanical engineer on traumatic brain injury
Report States:

It was obvious from this test that utilization of a hard hat would have had little or no effect upon the injury sustained by Jones. The nail penetrating the hard hat shell would have entered the brain of Jones though the depth of penetration would have been reduced by the depth of the hard hat suppression. (Written by mechanical engineer.)

Resulting Cross-examination:
Q. If a hard hat had been worn, the nail would not have penetrated Jones's head as deeply, is that correct?
A. Yes.
Q. It is your opinion, is it not, that the nail not going into Jones' brain as deeply would have had little or no effect on the injury Jones received?
A. Yes.
Q. How less deeply would the nail have penetrated had Jones been wearing a hard hat?
A. About an inch, I'd say.
Q. That extra inch of steel shot into Mr. Jones' brain didn't really matter then?
A. It wouldn't have made much of a difference.
Q. What if the nail had been longer and had shot deeper into his head, would he have had worse injuries?
A. Possibly.
Q. What is the difference between the cerebrum and the cerebellum?
A. I don't know.
Q. You are a mechanical engineer, not a medical doctor, isn't that true?

A. Yes.

Q. You don't have any medical training?

A. No.

Q. But you are being paid for your testimony today and are willing to give us the benefit of your medical wisdom?

A. Yes.

Comment: Stating opinions that are beyond one's true area of expertise can make *all* of the expert's opinions suspect. If opposing counsel can show that one of the expert's opinions should not be believed, she can suggest to the fact finder that none of the expert's opinions should be believed. This particular engineering expert was way out of his league when he began expressing opinions on traumatic brain injury. He would have been far better off limiting his opinions to his true area of expertise.

> It is my opinion, based on a reasonable degree of engineering certainty, that had Jones been wearing a hard hat, the nail penetrating the hard hat shell would have still entered the brain of Jones though the depth of penetration would have been reduced by the depth of the hard hat suppression. (Written by engineer.)

Experts should not give in to pressure from counsel or personal temptation to opine on areas beyond their true area of expertise. Consider the following example.

Example 9.24: Refusal to opine beyond area of expertise
Report States:

> I do not offer any expert opinions with regard to ABC or Main St. Clinic. The only opinion I feel qualified to offer is that as it relates to Dr. A. in his capacity as a family practice physician.

Resulting Cross-examination:

Q. You admit that you are not qualified to offer opinions on ABC or Main St. Clinic, correct?

A. Yes and I stated that in my report, counselor.

Comment: This expert acted wisely in limiting her opinions to those areas where she is truly qualified. This prudent self-restraint will help insulate the expert's opinions against attack on cross-examination.

9.3 Legal Terms

One of the many traps that experts often fall into is the use of legal terms in their reports and opinions.[2] An expert can expect to be questioned closely about any legal terms used in her report. The cross-examiner will attempt to

---

[2] If the expert is an attorney, judge, or other qualified person, she may properly use legal terms in a report.

show that the expert didn't really know what she was talking about when she employed legal terms. This can be used to lessen the expert's credibility by demonstrating that because the expert did not know what she was talking about in one area of her report, the rest of the report should also be called into question. The other implication is that if the expert was not qualified to use the legal term, maybe she is not qualified to give an opinion in the case.

It is good practice to avoid such legal terms. This can often be done without having to leave any facts out of the report.

Example 9.31: "Grossly negligent"
The following language appeared in a forensic engineering report. Note how, in the cross-examination that follows, the questioner zeroes in on the legal terms used in an attempt to attack the expert's opinion.

Report States:
Warren was also grossly negligent in regards to the collapse of the deck.

Resulting Cross-examination:
Q. Did you form an opinion as to the cause of the collapse of the deck?
A. Yes. As indicated in my report, it was directly due to the gross negligence of Rob Warren, the general contractor.
Q. Could you define what you mean by gross negligence?
A. Ah…well…I am not a lawyer, counselor, but more than regular negligence.
Q. Well, sir, could you define negligence?
A. Failure to use reasonable care.
Q. What are the four elements of negligence?
A. I don't know.
Q. What is the difference between gross negligence and ordinary negligence?
A. Gross negligence is a more serious action.
Q. Was there an intent to injure by Mr. Warren?
A. Not that I know of.
Q. If gross negligence was defined as an actual or constructive intent to injure, might that change the opinion expressed in your report that Mr. Warren was "grossly negligent"?
A. It might.

Comment: The expert in this example would have been better served by avoiding the legal term "grossly negligent." This is easily done without taking anything away from the idea the expert is trying to communicate. For example, the expert could have written, "The actions of the general contractor detailed above represent a grave and flagrant violation of reasonable construction practices."

The following additional examples also use legal terms or citations. Each could result in a close cross-examination focusing on the legal definitions. This is likely to show that the expert did not completely understand the word that was being used and will result in a loss of credibility.

Example 9.32: Citation to legal authority
Report States:

> The implied obligation to build in a good and workmanlike manner is contractual in nature and, when breached, gives rise to a breach of contract cause of action by an Owner.[3]

Resulting Cross-examination:
Q. You cited the case of *HMR Construction Company* in your report?
A. Yes.
Q. Do you have the full name of the case and the correct legal citation as it appears in the case reporter?
A. I don't know what you mean.
Q. Did you look up the case or was this quote provided to you by counsel?
A. I….was given the quote.
Q. Do you even know how to conduct legal research, sir?
A. No.
Q. Do you know if this case was reversed on appeal?
A. No.
Q. But you do know how to follow the instructions of counsel who retained you, correct?

Comment: This is a legal statement that cites legal authority. It is an invitation for trouble. It would be better for the expert to make his point while avoiding the legalities:

> The builder's work was not performed in a good and workmanlike manner.

Example 9.33: "Informed consent"
Report States:

> The signed nonspecific statement qualifies as informed consent for dental therapy.

Resulting Cross-examination:
Q. You found the statement sufficient legally for informed consent, correct?
A. Yes.
Q. Can you explain the four elements of informed consent?
A. No, not off-hand.
Q. The dentist would have to explain the nature of the procedure and treatment, correct?
A. Yes.
Q. Did that take place here?
A. I don't know.
Q. The patient should be informed about the expectations of the treatments and the likelihood of success?
A. Yes.

---

[3] *HMR Construction Company, Inc.,* 422 S.W.2d at 216.

Q. Is that contained in the form?
A. No.
Q. What about reasonable alternatives and probable outcome? Are those in the form?
A. No.
Q. What about the known inherent material risks? Is that in the form?
A. No.
Q. So, when you concluded that the signed, nonspecific statement qualified as informed consent for dental therapy, you were wrong, weren't you?

Comment: A statement less vulnerable to cross-examination would avoid the legal term "informed consent." For example, consider this:

> In my opinion, Dr. Jones did not fully and effectively communicate to Ms. Bailey all the information necessary for Ms. Bailey to make an intelligent decision on her course of treatment. The signed statement he obtained was vague and looked like just another standard form the patients sign.

Example 9.34: "Draft Copy. Attorney Work Product"
Report Cover Page States:
Draft Copy. Attorney Work Product.

Resulting Cross-examination:
Q. Your report is labeled "draft copy, attorney work product," correct?
A. Yes.
Q. This was your attempt to keep it out of the hands of opposing counsel, the judge, and jury?

Comment: This superfluous statement should be avoided altogether. It serves no use and can create a multitude of problems. The term "draft" is a red flag for attorneys and should be avoided (see section 14.4). "Draft" implies that the report was changed after discussions with retaining counsel and this can be extremely problematic. "Work product" is an extremely complex legal term dealing with the discovery process. Writing "work product" on the document does not make the document work product, but it does make it look like the expert is trying to hide something from the other party in the case.

Example 9.35: "Established and recognized case law"
Report States:
In preparing this report, I relied on my knowledge and experience as an institutional Sanitarian, established and recognized case law, and several documents.

Resulting Cross-examination:
Q. In preparing your report, you relied on what you called established and recognized case law, is that correct?
A. Yes.
Q. Can you please cite the exact cases you relied on?
A. I don't have them in front of me.

Q. Do you maintain a list of cases you relied on anywhere else in your file?
A. No. But the law is established.
Q. Do you consider yourself, a sanitarian, qualified to tell this jury under oath what is and what is not established case law?
A. In this area, yes.
Q. What is the legal definition of "established" law?
A. I really can't say.
Q. Is the case law you relied upon binding or persuasive?
A. I'm not sure what you mean by that.
Q. Prior to making this statement, did you do a search to see if any new case law has come down in this area subsequent to your preparing this report?
A. No.
Q. You're really not qualified to testify to this court on what is and is not established case law, are you?
A. No, I guess not.

Comment: This expert has just suffered a needless loss in credibility by getting into legalities in his report. This is a practice that is fraught with danger. This expert would have been better served by removing the reference to relying on "established case law" from his report.

Example 9.36: "Grossly negligent"
Report States:
> Based on the above findings, it is my opinion that the nursing staff was grossly negligent in the care of Mrs. Wilson.

Resulting Cross-examination:
Q. What is the legal definition of negligence?
A. I am not sure.
Q. What is the legal definition of gross negligence?
A. I am not sure.
Q. So, you used the term gross negligence in your report even though you don't know what it means?

Comment: The expert can be expected to be cross-examined on the meaning of gross negligence. (See example 9.31). The expert would have been better served by rephrasing her statement as follows:

> It is my opinion that the nursing staff was far below the applicable standard of care in its care of Mrs. Wilson.

9.4 Costs, Value, Money
Many times, making any estimate regarding costs or value is outside of the expert's true area of expertise. When an expert makes an unsupported financial prediction and is outside of his true area of expertise he will suffer an even greater loss of credibility. Please consider the following examples.

Example 9.41: Physician's cost estimate of future medical care
Report States:

> The permanent injuries described above will most likely require physician-directed supportive care conservatively estimated at an ongoing cost of $1,200.00 to $1,500.00 per year for a minimum of two years and on a possible lifetime basis.

Resulting Cross-examination:

Q. Your estimate is that the future medical expenses could be $2,400, or $3,000, or $95,000 for this 25-year old?
A. Yes.
Q. Can you tell us if he will need this medical care for 1 year, or 2 years, or 50 years?
A. No.
Q. Could you explain on what you based your $1,200–$1,500 per year estimate?
A. My years of training and experience.
Q. What training do you have in the accurate projection of future medical expenses?
A. None.
Q. Did you consult with an expert in the field before you came up with your estimate?
A. No.
Q. So, in fact, you have no objective guidelines or support for your figures, is that correct?

Comment: This expert's cost estimate is on extremely shaky ground. This expert did not appear to be qualified to comment in this area and he failed to provide objective justification for the cost estimates. This expert should have either refrained from offering an opinion in this area or should have provided objective evidence for his cost estimates.

Example 9.42: Engineer: "hundreds of thousands of dollars"
Report States:

> To this day the controls have never functioned properly, and it is predicted that the plaintiffs will have to spend hundreds of thousands of dollars to retrofit the continuing dysfunctional system.

Resulting Cross-examination:

Q. Do you know what is specifically wrong with the system?
A. No….
Q. So, you are not sure what needs to be done to fix it, correct?
A. It may need to be retrofitted.
Q. Have you put the job out to bid?
A. No.
Q. When you said in your report it is predicted that the plaintiffs will have to spend hundreds of thousands of dollars to retrofit the continuing dysfunctional system, was it you who predicted this?
A. No.

Q. Who was it who arrived at this figure?

A. I am not sure. That's the number we were working with.

Q. Sir, can you swear under oath that the cost would be "hundreds of thousands of dollars"?

Comment: Experts should not put cost predictions unsupported by hard data in their expert reports.

Chapter 10 Stating Opinions and Conclusions in a Defensible Manner

10.1 Executive Summary

The main reason an expert is involved in a case is to state her opinion. The principle reason an expert writes a report is to communicate that opinion. The opinion must be communicated effectively and must be expressed in a defensible manner. The authors recommend the following.

- Stating all opinions clearly, explicitly, and with confidence.
- Using the magic words "based upon a reasonable degree of (medical, engineering, legal, accounting, jewelry appraisal, or other field) certainty" or "based on a reasonable degree of (medical, engineering, legal, accounting, jewelry appraisal, or other field) probability" when expressing the opinion in the report.
- Avoiding hedge words, such as "it seems," "I think," and "I believe" when expressing opinions in the expert report.
- Stating the reasons that justify the opinion in concise bullet-point format.
- Avoiding expressing net opinions; that is, bare conclusions without supporting justification.
- Stating all of the opinions the expert expects to express at trial.
- Documenting a detailed and reliable methodology so that the report will not be challenged under *Daubert*.

10.2 State Opinions Clearly and with Confidence

The reason an expert report is prepared is so that the expert can express her opinion(s). These opinions should be stated clearly, explicitly, and confidently. For expert opinions to be admissible in most civil cases, the expert generally must believe that it is more likely than not that her opinion is correct (51% or more certainty). There are certain "magic words" that are commonly accepted as expressing the idea that the expert is 51% or more certain of her opinion. These include the expressions "based upon a reasonable degree of (medical, engineering, legal, accounting, jewelry appraisal, or other field) certainty" and "based on a reasonable degree of (medical, engineering, legal, accounting, jewelry appraisal, or other field) probability." It is good practice to use one of these phrases when stating an expert opinion in a report.

Hedge words, such as "it seems," "I think," and "I believe," should be avoided. Such words suggest that the expert does not have confidence in her opinion. Failure to state opinions clearly and with confidence will make the report and opinion vulnerable to attack on cross-examination and could possibly result in the report being stricken by the judge.

Example 10.21: "Could" and "possibility" insufficient to establish proof by a preponderance of the evidence

Perkins v. Entergy Corporation, 756 So.2d 388 (La.App. 1 Cir.,1999)
This case dealt with a flash fire at an air separation facility. The expert Schmidt concluded in his report:

> [D]uring highly abnormal pipeline operating conditions, which occurred during the early hours of April 6, 1994, circumstances *could* have developed which caused the movement of metallic particles through the piping network [of the ALAC facility]. Therefore, the potential availability of metallic particles within a piping system and the likelihood of particle impact or frictionally induced ignition becomes a *statistical possibility.* (Emphasis added.)

The court found the language on causation too indefinite and stated:

> This conclusion is clearly insufficient to establish cause in fact, which requires proof by a preponderance of the evidence. *See Dabog.* 625 So.2d at 493. One must prove what probably happened as opposed to what "could" have happened and what is a "statistical possibility."

Example 10.22: Overly vague opinion insufficient

Piascyk v. City of New Haven, 64 F. Supp2d.19 (D.Conn. 1999)
This case dealt with an ADA case filed by a police officer. The expert report was written by a physician, Shine. In support of the plaintiff's claim that he was substantially limited with regard to carrying, the plaintiff offered only Dr. Shine's statement in his report to the New Haven Workers' Compensation Division that plaintiff would have difficulty "carrying heavy loads...." The court rejected the indefinite language "carrying heavy loads" and stated:

> This statement is too vague to support a finding that plaintiff is significantly restricted in his ability to carry compared to the average person. *See Colwell,* 158 F.3d at 644 (testimony that plaintiff could not lift "very heavy objects" did not support a finding of substantial limitation).

Example 10.23: Failure to be clear and explicit

Report States:
> Although Buildem Engineering had no direct contractual responsibility for safety, Mr. Donnelley did recognize the hazard. It is true that Mr. Donnelley told Mr. First, the project engineer, of the danger he saw. I feel Mr. First should have responded. He should have advised Mr. Williams and verified that corrective action resulted. All engineering societies exhort members to hold safety paramount.

Resulting Cross-examination:
Q. When you say in your report, "he should have advised Mr. Williams" who are you referring to?

A. Mr. First.
Q. Do you know what corrective action should have been taken?
A. Yes.
Q. Do you specify the action in your report?
A. Well. . .I discuss that on page 7, but I don't detail it.
Q. So you did the same thing Mr. First did?
A. Huh?
Q. You knew what should have been done, but never told anyone?
A. I explained myself, maybe I could have expressed myself better.
Q. You don't know how many engineering societies there are, do you?
A. Well, it's over 50 but. . .no I don't know.
Q. So, when you wrote "all engineering societies exhort members to hold safety paramount" you just misspoke?
A. I should have been more precise with my language.
Q. Agreed.

Comment: The expert's opinions need to be stated clearly and explicitly. This was not done in this example. A clearer and more explicit way to state the expert's opinions in this case would be as follows:

> It is my opinion, based upon a reasonable degree of engineering certainty, that Mr. First failed to follow fundamental safety practices by failing to advise Mr. Williams of the danger at the site and failing to verify that corrective action took place.

Example 10.24: Failure to state opinion confidently: "cannot be ruled out"
Report States:
> Therefore, based upon the foregoing and a reasonable degree of engineering certainty, it is our opinion electrical failure cannot be ruled out as a possible cause of loss.

Resulting Cross-examination:
Q. So, your opinion is that electrical failure caused the loss?
A. No, that's not what I said.
Q. You qualified your opinion, correct?
A. Yes.
Q. In fact, you used three qualifiers in your opinion?
A. Three?
Q. A reasonable degree of engineering certainty would be what expressed in a percentage form?
A. 51 percent.
Q. Your use of the term "possible" indicated less than 51% certainty, correct?
A. Yes.
Q. And, the phrase "cannot be ruled out" even less certainty.
A. That's true.
Q. Would it be fair to say that there were several potential causes of the loss here?
A. Yes.
Q. In fact, how many potential causes of the loss could you "not rule out"?

A. Approximately seven.
Q. You're not even certain about this, sir?
A. Well, there are various degrees of certainty.
Q. Would it be fair to say that you cannot truthfully testify with a reasonable degree of engineering certainty as to what in fact caused the loss?
A. Yes, that's true.

Comment: Not only is this opinion highly vulnerable to cross-examination, the opinion may also be vulnerable to legal challenges.

> Therefore, based upon the foregoing and to a reasonable degree of engineering certainty, it is our opinion that electrical failure is more likely than not the cause of this loss.

Example 10.25: "It would seem to me" language takes away from opinion
Report States:

> It would seem to me, therefore, that the treatment rendered from August 31, 1998 to present was not reasonable or necessary.

Resulting Cross-examination:
Q. Are you certain that the treatment rendered from August 31, 1998 to present was not reasonable or necessary?
A. Yes.
Q. Sir, how old are you?
A. 53, but I don't see how that is relevant, counselor.
Q. Why didn't you say "it would seem to me" I am 53 years old?
A. Because I know precisely how old I am.
Q. As opposed to your opinion on the reasonableness of the treatment when you said, "it seems to me it was not reasonable or necessary"?

Comment: The weight the expert's opinion will likely be given is greatly lessened by his inclusion of the "it would seem to me" language. This language suggests uncertainty. This report would likely be given more weight had the expert used confident language to express his opinion:

> It is my opinion, based upon a reasonable degree of medical certainty, that the treatment rendered from August 31, 1998 to present was neither reasonable nor necessary. I base this opinion on the following:
>   1. ...

Example 10.26: "I do not think" language lessens weight report will be given
Report States:

> I do not think that the revision of the total knee arthroplasties that took place following his accident of 2/7/94 were necessitated by the accident itself.

Comment: This report would have been far better had it used more confident language:

> It is my opinion, based upon a reasonable degree of medical certainty, that the revision of the total knee arthroplasties that took place following his accident of 2/7/94 were not necessitated by the accident itself. I base this opinion on the following reasons.
>   1. …

Example 10.27: "I do not believe" language lessens weight report will be given

Report States:

> I don't believe that the laminectomies at T5 to T6 caused any significant increase in Mr. Collins's complaints.

Comment: The "I don't believe" language takes away from the expert's opinion.

> It is my opinion, based upon a reasonable degree of medical certainty, that the laminectomies at T5 to T6 did not cause any significant increase in Mr. Collins's complaints. I base this opinion on the following reasons:
>   1. …

Example 10.28: "The following conclusions can be made"

Report States:

> Based on the foregoing, and to a reasonable degree of engineering certainty, the following conclusions can be made.

Comment: This expert's conclusions would be more persuasive if the "can be made" language was replaced with more confident language.

> Based on the foregoing, and to a reasonable degree of engineering certainty, I have made the following conclusions:
>   1. …

Example 10.29: "It can be argued": expert now an advocate?

Report States:

> Thus it can be argued that Dr. A should have never been doing HIV testing/interpretation in the first place, based on his admitted lack of experience.

Resulting Cross-examination:

Q. You testified that "it can be argued that Dr. A should have never been doing HIV testing/interpretation in the first place, based on his admitted lack of experience"?
A. Correct.
Q. It could also be argued that he should have been doing the HIV testing, correct?
A. Yes.

Q. Thank you, no further questions.

Comment: The "it can be argued" language should not have been used. This language may make the expert either appear to be an advocate or unsure of himself. Better language follows.

> It is my opinion, based upon a reasonable degree of medical certainty, that Dr. A breached the standard of care in providing Mr. Jones HIV testing and interpretation. Dr. A had no training or experience in HIV testing and HIV test interpretation.

10.3 State Reasons for Opinions

The opinions expressed in the report should be supported with reasons that justify them. When the opinions are so supported, the weight that will likely be given to the expert's report will be increased significantly. If possible, the supporting reasons should be listed as a concise bullet-point list. Consider the following examples, which clearly and explicitly state the reasons for the experts' opinions.

Example 10.31: Detailed reasons to support opinion provided in bullet-point list

Report States:

> It is my opinion, based upon a reasonable degree of medical certainty that S.B., M.D. provided markedly substandard care in:
>
> (a.) Embarking on a course of very prolonged, poorly monitored lytic therapy in a case which required treatment by surgical thrombectomy because of the sensory and motor changes present;
>
> (b.) Having started therapy for whatever reason, failing to use an aggressive fragmentation, high concentration, directed lytic agent infusion; and for some reason starting and continuing therapy in a demonstrably non-essential, currently and previously non-collateralizing profunda femoris artery while the condition of the right foot and leg continued to deteriorate;
>
> (c.) Failing to recognize that the previously angiographically demonstrated major collateral, the DBrLCF was obstructed and that Mr. B.'s leg and foot were not in the same condition as before by-pass surgery and now had insufficient collateralization to maintain viability;
>
> (d.) Continuing the infusion in a non-essential artery for 11 hours after the current patient complaint began, before trying to clear the bypass graft of clot;
>
> (e.) Failing to pursue established principles of lytic therapy, and/or failing to observe the limitations, the indications and contraindications of the technique; and
>
> (f.) Failing to obtain adequate supervision of his performance from the surgeons in an area of treatment he claims is beyond his ability to evaluate and conduct.

It is my further opinion that because of each and all of these incidents of failing to render care to a current medically acceptable standard, Mr. B. unnecessarily suffered the loss of his right leg below the mid-thigh.

Comment: The expert's conclusions in this report are made more persuasive by the expert's inclusion of the reasons for his opinion. The bullet-points make the report easy to read and even more persuasive.

Example 10.32: Reasons to support opinion stated
Report States:

The claimant sustained severe closed head injury with persistent cognitive defects and post traumatic seizure disorder. The symptoms are all causally related to the claimant's last accident on June 14, 1995. The reason they are causally related are that the claimant sustained a head injury in the past. However, he never had any seizures as a result of any prior injury. Of note, one week following this last injury he suffered on the aircraft he did sustain seizures and they were poorly controlled.

Comment: The expert's conclusions in this report are made more persuasive by the expert's inclusion of the reasons for her opinion.

10.4 Net Opinions

Failure to state reasons for the expert's opinion makes the report less credible and may make it particularly vulnerable to legal challenges. "An expert's report which offers only a bare conclusion—nothing more than a bottom line—is insufficient to prove the expert's point."[1] This is what is known as a net opinion. Net opinions are inadmissible. Please consider the following examples.

Example 10.41: Overly vague opinion insufficient
Ohime v. Foresman, 186 F.R.D. 507 (N.D.Ind.,1999)
In this case, the proffered report of a psychiatric social worker, Nott, was found to be deficient. The court stated:

Mr. Nott's second report still is deficient under Rule 26(a)(2)(B). The report states a summary of Ms. Ohime's two meetings with Mr. Nott (arguably the data or other information on which Mr. Nott relied in making his report), but it contains only a three-sentence paragraph of vague conclusions as to his expert opinion of Ms. Ohime's condition. These conclusory determinations are insufficient under Rule 26(1).

Example 10.42: Overly vague opinion insufficient
Hemmen v. Atlantic City Medical Center, 758 A.2d 1145 (N.J.Super.L.,1999)
This was a medical malpractice case. The court found the expert's report an

---

[1] *SMS Systems Maintenance Services v. Digital Equipment Corporation,* 188 F.3rd11 24 (1999).

inadmissible net opinion and stated:

> I recognized that the expert may have been reporting that the medical community understands that of the cases of drug induced sciatic nerve damage, negligence is the most frequent cause. Such a report, however, must rest upon the expert's experience or upon textual support. *Connors v. University Associates*, 769 F.*Supp.* 578, 587 (D.Vt.1991) *aff'd* 4 *F.*3d 123 (2d Cir.1993). In the absence of such a basis, the opinion of the relative frequency of negligent and non-negligently caused damage would be an inadmissible net opinion, bereft of any factual underpinning.

Example 10.43: One-page conclusory report insufficient under Rule 26(a)(2)B
Bank Brussels Lambert v. Credit Lyonnais, 2000 WL 1762533 (S.D.N.Y. 2000) The court stated:

> The Perkins Report is a one page report that states a conclusion and offers no support for it. While it states that the conclusion is based on the "review of the brokers' reports and borrowing base reports" it does not explain the rationale that led to the conclusion nor does it set forth the testimony that will be provided at trial. As a result, the amount of information provided in the Perkins Report is not sufficient under Rule 26(a)(2)(B). Further, the Perkins Report fails to state that it is responding to the Boothman Sherwin Report.

10.5 Failure to Disclose Fact/Experiment in Report
An expert who files a pretrial report and fails to mention important information (for instance, that she conducted an out-of-court experiment) does so at her peril. Opposing counsel will argue that it was not adequately apprised of the basis for the expert's opinion and/or that the expert and counsel failed to supplement its discovery responses.

In *Metropolitan Life Insurance Company v. Tomchik,*[2] the court found the expert's report, which did specifically reveal an out-of-court experiment, was legally sufficient. The court stated:

> In the instant case, although Lurwig's report does not specifically state that an out-of-court experiment was conducted, it is apparent from the photographs and from the statement in the report that Lurwig had made a model work piece, that Lurwig's opinion was based, in part at least, on the results of an experiment regarding kerf marks. In addition, the report makes very clear that it was Lurwig's expert opinion that the amputation of appellant's thumb could not have occurred in the manner described by appellant. At trial, Lurwig did not change his opinion in this regard. The fact that Lurwig conducted an experiment in forming his opinion appears to be a nuance in his opinion, rather than the opinion itself. The report was sufficiently clear to apprise appellant as to Lurwig's opinion and to present appellant with a reasonable opportunity to prepare a defense against it.[3]

---

[2] 732 N.E.2d430 (Ohio App. 7 Dist., 1999).
[3] At 782, 783.

10.6 State All Opinions to Which Expert Will Testify

The expert's report should contain *all* of the opinions the expert expects to express at trial. Failure to include all opinions may result in the preclusion of the expert from offering at trial the opinions that were not included in the expert's report. Failure to include all opinions may also be a subject of pointed cross-examination.

Example 10.61: Some opinions omitted from report
Report States:
> This letter contains some of my opinions in the above referenced matter.

Resulting Cross-examination:
Q. You do have other opinions on this case which were not contained in your letter, correct?
A. Yes.
Q. Why did you omit these opinions?
A. I was asked to.
Q. By counsel who retained you?
A. Yes.
Q. This was after you shared these opinions with her?
A. Well, . . . yes.
Q. So, these opinions are ones you and counsel decided should not be shared with her honor and the members of the jury?
A. I was just. . ..
Q. Following orders?
A. Completing my assignment.
Q. Let's go through these opinions and see why it was decided that they should not be shared with the jury.

Comment: This language should be avoided because it can be made to appear as though the expert is intentionally withholding some of his opinions.

10.7 Conclusory Statements

When expert reports are offered with conclusory statements in lieu of the basis for the expert's opinions, they are stricken and found to be legally insufficient under Rule 26.

Example 10.71: Conclusory determinations
Ohime v. Foresman, 186 F.R.D. 507 (N.D.Ind. 1999)
The proffered report of a psychiatric social worker, Nott, was found to be deficient for being a conclusory determination. The court stated:

> Mr. Nott's second report still is deficient under Rule 26(a)(2)(B). The report states a summary of Ms. Ohime's two meetings with Mr. Nott (arguably the data or other information on which Mr. Nott relied in making his report), but it contains only a three-sentence paragraph of vague conclusions as to his expert opinion of Ms.

Ohime's condition. These conclusory determinations are insufficient under Rule 26(1).[4]

Example 10.72: Conclusory report inadmissible in Texas medical malpractice case

Hart v. Wright, 16 S.W.3rd 872 (Tex.App.-Fort Worth 2000)
This was a Texas medical malpractice case. The Medical Liability and Insurance Improvement Act contains expert report writing standards and was enacted to curtail frivolous claims against physicians and related healthcare providers.[5] The court dealt with and rejected a written report in affidavit form.

An expert report is defined as any report written by an expert that provides a fair summary of the expert's opinions as of the date of the report regarding: (1) the applicable standard of care; (2) the manner in which the care rendered by defendant failed to meet the standard of care; and (3) the causal relationship between that failure and the injury, harm, or damages claimed.

Appellants offered this written report of Dr. Maewal in affidavit form to comply with their obligation under the Act:

> My name is Hrishi K. Maewal. I am over the age of majority. I have never been convicted of a felony or a crime of moral turpitude, and I am in all things qualified to make this affidavit.
>
> I am a physician licensed to practice medicine in the State of Texas.
>
> I am currently practicing medicine and was practicing medicine on January 22, 1996.
>
> I am board certified in Internal Medicine, Pulmonary Disease, Cardiology, and Critical Care Medicine.
>
> I examined Bobby Hart at Harris Methodist Fort Worth Hospital on January 23, 1996.
>
> Based on the history obtained from the patient and his family members along with the supporting evidence of laboratory evaluation which showed an elevated creatine kinase of 1854 U/L, CK-MB 219.7 ng/ml and % relative index 11.9 at 10:41 a.m. along with an EKG which shows an inferior infarction with Q-waves, in my expert opinion, Mr. Hart was experiencing an acute myocardial infarction at approximately 5:00 p.m. on January 22, 1996 while a patient in the emergency room at Huguley Memorial Hospital.
>
> Based on the above analysis, Dr. Wright, the treating physician at Huguley Memorial Hospital, and Huguley Memorial Hospital departed from the acceptable standard of care for the diagnosis, medical care, and treatment of a patient with an acute myocardial infarction.

Appellants argue that even thought Dr. Maewal's report does not include all of the information required by section 13.01(r)(6), it nonetheless satisfies the definition of an expert report. We disagree because Dr. Maewal's report does not address a standard of care, deviation from that standard, or that a deviation from the standard caused injury or damages. *See id.* The report merely concludes that Mr. Hart demonstrated signs and symptoms of a heart attack at a time and place with which

---

[4] At 23.

[5] Tex.Rev.Civ. Stat. Ann. Art. 49501 Sec. 13.01(d)1.

Dr. Maewal had no connection. For Dr. Maewal to qualify as an expert, the report had to show that he had knowledge of the accepted standards of care for the diagnosis, care and treatment of the injury involved, how the applicable standard was breached, and how the alleged breach contributed to Appellants' injuries or damages. *See id.* §§ 13.01(r)(5), (6). While a party need not marshal all its proof, a good faith effort in preparing an expert report must, at a minimum, attempt to incorporate the three requirements found in section 13.01(r)(6). Here, the conclusory report is not the good faith effort required by the statute. We overrule issue one.[6]

Example 10.73: No reasons stated for this conclusion
Report States:
        Care by paramedics and intermediate EMS staff was appropriate.

Resulting Cross-examination:
Q. Your conclusion in your report is that care by the paramedics and EMS staff was appropriate?
A. Yes.
Q. Where in your report do you explain your reasoning and provide facts and the scientific rationale for this conclusion?
A. It's not in there.
Q. So, you are asking this jury to just accept this naked conclusion without any basis in fact or science?

Comment: Conclusions without supporting reasoning are not persuasive. Conclusions should always be supported with reasoning.

        Care by paramedics and intermediate EMS staff was appropriate. I base this conclusion on the following...

Example 10.74: Conclusion without support insufficient under Rule 26
Bank Brussels Lambert v. Credit Lyonnais, 2000 WL 1762533 (S.D.N.Y. 2000)
The court rejected a one-page conclusory report and stated:

        The Perkins Report is a one page report that states a conclusion and offers no
        support for it. While it states that the conclusion is based on the "review of the
        brokers' reports and borrowing base reports" it does not explain the rationale that
        led to the conclusion nor does it set forth the testimony that will be provided at trial.
        As a result, the amount of information provided in the Perkins Report is not
        sufficient under Rule 26(a)(2)(B). Further, the Perkins Report fails to state that it is
        responding to the Boothman Sherwin Report.[7]

---

[6] At 876, 877.
[7] At 2000.

Example 10.75: Net opinion inadmissible
Hemmen v. Atlantic City Medical Center, 758 A.2d 1145 (N.J.Super.L. 1999)
This was a medical malpractice case. The court found the expert's report an
inadmissible net opinion and stated:

> I recognized that the expert may have been reporting that the medical community
> understands that of the cases of drug induced sciatic nerve damage, negligence is the
> most frequent cause. Such a report, however, must rest upon the expert's experience
> or upon textual support. *Connors v. University Associates,* 769 F.*Supp.* 578, 587
> (D.Vt.1991) *aff'd* 4 *F.*3d 123 (2d Cir.1993). In the absence of such a basis, the
> opinion of the relative frequency of negligent and non-negligently caused damage
> would be an inadmissible net opinion, bereft of any factual underpinning.[8]

10.8 Vague, Equivocal, and Uncertain Reports Inadmissible

The courts continue to reject reports where the expert's opinion is expressed
vaguely, equivocally, or with insufficient certainty.

Example 10.81: "Could" and "possibility"
Perkins v. Entergy Corporation, 756 So.2d 388 (La.App. 1 Cir. 2000)
The court dealt with the case of a flash fire at an air separation facility. The
expert Schmidt concluded in his report:

> [D]uring highly abnormal pipeline operating conditions, which occurred during the
> early hours of April 6, 1994, circumstances *could* have developed which caused the
> movement of metallic particles through the piping network [of the ALAC facility].
> Therefore, the potential availability of metallic particles within a piping system and
> the likelihood of particle impact or frictionally induced ignition becomes a *statistical
> possibility.* (Emphasis ours.)[9]

The court found the language on causation too indefinite and stated:

> This conclusion is clearly insufficient to establish cause in fact, which requires proof
> by a preponderance of the evidence. *See Dabog.* 625 So.2d at 493. One must prove
> what probably happened as opposed to what "could" have happened and what is a
> "statistical possibility."[10]

Example 10.82: Vague report cannot support finding for plaintiff
Piascyk v. City of New Haven, 64 F.Supp.2d 19 (D.Conn. 1999)
The court dealt with an ADA case filed by a police officer. The expert report
was written by a physician, Shine.

> In support of his claim that he is substantially limited with regard to carrying,
> plaintiff has offered only Dr. Shine's statement in his report to the New Haven
> Workers' Compensation Division that plaintiff would have difficulty "carrying
> heavy loads...." (Shine Report, Plaintiff's Exhibit 11.)[11]

---

[8] At 280.
[9] At 407.
[10] At 407.
[11] At 29.

The court rejected the indefinite language "carrying heavy loads" and stated:

> This statement is too vague to support a finding that plaintiff is significantly restricted in his ability to carry compared to the average person. *See Colwell*, 158 F.3d at 644 (testimony that plaintiff could not lift "very heavy objects" did not support a finding of substantial limitation).[12]

10.9 Documenting a Reliable Methodology

Experts should be aware that their reports will be closely scrutinized under the *Daubert* doctrine to see if they are not only relevant but reliable. [See *Daubert v. Merrell Dow Pharmaceuticals, Inc.*, 509 U.S. 579, 113 S.Ct.2786 125 L.E.2d 469 (1993); *General Electric Co. v. Joiner*, 522 U.S. 136, 118 S.Ct. 512, 517, 139 L.E.2d 508 (1977); and *Kumho Tire Co. Limited v. Carmichael*, 526 U.S. 137, 119 S.Ct. 1167, 143 L.E. 2d 238 (1999).] Under the *Daubert* line of cases the judge will act as a gatekeeper to screen out and exclude unreliable expert testimony and reports. The judge will consider several factors, including:

1. whether the theory or technique used by the expert can be, and has been, tested,
2. whether the theory or technique has been subjected to peer review and publication,
3. the known or potential rate of error of the method used, and
4. the degree of the method's or conclusion's acceptance within the relevant scientific community.

An expert report will survive *Daubert* challenges if the report is based upon reliable methodology and if this methodology is spelled out clearly in the report. Please consider the following examples.

Example 10.91: Minimal examination, report stricken
Minisan v. Danek Medical, Inc., 79 F.Supp. 2d 970 (N.D.Ind. 1999)
This was a pedicle screw medical device case. The plaintiff offered the report of Dr. Lance Yarus, an osteopath, as her only evidence. The court rejected the report and proposed testimony. The court stated:

> Dr. Yarus states that he arrived at his conclusions based solely on an examination of Minisan's numerous medical records. He apparently never examined her, met with her, or even spoke to her. Neither did he examine or test the TSRH device. Dr. Yarus concludes that "both surgical interventions were the proximate cause of the non-unions and subsequent development of pain." (Def's Mem. In Supp., Ex. 0 at 4.) He also concludes that Minisan's continued disability is directly related to the metallic devices. (*Id.*) Under *Daubert*, the expert "must explain precisely how [he] went about reaching [his] conclusions and point to some objective source... to show that [he] has followed the scientific method..." *Daubert v. Merrell Dow Pharm.*, 43

---

[12] At 29.

F.3d 1311, 1317 (9th Cir.1995) (*Daubert II*). Similar to his reports provided in other bone screw cases, Dr. Yarus has failed to provide any explanation as to how he reached his conclusions. *See McCollin,* 50 F.Supp.2d 1119, 1126-27; *Hartwell,* 47 F.Supp.2d 703, 712-13; *Pulice,* 199 WL 613370 at * 5-9; *Moses v. Danek Medical, Inc.* No.CV 95-512, 1998 WL 1041279 at *7 (D.Nev. Dec. 11, 1998). Dr. Yarus has not met the standard set forth in *Daubert.* The court therefore concludes that Dr. Yarus' opinion is simply insufficient to create a material fact issue for trial with respect to the issue of causation.[13]

Example 10.92: Economic professor's review of General Motors' business plan reliable

Voilas v. General Motors Corp., 73 F.Supp. 452 (D.N.J. 1999)
The court dealt with an economics professor testifying as to the employer's financial plans regarding its decision to sell, close, or keep its automobile plant open. The court held that the expert's report was not unreliable and stated:

> Turning to GM's arguments, this Court disagrees that Dr. Tinari's liability report is unreliable because he employed no particular methodology, but merely reviewed GM's own analyses of disposition plans for the Trenton plant. Indeed, an experienced economist's clarification and summary of a large corporation's business plans could certainly prove helpful to the average juror who presumabl[y] lacks such experience in and knowledge about complex financial matters, even if doing so does not require employing any particular methodology but simply a straightforward review of the corporation's data. See *Downing, supra,* 753 F.2d at 1235 (quoting Federal Rule of Evidence 702 and recognizing that "[t]he touchstone of Rule 702…is helpfulness of the expert testimony, *i.e.,* whether it 'will assist the trier of fact to understand the evidence or to determine a fact in issue.'"). In this context of reviewing and summarizing GM's business plans, the Court is satisfied that Dr. Tinari's report is sufficiently reliable, entitling him to testify as to his review and summary of GM's financial analyses.

Example 10.93: Causation opinion based on anecdotal case reports rather than epidemiological studies unreliable

Brumbaugh v. Dandot Pharmaceutical Corporation, 77 F.Supp.2d. 1153 (D.Mont. 1999)
The court stated:

> The challenged expert, Dr. Iffy, opines that he believes Parlodel has caused a chronic seizure condition in plaintiff. To support his opinions, he relies not on epidemiological studies but on anecdotal case reports and his theory that Parlodel can act as a vasospastic agent instead of a vasodilator.[14]
>
> …
>
> Dr. Iffy recognizes the insufficiency of reliance on case reports or ADE's to establish causation when he states that controlled studies are necessary to show that a particular drug causes an event or a particular reaction. Yet, he has developed a hypothesis that plaintiff's seizure and other seizures reported in ADE's and case reports were caused by Parlodel-induced vasospasms. He admits that it is "simply a hypothesis" which has not been tested and may be impossible to test.[15]

---

[13] At 976, 977.
[14] At 1155.
[15] At 1156, or 1157.

. . .

Dr. Iffy is, in essence, opining that plaintiff's seizures are due to Parlodel because he believes that. He admits that this causation opinion is "simply a hypothesis." Since they lack the rigor imposed by scientific methodology, Dr. Iffy's opinions do not have the evidentiary reliability to be admissible and are therefore excluded pursuant to Fed.R.Evid. 702 and 703.[16]

Example 10.94: Inability to replicate or explain data, testimony barred
Koch v. Shell Oil Company, 49 F.Supp. 2d 1262 (D.Mont. 1999)
This case involved the impact that the feed additive Rabon had on a dairy herd and the farmer and his family. The court rejected the testimony of Dr. Ruth and stated:

> Thus, the court finds that all four of the *Daubert* factors weigh against the admissibility of Dr. Ruth's testimony. In particular, the court is extremely concerned with the scientific validity and reliability of the testing performed by Dr. Ruth, as discussed above in relation to the first *Daubert* factor. Dr. Ruth's testimony indicates that he himself cannot reconstruct the calculations that he performed to reach his results. Since Dr. Ruth is unable to reconstruct that information and believes that there are mistakes in his calculations, the court is unable to find that the results of his testing were valid and reliable. Therefore, the court concludes that Dr. Ruth's testimony is inadmissible pursuant to Fed.R.Evid. 104(a) and 702.[17]

Example 10.95: Ignorance of key facts, report stricken
United Phosphorus Ltd. V. Midland Fumigant, Inc., 173 F.R.D. 675 (D.Kan. 1997)
The court rejected the report of Dr. Richard Hoyt, explaining:

> The court determines, based on the foregoing, that Hoyt violated a fundamental principle of economics when he failed to consider in his report the actions of Midland in estimating a value for the Quick-Phos trade name. Hoyt did not read any of the depositions (notably of Fox, Lynn, or Estes) before he rendered his report. Consequently, he was required to evaluate the Quick-Phos trademark with little knowledge about the facts of the case, and no knowledge about the underlying admissions from Midland's president and sales managers. The court finds that such ignorance of undisputed facts violates *Daubert's* requirement that an expert report and opinions must be based on "scientific knowledge."[18]

Example 10.96: General report inadmissible, fails *Daubert* test
United States Equal Employment Opportunity Commission v. Rockwell International Corporation, 60 F.Supp.2d 791 (N.D.Ill. 1999)
The court dealt with the expert report of a vocational counselor, Brethauer. The court first found that the report failed the reliability requirements of *Daubert*.

> He performed analyses he would not normally perform. He included analyses that he would not normally include. He included calculations upon which he did not rely and did not fully believe should be followed. He relied on materials, reports and

---

[16] At 1157.
[17] At 1269.
[18] At 683.

summaries given to him by counsel, and failed to verify the information from reliable, independent sources.[19]

The court went on to discuss the fatal lack of specificity of the report.

> Additionally, the court concludes that Brethauer's report, like the report in *Zarzycki*, is too general to be of use to the jury. Like the expert in *Zarzycki*, Brethauer failed to take into account the specific job market in the geographical area to which the Claimants had access. Brethauer's report also fails to contain evidence on the approximate number of actual jobs from which the Claimants could be excluded because of the perceived impairment. Instead, Brethauer analyzed job titles contained in the DOT. Without any evidence of the number of jobs contained in each job title, Brethauer's report supplies no information from which a jury could determine the number of jobs from which the Claimants were considered excluded. Accordingly, the court holds that the report fails under *Daubert's* relevancy requirement.[20]

Example 10.97: Untested hypothesis, testimony barred
Oddi v. Ford Motor Company, 234 F.3rd 136 (C.A.3, Pa. 2000)
This was a crash-worthiness case in which the plaintiff was catastrophically injured when his truck struck a guard rail and bridge abutment. The expert, Noettl, was an engineer retained to testify about defective design.

> In his preliminary report, Noettl opined that the truck Oddi was driving rode up on the guard rail because of the failure of the left side of the front bumper...Had the bumper not significantly deformed back and inward the vehicle would have been deflected by the guard rail.
>
> It is also my opinion that the floor board allowed intrusion by the guard rail and possibly the concrete barrier into the occupant compartment in the area near the brake pedal and where the driver's feet and legs would be located. This intrusion was a direct cause of the injuries to Mr. Oddi.
>
> Had the bumper and the floor board been properly structurally designed the vehicle would not have gone over the guard rail and the occupant compartment would not have been intruded by the guard rail and concrete barrier. App. At 104-105.
>
> After he reviewed the deposition of defense expert Donald Edelen, Noettl submitted an amended report, dated December 4, 1997. In it he stated:
>
> > It is my opinion that [Ford] should have warned [Grumman] of the fact that the front bumper on their chassis is for decorative trim only and will not offer protection to the body and occupant in a collision. As a result of the design of the chassis and bumper, the front wheels of the vehicle become exposed in foreseeable accident situations. Ford should have specifically warned that the bumper was extremely weak due to the fact that it had no backing plate or brackets for reinforcement and because it had holes in the bumper placed immediately adjacent to the outside where the bumper mounted to the chassis.[21]

---

[19] At 797.
[20] At 797, 798.
[21] At 146, 147.

The court rejected his proposed testimony and stated:

Noettl posited two hypotheses. His first hypothesis was that the front bumper's design should have included either bracketry or a brace system that would have increased the bumper's rigidity, prevented the truck from ramping, and deflected the vehicle back onto the roadway after impact with the guard rail. His second hypothesis was that thicker and/or ribbed metal on the flooring of the cab would have retained the integrity of the cab. However, Noettl quite candidly testified that he never tested either hypothesis. Consequently, he has not satisfied the first of the *Daubert* factors. The Supreme Court has explicitly instructed, "[o]rdinarily, a *key* question to be answered in determining whether a theory or technique is scientific knowledge that will assist the trier of fact will be whether it can be (and has been) tested." *Daubert* at 593, 113 S.Ct. 2786. *[Emphasis added.]*[22]

---

[22] At 158.

Chapter 11 How to Use Citations to Texts, Guidelines, Codes, Articles, and Other Authority to Bolster a Report's Credibility

11.1 Executive Summary

Citations to authority that support an expert's opinions will bolster the credibility of the report. Such citations will also greatly increase the chances that the expert's report and opinion will be able to successfully survive a challenge under the *Daubert* line of cases. The authors recommend the following.

- The citations should be detailed and precise. They should include title, author, edition, publisher, and year published.
- A pinpoint cite should be used if specific pages are referenced.
- The expert should be prepared to be cross-examined on any authority cited in the report.
- When an expert fails to search the literature and authority, his report and testimony may be excluded.
- An expert report is less credible and more vulnerable to cross-examination if it does not cite supporting literature.
- Avoid general statements that the expert's conclusion is supported by the "weight of the literature" or "studies."
- Experts should attempt to use authority that is as recent as possible and avoid the use of dated authority.
- Quoting authority may bolster the report's credibility, but the expert should expect to be closely questioned about the quoted passage.
- Experts should avoid describing any authority as being authoritative.

11.2 Citing Authority Properly

Citations to authority that support an expert's opinions will bolster the credibility of the report. Such citations will also greatly increase the chances that the expert's report and opinion will be able to successfully survive a challenge under the *Daubert* line of cases. Citations to authority should be made with as much specificity as possible. The citations should include title, author, edition, publisher, and year published. A pinpoint cite should be used if specific pages are referenced.

The list of authorities should be detailed and precise. Such a detailed list makes the report much more credible than it would have been had the expert instead made a general statement that literature in the field was reviewed. Indeed, the lack of a detailed list of authorities that legitimately support the expert's conclusions may be an important factor that could support a judge's disallowance of the expert opinion and report under the *Daubert*[1] line of cases. Of course, if the expert does list the authority specifically, she can be expected to be cross-examined on the authority. The expert must be prepared for this by doing her homework. Please consider the following examples.

Example 11.21: Explicit list of articles reviewed
Report States:
> Various scientific/medical articles and references were consulted and reviewed.

Comment: This report would have been more credible if it had explicitly and precisely listed the articles and references that were consulted. Consider the following. Note the detailed citations used. Such detailed citations add credibility to the report.

The following scientific/medical articles and references were consulted and reviewed:

1. Straume, T. High-energy gamma rays in Hiroshima and Nagasaki: Implications for risk and W_R. Health Phys. 69: 954-956, 1995.
2. Gundestrup, M., and Storm, H.H. Radiation-induced acute myeloid leukemia and other cancers in commercial jet cockpit crew: a population-based cohort study. Lancet: 354: 2029-2031, 1999.
3. Fairlie, I., and Resnikoff, M. No Dose Too Low. Bulletin Atomic Scientists. Nov.-Dec.1997, pages 52-56.
4. Schottenfeld, D., and Fraumeni, Jr., J.F. Cancer Epidemiology and Prevention, 2nd ed, Oxford University Press, New York, 1996.
5. Dollinger, M.R., Rosenbaum, E.H., and Cable, G. Everyone's Guide to Cancer Therapy. Somerville House/Toronto and Andrews-McMeel/Kansas City, 1998.
6. Wilkinson, G.S., and Dreyer, N.A. Leukemia among nuclear workers with protracted exposure to low-dose ionizing radiation. Epidemiology 2: 305-309, 1991.
7. Band, P.R., et al. Cohort study of Air Canada pilots: mortality, cancer incidence, and leukemia risk. Am. J. Epid. 143: 137-143, 1996.
8. Stewart, A.M. Low-level radiation: the cancer controversy. Bull. Atomic Scientists. Sept. 1990, pp. 15-19.
9. Ellenhorn, M.J. Medical Toxicology: Diagnosis and Treatment of Human Poisoning. Chapter 70: Radiation poisoning. 2nd Ed. Williams & Wilkins, Baltimore, 1997.

---

[1] See *Daubert v. Merrell Dow Pharmaceuticals, Inc.* 509 U.S. 579, 113 S.Ct.2786 125 L.E.2d 469 (1993), *General Electric Co. v. Joiner* 522 U.S. 136, 118 S.Ct. 512, 517, 139 L.E.2d 508 (1977), and *Kumho Tire Co. Limited v. Carmichael* 526 U.S. 137, 119 S.Ct. 1167, 143 L.E. 2d 238 (1999).

10. Hall, E.J. Risk of Cancer Causation by Diagnostic X-rays. Supplement to Cancer Prevention, eds. DeVita, V.T. Hellman, S., and Rosenberg, S.A. March 1990.

11. Flodin, U., et al. Acute myeloid leukemia and background radiation in an expanded case-referent study. Arch. Env. Health. 45: 364-366, 1990.

12. Wing, S., et al. Mortality among workers at Oak Ridge National Laboratory: Evidence of radiation effects in follow-up through 1984. J.Am. Med.Assn. 265: 1397-1402, 1991.

13. Bonin, S.R., et al. Treatment-related myelodysplastic syndrome following abdominopelvic radiotherapy for endometrial cancer. Gynec.Oncology. 57: 430-432, 1995

14. Upton, Arthur C. The Linear-Nonthreshold Dose-Response Model: A Critical Reappraisal. Proceedings of the Thirty-Fifth Annual Meeting of the National Council on Radiation Protection and Measurements. Bethesda, MD, National Council on Radiation Protection and Measurements, 1999, pp 9-31.

15. Pederson-Bjergaard J. Radiotherapy- and chemotherapy-induced myeloysplasia and acute myeloid leukemia. A review. Leuk Res. 16:61, 1992.

16. Little, J. B. Ionizing Radiation *in* Holland, et al, <u>Cancer Medicine,</u> Fourth Edition, Williams and Wilkins, Baltimore, 1997.

17. Kouides, P.A., and Bennett, J. M., The Myelodysplastic syndromes, *in* Abeloff, M.D., et al Clinical Oncology Churchill Livingstone, New York. 2000

18. Stone, R.M., and Mayer, R.J., Acute Myeloid Leukemia in Adults, *in* Abeloff, M.D., et al Clinical Oncology Churchill Livingstone, New York. 2000

19. Upton, A.C. The linear-nonthreshold dose-response model: a critical reappraisal. Proc. of the thirty-fifth annual meeting of the National Council on Radiation Protection and Measurements. Bethesda, MD. National Council on Radiation Protection and Measurements, 1999, pp 9-31.

20. Gundestrup, M., Storm, H.H. Radiation-induced acute myeloid leukemia and other cancers in commercial jet cockpit crew: a population-based cohort study. Lancet: 354: 2029-2031, 1999

21. Wallace, R.W., and Sondhaus, C.A. Cosmic radiation exposure in subsonic air transport. Aviat. Space Environ. Med. 49: 610-623, 1978.

22. Hall, E.J. Risk of Cancer Causation by Diagnostic X-rays. Cancer Prevention [DeVita, Hellman, and Rosenberg, eds], p 1-9, March 1990.

23. Fairlie, I. Risk of radiation-induced cancer at low doses and low dose rates for radiation protection purposes. National Radiological Protection Board. Vol. 6: No. 1, 1995.

24. Portions of CFR: Department of Veterans Affairs, Ch.1 (7-1-97 Edition), pages 221-226 [alternatively sections 3.309 to 3.312], dealing with radiation exposure – related cancers in veterans exposed to radiation.

25. Dreyer, N.A., and Friedlander, E. Identifying the health risks from very low-dose sparsely ionizing radiation. Am. J. Pub. Health. 72: 585-588, 1982.

26. Martland, H.S, et al. Some Unrecognized Dangers in the Use and Handling of Radioactive Substances: J. Am. Med. Assn. 85: 1769-1776, 1925.

Example 11.22: Explicit list of authority reviewed
Report States:
REFERENCES
The following references were used in the technical review of data and to determine the customary practices and standards of care in land development engineering:

- Land Development Handbook, authored by Dewberry & Davis, published by McGraw-Hill.
- Standard Handbook for Civil Engineers, Third Edition, edited by Frederick Merritt, published by McGraw-Hill.
- Quality in the Constructed Project - Manual on Engineering Practice No. 73, published by American Society of Civil Engineers.
- Standard Handbook of Consulting Engineering Practice, authored by Hicks and Mueller, published by McGraw-Hill.
- Site Planning Standards, authored by DeChiara and Koppelman, published by McGraw-Hill.
- Real Estate Development, Workbook and Manual, authored by Zuckerman and Blevins, published by Prentice Hall.
- Time Saver Standards for Landscape Architecture, edited by Albert Fein and published by McGraw-Hill.

Comment: This detailed list shows that the report was the product of significant research. The listing itself is good, but would have been better had publication dates and editions been added to each citation. The author of this report would also need to prepare herself for cross-examination based on each of these references.

11.3 Consequences of Failure to Cite Authority Specifically
When an expert fails to search the literature and cite authority, his report and testimony may be excluded. Even if the expert's opinion is not thrown out, the failure to research and cite supporting literature will most likely be an area of close questioning on cross-examination, which can result in a loss of credibility.

Experts often state that their conclusions are supported by the "weight of the literature" or "studies." Experts may be called upon during cross-examination to give specific examples of the supporting studies or literature. This may be difficult to do under the pressure of giving testimony. It is, therefore, better practice to list at least a representative sampling of the specific literature relied upon. Please consider the following examples.

Example 11.31: Failure to cite authority, opinion disallowed under *Daubert* line of cases

Brumbaugh v. Dandot Pharmaceutical Corporation, 77 F.Supp.2d. 1153 (D.Mont. 1999)

In this case the court rejected as unreliable an expert's opinion where the expert had failed to rely on reliable authority. The court stated:

> The challenged expert, Dr. Iffy, opines that he believes Parlodel has caused a chronic seizure condition in plaintiff. To support his opinions, he relies not on epidemiological studies but on anecdotal case reports and his theory that Parlodel can act as a vasospastic agent instead of a vasodilator....
>
> Dr. Iffy recognizes the insufficiency of reliance on case reports or ADE's to establish causation when he states that controlled studies are necessary to show that a particular drug causes an event or a particular reaction. Yet, he has developed a hypothesis that plaintiff's seizure and other seizures reported in ADE's and case reports were caused by Parlodel-induced vasospasms. He admits that it is "simply a hypothesis" which has not been tested and may be impossible to test.
>
> Dr. Iffy is, in essence, opining that plaintiff's seizures are due to Parlodel because he believes that. He admits that this causation opinion is "simply a hypothesis." Since they lack the rigor imposed by scientific methodology, Dr. Iffy's opinions do not have the evidentiary reliability to be admissible and are therefore excluded pursuant to Fed.R.Evid. 702 and 703.

Example 11.32: Failure to search literature and list authority in report

Amtel Corporation v. Information Storage Devices, Inc, 189 F.R.D. 410 (N.D.Cal. 1999)

In this case the expert, Kern, was purportedly retained as an independent expert to help the jury determine the extent to which numerous manufacturing processes were "not generally known" during a three-year period beginning ten years before the date of trial, i.e., 1989–92. In carrying out his assignment, however, Mr. Kern did not search the relevant literature before he formulated his Rule 26(a)(2)(B) report. Nor did he refresh his recollection by reviewing technical articles, books, patents, or other publications that he had read before the end of 1992. Furthermore, he did not consult colleagues who were knowledgeable on the subject and time frame.

Cross-examination:

Q. Did you review any technical articles, books, patents or other technical publications before you formulated the opinions that you've expressed in your initial report, that we've marked as Exhibit 930, that Amtel's alleged trade secrets were not generally known?

A. No.

Q. Why not?

A. Primarily because the task I was faced with was forming an opinion, not doing any research in the area as to what I believed, or my opinion was, was the circumstances in that time frame relative to these specific items.

Q. Did you believe that your assigned task was to not do any research and to simply formulate an opinion in the absence of doing any research?

A. Yes.

Q. Why did you believe that was your task?

A. Because I had a discussion with Mr. Weed about what his expectations of me were, and those were the expectations.

Q. What did Mr. Weed tell you his expectations were?

A. His expectations were that I should evaluate these trade secrets and give my opinion on them, as I discussed earlier in the testimony, and not to spend a lot of time doing literature searches and research; that ISD would, in fact, if they believed there was literature that was counter to what my beliefs were, then we would address it in a rebuttal report.

Q. Mr. Kern, how did you arrive at your opinion with respect to each of the alleged trade secrets that you considered that each was not published or was not generally known?

A. Well, I don't think I had an opinion that they weren't published. I think not generally known. I arrived at my conclusions based on my familiarity with the field and what I had read during that time frame to determine whether I thought it was generally known or not.

Q. Did you go back and read the technical articles, books, patents or other publications that you had read during the 1989-92 time period?

A. No, I didn't.

Example 11.33: Failure to cite specifically

Report States:

> The National Association of Home Builders has been guiding members in their industry relative to ways to prevent injury on residential construction sites for many years. In forming my opinion I relied upon two of their publications. These are:
>
> - An Occupational Safety Program for Builders: Guidelines for Residential and Commercial Construction.
> - An Ounce of Prevention: Job Site Safety and Insurance for Builders and Remodelers.

Resulting Cross-examination:

Q. In forming your opinion and writing your report you relied upon certain publications by the National Association of Home Builders, did you not?

A. Yes.

Q. One of those publications was the "An Ounce of Prevention: Job Site Safety and Insurance for Builders and Remodelers"?

A. Yes.

Q. Did you note in your report which edition of that book that you relied on?

A. No.

Q. Why not?

A. I didn't think it was important.

Q. Did you note in your report what year the edition that you relied upon was published?

A. No.

Q. You didn't think that was important either?

A. Not particularly.

Q. Are you aware of the fact that there have been seven different editions of that book?
A. No, I wasn't.
Q. Do you know why a book like that is updated periodically with a new edition?
A. To keep it current.
Q. Is that because things change?
A. Yes.
Q. When each new edition is published, the old edition becomes outdated, does it not?
A. Yes.
Q. You don't know in this case whether or not you relied on outdated information, do you?
A. I guess not.

Comment: Use of a fuller citation makes the expert and her report more credible. Consider the following:

> The National Association of Home Builders has been guiding members in their industry relative to ways to prevent injury on residential construction sites for many years. In forming my opinion I relied upon two of their publications. These are:
>
> • An Occupational Safety Program for Builders: Guidelines for Residential and Commercial Construction.
> • An Ounce of Prevention: Job Site Safety and Insurance for Builders and Remodelers. (7th edition)

Example 11.34: The "literature is in agreement"
Report States:
> Accountability is a fundamental element in a construction safety program. OSHA's literature is in agreement with this principle in many places.

Resulting Cross-examination:
Q. In your report you state on page 3 that, and I quote, "Accountability is a fundamental element in a construction safety program. OSHA's literature is in agreement with this principle in many places." Am I reading that correctly?
A. Yes.
Q. Specifically, which literature are you referring to?
A. OSHA's literature.
Q. Let me ask again, specifically, which of OSHA's many publications are you referring to?
A. I can't say.
Q. Sitting here today in front of this jury, you can't specifically cite ANY OSHA document to support your conclusion, can you?
A. Not specifically, no, but—
Q. Thank you, sir.

Comment: If an expert broadly claims that the literature or "many studies" agree with his proposition, he can expect to be asked, as above, to cite specific examples. Such a difficult question will be much easier to answer when the specific citations of supporting literature are listed explicitly. Consider the following.

> Accountability is a fundamental element in a construction safety program. OSHA's literature is in agreement with this principle in many places. For example:
>
> 1. Construction Safety Guidelines, OSHA pamphlet, 1999.
> 2. Workplace Safety, OSHA pamphlet, 2000.
> 3. Development of a Construction Safety Program, OSHA pamphlet, 1997.

Example 11.35: "Studies consistently demonstrate"
Report States:
> Studies consistently demonstrate that reported mold on surfaces, water damage, and excessive moisture are strongly associated with excess reporting of upper and lower respiratory symptoms—wheeze, asthma, and other conditions.

Resulting Cross-examination:
Q. In your report you state on page 3 that, and I quote, "Studies consistently demonstrate that reported mold on surfaces, water damage, and excessive moisture are strongly associated with excess reporting of upper and lower respiratory symptoms—wheeze, asthma, and other conditions." Am I reading that correctly?
A. Yes.
Q. Specifically, which studies are you referring to?
A. I'd have to look them up.
Q. Sitting here today in front of this jury, you can't specifically cite ANY study to support your conclusion, can you?
A. No, but if I could have some time to research this, I'd get you what you are looking for.

Comment: If an expert generally cites "studies" or "the literature," he can expect to be asked to cite the specific studies or the specific literature.

> Studies consistently demonstrate that reported mold on surfaces, water damage, and excessive moisture are strongly associated with excess reporting of upper and lower respiratory symptoms—wheeze, asthma, and other conditions. Examples of such studies follow.
>
> 1. Excessive Building Moisture and Prevalence of Lower Respiratory Distress, *New England Journal of Medicine*...

11.4 Dated Authority

An expert should attempt to use authority that is as current as possible. Use of authority that is dated can and will be seized upon by opposing counsel.

Example 11.41: 1972 Edition

Report States:

> Since 1927, the Associated General Contractors of America have published their MANUAL OF ACCIDENT PREVENTION IN CONSTRUCTION. They point out in their 1972 edition of this manual the following:...

Resulting Cross-examination:

Q. In your report you rely on the 1972 edition of the MANUAL OF ACCIDENT PREVENTION IN CONSTRUCTION, is that correct?
A. Yes, I do.
Q. That was published in 1972 when Richard Nixon was president?
A. Yes.
Q. The US was still at war in Vietnam?
A. Yes.
Q. Cars ran on leaded gas?
A. Yes.
Q. How old are you, sir?
A. Thirty-six.
Q. How old were you when this was published?
A. Four.
Q. Did you cite in your report any more recent publications?
A. No.
Q. Were you involved in the construction industry in 1972?
A. No, of course not.
Q. There have been significant changes in construction techniques since 1972, have there not?
A. Certainly, yes.

Comment: Relying on outdated authority will undermine an expert's credibility. The expert should rely on recent authority.

> Since 1927, the Associated General Contractors of America have published their MANUAL OF ACCIDENT PREVENTION IN CONSTRUCTION. They point out in their 2000 edition of this manual the following:...

11.5 Quoting Authority

Expert reports often quote from one or more of the authorities relied upon. Such quotations, if taken in context, will help to bolster the expert's report. The expert needs to be prepared, however, to be closely questioned on other portions of the authority that may not support her opinion.

Example 11.51: Statements from text quoted

Report States:

The following statements from the current edition of Campbell's *Urology* would support Dr. Doe's management of Mr. Clark:

—It is uncertain whether residual urine volume indicates impending bladder or renal damage.

—Large residual urine volumes may predict a slightly higher failure rate with a strategy of watchful waiting. However, the threshold volume defining a poorer outcome is uncertain.

—There is no data documenting that the incidence of urinary tract infection is related to postvoid residual volume.

Resulting Cross-examination:

Q. In your report you quote three statements from Campbell's *Urology* that support your opinion, is that correct?
A. Yes.
Q. Do you consider that work authoritative?
A. Yes.
Q. How big is that book?
A. I'm not sure, but it's quite thick.
Q. Maybe 200,000 words?
A. Maybe, yes.
Q. Would you agree that there likely are statements in Campbell's that do not support your opinion?
A. Probably.
Q. You didn't quote any of the statements that didn't support your opinion, did you?
A. No.
Q. And out of the 200,000-word treatise, you carefully chose the 60 words that most support your opinion.
A. That's right.

Comment: Citing authority will bolster an expert's credibility and help defend against *Daubert*[2] attacks. There are two important caveats, however. One, the authority should in fact stand for the proposition that the expert is asserting that it does. Second, the expert should be prepared to be cross-examined on the entire authority, not just the sections specifically used by the expert. Experts need to assume that opposing counsel (with the help of her own expert) will thoroughly review the authority that the expert is relying on to verify that it does in fact stand for what the expert claims it does. Counsel will then review the authority and look for contradictory statements to use as ammunition for cross-

---

[2] See *Daubert v. Merrell Dow Pharmaceuticals, Inc.,* 509 U.S. 579, 113 S.Ct.2786 125 L.E.2d 469 (1993); *General Electric Co. v. Joiner,* 522 U.S. 136, 118 S.Ct. 512, 517, 139 L.E.2d 508 (1977); and *Kumho Tire Co. Limited v. Carmichael,* 526 U.S. 137, 119 S.Ct. 1167, 143 L.E. 2d 238 (1999).

examination. This particular citation would have been better had it listed the year and edition of Campbell's, instead of saying the "current edition."

11.6 Authoritative

An expert should not use the words "authoritative" or "reliable authority" and the like to describe any resources the expert relied upon in forming her opinion. (Please see section 14.2.) These terms may have a special legal significance under the Federal Rules of Evidence. Under the Federal Rules, experts may be cross-examined on any work that has been established as a reliable authority by expert testimony.[3]

Example 11.61: "Recognized to be authoritative"
Report States:
> Attached as Exhibit L are excerpts from an engineering design text written by George Dieter which describes in detail this methodology. This text is recognized to be authoritative in the field of engineering design and is used by many engineering schools in the United States.

Resulting Cross-examination:
Q. In your report you relied upon the Dieter engineering text, did you not?
A. Yes.
Q. You state in your report that this text is "recognized to be authoritative in the field of engineering design," is that correct?
A. Yes.
Q. Is this the book?
A. Yes.
Q. I direct your attention to page 274, third paragraph....

Comment: Calling the text that was relied upon "authoritative" was an engraved invitation by the expert to be cross-examined on the text. The expert may have been better served by omitting the "authoritative" language:

> In forming my opinion, I relied in part on the engineering design text written by George Dieter. Particularly relevant portions of this text are attached to this report as Exhibit L.

---

[3] "The following are not excluded by the hearsay rule, even though the declarant is available as a witness. **Learned Treatises.** To the extent called to the attention of an expert witness upon cross-examination or relied upon by the expert witness in direct examination, statements contained in published treatises, periodicals, or pamphlets on a subject of history, medicine, or other science or art, established as a reliable authority by the testimony or admission of the witness or by other expert testimony or by judicial notice. If admitted, the statements may be read into evidence, but may not be received as exhibits." Federal Rule of Evidence 803(18).

Chapter 12 Making Your Report Powerful, Persuasive, and Understandable

12.1 Executive Summary

There are numerous techniques that can be utilized to make an expert report powerful, persuasive, and understandable. The authors recommend the following.

- Stating things clearly and directly.
- Not speculating or guessing.
- Taking care if speculating about future costs or monetary values.
- Not using boilerplate language.
- Avoiding the use of absolute words, such as "always" and "never."
- Making sure the report is not vague, equivocal, or uncertain.
- Avoiding emphatic language, exclamation points, bolding, italics, and capital letters to emphasize findings or conclusions.
- Using the active voice.
- Using precise language.
- Writing with confident language and avoiding hedge words, such as, "it seems," "could," "apparently," and "I believe."
- Defining all technical terms and technical jargon.
- Using objective language and avoiding subjective characterizations to describe the investigation, findings, and conclusions.
- Explaining any abbreviations used.
- Avoiding argumentative language.
- Avoiding commenting on the credibility of witnesses.
- Making sure the report is internally consistent and consistent with any previous reports in the case or other cases.
- Avoiding any bias in the report.

12.2 State Things Clearly and Directly

An expert report is most effective when the expert uses clear language and states things directly. An expert's role is to state and provide an opinion, not to hide one. Consider the following example.

Example 12.21: Opinion not stated directly

Report States:

> The urokinase therapy was carried out in a manner for which I can see no logic: The catheter was placed in the profunda femoris artery which contains clots, but was not a primary conduit—why was this done?

Comment: This opinion would have been easier to read and more persuasive had the opinion been stated clearly and directly.

> The urokinase therapy was carried out in a manner that violated the standard of care in that the catheter was placed in the profunda femoris artery which contains clots, but was not a primary conduit.

12.3 Do Not Guess

Experts should not guess in their reports. Guesses undermine the credibility of the expert's report. Counsel will use an expert's guesses against the expert. Counsel will attempt to show that the expert's opinion is unreliable in that it relies upon guesses. Please consider the following examples.

Example 12.31: "In the arbitrary opinion of the undersigned"
Report States:

> The damage appraisal is not simply the difference between the average prices in each of those two months. One must adjust for market conditions. In the arbitrary opinion of the undersigned, a fair adjusting differential is $.60 per share.

Resulting Cross-examination:

Q. Sir, as I understand it, you offer two kinds of opinions—regular opinions and arbitrary opinions, correct?
A. No, that's not true.
Q. Sometimes you conclude your reports with the phrase, "In the opinion of the undersigned" and sometimes you say, "In the arbitrary opinion of the undersigned."
A. That's true for what it's worth, counselor.
Q. Do you know the definition of the word "arbitrary"?
A. No, not really.
Q. Could you read the definition from this American Heritage Dictionary?
A. "Determined by whim or caprice."
Q. This opinion you are offering to the jury is one of your arbitrary ones, is it not?
A. If you say so.
Q. It's not what I say, sir, it's what you said. Could you read the final line of your report?
A. "In the arbitrary opinion of the undersigned, a fair adjusting differential is $.60 per share."

Comment: Making arbitrary assumptions can be fatal to an expert's credibility. Any estimates an expert is forced to make should be based upon as much objective data as possible. This objective data should be stated explicitly in the report.

> The damage appraisal is not simply the difference between the average prices in each of those two months. One must adjust for market conditions.

A reasonable adjusting differential is $.60 per share. This is based upon the following five considerations...

       1...
       2...
       3...
       4...
       5...

Example 12.32: "I suspect"

Report States:

I have not been involved in [several documents listed]. I suspect that potential contractual violations by the Defendants may be found there.

Resulting Cross-examination:

Q. You do not know what is contained in the documents, correct?
A. Yes.
Q. That's because you were not involved with them, correct?
A. Yes.
Q. You never even had an opportunity to read them, did you?
A. I did not.
Q. So your suspicions are just educated guesses?

Comment: The use of the term "I suspect" is counterproductive in an expert's report.

Example 12.33: "I believe"

Report States:

He is presently taking Prozac and Percocet and takes both of these more or less on a p.r.n. basis. I believe that he had one of each today prior to me examining him.

Resulting Cross-examination:

Q. Doctor, you said, you "believe" that he had one of each pill today prior to your examination.
A. Yes.
Q. You said "believe" because you wanted to be fair and accurate in your report, correct?
A. That's correct.
Q. And, also, because you were not sure he actually had two pills?
A. That's correct.

Comment: Guessing will negatively affect the expert's credibility. Experts should objectively base their assumptions and never guess.

He is presently taking Prozac and Percocet and takes both of these more or less on a p.r.n. basis. He stated to me that he had one of each today prior to me examining him.

Example 12.34: "Must have...given the circumstances as described, no other scenario can be reasonably deduced"
Report States:

> Though he has no recollection of his finger position on the manual trigger, Macks must have unconsciously held the trigger in the depressed position while moving the gun to his side at the time that he struck Talley's head. This is because the response of the tool to depression if the contact tip occurs so rapidly...Given the tests that were conducted, Mr. Macks's recollection of the accident occurrence contains an observation error. Mr. Macks testified that he believed that the gun fired the second nail when the push lever was not in contact with the wood or anything else. We believe that it is far more likely that a recoil fire occurred due to involuntary muscle reaction on the part of Mr. Macks. Given the circumstances as described by Macks and the testing on the subject nailer, no other scenario of the accident can be reasonably deduced.

Resulting Cross-examination:

Q. When you say Macks "must have unconsciously held the trigger in the depressed position," that's not what he told you, correct?
A. That's true. That's what we deduced.
Q. Of course, you were not there to observe what actually happened, correct?
A. That's true.
Q. Mr. Macks was in fact there?
A. Absolutely.
Q. You're not saying that Mr. Macks is lying about what happened, are you?
A. No.
Q. You're saying that although he was there, he doesn't know what happened?
A. Yes.
Q. Your deduction is based upon:
   1. "his unconsciously holding the trigger,"
   2. "an observation error by Mr. Macks,"
   3. "an involuntary muscle reaction by Mr. Macks," and
   4. "a recoil fire occurring," correct?
A. That's correct.
Q. If any of the "deductions" are inaccurate, you have to reconsider your conclusions and opinions?
A. That is correct.

Comment: This expert's deduction is based upon objective facts that are listed in his report. It is, therefore, a more credible "guess" than it would have been had the objective factors upon which it was based not been spelled out. As this cross-examination shows, however, any guess or deduction, even when based upon objective facts, can still be easily challenged on cross-examination.

Example 12.35: Speculation regarding facts
Report States:
> Two other individuals were listed in this report that the plaintiff did not identify in her deposition as colleagues (perhaps they worked in a different sales department).

Resulting Cross-examination:
Q. You don't know if the two other individuals actually worked in a different sales department, do you?
A. No.
Q. You could have found this out simply by asking the store?
A. Yes.
Q. But you chose not to do so?

Comment: The expert's language in this report was used against him to make him look as though he did not conduct a thorough investigation. This expert would have been better served by not guessing as to where these two individuals worked.

> Two other individuals were listed in this report that the plaintiff did not identify in her deposition as colleagues.

Example 12.36: Speculation regarding what would have happened
Report States:
> It may prove difficult for her to achieve such goals given the aforementioned instability in home, work, and relationships coupled with her youth. It is therefore very unlikely that she would have stayed employed with Kelly Products or in the telemarketing industry for any great length of time under the best of circumstances.

Resulting Cross-examination:
Q. Can you define the term "unlikely" used in your conclusion in terms of percentages?
A. I am not sure I can express it in a percentage, counselor.
Q. What about "very unlikely," could you express that in a percentage?
A. No.
Q. So, you can't explain to the jury in a percentage form how improbable or unlikely or "very unlikely" was when used in your report?
A. I don't understand.
Q. Neither does anyone else.

Comment: This expert's opinion is based upon speculation as to what might have happened had things been different. It is therefore vulnerable on cross-examination. This expert might have mitigated the negative effect of his speculation had he used more precise language.

> It may prove difficult for her to achieve such goals given the aforementioned instability in home, work, and relationships coupled with her youth. It is therefore my opinion that it is more likely than not that she

would not have remained employed with Kelly Products or in the telemarketing industry for any great length of time under the best of circumstances.

Example 12.37: Facts determined by unreliable method

Report States:

Mr. Miller states that he has not filed income taxes since 1995; therefore, we reviewed his bank statements in order to determine earnings. Labor market surveys revealed that the automobile hauling industry has approximately 13% expense rate in relation to the yearly owner/operator gross earnings.

Resulting Cross-examination:

Q. You would agree that people who do not pay taxes often do not follow traditional bookkeeping, banking, and accounting practices?
A. Yes.
Q. They often get paid in cash.
A. Yes.
Q. The traditional 13% expense rate from the industry may not be directly applicable to them, correct?
A. It's some indication.
Q. Can you swear under oath, sir, that within a reasonable degree of certainty you know how much Mr. Miller's gross or net income was?
A. No.

Comment: In order for an expert's opinion to be credible it must be based upon reliable methodology. Experts should avoid unreliable methodology. Reports that use unreliable methodology are not defensible.

Example 12.38: "I think that they say"

Report States:

In any event, I examined the trucks there and those trucks were 34- to 36-wheel trucks, approximately 55 to 60 feet in length and carrying petroleum and gasoline fuel and diesel fuel. I think that they say the trucks carry about 14,000 gallons.

Resulting Cross-examination:

Q. When you say "I think" the trucks carry 14,000 gallons, that indicates you are not sure, correct?
A. Not absolutely.
Q. You also used "about" 14,000 gallons. That indicates additional uncertainty?
A. Yes.
Q. But you got this vague information from a reliable source, correct?
A. I don't understand.
Q. Who do you say in your conclusion provided you with this insight into the capacity of the trucks?
A. "They."

Q. You are not even sure that's what "they" actually said, correct?
A. Yes. No. The conclusion speaks for itself.
Q. Yes, it does. It says, "I think they say," correct?

Comment: Experts should base their opinions on precise data. If this is not done, the expert's report will not be defensible. A stronger report might have stated:

> According to the manufacturer's specifications, the truck in question was 34 feet long and carried 14,000 gallons of petroleum products.

Example 12.39: Imprecise measurements
Report States:
> There are three one-foot steps leading up to the cab of the truck, which is about four to five feet above the ground. It came up to my shoulder level and I am 5' 11".

Resulting Cross-examination:
Q. You are a safety analyst, correct?
A. Yes.
Q. You are familiar with devices to precisely measure feet and inches?
A. Yes.
Q. You didn't choose to do so in this case, correct?
A. I forgot my tape measure.
Q. So you "eyeballed" it?

Comment: By failing to take the time to measure properly, this expert makes himself look unprofessional. This report would have been far more credible had the expert properly measured and documented these measurements.

> There are three steps leading up to the cab of the truck, which I measured at 11 in. each. I measured the cab of the truck to be four feet 7 in. above the ground.

12.4 Guessing about Costs, Value, and Money

Estimated costs and monetary values can be particularly problematic. Experts are best served when they have objective and substantial justification for their financial estimates. Pure guessing in terms of costs or value can have an extremely detrimental effect on the credibility of the expert and her report. Many times, making any estimate as to costs or value is outside of the expert's true area of expertise. When an expert makes an unsupported financial prediction and is outside of her true area of expertise, she will suffer an even greater loss of credibility. Please consider the following examples.

Example 12.41: Guessing on action and speculative assumption

Report States:

> It is difficult to state with any certainty at all what De Soto would have done with the 2.615 million dollars, and what the results would have been. However…(report goes on to assume 19.64% rate of return for the money).

Resulting Cross-examination:

Q. You don't know what De Soto would have done with the $2.615 million, correct?

A. Well, we based our conclusions on assumptions.

Q. Could he have taken the money to Las Vegas and gambled it away?

A. Yes.

Q. What about investing it in a dot-com stock and losing 90% of its value? Could he have done that?

A. Yes.

Q. He could have invested it and had a return anywhere from -90% to +200%, correct?

A. Yes.

Q. You cannot state with any certainty what would have happened to the money?

A. That's true.

Comment: Any report that is based upon a speculative assumption will be difficult to defend. Experts should expect counsel to zero-in on any speculative assumptions made in the report. Experts are best served by having as much objective data as possible support their assumptions.

> Based upon De Soto's past history of financial dealings, what most prudent financial advisers would advise, and the average market returns in the years 1997 through 1999, it is my opinion and my best estimate that De Soto would have realized a 19.64 percent rate of return on the $2.615 million.

Example 12.42: Cost estimate unsupported by objective information

Report States:

> The permanent injuries described above will most likely require physician-directed supportive care conservatively estimated at an ongoing cost of $1,200.00 to $1,500.00 per year for a minimum of two years and on a possible lifetime basis.

Resulting Cross-examination:

Q. Your estimate is that the future medical expenses could be $2,400, or $3,000, or $95,000 for this 25-year old?

A. Yes.

Q. Can you tell us if he will need this medical care for 1 year, or 2 years, or 50 years?

A. No.

Q. Could you explain on what you based your $1,200 to $1,500 per year estimate?

A. My years of training and experience.

Q. What training do you have in the accurate projection of future medical expenses?

A. None.

Q. Did you consult with an expert in the field before you came up with your estimate?

A. No.

Q. So, in fact, you have no objective guidelines or support for your figures, is that correct?

Comment: This expert's cost estimate is on extremely shaky ground. Not only did he not provide objective justification for the cost estimates, but this expert didn't even appear to be qualified to comment in this area. This expert should have either refrained from offering an opinion in this area or provided objective justification for his cost estimates.

12.5 Avoid Boilerplate Language

It is not uncommon for experts to use boilerplate language when issuing their reports. While this may be a time saver and a way of "covering all the bases," not customizing reports and not reviewing them carefully can have devastating effects. Please consider the following examples.

Example 12.51: Boilerplate language referring to repealed statute
Estate of Hinz v. Commissioner of Internal Revenue, 2000 WL 5258 (US Tax Court 2000)
The tax court dealt with the expert testimony of a real estate appraiser, Atkinson, who spent about half his time testifying in court. The court's explanation of the errors in his report is instructive.

> Another matter that gives us concern about how carefully Atkinson reads the expert witness reports that he issues relates to the following statement which appears in each of his valuations of the Subject Properties. "This appraisal meets the certification requirements of the California Civil Code Section 1922.14 controlling persons preparing certified appraisals of real property." These valuations are dated from May 10, 1995 (Lafayette Property), to February 11, 1998 (Parker Property). At trial, Atkinson was confronted by the fact that the cited California Code provision had been repealed in 1990, the repeal taking effect no later than January 1, 1992. Atkinson acknowledged the repeal. When asked why his expert witness report relies on a statute that had been repealed years earlier, Atkinson replied as follows: "I think this is boilerplate that was put in by my secretary over the last—ever since 1992, and I have never taken it out." As a result of the obvious errors in Atkinson's expert witness report, we are hesitant to rely on Atkinson's judgement even as to those matters that do not involve obvious errors.

Example 12.52: Boilerplate language diminishes credibility
Prunty v. Florabunda, 1998 WL 409030 (E.D.Pa. 1998)
Please consider the negative impact of the use of boilerplate language in the

expert's report. The court in this case stated:

> Although Plaintiff called Norman Goldstein to testify to his opinion that the stairway did not present an unreasonable risk of harm, defense counsel's cross-examination of Mr. Goldstein cast considerable doubt on his testimony. Under cross-examination, Mr. Goldstein admitted that he had not reviewed all of the evidence in the instant case, including Plaintiff's deposition testimony. Furthermore, Mr. Goldstein admitted that he had been paid a substantial fee to testify in the instant action and had testified in several similar legal actions involving falls from stairways. Additionally, Mr. Goldstein admitted that his report in the instant case included several "boilerplate" statements which he had used in other expert reports prepared in connection with other actions.

Example 12.53: Warranty
Report States:
No warranty or guarantee, express or implied, is made.

Resulting Cross-examination:
Q. Is your five-page report accurate?
A. Yes.
Q. Is your five-page report truthful?
A. Yes.
Q. Can you guarantee for the jury the report's accuracy and truthfulness?
A. Yes.
Q. When you said on page five, last paragraph of your report, "no warranty or guarantee, express or implied is made," that's not true, is it?
A. No.
Q. That last statement was not accurate, was it?
A. It was not.
Q. Was it truthful?
A. No.
Q. Is the rest of your report filled with similar inaccuracies and untruths?

Comment: Major appliances come with a warranty, but expert reports should not. This type of boilerplate language is distracting and should not be included in the report.

Example 12.54: Not responsible for the accuracy of information provided
Resulting Cross-examination:
Q. You are not responsible for the accuracy of information provided?
A. That's correct.
Q. That includes only parts of your seven-page report, correct?
A. No, counselor, that's for the entire report.
Q. So that includes your factual assumptions?
A. Yes.
Q. Your analysis?
A. Yes.
Q. Your testing?
A. Yes.

Q. Your measurements?
A. Yes.
Q. Your opinions?
A. Yes.
Q. And your conclusions?
A. Yes.
Q. So, if there is anything wrong with this seven-page report, it's not your fault, correct?
A. That's correct.
Q. Who signed this report?
A. I did.
Q. And that's your professional license number next to your signature, 123456-01?
A. Yes.
Q. As I understand it, the same person who wrote the report, signed it, and got paid for it is not responsible for the accuracy of the information provided?

Example 12.55: Reserve the right to amend
Report States:
> This report does not necessarily embody the details of all of my opinions. I reserve the right to amend and add to my opinions upon further review of records.

Resulting Cross-examination:
Q. Which opinions did you leave out of your nine-page report?
A. None.
Q. Which details of your opinions did you leave out?
A. The unimportant ones.
Q. The ones that were so unimportant that you specifically and in writing reserved the right to amend them?
A. That's just a phrase I use in all my reports.
Q. In other words, boilerplate language?
A. Standard language.
Q. You use it sometimes when it really doesn't apply to the report?
A. It's always in there.
Q. Do you have other standard language in your reports?
A. Yes, some.
Q. Could you go through this nine-page report and highlight with this yellow marker all of the standard language?
A. That would be difficult to do.
Q. Would it help you if I provided you with six other reports you issued with paragraph after paragraph of boilerplate language?

Comment: This example also shows how boilerplate language most often does more harm than good.

12.6 Avoid Absolute Words

It is a mistake to use absolute language such as "always" or "never" in an expert report. Use of absolute language leaves the expert wide open to damaging cross-examination. When absolute language is used, all the cross-examiner has to do is to present the expert with a single counterexample where the expert's statement is not correct. Once this is established it will then also be established that the expert was either exaggerating or flat out wrong when the absolute language was used. In either event, the expert will lose credibility. Consider the following examples.

Example 12.61: "No experience whatsoever"
Report States:

> At the time of her divorce, Jill De Soto had no experience whatsoever in the world of investment or finance. Fortunately, it appears that she was wise enough to realize how little, if anything, she knew about these matters….Ms. De Soto had a total lack of investment experience or knowledge.

Resulting Cross-examination:

Q. Is a deposit in a savings account an investment?
A. Yes.
Q. Is a mortgage a method of finance?
A. Yes.
Q. Jill De Soto had owned and managed her own savings account before her divorce, did she not?
A. Yes.
Q. And she paid the couple's monthly mortgage, did she not?
A. Yes.
Q. When you say in your report that, "At the time of her divorce, Jill De Soto had no experience whatsoever in the world of investment or finance" and "a total lack of investment experience," that was an exaggeration, was it not?
A. Maybe somewhat, technically speaking of course.
Q. Technically speaking, it wasn't 100% accurate, was it?
A. No, I was just trying to make a point.
Q. Yes, you helped me do the same. Thank you.

Comment: This expert was forced to admit that he had exaggerated. This willingness to exaggerate will damage the expert's credibility. The expert would not have been open to this attack had he not used absolute language.

> At the time of her divorce, Jill De Soto had minimal experience in the world of investment or finance. Fortunately, it appears that she was wise enough to realize how little, if anything, she knew about these matters….Ms. De Soto had a total lack of investment experience or knowledge.

Example 12.62: "All…without limits…complete recovery"
Report States:

> He is capable of return to full and unrestricted employment in his position of truck driving. He can pursue all vocational and avocational activity at this time without restriction as a result of the completion of this

examination which was entirely within normal limits. He has recovered completely and it was exhibited throughout this examination.

Resulting Cross-examination:
Q. In your opinion the employee can pursue all vocational and avocational activities at this time?
A. Well, yes, as a truck driver.
Q. You didn't limit him to that restriction in your report, did you?
A. Well, no, not in those words.
Q. You didn't do it in any words, did you?
A. No.
Q. Did you intend to release him for *all* vocational activities from airplane pilot to x-ray technician?
A. No.
Q. Did you intend to release him to pursue all avocational activities from bungee jumping to skydiving?
A. No.
Q. Why don't you tell us what you really meant, sir?

Comment: Absolute language is easy to poke holes in. The expert would have been better off toning down the absolute language in the report to refer to only the subject's previous usual and customary activities.

He is capable of return to full and unrestricted employment in his position of truck driving. He can pursue his previous usual and customary vocational and avocational activity at this time without restriction as a result of the completion of this examination which was entirely within normal limits. He has recovered completely as exhibited throughout this examination.

Example 12.63: "Never functioned properly"
Report States:
To this day the controls have never functioned properly.

Resulting Cross-examination:
Q. How many times did you check the controls?
A. Twice.
Q. So when you say, "To this day the controls have never functioned properly," you mean during the two times you checked them, correct?
A. Yes.

Comment: Less absolute language is more easily defensible.

To this day there continue to be problems with the controls.

Example 12.64: Absolute confidence in opinion: "There is no question"
Report States:

> There is no question but that the arthritis at the base of the thumb is an aging phenomenon. I do not really think that the use of the thumb as a bank teller caused this.

Resulting Cross-examination:

Q. One of the issues in this case was the etiology of the arthritis at the base of the thumb, correct?

A. Yes.

Q. That was one of the questions disputed by the medical experts?

A. Yes.

Q. It was your opinion that it did not result from the use of the thumb as a bank teller?

A. That's correct.

Q. Did you review the job title for a bank teller?

A. No.

Q. Did you review the dictionary of occupational titles for the duties of this position?

A. No.

Q. If you do not know what the job consisted of, are you in the best position to express an opinion as to whether the arthritis resulted from her work as a bank teller?

Comment: This expression of absolute certainty can be used to make the expert appear closed minded. This will lessen the expert's credibility. The expert report would have been better had it avoided the absolute language.

> It is my opinion, based on a reasonable degree of medical certainty, that the arthritis at the base of the thumb is an aging phenomenon. It is my opinion, based on a reasonable degree of medical certainty, that the use of the thumb as a bank teller did not cause the arthritis.

12.7 Avoid Vague, Equivocal, and Uncertain Reports

The courts continue to reject reports where the expert's opinion is expressed vaguely, equivocally, or with insufficient certainty.

Example 12.71: "Could" and "possibility"
Perkins v. Entergy Corporation, 756 So.2d 388 (La.App.1 Cir. 1999)
The court dealt with the case of a flash fire at an air separation facility. The expert Schmidt concluded in his report:

> [D]uring highly abnormal pipeline operating conditions, which occurred during the early hours of April 6, 1994, circumstances *could* have developed which caused the movement of metallic particles through the piping network [of the ALAC facility]. Therefore, the potential availability of metallic particles within a piping system and

the likelihood of particle impact or frictionally induced ignition becomes a *statistical possibility.* [Emphasis ours.][1]

The court found the language on causation too indefinite and stated:

This conclusion is clearly insufficient to establish cause in fact, which requires proof by a preponderance of the evidence. *See Dabog.* 625 So.2d at 493. One must prove what probably happened as opposed to what "could" have happened and what is a "statistical possibility."[2]

Example 12.72: Vague report cannot support finding for plaintiff
Piascyk v. City of New Haven, 64 F.Supp2d 19 (D.Conn. 1999)
The court dealt with an ADA case filed by a police officer. The expert report was written by a physician, Shine.

In support of his claim that he is substantially limited with regard to carrying, plaintiff has offered only Dr. Shine's statement in his report to the New Haven Workers' Compensation Division that plaintiff would have difficulty "carrying heavy loads...." (Shine Report, Plaintiff's Exhibit 11.)[3]

The court rejected the indefinite language "carrying heavy loads" and stated:

This statement is too vague to support a finding that plaintiff is significantly restricted in his ability to carry compared to the average person. *See Colwell,* 158 F.3d at 644 (testimony that plaintiff could not lift "very heavy objects" did not support a finding of substantial limitation).[4]

12.8 Do Not Use Emphasis When Expressing Findings or Conclusions
Experts often use various methods such as emphatic language, exclamation points, bolding, italics, and capital letters to emphasize their findings or conclusions. A well-written report will not need such emphasis. A seasoned trial attorney will use an expert's use of emphasis against that expert. The trial attorney may attempt to show that the expert's use of emphasis is a sign of bias.

Example 12.81: "Thoroughly derelict in its duty"
Report States:
Warren Financial was thoroughly derelict in its duty to recognize that the De Soto portfolio was in extreme jeopardy.

Resulting Cross-examination:
Q. Your opinion is that Warren should have known that the De Soto portfolio was in jeopardy, correct?
A. Absolutely.

---

[1] At 407.
[2] At 407.
[3] At 29.
[4] At 29.

Q. The terms "thoroughly derelict in his duty" and "extreme jeopardy" used in your report have no specific accounting definitions, do they?
A. That's correct.
Q. But you used them in the conclusion of your opinion to show how sloppy Warren Financial was?
A. Yes.
Q. In fact, you made these terms up to exaggerate your conclusion, correct?
A. Absolutely not—just to emphasize them.
Q. If your opinion and conclusions were correct, why did you need to "emphasize" them?

Comment: Emphasis can and will be used against the expert. Here, the expert's use of emphasis makes the expert appear to be biased. The expert would have been better served by avoiding the emphasis and using more objective language.

> Warren Financial's management of the portfolio was below the standard of care expected from a reasonably prudent financial manager.

Example 12.82: Underlining
Report States:
> However, again, <u>there is not the slightest appearance of the word "suicide" anywhere in the materials.</u> This is an unimaginable omission, given his case and his presentation to these caretakers.

Resulting Cross-examination:
Q. You underlined parts of your conclusion to make sure that the reader would not miss these words, correct?
A. Yes.
Q. You selected only the key words?
A. The important ones.
Q. So you didn't feel the rest of your three-page, single-spaced report was important, or was it that you didn't feel the judge and jury were smart enough to figure out what was important for themselves?

Comment: A well-written report does not need emphasis of this type. This report would have been far more effective without the emphasis.

> The records do not in any place mention the word "suicide." Under the circumstances, this is a breach of the standard of care.

12.9 Use Active Voice
Experts should write their reports in the active as opposed to the passive voice. Sentences that use the passive voice are more likely to be ambiguous. Sentences that use the passive voice also tend to sound awkward. Active voice sentences are clearer and sound more persuasive. Consider the following examples.

Example 12.91: Passive voice creates ambiguity
Report States:
> After being examined by both Dr. Lang and Dr. Gerald and discussing with Dr. O'Neill, a decision was made to admit Mrs. Elderly.

Resulting Cross-examination:
Q. Your report indicates, page 5, paragraph 3 that, "After being examined by both Dr. Lang and Dr. Gerald and discussing with Dr. O'Neill, a decision was made to admit Mrs. Elderly." Is that correct?
A. Yes, that's right.
Q. Who, in your opinion, made the decision? Was it Dr. Lang, Dr. Gerald, or Dr. O'Neill?
A. Dr. O'Neill made the decision as he was her treating physician.
Q. Does your report indicate what time Mrs. Elderly arrived at the emergency room of the Memorial Hospital?
A. Yes. "By 9:55 P.M."
Q. Doctor, was that at 8:00 P.M., 8:30 P.M., 9:00 P.M., or 9:55 P.M.?
A. Sorry. It was at 9:55 P.M.
Q. Does your report indicate whether a chest x-ray should have been performed and laboratory data collected?
A. Yes, it does.
Q. What does your report indicate?
A. "I see no reason for a chest x-ray or laboratory data to be collected in this patient. No indication existed."
Q. Doctor, can you explain or clarify that?
A. Sure. What I meant to say was that there was no reason for a chest x-ray or laboratory data to be collected in this patient, no indication existed. The standard of care in emergency room medicine does not call for testing to be performed without a clear indication.
Q. Thank you, doctor.

Comment: Rewriting this report segment in an active voice makes the report clearer and more persuasive.

> Dr. Lang and Dr. Gerald examined Mrs. Elderly. Immediately following these examinations, Dr. O'Neill consulted with Drs. Lang and Gerald. Dr. O'Neill then decided to admit Mrs. Elderly. Mrs. Elderly was admitted at 9:55 P.M.

Example 12.92: Passive voice is awkward
Report States:
> Method used to evaluate the conduct of the defendants in this case was to compare their conduct to the principles and practices of construction safety management and injury prevention established by safety authorities. It was also to compare their conduct relative to compliance with OSHA regulations and the requirements of the contracts.

Comment: The passive voice in this example makes the report sound awkward. Rewriting this report segment in an active voice makes the report less awkward and, therefore, more persuasive.

> This report compares the defendants' conduct to various safety authorities' principles and practices of construction safety management and injury prevention. It also compares their conduct relative to compliance with OSHA regulations and the requirements of the contracts.

Example 12.93: Active voice clearer and more persuasive
Report States:

> It was learned from the documents produced by Moorings Corp. in the instant case that a discussion on January 25, 1993 had ensued with regard to tool safety.

Comment: This sentence is clearer and more persuasive when written in an active voice.

> According to documents X, Y, and Z produced by the defendant, a discussion with regard to tool safety took place on January 25, 1993.

12.10 Use Precise Language

Precise language should be used in expert reports where possible. The use of precise language will make the report more credible. On the other hand, the use of imprecise language will make the expert report less credible.

Example 12.101: Imprecise language
Report States:

> A review of the construction safety literature will find fundamental agreement with the following principles:...

Comment: More precise language would make this report more credible.

> My opinions are supported by the following construction safety literature, which I reviewed prior to drafting my report.
> > 1. Fundamentals of Construction Safety, Smith, RJ, Fictional Press, 2001.
> > 2. Construction Safety Today,...

Example 12.102: Imprecise language, missing object
Report States:

> Thank you for referring the above examinee for plaintiff medical evaluation. I explained that I was a certified independent medical examiner. I also explained that this evaluation did not constitute a doctor/patient relationship, and that I would not be a treating physician.

Resulting Cross-examination:
Q. Your report indicates, page 1, paragraph 1, that, " I explained that I was a certified independent medical examiner." Is that correct?
A. Yes, that's right.
Q. I'm confused. It is unclear to me who this is being addressed to. Is it the reader or did you say this to the plaintiff?
A. The plaintiff.
Q. OK. Now, just to clear up some more confusion, when you say in the very next sentence, "I also explained that this evaluation did not constitute a doctor/patient relationship, and that I would not be a treating physician" you were again reporting something you said to the plaintiff?
A. Yes.

Comment: This type of "I'm confused" cross-examination is not earth-shattering, but it can be effective in eroding an expert's credibility. The expert would have been better off using more precise language.

> Upon meeting the plaintiff I introduced myself and explained to him that I was a certified independent medical examiner. I also explained to the plaintiff that the evaluation I was about to conduct did not create a doctor/patient relationship, and that I would not be giving him any treatment or advice.

12.11 Use First-person Singular

Experts should use the first-person singular when referring to themselves. Some experts use the third person when describing their qualifications in a report. This is awkward, can be used to make the expert sound pompous or silly, and should be avoided. Jurors do not commonly refer to themselves in the third person and may not relate well to someone who does. Consider the following example.

Example 12.111: Use of third person to describe qualifications
Report States:
> Tom Thompson has been in the securities industry since 1969 (CV attached).

Resulting Cross-examination:
Q. Is this a copy of your report, sir?
A. Yes.
Q. Are you the author of this report?
A. Yes.
Q. The only author?
A. Yes.
Q. I refer you to page 1 of your report, paragraph 3, line 1. It states, "Tom Thompson has been in the securities industry since 1969." Am I reading that correctly?
A. Yes.
Q. Who wrote that description of you?
A. I did.

Q. Do you normally refer to Tom Thompson in the third person?
A. No.
Q. Did you think your qualifications would sound better that way?
A. I guess so.

Comment: The expert's use of the third person when referring to himself is a needless distraction that may make the report seem as though it was at least partially written by someone else. It may also make the expert look pompous. Experts should instead use the first person when referring to themselves.

I have been in the securities industry since 1969 (CV attached).

12.12 Use Confident Language and Avoid Hedge Words

The purpose of an expert report is to communicate the expert's findings and opinions. These findings and opinions should be stated in a clear, confident manner. Hedge words such as "it seems," "could," "apparently," and "I believe" indicate that the expert does not have confidence in her findings and opinions. They may even make the expert's report insufficient as a matter of law.[5] Use of such hedge words will decrease the persuasiveness of the expert's report and should be avoided. Consider the following examples.

Example 12.121: Hedge word "could" results in summary judgment
Samos Imex Corporation v. Nextel Communications, 194 F.3d 301 (C.A.1 [Mass.] 1999)

The expert in this case, John Carota, was a structural engineer. Prior to the suit being filed, John Carota, a structural engineering expert, gave Samos Imex a report evaluating the condition of the building, recommending repairs, and identifying "the probable cause" of the damage to the building and the freight elevator. The probable cause section of the report began by concluding that "[t]he probable cause of the recent movement and racking [*i.e.,* shifting] [of] this three story brick building...can be directly attributed to the building responding to the effects of constructing the monopole project." The report then identified various "aspects" of the antenna project that "either singularly or in combination *could* (emphasis added) have caused the failed elevator and cracked building support columns and walls."

As a result of the expert's language, the trial judge dismissed the case on summary judgment. Counsel was later able to save the case by his offer of proof explaining what the expert meant and what he would testify to if permitted.

Even if the legal challenge to such hedge language is met, such language frequently results in additional and unnecessary cross-examination.

Q. You stated that the construction project could have caused the failed elevator and cracked building?
A. That's correct.
Q. Other factors could have caused them as well?

---

[5] See *Samos Imex Corporation v. Nextel Communications* 194F.3rd 301 (1999).

A. Yes.

Q. As a matter of fact, there were multiple probable causes which singly or in combination could have caused the failed elevator and cracked building, correct?

A. That's correct.

Q. Why don't you list all of the potential causes so we can go through them one at a time....

Example 12.122: "It seems"

Report States:

> In summary, it seems that the conversations Ms. De Soto had with Mr. Warren covered two broad topics.

Resulting Cross-examination:

Q. Are the substance of the conversations between Ms. De Soto and Mr. Warren relevant to your opinion?

A. Yes.

Q. But you're not really sure about the exact nature of those conversations, are you?

A. I wasn't there if that's what you mean.

Q. In your report on page 3, paragraph 2, line 1, you wrote that, "*it seems* that the conversations Ms. De Soto had with Mr. Warren covered two broad topics." Am I reading that correctly?

A. Yes.

Q. Your use of the words "it seems" indicates that you don't know the exact nature of those conversations, is that a fair statement?

A. Yes.

Comment: This language would have been stronger without the hedge words.

> The conversations Ms. De Soto had with Mr. Warren covered two broad topics.

Example 12.123: "Apparent" and "perceived"

Report States:

> This report is intended to express the writer's perceived impression of the apparent performance of the items viewed during the time frame noted above.

Resulting Cross-examination:

Q. You planned to express your opinion in this report, did you not?

A. Yes.

Q. Did you in fact present it?

A. I don't understand.

Q. When you say, "this report is intended to express my impression," it would be more accurate to say "it expresses my impression," would it not?

A. Yes, I guess I was not clear.

Q. Did you express your "impression of the performance" in this report?

A. I tried to.

Q. Didn't you write this was your "perceived impression"?
A. Yes.
Q. Is this precisely the same as your direct impression?
A. No.
Q. What is the difference?
A. That's hard to say.
Q. Apparently so…did you report on the actual performance here?
A. Yes…I take that back…No, on the "apparent performance."
Q. The difference being?
A. What appeared to me to be the performance.
Q. As opposed to what actually was the performance?

Comment: The use of these multiple hedge words make this report nearly useless. The expert needs to use more confident language that indicates that the expert is confident in her findings and conclusions.

In this report I will express my professional opinion to a reasonable degree of certainty regarding the performance of the following items:…

Example 12.124: "I believe"
Report States:
Consequently, I believe that the defendant's actions were below the standard of care and have a causal role in this unfortunate man's suicide.

Resulting Cross-examination:
Q. Do you believe in God, sir?
A. Yes.
Q. Have you ever seen God?
A. Of course not.
Q. Do you know of any objective or scientific proof supporting the existence of God?
A. No. I have faith.
Q. You use the words "I believe" in your report to describe your feeling that Dr. Smith caused the death of the Mr. Jones, don't you?
A. I'm not sure what exact words I used.
Q. You state on page 3, and I quote, "Consequently, I believe that the defendant's actions were below the standard of care and have a causal role in this unfortunate man's suicide." Am I reading that correctly?
A. That's what I wrote.

Comment: The careless use of "I believe" will lessen the weight given to the expert's report and opinion. This hedge term should have been omitted.

It is my opinion, based on a reasonable degree of medical certainty, that Dr. Smith's actions were below the standard of care and were the proximate cause of Mr. Jones's suicide.

Example 12.125: "Apparently"
Report States:
    Now, apparently, an infusion of urokinase was started at 05:30 on 8/12/99.

Resulting Cross-examination:
Q. When you say, "apparently," you are indicating you are not certain of that fact. Correct?
A. That's what it says in the records.
Q. Are you 100% certain that an infusion of urokinase was started at 05:30 on 8/12/99?
A. No. I wasn't there, counselor.
Q. Are you 95% certain?
A. No.
Q. Are you 85% certain?
A. No.
Q. So you really don't know if in fact an infusion of urokinase was started at 05:30 on 8/12/99?
A. That's correct, but it does say that in the records.

Comment: The term "apparently" implies to the reader that the expert was not sure of the facts. This is unnecessary. Consider how this could have been expressed in more confident language.

    According to the records, an infusion of urokinase was started at 05:30 on 8/12/99.

Example 12.126: "I do not believe"
Report States:
    I do not believe there was a basic understanding of the principles on his part.

Comment: Using "I do not believe" lessens the credibility of this report. The expert should have used more objective and confident language.

    His deposition testimony is inconsistent with a basic understanding of the involved principles.

Example 12.127: "Appears...probably should"
Report States:
    Clinically, her difficulty appears to represent a carpal tunnel syndrome at this point for which a cortisone injection should probably be considered.

Resulting Cross-examination:
Q. Does the patient's difficulty represent a carpal tunnel syndrome?
A. Yes, that's what I said in my report.
Q. You said it "appears" to represent, didn't you?
A. That's what I meant.
Q. That it seems possible that the difficulty represented a carpal tunnel syndrome?

151

A. No…No…more than possible.
Q. But less than absolute certainty?
A. Yes.
Q. Did you say in your report who should consider the cortisone injection?
A. Yes.
Q. Where is that? What line?
A. It's clearly implicit in my report.
Q. Just to make it a little easier for the fact finder, could you be more specific?
A. The patient…and I guess the doctor also.
Q. The injection should presumably be considered?
A. No, I said probably be considered.
Q. The difference being, just a matter of wording?
A. If you say so.

Comment: The language in this report makes it sound as if the expert is not at all sure of herself. If the expert is not confident in her opinion, why should the reader be? Consider a better way to write this.

> It is my opinion, based on a reasonable degree of medical certainty, that Ms. Smith's impairment is caused by a carpal tunnel syndrome. It is my opinion, based on a reasonable degree of medical certainty, that a cortisone injection should be given to Ms. Smith to treat this condition.

Example 12.128: "Suggests"
Report States:
> The review of the reports suggests that the cause is related to the heave of the clay subgrade soils.

Resulting Cross-examination:
Q. You state in your report that a review of the reports *suggests* that the cause is related to the clay upgrade soils, do you not?
A. Yes.
Q. That is what the reports *suggested* to you?
A. Yes.
Q. And you consider your opinion to be based on a reasonable interpretation of what the reports suggest to you?
A. Yes.
Q. Is it fair to say that it is possible that these reports may suggest other reasons for the cause of the accident to other reasonable engineers?
A. Yes.

Comment: Use of the term "suggests" red flags the point to counsel that these reports may be open to different interpretations. It would have been better to avoid the "suggests" language.

> It is my opinion, based on a reasonable degree of engineering certainty, that the cause of the failure is the heave of the clay subgrade soils.

12.13 Define Technical Terms and Jargon

Expert reports are designed for a lay audience. To make reports easy to understand and read and as persuasive as possible, experts should define technical terms that the lay reader may not be familiar with. This will make the report much more valuable and bolster the report's effectiveness. Consider the following examples.

Example 12.131: Defining a technical term
Report States:

Bone marrow examination revealed aplastic anemia (failure of bone marrow to make blood cells)...This showed a "dyplastic marrow with excess blasts consistent with conversion to acute leukemia." (Blasts are the earliest blood cells in the bone marrow and may normally be up to 5% of the marrow cells. An excess of blasts is a sign of acute leukemia or a related disorder.)

Comment: The expert in this case did an excellent job explaining technical medical terms. His report is understandable and, therefore, more likely to be persuasive to the reader.

Example 12.132: Defining a technical term
Report States:

Sequential operation of these types of tools is well known in the industry. Sequential operation means that the push lever must be depressed first and then the manual trigger is pulled.

Comment: The expert's definition of the term "sequential operation" in this report makes the report effective and persuasive.

12.14 Use Objective Language

Expert reports should be written using language that is as objective as possible. Subjective characterizations should be avoided. Most commonly, experts add characterizations to describe the expert's investigation, findings, and conclusions. Such subjective characterizations seldom add anything of substance to the report and make the report less, as opposed to more, credible. Subjective characterizations provide fertile ground for cross-examination. Consider the following examples.

Example 12.141: "Complete absence" and "manifestly and egregiously"
Report States:

The complete absence of any comments about suicidality are manifestly and egregiously below the standard of care for mental care treaters.

Resulting Cross-examination:

Q. Doctor, can you explain the difference between "absence of any comments" and "complete absence of any comments" in your report?
A. There is no difference, Counselor. I was just trying to emphasize the point.
Q. Care below the standard of care for mental care treaters is malpractice, correct?

A. Yes.

Q. So, you added the modifiers "manifestly" and "egregiously" in your report for what reason, Doctor?

A. To explain the care.

Q. Can you quantify "manifestly" below the standard of care?

A. Well, no. It's just apparent.

Q. To whom, Doctor?

A. To me.

Q. The same for "egregiously"?

A. Yes.

Q. If ten different mental care treaters looked at this case, how many would describe it as "manifestly and egregiously below the standard of care"?

A. I don't know.

Q. That's because they would all describe it in a different way, or in their own way?

A. Yes.

Q. We would have 11 different doctors with 11 different descriptions?

A. Yes, right.

Q. So, in fact, these descriptions are subjective characterizations of the care here?

A. It doesn't change my opinion, Counselor.

Q. So, your opinion is engraved in stone?

A. Yes, absolutely.

Comment: The "manifestly" and "egregiously" characterizations used by the author of this report commit the expert and retaining counsel to proving more than the law requires. These characterizations may also be used to suggest that the expert is a hired gun who is making any statements necessary to help "his" team win. In either case, these characterizations make defending the report on cross-examination much more difficult. This expert would have been better served by leaving the characterizations out of his report.

> In my opinion, based on a reasonable degree of medical certainty, the absence of comments about suicidality in the records is below the standard of care for mental care treaters.

Example 12:142: "Complete and thorough"
Report States:

> Examination of the plaintiff involved the following interview and clinical diagnostic procedures:
>> —Complete and thorough intraoral and extraoral dental examinations

Resulting Cross-examination:

Q. This examination was no different from any other of your examinations, correct?

A. I don't follow.

Q. This exam "was complete and thorough" was it not?

154

A. Yes.

Q. As are all of your examinations, correct?

A. Yes.

Q. So, in fact, the exam was no different from any of your examinations, correct?

A. Yes, that's correct.

Comment: This expert has set a very high standard for her examinations. She then must defend this standard on cross-examination. She would have been better served by not including the self-serving characterization of her own investigation.

> Examination of the plaintiff involved the following interview and clinical diagnostic procedures:
> —intraoral and extraoral dental examinations

Example 12.143: "Detailed measurements"

Report States:

> We conducted a site investigation on March 26, 1999. During this investigation, we took detailed measurements, photographs, and made observations.

Comment: This expert would have been better served by not characterizing the measurements that he took as part of his investigation.

> We conducted a site investigation on March 26, 1999. During this investigation, we took measurements and photographs and made observations.

Example 12.144: "Grossly inadequate" and "seriously lacking"

Report States:

> The Table of Contents in the Project Close Out Documentation Manual, Bate Stamp Nos. 1048-1550, is grossly inadequate and does not satisfy the disclosure of all sub-subcontractor participants...Further, the "Manual" is seriously lacking in providing the owner with all maintenance and repair instructions....

Comment: Language that is more toned-down and objective is likely to be more effective in driving home the expert's point. An expert who uses language that is very strong, as in this example, may appear to a jury to be biased and likely to say anything so that his side will win.

> The Table of Contents in the Project Close Out Documentation Manual, Bate Stamp Nos. 1048-1550, is inadequate and does not satisfy the disclosure of all sub-subcontractor participants...Further, the "Manual" is unreasonably lacking in providing the owner with all maintenance and repair instructions....

Example 12.145: "Lengthy, careful, and objective"
Report States:

A lengthy, careful, and objective examination was made of EXHIBIT 1 and EXHIBIT 2 with the aids of a stereoscopic microscope, enlargement of documents, and transparencies along with various optical and measuring devices/gauges. A comparison was then made between them in order to determine whether or not EXHIBIT 2 was altered in any way.

Resulting Cross-examination:

Q. What percentage of your examinations are done carefully?
A. 100% of the time.
Q. How often do you do them objectively?
A. 100% of the time.
Q. I have 6 of your prior reports. Can you explain why in none of the 6 reports do you say the exam was done "carefully and objectively"?
A. Well, not really. Just to…save time, I guess.
Q. Talking about time…how much do you charge per hour?
A. $300.00 an hour.
Q. So, the longer the examination, the more money you charge, correct?
A. Yes.
Q. And in this case you were able to charge for how many hours?
A. 50.
Q. So, your "lengthy examination" has resulted in payment of fees of $15,000?
A. Well, I have been only paid $12,500 to date.
Q. You will get additional fees after you testify objectively here today?
A. Yes.

Comment: This expert report would have been stronger had the expert described his examination in objective, rather than subjective, terms.

EXHIBIT 1 and EXHIBIT 2 were examined on March 1, 2001. This examination took over five hours and was conducted with the aids of a stereoscopic microscope, enlargement of documents, and transparencies along with various optical and measuring devices/gauges. A comparison was then made between them in order to determine whether or not EXHIBIT 2 was altered in any way.

Example 12.146: "Unjustifiable"
Report States:

It is unjustifiable that only one area yard drain, in Photo Nos. 12 and 30, was installed to handle large volumes of storm water….

Comment: The use of objective terms in stating the expert's opinion would make this report more credible and persuasive.

The design of the sewer system was improper in that only one area yard drain was installed to handle large volumes of storm water…

Example 12.147: "Unconscionable"
Report States:

> From the depositions, we know that Mr. De Pau made some initial site visits and that Mr. Coolidge did not. To engineer a subdivision without ever setting foot on the land is unconscionable in this writer's opinion.

Comment: Objective language would make this expert's opinion sound less like it was a bought and paid for commodity.

> It is my opinion, based on a reasonable degree of engineering certainty, that Mr. Coolidge's engineering of the subdivision without ever having personally set forth on the land is a deviation from the standard of care which should be employed by a reasonably prudent engineer. I base this opinion on the following:
> 1....

Example12.148 "Carefully reviewed"
Report States:

> I have carefully reviewed all of the medical records in this case.

Comment: This expert has set himself up to be cross-examined on the contents of all of the lengthy medical records in the case. She would have been better off removing the self-serving "carefully" characterization.

> I have reviewed the medical records in this case.

Example 12.149: "Ridiculous"
Report States:

> Furthermore, the physician's responsibility included informing the patient of the results in a clearly understood and confidential manner. For Dr. A to simply dismiss Mr. Jackson as "he wasn't my patient," is ridiculous.

Comment: More objective language would be more persuasive.

> It is my opinion, based on a reasonable degree of medical certainty, that Dr. A deviated from the standard of care by failing to inform Mr. Jackson of the results in a clearly understood and confidential manner.

Example 12.1410: "Conscious indifference"
Report States:

> The staff at Manor Nursing Home displayed a conscious indifference to Mr. Lee's safety by failing to take action when it was apparent that he was severely nutritionally compromised.

Resulting Cross-examination:

Q. Is it your testimony that the staff intentionally tried to starve Mr. Lee?
A. No, but they should have been more careful.
Q. When you say "apparent," apparent to whom?
A. To the staff.

Q. So they should have noticed this?
A. Exactly.
Q. But they didn't?
A. Correct.
Q. So, it was not apparent to them, correct?
A. It should have been.
Q. But it wasn't?
A. Correct.
Q. If they were unaware of the problem, they could not be "consciously" indifferent to it, could they?
A. They should have noticed it.
Q. But they didn't, did they?
A. Yes. But that's not an excuse. You're twisting my words.
Q. You did use the words "apparent," "conscious," and "indifference" in your report?
A. Yes. But that's not what I meant…I mean….
Q. Would you like to restate your opinion using different words?

Comment: This original sentence from the report is full of subjective characterizations that the author would have been better off replacing with more objective language.

> The staff at Manor Nursing Home violated the standard of care by failing to take action after Mr. Lee became nutritionally compromised.

Example 12.1411: "Independently review," "very complex case"
Report States:
> Thank you for asking me to independently review and opine on this very complex case.

Comment: These subjective characterizations can and will be used against the expert. They should not have been included in the expert's report.

12.15 Explain Explicitly the Meaning of Abbreviations
An expert report is written to communicate the expert's findings and conclusions to lay people such as attorneys, judges, jurors, and others. These lay people may not readily understand all of the technical jargon and abbreviations in the expert's field. It is therefore recommended that experts not use abbreviations in their reports without explaining explicitly the meaning of the abbreviation the first time it is used in the report. The best practice is to write the term out longhand the first time it is used and to follow the terms with a parenthetical reference to the abbreviation that the author will use in the remainder of the report.

Example 12.151: Explanation after abbreviation
Report States:
> ACEP's cost containment committee verifies that chest x-rays and labs that have no clinical indication should not be done....Chest compressions during ACLS treatment lasted for 69 minutes.

Resulting Cross-examination:
Q. ACEP is an abbreviation for what?
A. American College of Emergency Physicians.
Q. Why did you abbreviate it?
A. Because I assumed everyone would know what it meant.
Q. I didn't.
A. Sorry.

Comment: This report would have been more readily understandable to a lay reader, and thus more persuasive, had the expert included explanations of the meanings of the abbreviations used.

> The American College of Emergency Physicians (ACEP) cost containment committee verifies that chest x-rays and labs that have no clinical indication should not be done....Chest compressions during Advanced Cardiac Life Support (ACLS) treatment lasted for 69 minutes.

Example 12.152: Hereinafter parenthetical
Report States:
> Screening items were within normal limits (hereinafter "WNL") for accuracy but times tests were slow.

Comment: If an expert wants to use abbreviations, it is best to write the term out longhand for its first use followed by a parenthetical reference to the abbreviation that the author will use in the remainder of the report.

12.16 Avoid Argumentative Language

The tone of the expert report should always be formal and objective. Argumentative language should be avoided. Argumentative language makes the expert appear as though she has an interest in the case. This will result in a loss of credibility. Consider the following example.

Example 12.161: "Makes this argument moot"
Report States:
The excuse given for not providing bed linens is that sheets are a fire hazard. Although this is not true, the fact that these facilities are now smoke-free and inmates are no longer permitted matches, makes this argument moot.

Resulting Cross-examination:
Q. Inmates get sent to prison because they do things they are not supposed to?
A. I suppose so.
Q. Do you suppose that some inmates may smuggle matches and cigarettes even if it is against the rules?

A. Yes.

Q. You are supposed to be an impartial and unbiased expert?

A. I am impartial and unbiased.

Q. Is your assignment to take counsel's arguments and disprove them?

A. No.

Q. But, that is what you are doing in your report when you try to "moot out" the bed linen argument, correct?

Comment: This report would have been more persuasive had it not contained the above argumentative language.

> In my opinion, sheets and linens are not a fire hazard. This is especially true because the prisoners are no longer allowed cigarettes and matches.

12.17 Beware of Commenting on the Credibility of Witnesses

Experts often comment explicitly or implicitly regarding the veracity of others involved in the case. This includes witnesses and other experts. Generally speaking, it is the duty of the jury, not the expert, to determine the veracity of the witnesses in the case. When experts comment about the veracity of others in a report, they may appear to be biased and thus lose credibility. Such statements may also be subject to redaction. Please consider the following examples.

Example 12.171: Opposing expert untruthful
Report States:

> Plaintiff's expert would have us believe that the National Electric Safety Code (NESC) specifies the design of protection systems for utilities. This couldn't be further from the truth.

Resulting Cross-examination:

Q. You're accusing the plaintiff's expert of lying about the NESC Code, correct?

A. No. But he is wrong.

Q. You said his report's conclusion could not be further from the truth, didn't you?

A. Yes.

Q. If he is intentionally not telling the truth, he is lying, correct?

A. Yes. But I didn't say his error was intentional.

Q. It's your opinion that he is wrong?

A. Correct.

Q. And it is his opinion that you are wrong?

A. You would have to ask him that.

Q. Counsel who retained you asked you to comment on the opposing expert's veracity, correct?

A. Yes.

Q. And you accommodated her with this personal attack accusing him of lying?

Comment: The expert's comment regarding the other expert's veracity makes the initial expert seem partisan and biased. This comment should have been avoided. The expert would have been better served with more objective and less inflammatory language.

> The National Electric Safety Code (NESC) does not specify the design of protection systems for utilities.

Example 12.172: Eyewitness wrong but expert deduction correct

Report States:

> Given the tests that were conducted, Mr. Macks' recollection of the accident occurrence contains an observation error. Mr. Macks testified that he believed that the gun fired the second nail when the push lever was not in contact with the wood or anything else. We believe that it is far more likely that a recoil fire occurred due to involuntary muscle reaction on the part of Mr. Macks. Given the circumstances as described by Macks and the testing on the subject nailer, no other scenario of the accident can be reasonably deduced.

Resulting Cross-examination:

Q. Who was the only eyewitness to the accident?

A. Mr. Macks.

Q. Who was the only person in position to see what actually happened?

A. Mr. Macks.

Q. Where were you on September 17, 2001, at noon when the accident happened?

A. Well, I would have to consult my date book, but I believe I was in Los Angeles.

Q. Some 3,000+ miles away?

A. Yes.

Q. After you returned from LA, how long was it before you formed your opinion in this case?

A. Approximately seven months later.

Q. Your opinion was based on your reconstruction of the accident and your observation during the reconstruction, correct?

A. Yes.

Q. During your reconstruction you tried to simulate as closely as possible the actual accident?

A. Yes.

Q. At your simulation, you were still not able to come up with an alternate cause until you started your deductive process, correct?

A. Yes.

Q. Is it your testimony here under oath and before this jury that you are 100% correct and there is absolutely no way other than what you deduced as to how this accident happened?

A. Yes.

Q. So, when you said in your report no other scenario of the accident can be "reasonably" deduced, you didn't really mean that, did you?

A. Well, there is always a small chance....

Q. That Mr. Macks is correct?

Comment: This expert would have looked a lot less biased had he used language that was less strong.

> Given the tests that were conducted, Mr. Macks's recollection of the accident occurrence most likely contains an observation error. Mr. Macks testified that he believed that the gun fired the second nail when the push lever was not in contact with the wood or anything else. In my expert opinion it is far more likely that a recoil fire occurred due to involuntary muscle reaction on the part of Mr. Macks.

Example 12.173: Ridiculing the veracity of the defendant

Report States:

> SB, MD, claims that a repeat test in two hours was requested of surgeons. (There is no chart note of such, no order; or no attempted follow-up documented.) SB, MD, continues that, "Clinical Condition precluded return earlier than 11:00am." There is no corroboration of this statement by any physician testimony, or physicians' or nurses' note. What prompts recall of this event by SB, MD, when nothing else is recalled about the patient, by him or most of the physicians, except the patient's young age? He doesn't remember who placed the catheter (pg 64.). He doesn't recollect any history or ischemic symptoms relayed to him (pg. 58), but "I recall that his pulses were absent...he was able to move the foot" (pg. 63). How does he recall, "The surgical resident told us that his leg is still cold?" (pg. 101).

Resulting Cross-examination:

Q. Do you have absolute recall, Doctor?
A. No.
Q. Some things you remember and some things you do not?
A. Yes, that's correct.
Q. Just like SB, MD, in this case?
A. No. He has a selective memory.
Q. So, as an unbiased and impartial expert, it is your testimony here, today, that you can tell this jury which statements Dr. SB recalls and which he does not?
A. It's just hard for me to believe that is his memory of the situation.
Q. Just like it is hard for us to believe that you can, with a reasonable degree of medical certainty under oath, testify as to what another physician remembers?

Comment: This expert's report sounds more like an attorney's closing argument than it does a forensic report. This type of language should be avoided because it makes the expert appear biased.

12.18 Maintain Consistency in and amongst Reports

An expert report needs to be internally consistent. If the expert has issued more than one report, these multiple reports need to be consistent. Counsel who can point out significant internal inconsistencies or discrepancies between an expert's own reports can cast significant doubts about the expert's credibility. The effectiveness of this technique is magnified when counsel can show that the discrepancies may be a result of the use of the expert's reports in different legal forums to achieve different results. It is more and more likely today that counsel will be able to obtain an expert's reports from other cases to check for inconsistencies; for example, if a physician in one case wrote that fibromyalgia does not exist and in a subsequent case diagnosed a patient with fibromyalgia.

Example 12.181: Discrepancies in and amongst reports
Sita v. Danek Medical, Inc., 43 F.Supp.2d 245 (E.D.N.Y. 1999)
The court closely examined apparent discrepancies in and amongst an expert's reports.

> Plaintiff has also failed to explain a number of discrepancies within and between Dr. Einhorn's May 1995 and 1997 reports. First, the May 1995 report is internally inconsistent. When asked to examine plaintiff for the purpose of assessing plaintiff's entitlement to Workers' Compensation benefits, Dr. Einhorn diagnosed plaintiff with pseudarthrosis (non-union or failure of the bone to fuse). *See* Einhorn Letter, dated 5/16/95. However, Dr. Einhorn had earlier in the same report observed that he could not tell whether the bone from any of plaintiff's spinal surgeries had fused. *See id.* Thus, Dr. Einhorn's finding that plaintiff suffered from pseudarthrosis is implausible.
>
> There are also several discrepancies between the May 1995 and September 1997 reports. In his September 1997 report, Dr. Einhorn noted that "[his]...[that] one of the lower pedicle screws was broken." Einhorn Report, dated 9/29/97. Dr. Einhorn did not make this finding in his May 1995 report, perhaps because the fact of the broken pedicle screw would not have been important to a Workers' Compensation determination. Nor did Dr. Einhorn then conclude that any of defendant's TSRH screws had caused or contributed to plaintiff's pain, as he did in his 1997 report. Again, this discrepancy might be explained away because in a Workers' Compensation proceeding, medical causation of the type at issue here may not be material. However, Dr. Einhorn did not, in May 1995, indicate, as he did in his September 1997 report, that plaintiff had a fractured pedicle, a fact that might well have been important to a Workers' Compensation determination. These unexplained inconsistencies—the finding of pseudarthrosis without evidence of non-union and the failure to diagnose a fractured pedicle in May 1995—cast a shadow of doubt upon the credibility of Dr. Einhorn's report.[6]

Example 12.182: Two reports, two different opinions
Cross-examination:
Q. You issued a report dated 9/15/2000 in this case, correct?
A. Yes.
Q. Your opinion was that the accident was caused by a defectively designed latch bracket, correct?
A. Yes.
Q. Prior to formulating this opinion, which documents did you review?

---

[6] At 253.

A. The operation catalog, and service manual of the machine, the complaint, response to production of documents, answers to interrogatories, photos of the machine, and the deposition transcript of Mr. Allen and Mr. Stevens.

Q. What other work did you perform prior to formulating your opinion expressed in your 9/15/2000 report?

A. I inspected and tested the machine and reviewed the ANSI and OSHA safety standards and analyzed this information.

Q. You issued a second report on 1/17/2001, correct?

A. Yes. That's correct.

Q. In your second report you stated that the cause of the accident was, in fact, the failure to provide an appropriate point-of-operation interlocked barrier guard?

A. That's correct.

Q. What additional testing did you do between 9/15/2000 and 1/17/2001?

A. No additional testing, but I did review the final investigative OSHA report.

Q. Where did you obtain this from?

A. Attorney Jones sent it to me.

Q. Based upon that, you changed your opinion on the cause of the accident?

A. Yes. Based upon the report and my analysis of same.

Q. Sir, if OSHA changes their report or issues a new report, will you again change your opinion as to the cause of the accident?

A. It would depend....

Q. On what is in the report?

A. Yes.

Q. So, your opinion is flexible and not yet final?

Comment: Experts can expect to be questioned closely about any inconsistencies between their multiple reports. Inconsistencies will result in a loss of credibility.

Example 12.183: Affidavit not a sham in light of previous report
Hill v. Martinez, 87 F.Supp.2d 1115 (D.Colo. 2000)
The court examined the expert's prior report in determining if his affidavit was a sham created to defeat a motion for summary judgment. The court stated:

> Defendants argue in effect that I should disregard Dr. Richie's affadivit because it is a sham. As support, Defendants cite apparent inconsistencies between Dr. Richie's affidavit, and both a written report he authored on November 7, 1995 (1995 Report), and his deposition testimony. The Tenth Circuit permits an affidavit that conflicts with earlier sworn testimony be disregarded when it constitutes an attempt to create a sham fact issue. *See Franks v. Nimmo*, 796 F.2d 1230, 1237 (10th Cir.1986). In *Franks*, the Tenth Circuit held that the utility of summary judgment as a procedure for screening out sham fact issues would be greatly undermined if a party could create an issue of fact merely by submitting an affidavit contradicting his or her own prior testimony. *Id.* Factors relevant to the existence of a sham fact issue include whether the affiant was cross-examined during his earlier testimony, whether the affidavit was based on newly discovered evidence, and whether the earlier testimony reflects confusion which the affidavit attempts to explain.[7]

---

[7] At 1127.

The court concluded there was no direct conflict and/or sham and stated:

> I cannot conclude that Dr. Richie's affidavit is a sham created for the purpose of avoiding summary judgment. In his deposition, Dr. Richie stated both that he did not disagree with the findings of the individual who performed the autopsy of Preston Hill, Dr. Deter, *see Defendants' Motion for Summary Judgment,* Ex. E at 78, and that he could not render an opinion regarding exactly how Preston Hill was killed. *Id.* at 62. Because the autopsy report did not draw any conclusion regarding the events that led to Preston Hill's death, *see Plaintiffs' Response,* Ex. 8, Dr. Richie's affidavit does not directly conflict with his deposition testimony.[8]

Example 12.184: Cross-examination permitted on discrepancies between reports
People v. Gregg, 732 N.E.2d 1152 (Ill.App.1 Dist. 2000)
In this case, the court permitted the cross-examination of the expert regarding discrepancies between his two reports. The court stated:

> Furthermore, any additional reports that defendant produced from Dr. Schwartz and that contradicted Dr. Schwartz's previous report were properly used by the State for impeachment. The credibility of a witness is put in issue when the witness testifies during trial. *People v. Bull,* 185 Ill.2d 179, 235 Ill.Dec. 641, 705 N.E.2d 824 (1998). Here, Dr. Schwartz prepared two reports, one dated October 1995, and the other, August 1998. The 1998 report included pertinent information not contained in the 1995 report. As such, the State had a right to cross-examine Dr. Schwartz regarding the discrepancies in the two reports, including the omissions in the 1995 report and the new information in the 1998 report which was submitted closer in time to trial.

12.19 Avoid Drafting Reports that Appear Biased or Partisan
An expert's report that evidences bias, lack of impartiality, or the selective use of data to support a theory will normally be discounted, discredited, or stricken.

Example 12.191: Biased expert report disallowed
Derrickson v. Circuit City Stores, Inc., 84 F. Supp. 679 (D.Md. 2000)
In this case, the court dealt with a Title VII discrimination suit. The expert, Medoff, was a Harvard professor and offered as part of his report his essay on "Enlightened Equal Employment Opportunity Practices." The court struck this portion of the report and stated:

> The court will GRANT the motion to exclude the third part of Dr. Medoff's report. The essay on "enlightened" employment practices is nothing more than a five-page summary of Dr. Medoff's experiences providing consulting services for IBM and the Boston Globe. Through these experiences, Dr. Medoff develops a theory of what employment practices may prevent discriminatory actions. In its final page, Dr. Medoff provides a sole conclusory opinion with regard to Defendant:
>
> > I have reviewed documents and depositions relating to Circuit City's employment policies and practices. From this review, it is not surprising to me that a quantitative analysis of Circuit City's employment statistics

---

[8] At 1128.

indicates that black employees at the company do not have the same employment opportunities as their white counterparts.

The court finds that Dr. Medoff's opinion on what employment practices at IBM and the Boston Globe reduced discrimination is irrelevant to whether Circuit City discriminated in violation of Title VII and § 1981. In fact, the essay's only possible relevance to this case is that it may show Dr. Medoff's bias to put forth data that supports his own "enlightened" employment theory. Further, Dr. Medoff admits in his deposition that he is not an expert in, or even familiar with, Circuit City's employment practices, the ones at issue in this case. Therefore, the court will exclude this document as both irrelevant and unreliable for the purposes of Plaintiffs' proof.[9]

Even court-appointed experts can and do issue reports that bring their impartiality into question.

Certainly an appointed expert who is not only seen as partial but who also appears to be working toward a particular outcome in a case will be ineffective in either an evaluative or facilitative settlement role. The problem is illustrated by a controversial Illinois case, Edgar v. K.L., brought by the American Civil Liberties Union against the state Department of Mental Health and Developmental Disabilities challenging conditions in mental hospitals. The parties jointly requested appointment of an expert panel to evaluate the hospitals with the expectation that their findings would lay the groundwork for a settlement. They had reason to believe that the procedure would work, because it had been successful in an earlier suit against a state agency with responsibility for abused and neglected children in state custody. Evaluation, however, did not lead to acquiescence or compromise in the mental health case. The experts' report, described by the press as a "blistering expose" of the state mental health system, was immediately countered by an agency study criticizing the methodology and rejecting its findings. The intemperance of the experts' report seems to have been enough to destroy their usefulness in fostering settlement. But, in addition, one of the experts went beyond offering an opinion and assumed an overtly partisan role in the litigation. He urged the district judge to release the report at a time designed to maximize political pressure on the state government. Statements in his letter to the judge such as "(t)his fight needs to be won on the street, not just in court," caused the court of appeals to conclude that the expert was not neutral and that "the (expert) panel can no longer claim the mantle of judicial appointment."[10]

---

[9] At 688, 689.

[10] Ellen E. Deason, "Managing the Managerial Expert," 1998 U. Ill. L. Rev. 341, (400, 401).

Chapter 13 Damaging Superfluous Language and Information that Should Not Be Included in Expert Reports

13.1 Executive Summary

The only language that should appear in expert reports is language that objectively states or objectively supports an expert's findings and conclusions. All other information is superfluous and should not be included in the report.

Including superfluous language in a report is one of the most common mistakes experts make. This mistake can cost the expert's credibility dearly. Superfluous language often provides fertile grounds for cross-examination that will damage the expert's credibility. The authors recommend the following.

- Avoid "friendly" language to counsel that thanks them for the assignment, invites comments or questions, or makes personal salutations.
- Do not include speeches in the expert report that espouse the expert's beliefs.
- Make sure letterhead does not include references to being an "expert witness."
- Cover letters accompanying reports should be short and formal. One sentence is ideal.
- Do not document in the expert report discussions with retaining counsel unless they are relevant.
- Experts should self-edit their reports aggressively to remove any and all other superfluous language.

13.2 "Friendly" Language Directed at Counsel

Experts often make the mistake of including language to counsel that thanks them for the assignment, invites comments or questions, or makes personal salutations. Even seemingly innocuous language can damage an expert's credibility. It is best to avoid such language. Consider the following examples.

Example 13.21: Personal salutation
Report States:

P.S.: I hope that you, Jean, and the kids have a very Merry Christmas and a Happy New Year!

Resulting Cross-examination:

Q. You have a professional relationship with counsel who retained you in this case, correct?

A. Yes.

Q. You also have a warm, personal relationship with counsel, his wife, Jean, and their three children?

A. Well, I don't know if I would call it a "warm, personal relationship."

Q. You meant what you said in your P.S.—"I hope you, Jean, and the kids have a very, Merry Christmas and a Happy New Year," didn't you?

A. Yes.

Q. You don't include a P.S. like that in all of your letters to lawyers, do you?

A. No, I don't.

Q. The reason being...?

A. I don't know them well enough to say something like that.

Comment: This language can be used to show that the expert may be biased in favor of his personal friend, retaining counsel. This language should have been omitted from the report.

Example 13.22: "Thank you...please call" with questions
Report States:

> Thank you for the opportunity to prepare this report. If you have any
> questions regarding the detail and content, please call.

Resulting Cross-examination:

Q. You are happy to answer questions of retaining counsel about the preliminary report that you issued?

A. Correct.

Q. You discuss detail and content?

A. Yes.

Q. Sometimes you modify your preliminary report when you issue your final report?

A. Yes, sometimes.

Q. That would take place after you sent them a letter saying, "Thank you for the opportunity to prepare this report. If you have any questions regarding the detail and content, please call."

A. Yes.

Q. And after you discuss the report with retaining counsel?

A. Yes.

Q. Then you issue your impartial, unbiased, final report?

A. Yes.

Comment: Even this seemingly innocuous superfluous language can be used against an expert. This language is unnecessary. No expert should think that retaining counsel needs a written invitation to call the expert with a question.

Example 13.23: "I trust this information will be of help"
Report States:

I trust this information will be of help.

Resulting Cross-examination:
Q. You gave the benefit of the doubt to counsel who retained you when arriving at your opinion, didn't you?
A. No, I did not.
Q. Did you say in your report, "I trust this information will be of help"?
A. Yes.
Q. You knew what counsel needed you to say for her to make her case, correct?
A. Yes.
Q. That's because of the number of times you have testified and the discussion with counsel?
A. I talked to counsel.
Q. She trusted you to do a good job?
A. Yes.
Q. And you did not betray her trust?
A. I don't understand.
Q. You gave her what she wanted and then said, "I trust this information will be of help," correct?

Comment: This statement does not support or express the expert's findings and conclusions and should not have been included in the report.

Example 13.24: Wants to satisfy counsel's needs
Report States:

I trust the above are sufficient for your needs at this time. If I can be of any further assistance, please do not hesitate to call on me.

Resulting Cross-examination:
Q. You were retained by counsel to issue a report, correct?
A. Yes.
Q. And you did so in accordance with the instructions of counsel?
A. I answered the questions she asked.
Q. You only expressed opinions in the areas she instructed you to do so, correct?
A. Yes.
Q. You tried to be helpful?
A. Yes, within the bounds of the ethics of my profession.
Q. You tried to meet counsel's needs?
A. Yes.
Q. Bottom line—counsel needs to win, correct?
A. I guess that's true.
Q. And you gave her an opinion sufficient to meet her needs to win?
A. You are making it sound sinister, counselor.
Q. Aren't you the one who said in your report, "I trust the above are sufficient for your needs at this time"?

A. Yes, I did.

Comment: This statement does not support or express the expert's findings and conclusions and should not have been included in the report.

13.3 Speeches

An expert report is no place to make speeches espousing the expert's beliefs. Such speeches are irrelevant, subjective, and will make the expert appear as though he has interests beyond an objective evaluation of the case. Even court-appointed experts can put their credibility into serious question by using the expert report as a platform of opportunity to make a speech. Such experts can and do issue reports that bring their impartiality into question.

> Certainly an appointed expert who is not only seen as partial but who also appears to be working toward a particular outcome in a case will be ineffective in either an evaluative or facilitative settlement role. The problem is illustrated by a controversial Illinois case, Edgar v. K.L., brought by the American Civil Liberties Union against the state Department of Mental Health and Developmental Disabilities challenging conditions in mental hospitals. The parties jointly requested appointment of an expert panel to evaluate the hospitals with the expectation that their findings would lay the groundwork for a settlement. They had reason to believe that the procedure would work, because it had been successful in an earlier suit against a state agency with responsibility for abused and neglected children in state custody. Evaluation, however, did not lead to acquiescence or compromise in the mental health case. The experts' report, described by the press as a "blistering expose" of the state mental health system, was immediately countered by an agency study criticizing the methodology and rejecting its findings. The intemperance of the experts' report seems to have been enough to destroy their usefulness in fostering settlement. But, in addition, one of the experts went beyond offering an opinion and assumed an overtly partisan role in the litigation. He urged the district judge to release the report at a time designed to maximize political pressure on the state government. Statements in his letter to the judge such as "(t)his fight needs to be won on the street, not just in court," caused the court of appeals to conclude that the expert was not neutral and that "the (expert) panel can no longer claim the mantle of judicial appointment."[1]

Consider the following additional examples of expert witness speechmaking in reports.

---

[1] *Managing the Managerial Expert,* Ellen E. Deason, 1998 U. Ill L. Rev. 341 at 400-401.

Example 13.31 Speech on safety
Report States:
> Safety professionals, construction industry managers and others believe that it is not only morally and ethically responsible to control workplace hazards that could otherwise lead to catastrophic injury and death, it is also good business. That is, we believe that it is much more cost effective to pay for the added costs to prevent injury and death than it is to cut corners, save safety costs and time, and expose workers to dangers and hope that no injury will occur. When injury does occur, the costs to society are significantly higher than the costs to prevent the injury. Certainly, an "ounce of prevention" is worth a pound of "cure" in the construction industry.

Resulting Cross-examination:
Q. Sir, how many safety professionals are there in the United States?
A. Well, depending on how you define it, 15,000–20,000.
Q. And how many construction industry managers?
A. Again, depending on your definition, 7,000–9,000.
Q. How many "others" are there?
A. Others?
Q. Yes, as you used the term in your report.
A. Well, that would be impossible to say.
Q. Have you been elected or selected as a leader or spokesperson for these 20,000 safety professionals, 9,000 construction managers, and untold others, sir?
A. No.
Q. So, when you say "we believe" in paragraph one, page 3 of your report, you are just expressing your thoughts, correct?
A. Yes.

Comment: This language is superfluous and should not be in the expert's report.

Example 13.32: Moral responsibility to pay
Report States:
> There are significant costs associated with workplace injury. But it is much cheaper and it is morally responsible for the entity that creates the hazard, or the company that benefits from not spending the money, to bear all of the costs. These companies should pay the full costs of injury and death because, otherwise, there would be little incentive to prevent injury.

Resulting Cross-examination:
Q. The company who is legally responsible is always the same as the one who is morally responsible for an injury, correct?
A. No, absolutely not.
Q. It is your belief that it is not the company who is legally responsible but the company who is morally responsible who should pay for the cost of injury and death?
A. No.

Q. Didn't you say in your report, "… it is morally responsible for the entity that creates the hazard, or the company that benefits from not spending the money to bear all of the costs"?
A. Yes.
Q. Who decides who is legally responsible?
A. The courts and the judicial system.
Q. Who do you propose decides who is morally responsible?

Comment: This superfluous language makes the expert appear as though he is a crusader on a mission. This will damage the expert's credibility because it indicates that the expert has an agenda of his own to advance. This language has no place in an expert report.

Example 13.33: Essay on enlightened equal employment opportunity practices irrelevant and unreliable

Derrickson v. Circuit City Stores, Inc., 84 F. Supp.2d 679 (D.Md. 2000)
In this case, the court dealt with a Title VII discrimination suit. The expert, Medoff, was a Harvard professor and offered as part of his report his essay on "Enlightened Equal Employment Opportunity Practices." The court struck this portion of the report and stated:

> The court will GRANT the motion to exclude the third part of Dr. Medoff's report. The essay on "enlightened" employment practices is nothing more than a five-page summary of Dr. Medoff's experiences providing consulting services for IBM and the Boston Globe. Through these experiences, Dr. Medoff develops a theory of what employment practices may prevent discriminatory actions. In its final page, Dr. Medoff provides a sole conclusory opinion with regard to Defendant:

>> I have reviewed documents and depositions relating to Circuit City's employment policies and practices. From this review, it is not surprising to me that a quantitative analysis of Circuit City's employment statistics indicates that black employees at the company do not have the same employment opportunities as their white counterparts.

> The court finds that Dr. Medoff's opinion on what employment practices at IBM and the Boston Globe reduced discrimination is irrelevant to whether Circuit City discriminated in violation of Title VII and § 1981. In fact, the essay's only possible relevance to this case is that it may show Dr. Medoff's bias to put forth data that supports his own "enlightened" employment theory. Further, Dr. Medoff admits in his deposition that he is not an expert in, or even familiar with, Circuit City's employment practices, the ones at issue in this case. Therefore, the court will exclude this document as both irrelevant and unreliable for the purposes of Plaintiffs' proof.

13.4 Letterhead

Experts should be careful about what is contained on their letterhead. Their letterhead should not contain any reference to the professional being an "expert witness." Such references can result in a completely avoidable loss of credibility. Please consider the following examples.

Example 13.41: "Expert witness"
Report States:
> Expert Witness for Construction Personal Injury & Premise Liability
> Expert.

Resulting Cross-examination:
Q. You are a civil engineer, correct?
A. Yes.
Q. Your degree and license are in civil engineering?
A. Yes.
Q. But your letterhead doesn't say anything about civil engineering, does it?
A. It speaks for itself.
Q. Actually, it speaks for you, sir. It says, "Expert witness for construction, personal injury, and premise liability expert," correct?
A. Yes.
Q. So you promote yourself as an expert witness for hire, correct?
A. Yes, I am an expert.
Q. But your stationery makes it clear that you are not just an expert, but an "expert witness," correct?
A. Yes.
Q. You do this expert witness work as a business for money, correct?
A. Yes.
Q. The object in your expert witness business is to make as much money as possible?
A. Yes.
Q. Sir, when did you stop being a civil engineer and become an "expert witness"?

Comment: References to being an "expert witness" should not be contained on the expert's letterhead. If such a reference is contained in the letterhead, the expert is likely to face a line of questioning similar to the above.

Example 13.42: "Pro-Witness Forensic Consulting: Expert Witness Testimony"
Report States:
> Name of Business is "Pro-Witness Forensic Consulting: Expert Witness
> Testimony, Playground Accidents." (Actual language used by expert.)

Resulting Cross-examination:
Q. The name of your business listed prominently in large block letters on your letterhead is "Pro-Witness Forensic Consulting"?
A. That's correct.
Q. The "Pro" stands for?
A. Professional.
Q. So you advertise and promote yourself as a "Professional Witness," sir?

Comment: This expert's choice of a name to do business under implies that she is a professional witness. This will damage her credibility. Putting that name on her report will damage it even more.

13.5 Cover Letters

The cover letter accompanying an expert's report should be short, formal, and contain nothing that can later be used against the expert on cross-examination. If this is not done, the cover letter will itself become a fertile area of contention and provide ammunition for unnecessary cross-examination. Consider the following examples.

Example 13.51: Cover letter to attorney
Cover Letter States:

> Re: *Smith v. Jones*
>
> Dear Attorney Johnson:
>
> Enclosed please find my seven-page written report dated September 28, 2001, in the above-referenced matter.
>
> Very truly yours,
> John Q. Expert

Comment: This is a well-written cover letter. It serves its purpose as a cover letter yet provides no ammunition for the cross-examiner to use against the expert.

Example 13.52: Informality and extraneous information in cover letter
Cover Letter States:

> Re: *Smith v. Jones*
>
> Dear Teddy:
>
> Thank you for referring this fascinating case to me. Enclosed please find my written report. I hope it was what you were looking for. Please do not hesitate to contact me if you have any questions, comments, or concerns.
>
> Warm Regards,
> John Q. Expert
>
> PS: And I hope that you, Sally, and the kids have a very happy holiday season.

Resulting Cross-examination:
Q. Your report is impartial and unbiased, correct?
A. Yes.
Q. Despite the fact that you are a close personal friend of plaintiff's counsel?
A. Well, I don't know if I would call him a close personal friend.
Q. You do call him Teddy in your cover letter?
A. Yes.
Q. You also in the cover letter inquire about his wife, Sally, and his children?
A. Yes, but I was trying to be....

Q. Friendly?
A. Polite.
Q. Were you just being polite when you told "Teddy" "I hope it was what you were looking for"?
A. Yes.
Q. Is it your testimony that you never altered, changed, modified, or corrected reports at the request of retaining attorneys with whom you were personal friends?

Comment: Had this expert used a short, formal, no-nonsense cover letter, he would have avoided the above line of questioning.

Example 13.53: Superfluous language in cover letter
Cross-examination:
Q. Your cover letter of March 6, 2000, states that the appraisal report is "intended as an estimate of fair market value," correct?
A. Correct.
Q. So, the figure of $15,697.34 you arrived at is not a precise figure?
A. It's an estimate.
Q. By "estimate," you mean there is a margin of error?
A. Yes.
Q. What is the margin of error for your entire appraisal?
A. I didn't compute that.
Q. Could it be 5%?
A. It could be.
Q. Could it be 10%?
A. Yes.
Q. What about 20%?
A. Yes.
Q. What about 25%?
A. No, that's too high.
Q. So your appraisal could be off by as much as 40%?
A. No, I said 20%.
Q. But that's 20% on the low side or 20% on the high side, so that's a range of up to 40%, correct?
A. That's correct.
Q. You would agree that your appraisal is "subjective," correct?
A. No, I don't.
Q. Do you not say in your cover letter of March 6, 2000, "an appraisal is a subjective professional assessment"?
A. Yes, but it is not totally subjective.
Q. Could you express in a percentage form the degree of subjectivity in an appraisal of this sort?
A. No, I could not.
Q. You gave counsel who retained you exactly what she was looking for, correct?
A. I gave her my honest appraisal.

Q. Did you not say in your cover letter of March 6, 2000, "I was glad to be of service to you and if I can assist you in any other way in this case, please do not hesitate to call me"?

A. Yes, but I was just being polite.

Q. But you do anticipate additional "service" on this matter to counsel, correct?

A. I am not sure what you mean.

Q. In addition to saying, "If I can assist you in any other way in this case, please let me know," you go on to state, "If I am called upon to testify in this matter, I shall be compensated at my standard fee," correct?

A. Yes.

Q. You would normally only be called upon to testify if counsel was pleased with the report you furnished her?

A. Well…I guess that's true.

Q. And when you don't give counsel what they want they normally do not call upon you to testify?

A. Well…ah, I am not sure.

Q. So you have a direct pecuniary interest in pleasing counsel with your subjective estimate?

A. I am not sure how to answer that.

Q. You just did. Thank you.

Comment: This expert could have avoided this entire damaging cross-examination by writing a simple one-sentence cover letter. In the case of cover letters, less is more.

13.6 Discussions with Retaining Counsel

Retaining counsel and the expert often have many conversations discussing the case at hand. These conversations are perfectly legitimate, however, it is usually not good practice to document them in a forensic report. Opposing counsel zero-in on such references and try to make it look as if retaining counsel improperly influenced the expert's opinion. Please consider the following example.

Example 13.61: Verbal report mentioned in written report
Report States:
> After a verbal report, a request was made to reduce to writing the main points of that verbal report.

Resulting Cross-examination:

Q. You gave a verbal report to counsel prior to reducing it to writing?

A. Yes.

Q. Did counsel ask you to do this?

A. Yes.

Q. So, counsel could "preview" the report without actually receiving something in writing she would have to share during discovery?

A. You would have to ask her about the reason.

Q. The verbal report you gave counsel was essentially the same as the one reduced to writing?

A. Yes.

Q. Did you memorize this seven-page, single-spaced report, or did you have notes when you discussed it with counsel?

A. I had notes.

Q. Can I see them?

A. I destroyed them once the report was typed up.

Q. As a result of your discussions with counsel, did you alter, change, modify, or revise your report when it was typed up?

A. Yes.

Q. Let's go through all the changes you made. Tell me how it was before the oral report, how it was changed, and why you made the changes, sir.

Comment: This expert would have been better served by not documenting in his report the fact that a verbal report had first been made to retaining counsel.

13.7 Additional Examples of Superfluous Language

Experts need to self-edit their reports to remove any and all superfluous language. Failure to do so will result in damaging cross-examinations that will negatively affect the expert's credibility. Please consider the following additional examples.

Example 13.71: MENSA member
Report States:
Member: MENSA

Resulting Cross-examination:

Q. Ms. Curran, on page 7 of your report above your signature, you indicate that you are a member of MENSA, is that correct?

A. Yes.

Q. Why did you put that in your report?

A. It is part of my background that I think people would be interested in.

Q. MENSA is a high IQ group only open to people with IQs over 140, correct?

A. No, it's 150.

Q. You feel you are smarter than your fellow experts, don't you?

A. Well…no…not really.

Q. Only 3% of people have IQs over 150, correct?

A. Yes, but there are all kinds of intelligence. IQ is just one measurement.

Q. Ms. Curran, are you smarter than our 12 jurors?

A. I have no way of knowing that. Is that important, counselor?

Q. My point exactly, Ms. Curran.

Comment: This expert report would have been more defensible had the expert removed her reference to her membership in MENSA.

Example 13.72: Piling on: "plaintiff bears no responsibility"
Report States:

> We therefore conclude that Mr. Macks's injury resulted from a reasonably foreseeable action scenario involving involuntary recoil firing of the tool as reflected in his deposition testimony. He therefore bears no responsibility for the injury he sustained.

Resulting Cross-examination:

Q. The action scenario that occurred was "reasonably foreseeable," was it not?
A. Yes, it was.
Q. By "reasonably foreseeable," you mean a reasonably prudent person would have foreseen the injury?
A. Well,....yes.
Q. Mr. Macks did not foresee the injury, did he?
A. No he did not.
Q. So, Mr. Macks was not in fact reasonably prudent, was he?
A. Well,....you would have to ask him that.
Q. Should I also ask him how much of the responsibility he bears for the injury?
A. Suit yourself, counselor.
Q. Could he in fact bear 1% responsibility for the injury he sustained?
A. Well,....yes, maybe 1% to 2%.
Q. What about 3%?
A. I do not want to go down that road, counselor.
Q. I can see why.

Comment: The second sentence in this excerpt is superfluous. It can be used to indicate that the expert is biased and will say anything to help his side win. Superfluous sentences should not be included in expert reports.

Example 13.73: Setting a very high standard for investigation/opinion
Report States:

> Four things contribute to a reliable conclusion for an expert's opinion in forensic document examination. 1) Physical observations are accurately and objectively demonstrated. 2) The explanation of scientific theories are reasonable and based on proper theory and objective sources. 3) Crisp and impeccable logic is applied. 4) Precise definitions of terminology are used.

Resulting Cross-examination:

Q. Can you give me a precise definition of "crisp and impeccable logic" in forensic document examination?
A. Well...that would depend on a number of circumstances and variables, counselor.
Q. So, you would want to do that on a case-by-case basis?
A. Yes.
Q. So, you need crisp and impeccable logic and precise definitions of terminology for an expert opinion in forensic document examination?
A. Yes, precisely.

Q. As you can't define what you mean by crisp and impeccable logic, does that seem logical to you?

Comment: This expert needlessly set a very high standard for her testimony.

Example 13.74: Expert's personal feelings
Report States:
> There were some disturbing elements to this case. We have not been given any of Dr. Henkels's personal records other than his operative report. Solely on the basis of what Ms. Adams stated and the magnitude of the injury we found, his initial planning appeared to have been seriously flawed.

Resulting Cross-examination:
Q. Were you completely objective and non-judgmental when you started working on this case?
A. Yes, absolutely.
Q. You became "disturbed" when you were not furnished with Dr. Henkels's personal records?
A. Well....it was somewhat disturbing.
Q. That's because you assumed he, or someone on his behalf, was trying to hide or cover-up something?
A. One could draw that inference.
Q. And you did, correct?
A. Yes, to some degree.
Q. You in fact had good reason to be disturbed, correct?
A. Yes, I did.
Q. Did you try to remain completely objective and non-judgmental once you inferred a cover-up because of the missing records?
A. Yes, I tried.
Q. In all honesty, you were not completely objective and non-judgmental once you settled on your cover-up theory?
A. Yes, that's fair.

Comment: By including his personal feelings of being disturbed, this expert can be made to seem as no longer objective.

Example 13.75: Legal advice: defendant should settle
Report States:
> Therefore, he probably cut the median nerve, mistaking it for the palmaris longus tendon...and that, sirs, does not meet an acceptable standard of care. Notwithstanding Dr. Henkels's optimism, both in his operative report ("the repair was noted to be excellent") and in his post-operative summary ("She is quite happy now"), he would best be advised to settle.

Resulting Cross-examination:
Q. You were hired as a medical expert in this case, correct?
A. Yes.
Q. And you rendered your expert medical opinion?

A. Yes.

Q. Then you rendered your legal opinion as well?

A. I did no such thing, counselor.

Q. When you state in your report, "He would best be advised to settle," is that a medical opinion?

A. No, not strictly.

Q. In fact, you are commenting on the relative chances of success in the legal action, correct?

A. Well….it was just an off-the-cuff, innocent remark.

Q. If Dr. Henkels followed your advice and spent millions of dollars to settle this case, would you feel responsible for his actions?

A. Absolutely not. He would be foolish to rely on my advice. After all, I am not a lawyer.

Q. Precisely—just as foolish as you were in offering the advice, correct?

Comment: This is advice a lawyer gives, not an expert.

Example 13.76: Marketing service name
Report States:
> If you have any further questions, please contact me through Medical Experts for Hire, Inc.

Resulting Cross-examination:

Q. Does the name of the expert witness service you work for accurately depict what the service provides?

A. Yes.

Q. And that is "Medical Experts for Hire"?

A. Inc.

Q. "Medical Experts for Hire, Inc."

A. Yes.

Q. The service rents out physicians like yourself to lawyers who need medical opinions to help their cases?

A. Yes, but I am impartial and objective.

Q. How many non-favorable reports issued by you would it take before the service stopped using you?

A. I don't know.

Q. That's because you haven't been offering non-favorable reports to Medical Experts for Hire, Inc., correct?

A. That is an absolute lie. I tell the truth!

Q. Name me two cases in which you offered non-favorable opinions to Medical Experts for Hire, Inc.

A. Well….it's hard to remember them.

Q. Could that be because they do *not* exist?

Comment: There is no reason the expert needs to include the potentially damaging information that he receives work through an expert witness marketing organization. This language should not have been included in the report.

Example 13.77: Snide comment
Report States:
>   In the opinion of the undersigned, setting price targets was an unfounded and amateurish thing to do.

Resulting Cross-examination:
Q. You felt that setting target prices was a mistake, correct?
A. Yes.
Q. But that's not what you said in your report, is it?
A. I said it was unfounded and amateurish.
Q. Would you agree that those are your characterizations of what was done?
A. To some degree…yes.
Q. Those are not strictly facts, are they?
A. No, but I stand behind what I said.
Q. Other experts would characterize this in their own way, wouldn't they?
A. Yes.
Q. Would they also be mistaken?

Comment: Calling the defendant an amateur makes the expert look opinionated and pompous. This is an unnecessary statement and can be used effectively against the expert.

Chapter 14 Red-flag Words to Avoid

14.1 Executive Summary

Using certain words in reports will raise red flags with an attorney whose job it is to undermine the expert, her credibility, and her opinions. These red-flag words should be avoided. This chapter discusses some of the most common red-flag words. They include:

- "Authoritative" to describe a text. This term has special legal significance that may allow a cross-examining attorney to question the expert about everything in the text.
- "Legal" or "legally." What is and is not legal is usually outside of the area of expertise of most experts.
- "Draft." This term alerts counsel to the existence of draft reports that are usually extremely fertile grounds for cross-examination.
- "Work product," "confidential," or "privileged." These terms make it appear as though the expert is trying to hide something.
- "Probable" and "possible." These ambiguous words should be avoided.
- "Substantially." This is another ambiguous word to avoid.
- "Obviously" and "clearly." These terms can be used to make the expert appear patronizing or presumptive.
- "Appears," "presumably," "supposedly," "is said," and "evidently." These terms imply uncertainty.
- "He," "she," "it," "they" and other pronouns. Pronouns are uncertain. It is best to use a proper noun.
- Royal "we." This can be used to make the expert look silly, pompous, or even dishonest.
- "It seems," "could," "apparently," "I believe," and other hedge words. It is always best to use confident language.
- "Complete," "thorough," "meticulous," "exhaustive," and other such words. These self-serving words will hold the expert and her report to an extremely high standard.

14.2 "Authoritative"

Stating that a certain reference is authoritative will usually allow the cross-examiner to question an expert about anything contained in the text in question. It is, therefore, usually best to exercise caution before admitting that any reference is "authoritative."

Example 14.21: Authoritative text
Report States:

> This impairment evaluation was performed according to the American Medical Association's *Guides to the Evaluation of Permanent Impairment*, which is an authoritative text in the area of impairment evaluation.

Resulting Cross-examination:

Q. Doctor, your report indicates that the impairment evaluation was performed according to the AMA *Guides*, correct?
A. Yes.
Q. You, of course, recognize the AMA *Guides* as an authoritative text?
A. Yes.
Q. Which edition?
A. The 4th edition.
Q. The 5th edition is an authoritative text as well?
A. Yes.
Q. Doctor, could you read the highlighted portion of the first paragraph of page 2 of the 5th edition?
A. "The 5th edition includes most of the common conditions…since this edition encompasses the most current criteria and procedures for impairment assessment, it is strongly recommended that physicians use this latest edition, the 5th edition, when rating impairment."
Q. You accept this strong recommendation as authoritative, correct?
A. Yes.
Q. But you did not follow it when performing your impairment evaluation?

Comment: If an expert states in his report that a text is "authoritative," he can expect questions similar to those in this example. It is better practice to exercise caution before admitting a text is authoritative.

> This impairment evaluation was performed according to the American Medical Association's *Guides to the Evaluation of Permanent Impairment.*

14.3 "Legal" or "Legally"

Most experts are getting beyond their true area of expertise when they discuss what is and is not legal in their reports. The expert's role is to assist the trier of fact. Legalities are best left to the attorneys and judge.

Example 14.31: Using the "'legal" definition
Report States:

> Using the "legal" definition, participants in futures markets who are not "hedgers" are speculators.

Resulting Cross-examination:

Q. According to your report, the legal definition of speculators are those who participate in futures markets who are not hedgers?
A. Yes.
Q. Can you please identify the text I am handing you?

A. Black's Law Dictionary. Sixth Edition.
Q. How many pages is this text?
A. It appears to be over 1,600.
Q. Can you please look up the term "speculator" in this 1,600-plus-page legal dictionary and read the definition you find to the court?
A. I can't find it.
Q. It's not in there, is it?
A. No.
Q. Where did you come up with your so-called legal definition of the term "speculator"?
A. It's common knowledge in my field.
Q. You didn't look up the term in a legal dictionary before using it?
A. No.
Q. And your report doesn't cite where you obtained this definition?
A. No, it doesn't.
Q. There really isn't a "legal" definition of the term "speculator," is there?

Comment: This expert would have been better served by removing the red-flag word "legal" from his report. A good cross-examiner will suspect that most experts are on very thin ground as compared to a competent attorney when legality is the topic. This expert would have been better off dropping the word "legal" from his report as follows:

> Participants in futures markets who are not hedgers are speculators.

14.4 "Draft"

Opposing counsel will immediately be alerted by the use of the term "draft" in an expert report. The use of this term immediately raises a number of questions. Were there any changes made subsequent to the issuance of the draft report? Why were these changes made? Did retaining counsel have any improper influence on any changes made? It is best to avoid these types of questions by not using the term "draft" in an expert's report.

Example 14.41: Draft—8/1/2001
Report States:
Draft—8/1/2001

Resulting Cross-examination:
Q. This is your 8/1/2001 draft report, correct?
A. Yes.
Q. This is not the first draft of the report, correct?
A. Yes, that's true.
Q. How many prior drafts were there?
A. Three.
Q. After you did each draft you sent them to Attorney Rogers, correct?
A. Yes.
Q. You then discussed them with her?
A. Yes.
Q. You made changes after those discussions?

A. Yes.

Q. Were any of these changes ones that Attorney Rogers did *not* ask you to make?

A. No.

Q. Did she put her suggested changes in writing?

A. No.

Q. Ever ask why not?

A. No.

Q. Did you correct typos at her suggestions?

A. Yes.

Q. Did you add sections that were missing?

A. Yes.

Q. Did you take out sections that were not supposed to be in there?

A. Not that I can remember.

Q. Well, let's take a look at them. Could you show me drafts one, two and three? The ones that were done before Attorney Rogers reviewed them?

A. There are not available.

Q. Where are they?

A. I destroyed them as a regular course of business.

Q. Did you discuss this with Attorney Rogers before you destroyed them?

A. Yes.

Q. Are they still on your computer hard drive?

Comment: Draft reports should not be issued to counsel. As the above example demonstrates, a draft report is an invitation for trouble.

14.5 "Work Product," "Confidential," or "Privileged"

Experts sometimes attempt to protect the confidentiality of their reports by including a clearly written notice that the document is subject to attorney client or work product privilege. Unfortunately, such a notice is not likely to have much effect on whether the forensic report will be protected from discovery. Worse, such a notice can be used against the expert to make it appear as though the expert has something to hide.

Example 14.51: Attorney work product
Report States:
> CONFIDENTIAL: ATTORNEY WORK PRODUCT

Resulting Cross-examination:

Q. Your report is stamped, "Confidential: Attorney Work Product"?

A. Yes.

Q. You are a testifying expert in this case?

A. Obviously.

Q. This is despite the fact that the court has ordered your work produced and discoverable.

A. I am not a lawyer, sir.

Q. But you attempted to hide your draft reports, chronology, statements, and investigation by stamping them, "Confidential: Attorney Work Product"?
A. I did what I was told to by counsel.
Q. Did you also follow counsel's instructions when forming your independent conclusions and opinions?

Comment: Writing "confidential" on a report will give the reader the impression that one has something to hide. It will have little, if any, effect on whether the report will ultimately be discoverable. It is, therefore, best to avoid labeling expert reports as "confidential," "privileged," or "work product."

14.6 "Probable" and "Possible"

The words "probable" and "possible" are ambiguous in nature and should be avoided. The expert would be better served by more precise language.

Example 14.61: "Probable"
Report States:
> It is probable that his injuries would have been substantially lessened.

Resulting Cross-examination:
Q. Your report indicates that it is "probable" that his injuries could have been substantially lessened, correct?
A. Yes.
Q. When you say "probable," you are not 100% certain, correct?
A. Yes, 51% or more sure.
Q. So, there is a 49% chance you are wrong?

Comment: This report would have been more persuasive and less vulnerable to attack had the expert used more precise language.

> It is my opinion, based upon a reasonable degree of medical certainty, that his injuries would have been lessened.

Example 14.62: "Possible"
Report States:
> The purpose of our investigation was to opine as to the possible cause and origin of water damage at the aforementioned premises.

Resulting Cross-examination:
Q. You opined in your report about the "possible" cause and origin of the water damage, correct?
A. Yes.
Q. Are you aware of the fact that the term "possible" in law means less than 51% and is legally insufficient for an opinion?

Comment: The word "possible" should be avoided.

> The purpose of our investigation was to opine as to the cause and origin of water damage at the aforementioned premises.

14.7 "Substantially"

"Substantially" is another ambiguous word which should be avoided. More precise, and therefore more persuasive, language should be used.

Example 14.71: "Substantially"
Report States:
> It is probable that his injuries would have been substantially lessened.

Resulting Cross-examination:
Q. How would you describe "substantially lessened" in a percentage form?
A. I am not sure.
Q. "Substantially" is not a medical term?
A. That's correct.
Q. Would it be more than 1%?
A. Yes.
Q. More than 2%?
A. Yes.
Q. More than 10%?
A. Yes.
Q. More than 50%?
A. Probably.
Q. Your opinion is more like an educated guess than a scientific, precise opinion, correct?

Comment: This report would have been more persuasive and less vulnerable to attack had the expert used more precise language.

> It is my opinion, based upon a reasonable degree of medical certainty, that his injuries would have been lessened to a degree whereby he would have had no permanent injury.

14.8 "Obvious"

The term "obvious" is another red flag for attorneys. A talented cross-examiner can use the expert's use of this term to make the expert appear patronizing and presumptive. Accordingly, this term should be avoided.

Example 14.81: "Obvious" what prevented return to work
Report States:
> It is obvious that this patient's severe cardiac status coupled with his myocardial infarction and open heart surgery are the major factors in prohibiting his return to work and his ongoing problems.

Resulting Cross-examination:
Q. You say it is "obvious" that the patient's severe cardiac status and his MI and open heart surgery prohibit his return to work, correct?
A. Yes.

Q. Dr. Arthur does not think that is obvious. As a matter of fact, he disagrees with your conclusion, doesn't he?
A. Yes, but he is wrong.
Q. Just like Dr. Cooper?
A. Yes.
Q. And Dr. Ralley?
A. Yes.
Q. And Dr. Kaline?
A. Yes.
Q. And the Social Security Administration, which concluded he could return to work?
A. Yes.
Q. It appears that the only physician who examined this patient and reached the conclusion he was disabled was you, correct?
A. Yes.
Q. Yet, in the face of all of this conflicting medical opinion, you stated he was "obviously" disabled?
A. It was obvious to me.
Q. Exactly, "obvious" to you and only you, correct?

Comment: A better way to present this opinion avoids the use of the term "obvious."

> It is my opinion, based upon a reasonable degree of medical certainty, that this patient's severe cardiac status coupled with his myocardial infarction and open heart surgery are the major factors in prohibiting his return to work and his ongoing problems.

14.9 "Appears"

The word "appears" implies to the reader that the writer is unsure of the facts. This uncertainty will lessen the persuasive value of the expert's report. Instead, more confident language should be used.

Example 14.91: "It appears that"
Report States:

> It appears that Mr. Hall's problems, particularly with his upper and lower back, are related to a chronic weakness of the musculature coupled with what appears to be some sort of fibromyalgia syndrome.

Resulting Cross-examination:
Q. Are you sure that Mr. Hall's symptoms are coupled with fibromyalgia syndrome?
A. Yes.
Q. But when you say it "appears" that they are, you are indicating less than 100% certainty?
A. Yes.
Q. How much less?
A. That's hard to say.
Q. Here you use the term "appears" twice when stating your diagnosis.

A. Yes.
Q. That would indicate even less certainty, correct?
A. Yes.
Q. How much less certainty?
A. That's hard to say.
Q. Apparently so.

Comment: This expert should have used more confident language.

> It is my opinion, based upon a reasonable degree of medical certainty, that Mr. Hall's problems, particularly with his upper and lower back, are related to a chronic weakness of the musculature coupled with what appears to be some sort of fibromyalgia syndrome.

14.10 "Presumably"

To presume is to assume. Invalid assumptions can call an expert's opinions into question. Experts should avoid making presumptions whenever possible. Their reports should be based upon verifiable facts.

Example 14.101: "Presumably"
Report States:
> Presumably, this did not include 1997 when she was at Nashville, TN.

Resulting Cross-examination:
Q. When you say "presumably," you are assuming that this did not include her 1997 stay in Nashville?
A. Yes.
Q. If this assumption is incorrect, you would change your opinion?
A. I would consider changing it.
Q. Why?
A. Because I based my opinion, in part, on this assumption.
Q. I show you this affidavit dated 7/11/2001 indicating, in fact, she was in Nashville in 1997 and had an incident there. Will you change your opinion?

Comment: This report would be more persuasive if it were based upon facts and not presumptions.

> According to the plaintiff's sworn deposition testimony (at 7), this did not include 1997 when she was at Nashville, TN.

14.11 "Evidently"

"Evidently" is another commonly used term that implies uncertainty. The expert's opinion will be more persuasive if the language in the report does not imply uncertainty.

Example 14.111: "Evidently"
Report States:
> Evidently x-rays of the entire spine were eventually taken and these are reported as being negative.

Resulting Cross-examination:
Q. You would agree that either the x-rays of the entire spine were taken or they were not?
A. Yes.
Q. If they were not taken, could they be negative?
A. No.
Q. So when you say "evidently" they were taken and were negative, what do you mean?
A. I was not there, counselor. I am just repeating what I was told by the patient.
Q. The patient is not a medical doctor?
A. Correct.
Q. He may be confused or mistaken about what some x-ray technician told him three years ago?
A. Yes.
Q. You cannot testify under oath here today that the x-rays of the entire spine were taken and they were, in fact, negative, can you?
A. Evidently not.

Comment: More certain language would have been more persuasive.

> X-rays of the entire spine were taken on June 6th, 1994. These x-rays were negative.

14.12 "Supposedly"

Experts often use the term "supposedly." This is yet another term that implies uncertainty and should therefore be avoided.

Example 14.121: "Supposedly"
Report States:
> These were supposedly to act as ineffective gutters to drain storm water.

Resulting Cross-examination:
Q. Someone told you that "these were supposedly" to act as ineffective gutters to drain storm water?
A. Yes.
Q. Who told you that?
A. My report doesn't indicate that.
Q. How many people did you talk to during the course of your investigation?
A. Approximately 17.
Q. Could it have been any one of them?
A. Yes.
Q. Could you have read it in some of the technical papers you looked at?
A. Yes.

Q. So, when you say "supposedly" they were to act as ineffective gutters, you have no real idea where they came from, do you?
A. As I stand here today, no.

Comment: This would have been better written and more persuasive had the expert not used the uncertain language. Instead, the expert should have provided a source for the reported information.

> According to the December 27, 1999, plans prepared by XYZ Engineering, these were to act as ineffective gutters to drain storm water.

14.13 "Is Said"

The term "is said" also implies uncertainty. The use of this term makes it appear as though the expert is obtaining the crucial facts upon which he bases his opinion from hearsay and rumor. This will negatively affect the persuasive value of the expert forensic report. The term "is said" should, therefore, be avoided and the specific source of information upon which the opinion is based should be laid out explicitly in the report.

Example 14.131: "Is said"
Report States:
> The system is said to be 40 years old.

Resulting Cross-examination:
Q. Is the age of the system significant in this case?
A. Yes.
Q. Who said the system is 40 years old?
A. I don't know.
Q. Did you rely on the assumption that the system is 40 years old in forming your opinion?
A. In part, yes.
Q. What steps, if any, did you take to verify the actual age of the system?
A. None.
Q. Do you normally accept unknown sources to supply you with significant facts upon which you base your conclusions and opinions?

Comment: "Is said" should not have been included in this report. The source of the expert's belief that the system was 40 years old should have been explicitly spelled out.

> According to my interview with Mr. Smith, the shop foreman, the system is approximately 40 years old. This interview was conducted on the day of my physical inspection of the premises, Sept. 6, 2001.

14.14 "He," "She," "It," "They," and Other Pronouns

The use of pronouns should be avoided. Pronouns make expert reports less explicit and can generate unnecessary confusion. It is better practice to identify all nouns explicitly.

Example 14.141: "She"

Report States:

> Ms. Paulson had shortness of breath at the scene and when her daughter, Lori, got to the scene, the situation had worsened and she had to be transported to the emergency room with a suspected myocardial infarction.

Resulting Cross-examination:

Q. Your report indicates on page 3, last paragraph, "Ms. Paulson had shortness of breath at the scene and when her daughter, Lori, got to the scene, the situation had worsened and she had to be transported to the emergency room with a suspected myocardial infarction." Is that correct?
A. Yes.
Q. Was it Ms. Paulson that was suspected of having a myocardial infarction?
A. No, it was her daughter Lori.
Q. So, when you say, "she had to be transported...," you were referring to Ms. Paulson or her daughter?
A. Sorry for the ambiguity. It was Lori, her daughter.

Comment: Who is "she"? Where, like here, there is more than one woman discussed in the report, it is not clear who "she" refers to. Clarity makes an expert report more valuable and reflects positively on the expert's credibility. The pronoun in this example should have been replaced with the actual name of the woman in question.

> Ms. Paulson had shortness of breath at the scene and when her daughter, Lori, got to the scene, the situation had worsened and Lori had to be transported to the emergency room with a suspected myocardial infarction.

Example 14.142: "It"

Report States:

> The incident occurred on August 1, 2001. There was water in the bottom of the trench. The soil was silt, sand, and clay. It was dry. This work involved the installation of 8-inch sanitary sewer.

Resulting Cross-examination:

Q. Page two of your report states, "There was water in the bottom of the trench. The soil was silt, sand, and clay. It was dry." Am I reading that correctly?
A. Yes, sir.
Q. There was water in the bottom of the trench?
A. Yes.
Q. And "it" was dry?
A. Yes.

Q. Now please forgive me as I'm not an expert like yourself, but could you please explain how soil under water is dry?
A. It isn't. What I was referring to was the other soil in the trench, not the soil on the bottom.
Q. You didn't say that though, did you? What you said was "it" was dry?
A. Yes, but it was implied.
Q. Did you intentionally not specify which soil you were referring to?
A. That's just the way I wrote it.
Q. Was it your intent to confuse people or were you just sloppy?
A. That's just the way I wrote it.
Q. Did you care whether or not anyone was confused?
A. I never really gave it any thought.

Comment: The use of the pronoun "it" in this example made the expert's report less precise. The report would have been much better if the expert had avoided the use of the pronoun and drafted his report with more precise language.

> The incident which resulted in Mr. Jones's death occurred on August 1, 2001. There was water in the bottom of the trench. The soil on the sides of the trench consisted of silt, sand, and clay. The soil on the sides of the trench was dry. The work Mr. Jones was participating in involved the installation of 8-inch sanitary sewer.

14.15 Royal "We"

Some experts use the word "we" when describing an investigation or conclusion that only they were involved in. This is known as the royal "we" and should be avoided. The royal "we" is not commonly used and use of it can make the expert look silly, pompous, or even dishonest. Unless more than one person was involved in forming the opinion, reports should be written in the first-person singular. Consider the following examples.

Example 14.151: Royal "we" for a one-person firm
Report States:
> After conducting an inspection, we came to the conclusion that the masonry work was defective and not up to code.

Resulting Cross-examination:
Q. Paragraph 2 of the report you signed indicates on the final page under the conclusion, "After conducting an inspection, we came to the conclusion that the masonry work was defective and not up to code." Is that correct?
A. Yes.
Q. What is the name of your engineering company, Mr. Evans?
A. Evans & Associates.
Q. How many associates accompanied you on that inspection, Mr. Evans?
A. None.
Q. So, when you used the term "we," is that a misstatement or the royal "we"?
A. I used the term "we" because it was a firm report of Evans & Associates.

Q. How many associates did you consult with in forming your conclusion?
A. None...It was just me.
Q. How many full-time associates are there in your firm?
A. None. We have part-timers.
Q. How many part-time employee associates are there in your firm?
A. Well...see...we call them in as consultants and contractors when needed.
Q. Did you say "we" call them in?
A. I...I call them in.
Q. Would it be fair to say, Mr. Evans, that "Evans & Associates" is essentially a one-man show?
A. Yes.

Comment: Counsel was very effective here in making the expert look dishonest by his use of the word "we." This report should have been written with the word "I."

> Based on a reasonable degree of engineering certainty, I concluded that the masonry work in question was defective and not up to code.

Example 14.152: "It was our information"
Report States:
> It was our information that Mr. Thomas was employed by TNT Builders and was working as a laborer in the construction of a home.

Comment: If only one person worked on this report it is far better to say:

> The information available to me indicates that Mr. Thomas was employed by TNT Builders and was working as a laborer in the construction of a home.

Example 14.153: "We"
Report States:
> We reconstructed the impact speeds of both the Mercury Sable and the Ford truck.

Comment: Avoid the royal "we."

> I reconstructed the impact speeds of both the Mercury Sable and the Ford truck.

14.16 "It Seems," "Could," "Apparently," "I Believe," and Other Hedge Words
Please see chapter 12 on using confident language and avoiding hedge words.

14.17 "Clearly" and "Obviously"
The use of the terms "clearly" and "obviously" may make the expert appear to be cocky, overconfident, or arrogant. They may also make the expert

appear to be acting as an advocate. In any event, these words do not add meaning to the forensic report and should be avoided.

Example 14.171: "Clearly"
Report States:

> ...[this] clearly reveals that the required feedback and evaluation step was lacking at Brown and Drecker.

Resulting Cross-examination:

Q. What is the difference between "reveals" and "clearly reveals" in terms of scientific certainty?
A. There is no difference, counselor, it's just an expression.
Q. So, this is your attempt to bolster your opinion and impress the jury without the benefit of any additional scientific evidence?

Comment: This report would have been more effective had the expert not "piled on" with the inclusion of the word "clearly." Deleting the word "clearly" makes this report seem more objective, less biased, and more credible.

> ...[this] reveals that the required feedback and evaluation step was lacking at Brown and Drecker.

Example 14.172: "Obviously"
Report States:

> It is clear that the discussion of "alternative type safety" envisioned the application of sequential trigger mechanisms to the ACME tool line. ABC and ACME personnel were obviously well aware of the enhanced safety of operation of pneumatic nailers when sequential trigger mechanisms were utilized.

Resulting Cross-examination:

Q. In your opinion, the ABC and ACME personnel knew of the safety effect of the sequential trigger mechanisms comment?
A. Yes.
Q. They were aware of them?
A. Yes.
Q. You used the words "well aware" merely as emphasis, correct?
A. Yes.
Q. "*Obviously* well aware" was also used for additional emphasis?
A. Yes.
Q. This was done to flag this for the judge and jury?
A. To emphasize it, yes.
Q. In case they overlooked it?
A. Well, yes.
Q. Do you think her honor and the good men and women of this jury needed this "help" to understand your opinion?

Comment: This expert's use of emphasis makes his report look less objective and therefore less credible. This expert would have been better served by avoiding the use of emphatic language.

The discussion of "alternative type safety" envisioned the application of sequential trigger mechanisms to the ACME tool line. ABC and ACME personnel were aware of the enhanced safety of operation of pneumatic nailers when sequential trigger mechanisms were utilized.

14.18 "Complete," "Thorough," "Meticulous," "Exhaustive," and Other Such Words

Words such as "complete," "thorough," "meticulous," and "exhaustive" when used to describe the expert's investigation and analysis can be extremely problematic. One problem is that the expert holds himself up to a very high standard when he uses these terms. Because these words generally do not make the report more persuasive, they should be avoided.

Example 14.181: "Complete and thorough"
Report States:
> The following opinion is based upon a complete and thorough examination of the documents submitted to me for this purpose. Any conclusions resulting therefrom can be based only upon the data submitted to me and an examination of same.

Resulting Cross-examination:
Q. You do two kinds of document examination, an incomplete and hasty one and a complete and thorough one, correct?
A. No.
Q. All of your document examinations are complete and thorough, correct?
A. Yes.
Q. You get paid by the hour?
A. Correct.
Q. So, the more complete and thorough, the more you get paid?
A. I get paid for the time I spend.
Q. The more time you spend, the more you get paid?
A. Yes.
Q. Are you certain that your examination was 100% complete and thorough?
A. Yes, I stated that already.
Q. Did you utilize the electrostatic detection apparatus (ESDA) to help decipher the indented writings?
A. No.
Q. Did you utilize thin layer chromatography to determine the kind of ink used?
A. No.
Q. What about paper chromatography electrophenisis, chemical spot tests, gas chromatography, or fourier transform infrared spectroscopy?

Comment: Self-serving descriptions of an investigation, such as "complete and thorough," do nothing to add to the persuasiveness of a report. Instead, the descriptions open up the expert to additional cross-examination. Such words should be avoided.

The following opinion is based upon my examination of the documents submitted to me for this purpose. Any conclusions resulting therefrom can be based only upon the data submitted to me and an examination of same.

Chapter 15 Proofreading for Mistakes

15.1 Executive Summary

Experts need to carefully proof their reports for mistakes. Each mistake made in a report will lessen the expert's credibility. Opposing counsel will argue that if the expert could make one mistake in his report, he may have made other mistakes and his entire report may be suspect. Common mistakes that need to be corrected in the proofreading process include:

- substantive mistakes,
- bad grammar,
- typographical errors, and
- misspelled words.

15.2 Substantive Mistakes

Outright mistakes by experts in their reports may not only result in their reports/testimony being excluded, but they may also be a permanent albatross hung on the experts' professional careers.

Example 15.21: Report with multiple mistakes stricken
In Re Bonham, 251 B.R. 113 (Bkrtcy.D.Alaska 2000)
The court showed its displeasure with an otherwise highly qualified expert and struck his report, which contained numerous mistakes.

> Elggren uses arguments which are undeniably fallacious or unsubstantial. For example, it is sophomoric to compare the high profits *realized* by certain mutual funds to those *promised* by debtors. And, suggesting that the debtors did not operate a Ponzi scheme because most Ponzi operations do not last seven years is a weak argument. There are a number of cases in which Ponzi schemes have lasted at least that long.
>
> …
>
> In short, I find that Elggren's report is based on substantial factual mistakes, speculation, innuendo, and inferences which are not supported by full explanations and analysis. It is not worthy of an expert of his caliber, nor worthy of admission as evidence in this case.
> His expert opinion will be excluded.[1]

15.3 Bad Grammar

Experts should check the grammar in their reports. Bad grammar in a report can be used by opposing counsel during cross-examination to lessen an expert's credibility. Opposing counsel will try to show that the bad grammar is a result of rushing, sloppiness, ignorance, or worse. Bad grammar in a report will also damage the expert's standing with and value to retaining counsel. To avoid grammatical errors, experts should have their reports

---

[1] At 135, 136.

proofed for grammar by both their computer word processor and a third person, such as a competent assistant.

Example 15.31: Sloppiness
Report States:
> EMTs arrived at the accident 4:47 P.M. to include Carol Stephenson, paramedic and Charlie Hess, intermediate.

Comment: This is sloppy work and damages the expert's credibility. The damage to credibility is avoided with a little grammatical proofing.

> The EMTs arrived at 4:47 P.M. The EMTs consisted of Carol Stephenson, paramedic, and Charlie Hess, intermediate.

Example 15.32: Improper tense
Report States:
> 1. Care by paramedics and intermediate EMS staff was appropriate.
> 2. All care provided by the Midland Medical Center staff including John Johnson is appropriate

Resulting Cross-examination:
Q. Can you please describe for the jury the treatment the plaintiff is currently receiving at the Midland Medical Center?
A. I'm not aware that he is continuing to receive any treatment at Midland.
Q. Doctor, I refer you to page 7 of your report, third paragraph, number 1: "Care by paramedics and intermediate EMS staff was appropriate.
All care provided by the Midland Medical Center staff including John Johnson *is* appropriate."
A. I apologize, that's just a little mistake. What that means to say is that the treatment provided *was* appropriate.
Q. You consider it a little mistake when you sit in judgment of a colleague with a distinguished twenty-five-year career and write in your report that the plaintiff is continuing treatment at a medical center that he hasn't been to in over three years?
A. It was a typo.

Comment: There is no getting away from the fact that the expert made a mistake. The mistake in his report will be used to show that the expert may have made other mistakes. The result is a needless loss of credibility. This could have been avoided with careful proofing.

Example 15.33: Missing apostrophe
Report States:
> Patients repeated serial examinations were unremarkable.

Resulting Cross-examination:
Q. What is the relevance of the other patients in this case?
A. Other patients?

Q. Doctor, I refer you to page 4 of your report, fourth paragraph, "Patients repeated serial examinations were unremarkable." Am I reading that correctly?
A. Yes, that should be "patient's" with an apostrophe. I am only talking about one patient.
Q. That's not what you wrote in your report, however. Your refer to "patients," plural, in your report.
A. That appears to be incorrect. I'm sorry for the confusion.
Q. That's not the only reason I'm baffled by your report. On page 6....

Comment: Here the expert is forced to apologize for confusing counsel. This is not a high point in his cross-examination testimony.

Example 15.34: Bad grammar
Report States:

> Dr. Davis examination of Mrs. Elderly was timely and complete in the privacy of her own home. Dr. Davis, not only a competent community physician but also a close personal friend of the family.

Comment: These sentences are unacceptable.

15.4 Typographical Errors
Experts should proof their reports carefully for typographical errors. Then they should have someone else proof their reports. Typographical errors in an expert report may indicate to the reader that the expert was rushed, sloppy, or did not take her assignment seriously. Consider the following examples.

Example 15.41: 12 packs of cigarettes per day
Report States:

> 12 packs of cigarettes per day for past 20 years.

Resulting Cross-examination:
Q. You took a careful history in this case, correct?
A. Yes.
Q. Did you take it yourself?
A. Yes.
Q. Did you carefully review the report after it was typed up?
A. Yes.
Q. Do you stand behind the accuracy of this report?
A. Yes.
Q. Your report says the examinee smoked 12 packs of cigarettes a day, correct?
A. No, that's a mistake.
Q. It may be a mistake, but that is what it says, correct?
A. Yes. It should read 1-2 packs of cigarettes a day.
Q. Can you tell us how many other mistakes there are in this report?

Comment: Typographical errors are 100 percent avoidable and absolutely must be eliminated from an expert report.

Example 15.42: Incorrect date
Report States:
> On 6/1/697 the neck mass was noted to be much smaller with no tenderness and the patient was instructed not to return in 2-3 months.

Resulting Cross-examination:
Q. Your report is replete with sloppy typographical errors, is it not?
A. No. That's just not true.
Q. When it reads, "on 6/1/697 the neck mass was…," that's a typo, correct?
A. Yes.
Q. On the next line when it says, "the patient was instructed not to return in 2-3 months," that's a typo, correct?
A. Yes. I had a new transcriptionist and she was not used to my style.
Q. Your report is in fact replete with typographical errors, correct?

Comment: Careful proofreading would have eliminated this embarrassing and damaging line of questioning.

> On 6/1/97 the neck mass was noted to be much smaller with no tenderness and the patient was instructed to return in 2-3 months.

15.5 Spelling

Spelling mistakes in an expert report are inexcusable. Because it is often difficult to proof one's own work, two persons, including the expert herself, should personally proof each report before it is signed. Any spelling error that is not caught will make the expert look sloppy or stupid and needlessly damage the expert's credibility. Consider the following example.

Example 15.51: Misspelling
Report States:
> This is exactly the seneiro in this patient.

Resulting Cross-examination:
Q. Doctor, did you conduct a careful investigation before forming your opinions and issuing your reports?
A. Yes.
Q. Did you feel that you were rushed in any way?
A. No.
Q. Did you carefully review your report for errors before it was submitted?
A. Yes, of course.
Q. Page 3 of your report, second line, states, "this is exactly the seneiro, s-e-n-e-i-r-o, in this patient." Am I reading that correctly?
A. Yes.
Q. What's a seneiro, doctor? I couldn't find the word in my dictionary.
A. That's just a typo, it is supposed to say "scenario."
Q. So what you're saying is that that's a mistake in your report, is that correct?
A. Yes.
Q. The report that you just testified was carefully reviewed by you?

A. Yes.

Q. Are there any other mistakes in your report?

A. I don't know.

Comment: The expert should have proofed the report and corrected the spelling error prior to signing the report.

This is exactly the scenario in this patient.

15.6 Run-on Sentences

Run-on sentences make an expert report difficult to read and may result in a needless loss of credibility. Please consider the following example.

Example 15.61: Run-on sentence

Report States:

It is my opinion that the design of the Brown and Drecker miter saw involved in Mr. Levon's incident was defective and inadequate from an engineering standpoint, and that Brown and Drecker was negligent in failing to use a proper guard to protect the user from foreseeable injuries in the expected, foreseeable use of this saw, in that Brown and Drecker failed to provide an adequate and effective lower blade perimeter and/or wraparound guard which would prevent exposure to the user in foreseeable uses, and which would be designed in such a way that it would not easily pivot out of position during cutting, including foreseeable kickback type incidents.

Resulting Cross-examination:

Q. In line eight of this sentence in your report you used the word "it," correct?

A. Yes.

Q. Could you tell us if the "it" refers to the saw or the guard, the user, Brown and Drecker, the lever blade, or the wraparound guard?

A. The saw.

Q. It's a little hard to tell due to the run-on sentence and lack of proper punctuation?

A. Yes. It could have been better written.

Q. Was this done intentionally to confuse the jury, or was it the result of sloppy work?

Comment: This damaging line of questioning would have been avoided had the expert taken the time to proofread his report and eliminate this run-on sentence.

It is my opinion that the design of the Brown and Drecker miter saw involved in Mr. Levon's incident was defective and inadequate from an engineering standpoint. Brown and Drecker was negligent in failing to use a proper guard to protect the user from foreseeable injuries in the expected, foreseeable use of this saw. Brown and Drecker failed to provide an adequate and effective lower blade perimeter and/or wraparound guard, which would prevent exposure to the user in foreseeable uses. This should have been designed in such a way that the saw would not easily pivot out of position during cutting, including foreseeable kickback type incidents.

Chapter 16 Defeating Counsel's Tactics

16.1 Executive Summary
Experts can expect counsel to use a variety of tactics when cross-examining them about their reports. What follows are 40 of the most frequently used tactics that the authors have encountered. Experts reading this chapter should keep in mind the following points:

- always tell the truth while testifying,
- take a moment when necessary to think about the tactic and its implication, and
- answer the question simply and directly.

The authors suggest that experts are best served by not trying to memorize the following tactics and replies. It is best to study the manner in which the replies are formulated to develop a style to handle the tactics one is likely to face. Experts can answer even the most difficult questions truthfully and, at the same time, artfully.

16.2 Tactics
Tactic 1: Dictated but not read
Counsel will try to make this simple, but ill-advised, statement into a major problem. If he can put the expert on the defensive and make her try to explain it away, i.e. "I was too busy to read the report," the expert can be made to look arrogant, sloppy, or even like a hired gun. The expert is advised to read and sign the report herself. If trapped by counsel with a prior report that is "dictated but not read," the expert should admit this was a prior practice that she no longer follows.

Example 16.21: "Dictated but not read"
Cross-examination:
Q. You were so interested in accuracy and professionalism that you did not bother to even read or sign this report, but you had your secretary do it?
A. That was my practice at that time. I changed that two years ago. I now read and sign all my reports to assure their accuracy.

Comment: Here the expert admitted his past practice and did not try to blame it on anyone else or offer excuses for it. This practice will help him avoid this tactic in the future.

Tactic 2: Counsel told expert what to say
Counsel can seriously undermine the integrity of the expert's report if she can demonstrate that the retaining attorney told the expert what to say. This tactic is a frontal assault on the credibility of the expert and should not be

permitted to go unchallenged. Experts are well advised to make sure the jury or fact finder understands the truth—that they and they alone are responsible for the opinions and conclusions in the report. If trapped by counsel, the expert needs to fight back.

Example 16.22: Counsel told expert what to say
Cross-examination:
Q. Attorney Jones retained you at $350 an hour, met with you on three occasions, explained what he needed in a report, and you gave it to him, didn't you?
A. I am being paid for my time and did meet with counsel. If you are suggesting that this led to my giving a false, dishonest, or misleading report, you are wrong. I have a 24-year history of integrity and professionalism and my integrity is not for sale, counselor.

Comment: The expert recognized this frontal assault and met it head on with one of his own. He did not permit counsel to leave the damning impression that retaining counsel told him what to say.

Tactic 3: Reliance on other expert's records
Counsel may try to trap the unwary expert by bringing into question his reliance on the reports of other experts in formulating his own report. Experts should be aware that under Rule 703 of the Federal Rules of Evidence, they are permitted to "reasonably rely upon the experts in the particular field in forming opinions or inferences upon the subject." If trapped by counsel, the expert need not fear admitting he relied on the reports of other experts.

Example 16.23: Expert did not read diagnostic study
Cross-examination:
Q. So you didn't read the CAT scan or mylogram yourself prior to commenting on it in your report, correct?
A. That's correct. As physicians, we customarily rely on such reports while treating patients.

Comment: The expert who understands that she can reasonably rely on reports of others in formulating her own opinion and report will not need to be defensive about doing so.

Tactic 4: Incomplete investigation
Counsel may attempt to discredit an expert, her report, and/or her credibility by attacking an alleged "incomplete investigation." To defeat this tactic, the expert should complete the investigation undertaken and be prepared to answer questions about what was done and why as well as what was not done and why. The expert need not concede that her investigation was incomplete

if that was not the case. If trapped by counsel with mistakes or omissions, the expert should concede the point and force counsel to move on.

Example 16.24: Did not personally measure the yaw marks
Cross-examination:
Q. When you went to the accident scene, did you measure the skid marks yourself?
A. Yes, I did.
Q. What about the yaw marks? Did you measure them yourself?
A. No, I didn't. I relied on the state troopers' measurements of the yaw marks.
Q. As your investigation was incomplete, why should I accept your conclusions and opinions?
A. My investigation was not "incomplete." I measured the skid marks, tire imprints, scuff marks, scratches, gouges, and holes myself. I relied on the state trooper accident reconstructionist for the yaw marks as I was not able to get at them because of the instability of the road.

Comment: When questioned about an "incomplete investigation," the expert should state what he did and did not do. The expert should not readily accept counsel's characterization of an incomplete investigation.

Tactic 5: Cross-examiner acts confused about statements in the report
Counsel may take the "Columbo" approach to cross-examination; that is, counsel might act bumbling or confused about the report. Counsel, using this tactic, is trying to elicit one of several responses from the expert:

- a long, detailed response that will provide additional information or material for cross-examination,
- a quick, inaccurate reply borne out of frustration, or
- a correction or a reframing of the question by the expert.

To defeat this tactic, the expert should remember that if counsel is confused, that is his problem. If trapped by counsel, the expert need not help counsel frame more precise or difficult questions.

Example 16.25: Expert does not volunteer information
Cross-examination:
Q. Latent fingerprints discussed in your report may be only of two kinds, correct?
A. No.
Q. You do mention plastic prints and visible prints in your report?
A. Yes.
Q. These are two kinds of latent fingerprints, correct?
A. Yes.
Q. Are there other kind of latent fingerprints not mentioned in your report?
A. Yes.

Comment: Here the expert did not fall for the confused counsel tactic. He did not try to help the lawyer better frame his questions. If, in fact, counsel knows about invisible prints, then it is a trap. If he doesn't, it is not the expert's obligation to inform or educate him.

Tactic 6: Royal "we," "and associates"

Counsel may pounce on a word or two in a 7-page report (for example "we" or "and associates") in an attempt to show the expert is exaggerating, sloppy, or lying. To defeat this tactic, an expert should not attempt to make his firm, investigation, or report sound more impressive by the use of these terms. If the expert conducted an investigation and/or writes a report himself, he should say, "I did...," not, "we did...." Similarly, if there are no employees or associates in a firm, the firm name should not read "Jones and Associates." If trapped by counsel, the expert should admit his mistake and force counsel to move on.

Example 16.26: "We" used in report prepared by one person
Cross-examination:
Q. You said "we" conducted a complete investigation. How many other associates of your firm were with you when you did the investigation?
A. None. It was just me.
Q. How many associates are there in your firm Jones & Associates?
A. It is just me.

Comment: Experts should avoid the royal "we" and the "and associates" in their reports and firm names when they are inaccurate or misleading. Having made that mistake, experts need to admit it without trying to justify the error.

Tactic 7: Meaning of term in report

Counsel may use a technical term in an expert's report to cast doubt on the expert's knowledge, expertise, or credibility. To defeat this tactic, experts should only use terms that they fully understand in reports. If trapped, the expert needs to be able to explain the term simply and precisely.

Example 16.27: Definition of "reasonable degree of medical certainty"
Cross-examination:
Q. You found permanent and total disability within a reasonable degree of medical certainty, correct?
A. Yes.
Q. Could you define reasonable degree of medical certainty?
A. Yes, more likely than not.

Comment: An expert who does not understand a technical term should not use it in her report. Likewise, experts should not use terms they cannot explain in their reports. Experts who understand terms and can articulate their definitions are better prepared to defend their reports.

Tactic 8: Unexplained abbreviations

Counsel can use unexplained abbreviations in an expert's report to attack both the expert and the report. The expert can be made to look arrogant or at least out of touch with the jury or fact finder who is desperately trying to understand the abbreviation. If counsel is able to show that the expert does not know precisely what the abbreviation stands for, his entire report and credibility can be called into question. To defeat this tactic, the expert should not assume that the readers know what abbreviations stand for and should spell them out in the report. If trapped by this tactic, the expert should apologize for the oversight and force counsel to move on.

Example 16.28: "ICSD"

Cross-examination:

Q. You stated in your report that the ICSD lists 14 different sleep disorders?

A. Yes, that's correct.

Q. What does ICSD stand for?

A. The International Classification of Sleep Disorders. Sorry, I should have spelled that out in the report.

Comment: Experts need to explain their abbreviations and be able to quickly and accurately define them. When an oversight is made, one should admit it graciously and force counsel to move on.

Tactic 9: Use of the third person

Counsel may bring up the fact that the expert's report is written in the third person (for example, "Professor Smith conducted DNA typing using the PCR process"). Counsel will use this awkward drafting to try and ridicule the expert. It is an attempt to make the expert look foolish and self-important and maybe to get him angry enough to make a testifying mistake. To defeat this tactic, the expert is well advised not to refer to himself in the third person in his report. If trapped by counsel, the expert should stay calm, smile, and admit his error.

Example 16.29: "Professor Smith conducted"

Cross-examination:

Q. You did write "Professor Smith conducted DNA typing using the PCR process" in your report on page 3, paragraph number one, correct?

A. Yes.

Q. Are you the Professor Smith you are referring to here?

A. Yes.

Q. Do you normally refer to yourself in the third person?

A. No (smiling), that was an error. It should read, "I conducted DNA...."

Comment: When questioned about this point, the expert recognized the tactic and its potential implications, stayed calm, and admitted her error. She did not exacerbate the issue by trying to defend her choice of words, blame others, or explain away the mistake.

Tactic 10: Expert's spelling attacked

Counsel employing this tactic will use one or more spelling errors in the report to make the expert look silly, sloppy, or indifferent. If counsel can accomplish any one of these three objectives, the expert's credibility can be damaged. To defeat this tactic, the expert should use spell-check, proofread the report, and, when possible, have another person proofread the report. If trapped, the expert, when questioned, should admit the mistake without being arrogant or getting into a protracted dialogue with counsel.

Example 16.210: "Egregious"

Cross-examination:

Q. In your report you concluded that the actions of the defendant were egergious....Is that a new technical term I am not aware of?

A. No. That is a typographical error. It should read "egregious."

Comment: The expert admits the error, forcing counsel to move on. Counsel who persists to question the expert about a typographical error runs the substantial risk of alienating the jury or fact finder by appearing petty.

Tactic 11: Hedge words attacked

Counsel will almost always pounce on an expert's report when it contains the hedge words "it seems" or "could." Counsel may often be successful in showing that the expert used these terms because she was unsure of her facts, assumptions, opinions, or conclusions. This line of cross-examination, if successful, can completely undermine the credibility of the expert and may lead to an outright rejection of her testimony as being speculative and thus inadmissible. To defeat this tactic, the expert should diligently avoid the hedge words "it seems" or "could" in reports or testimony. If trapped by counsel, the expert needs to briefly and succinctly explain what she meant and, if need be, that it was an error.

Example 16.211: "It seems"

Cross-examination:

Q. You state in your report on page 6 that "it seems" that the electrical fire was caused by overcurrent?

A. My opinion is that the electrical fire was caused by overcurrent.

Q. So the "it seems" portion of your report was written in error?

A. Yes. The report should read, "My opinion is that the electrical fire was caused by overcurrent.

Comment: The expert quickly recognized her mistake, the tactic, and its potential devastating implications. Admitting her error quickly and without permitting counsel to conduct a protracted and dramatic cross-examination was her best course of action.

Tactic 12: Investigation characterized as careful, detailed, and thorough
Counsel will use these self-serving comments in an expert's report to make
the expert look like he is immodest, exaggerating, mistaken, or even worse,
lying. The expert invites two substantial lines of cross-examination by these
characterizations:

> 1. proof that the expert mischaracterized the investigation, i.e., it
> was not, in fact, complete and thorough, or
> 2. that these words are without real meaning and were just used to
> make his report sound better.

To defeat this tactic, the expert should avoid characterizing his
investigation, analysis, forensic work, etc. in his report. If trapped by
counsel, the expert may be best served by "backing off" the characterization.

Example 16.212: "Careful, detailed, and thorough investigation"
Cross-examination:
Q. You state in your report that you conducted a careful, detailed, and
thorough investigation in this case?
A. Yes.
Q. You mention this because sometimes you do a careful job and sometimes
you don't?
A. No. I always conduct the most careful, detailed, and thorough
investigations and I note my reports with this fact.

Comment: Here the expert recognized the tactic and subtly backed off from the
comment. He did so without the need for a long explanation or any substantial
admissions or concessions.

Tactic 13: Expert reveals feeling
Counsel will use any statement in the report that tends to indicate bias or lack
of impartiality on the part of the expert. Three or four intemperate words in a
report can potentially taint the entire report and destroy the expert's
credibility. To defeat this tactic, experts are well advised to avoid these types
of remarks in their reports. If trapped by counsel, the expert will be forced to
either defend his impartiality and hang tough on his assessment or back off
his intemperate remark.

Example 16.213: "Defendant's conduct revolting"
Cross-examination:
Q. Your impartial and unbiased report states that you found the defendant's
conduct revolting?
A. Yes. A coach providing anabolic steroids to high school football players is,
in my opinion, revolting.

Comment: The expert is almost always better served by providing concrete, objective evidence in his report and letting the fact finder draw her own conclusions.

Tactic 14: Boilerplate language

Counsel will attack the use of boilerplate language in an expert's report to show that the expert's reports:

- are all the same,
- are interchangeable,
- are part of a hired-gun assembly line, or
- are ultimately not to be trusted or believed.

To defeat this tactic, the expert should limit or eliminate the use of boilerplate language in his report. If a certain amount of boilerplate language is required by necessity, custom, or the professional association the expert belongs to, the expert is well advised to:

- customize the language for each report,
- eliminate inapplicable boilerplate language on a case-by-case basis, and
- be able to articulate the meaning of the language and the reason it is used repeatedly.

If trapped by counsel, the expert needs to explain the reason for the use of the phrase, sentence, or paragraph, or admit his error and force counsel to move on.

Example 16.214: Report not reviewed to delete inapplicable boilerplate
Cross-examination:
Q. Your report indicates on page 4 that you personally examined the described articles and found them in good condition as listed in the appraisal, correct?
A. Yes.
Q. But this was a hypothetical appraisal so you didn't personally examine them did you?
A. No, I didn't. That phrase is in there because almost all of my appraisal work involves personal examinations. In this case, it should not have been in the report. It is my mistake.

Comment: The expert needs to carefully review her report for inappropriate boilerplate language.

Tactic 15: Prediction of future challenged

Counsel will attack predictions found in an expert's report in an attempt to show:

- the expert is outside her area of expertise,
- the prediction is no more than an educated guess and is therefore speculative and inadmissible, and
- the expert is imprecise or sloppy in one part of her report and thus her conclusions and opinions are not to be trusted or relied upon.

To defeat this tactic, experts should be cautious in offering predictions in their reports. If predictions cannot be supported by objective data to a reasonable degree of scientific certainty, they should not be included in the report. As a practiced matter, counsel who retained the expert will often push or pressure the expert for these types of predictions. Experts who wish to maintain their integrity, credibility, and be in the best position to defend their reports will not be bullied by retaining counsel into guessing about the future. If trapped by counsel, the expert needs to either support the prediction with hard scientific data or back off the prediction.

Example 16.215: Future medical care

Cross-examination:

Q. You said in your report that the plaintiff will likely require $100,000 of future medical care over the course of his lifetime based on $2,000 a year and a 50-year life expectancy.

A. Yes.

Q. That's assuming he does not get better, stop treatment, have corrective surgery, or die?

A. Yes.

Q. So, your $100,000 figure is just an educated guess?

Comment: Experts are best served by leaving predictions to psychics with 900 numbers.

Tactic 16: Failure to include all opinions in report questioned

Counsel will attack an expert's report that intentionally or unintentionally fails to include all of the expert's opinions. Here counsel will attempt to show that the expert:

- was following the instructions of counsel who retained him,
- had not completed his work when the report was filed,
- was trying to evade the disclosure requirements of Federal Rule of Civil Procedure 26 2(B), or
- was sloppy in his report.

To defeat this tactic, experts should generally include all of the opinions requested by counsel in their reports. Experts can add the following caveat to their reports: "if additional information becomes available, such information may change the opinions rendered in this report." If trapped by counsel, the expert should be prepared to explain why certain opinions were omitted from his report.

Example 16.216: Standard of care not addressed
Cross-examination:
Q. As an experienced expert you understand your legal obligations to disclose a "complete statement of all opinions to be expressed," correct?
A. Yes.
Q. Does your 4-page, single-spaced report include your opinion on the standard of care?
A. No, it doesn't.
Q. Why is that?
A. Because I will not be expressing an opinion on the standard of care, counselor.

Comment: Experts need to know prior to writing their reports what they will and will not testify to at trial. Experts will normally express the opinions they intend to offer at trial in their reports.

Tactic 17: Failure to state reasons for opinions
Counsel will closely question experts who fail to include the reasons for their opinions in their reports. Here counsel will try to show that the expert was being evasive, sloppy, trying to hide something, or playing cat and mouse with the legal system. To defeat this tactic, experts are best served by expressing their opinions with at least the basic reasons and rationale supporting the opinions. If trapped by counsel, the expert needs to be able to express a truthful, reasonable, and believable explanation of why she did not include her reasons for her opinions. The failure to do so could adversely impact one's credibility as an expert.

Example 16.217: Basis of opinions
Cross-examination:
Q. You expressed your opinion about the interpretation of the blood splatter patterns on page 2 of your report, correct?
A. Yes.
Q. You did not express the basis and reasons for this opinion in your report as required, correct?
A. That's not correct, counsel, my reasons for my opinions are expressed on pages 3, 4, and 7 of the report. They were not included under the opinion paragraph and perhaps that is why you missed them.

Comment: Experts need to be aware of and comply with the requirements of FRCP 26B(2) dealing with the disclosure of expert testimony: "The report shall contain a complete statement of all opinions to be expressed and the basis and reasons therefore; the data or other information considered by the witness in forming the opinions…."

Tactic 18: Disclaiming or limiting liability

Experts who attempt to limit their liability by putting disclaimers in their reports should anticipate close questioning by counsel about these disclaimers. Counsel will try to show, or at a minimum, imply that the expert is:

- unsure about her work,
- trying to escape potential legal liability,
- responding to past legal problems, or
- using boilerplate language.

To defeat this tactic, experts are advised to check with private counsel to see if the disclaimer would be effective. It is then and only then that the expert can intelligently perform a cost-benefit analysis and see if inserting the disclaimer is the best course of action. If trapped by counsel, the expert needs to be prepared to explain the disclaimer in a simple, yet forceful manner.

Example 16.218: Expert cannot be responsible for report

Cross-examination:

Q. You wrote a detailed 8-page report and stand by your opinions and conclusions, correct?

A. Yes.

Q. In the last paragraph you distance yourself from the report by saying, "Neither this appraiser, its parent company, nor any of its employees can be responsible for any action that may be taken on the basis of this report." This indicates that you don't stand behind your report?

A. This is the language adopted by the National Association of Jewelry Appraisers and, as I am a member, I include the phrase in my reports.

Comments: Experts should exercise caution when attempting to use disclaimers in their reports. In some cases they may do more harm than good.

Tactic 19: Personal note to counsel

Counsel will attack any personal notes experts include in their reports or cover letters. Counsel will try to show, or at the very least imply, that the expert is too friendly with retaining counsel. If counsel can convince the fact finder that the expert is biased or not taking his responsibilities seriously, the credibility of the expert can be eroded. To defeat this tactic, the expert should refrain from adding these personal notes, salutations, or other friendly passing remarks. If trapped by counsel, the expert will need to explain simply and quickly why the remark was made. Attempts to deny friendships or long-standing working relationships are usually a recipe for disaster.

Example 16.219: "Dear Teddy"
Cross-examination:
Q. Your impartial and unbiased professional report about Mr. Cooley, who lost his right arm in this accident starts off, "Dear Teddy"?
A. That's correct. I have the utmost respect for Mr. Cooley. I have known Attorney Jones for 10 years and he is a friend. That's why I didn't say, "Dear Mr. Jones" in my report.

Comment: Here the expert admitted the obvious without permitting counsel to conduct a dramatic cross-examination culminating with the admission of friendship.

Tactic 20: Opinion attacked as beyond the expert's true area of expertise
Experts can expect to be closely questioned about any opinions they express in their reports that are outside their true area of expertise. The further the expert moves out of his "sandbox" of expertise, the more vulnerable the expert becomes.

To defeat this tactic, the expert should stay within the area of expertise he feels most comfortable in. If trapped outside his area of expertise the expert has two choices:

- recede into his area of expertise while admitting he is not an expert in the controverted area, or
- hang tough while explaining why he does indeed have the requisite knowledge to opine in the area.

Example 16.220: Neurologist defends depressive disorder opinion
Cross-examination:
Q. As a neurologist, you were outside your area of expertise when you expressed the opinion in your report about the plaintiff's depressive disorder, correct?
A. No. I don't agree. As approximately 25% of my patients suffer from depression, I take continuing education psychiatric courses concentrating in depression. I teach my medical students about depression in the practice of neurology. I have co-authored two peer-reviewed medical journal articles on the topic and I am familiar with the mood disorders section of DSM IV. As I teach, write, conduct research, and treat patients with depressive disorders, I am an expert in the area.

Comment: Here the expert was able to articulate why, despite the fact that he is not a psychiatrist, he was testifying within his area of expertise.

Tactic 21: Superfluous remarks

Counsel will target seemingly innocuous statements in reports to show that the expert is too eager to please the retaining attorney. Counsel can then infer that the expert who is too eager to please the attorney is not impartial and may have given the benefit of the doubt to the retaining attorney. This is a serious accusation or implication and needs to be avoided or addressed. Counsel can be expected to inquire about the relationship with retaining counsel, past and future work for counsel, and the amount of money to be made if an ongoing relationship with counsel is maintained. To defeat this tactic experts should refrain from letting these types of remarks creep into their reports. If trapped by counsel, the expert can attempt to explain in a succinct fashion that she was just being polite.

Example 16.221: "I hope you find this helpful"
Cross-examination:

Q. You wrote this report to help counsel who retained you and who is paying your bill, correct?

A. No. I wrote the report to express my opinions.

Q. You do state in your report, "I hope you find this helpful," correct?

A. I did say that in the last line of my 13-page report. It is part of the salutation I have used for the past 17 years. I grew up in the Midwest and I was taught to be polite.

Comment: Here the expert was able to provide an innocent explanation for her comment.

Tactic 22: Opinions formed without the benefit of all the records/reports

Counsel can be expected to attack the foundation of the expert's opinions expressed in the report when the expert does not have access to all of the pertinent records/reports. Here counsel will attempt to get the expert to admit that:

- the reports/records may be important,
- the expert would have liked to have seen them,
- the reports/records could impact the expert's conclusions and opinions,
- counsel provided the records but omitted or failed to include the missing reports/records and, perhaps,
- the expert should have taken action to obtain the missing reports/records.

To defeat this tactic, experts are best served by listing in their report reports/records they reviewed and an explanatory comment dealing with the missing reports/records.

Example 16.222: Three key records missing
Cross-examination:
Q. You were missing three key records when you formed your opinion and issued this report, correct?
A. Yes. I stated in my report, page 4, last paragraph: "The records identified as missing should be identified and reviewed. If they become available at a later date, an additional report may be requested. The additional information may or may not change the opinions stated in this report."

Comment: While somewhat self-serving, the inclusion of the above statement dealt with the missing records and gave the expert the flexibility he needed when testifying.

Tactic 23: Blanket statements regarding literature
Counsel will target unsupported blanket statements in reports, i.e., that the expert's findings, conclusions, or opinions "are supported" by the literature. Counsel will try and show that:

- the expert is in fact unfamiliar with the literature,
- the blanket statement is an exaggeration or false, or
- in fact, the literature supports the opposite findings, conclusions, or opinions.

To defeat this tactic, experts should avoid making unsubstantiated comments in their reports about the state of the literature. Experts are better served by omitting references to the "literature" or, alternatively, by attaching a list of their references to their reports. If trapped by counsel, the expert needs to be able to testify effectively about the literature he referenced.

Example 16.223: Asked to specifically cite literature
Cross-examination:
Q. Your report indicates that in your opinion the birth injuries were a result of shoulder dystocia, correct?
A. Yes.
Q. You further state that this opinion is supported by the literature in the area?
A. Yes.
Q. Which literature is that?
A. Williams on *Obstetrics,* 2nd Edition, Allen, "Risk Factors for Shoulder Dystocia," *Obstetrics & Gynecology* (1991), and Megadari, "Engineering Analysis of Shoulder Dystocia in the Human Birth Process," *New England Journal of Medicine* (1992).

Comment: Here the expert was prepared to answer the inevitable questions about the state of the literature.

Tactic 24: Use of "I believe"
Counsel will attack an expert's report when the expert uses "hedge words" such as "I believe." Here counsel will try to show:

- that the expert is not sure of her facts, conclusions, or opinions,
- the testimony lacks the requisite scientific certainty to be admissible, i.e., reasonable degree of scientific certainty, or
- the expert is most likely mistaken.

To defeat this tactic, experts should make sure that they do not inadvertently let hedge words like "I believe" creep into their reports. When trapped by counsel the expert should be prepared to testify in such a manner as to clear up any ambiguity.

Example 16.224: "I believe"
Cross-examination:
Q. You stated in your report that you believe that the punch press was defective and unreasonably dangerous.
A. Yes. It is my opinion to a reasonable degree of engineering certainty that the punch press was defective and unreasonably dangerous.

Comment: Here the expert quickly recognized her poor drafting and the trap laid by counsel. She immediately corrected her report by using the correct phraseology in her testimony.

Tactic 25: Legal terms
Counsel can be expected to closely cross-examine experts who include legal phrases, opinions, or conclusions in their reports. Efforts may be made to prohibit the expert from so testifying at trial. Here counsel will try to show that:

- the expert has stepped outside of his impartial role as an expert and has assumed the role of an advocate,
- the expert is biased,
- the expert is a hired gun who has inadvertently slipped into legalese,
- the expert is not qualified to reach legal conclusions or opinions, and
- the expert cannot explain or define the term he has used.

To defeat this tactic, experts should stay within their areas of expertise and not offer legal opinions or conclusions in their reports. If trapped by counsel, the expert will either have to back off his legal characterization or back up his testimony with the correct explanation.

Example 16.225: "Grossly negligent"
Cross-examination:
Q. You stated in your report that you found the defendant's conduct was grossly negligent?
A. That's correct.
Q. Can you list the four basic elements of negligence?
A. Certainly—duty, breach, causation, and damages.
Q. Can you define gross negligence?
A. Yes. That's an actual or constructive intent to injure.

Comment: Here the expert was familiar with the legal phrase he used in his report.

Tactic 26: Speeches
Experts who make speeches or express personal opinions or beliefs in their reports (for instance, "Big polluters need to be held responsible or the planet as we know it is doomed") should expect close questioning about these comments. Here counsel will try to show that the expert:

- has an ax to grind,
- has let personal beliefs interfere with her professionalism,
- has beliefs that are opposed by some members of the jury, or
- is unscientific and exaggerating and is not to be trusted.

To defeat this tactic, experts should avoid expressing personal beliefs and their value systems. In addition, experts should avoid making speeches in their reports. If trapped by counsel, the expert needs to testify convincingly that her statement did not interfere with her impartial investigation, analysis, conclusions, and opinions.

Example 16.226: "Big polluters need to be held responsible"
Cross-examination:
Q. It's your opinion that big polluters need to be held responsible, correct?
A. I believe in rigorous scientific analysis prior to arriving at my professional opinions. If the defendant is found to be responsible for polluting, it is up to the jury to decide its fate.

Comment: The expert here attempts to deflect the fallout from his pronouncement. The expert would likely face additional follow-up questions.

Tactic 27: Examination or inspection took place long after the accident
Counsel can be expected to question experts who report on examinations or inspections that take place long after an accident. Here counsel is trying to show:

- the site has changed substantially,
- the expert or counsel was at fault for waiting so long to authorize the examination/inspection, or
- the examinations or inspections performed contemporaneously are more accurate than ones performed months or years later.

To defeat this tactic, the expert should try to do the exam/inspection as soon as practicable. Alternatively, if circumstances beyond his control force a delay, the expert needs to be able to accurately portray any changes or modifications that were made to the scene. If trapped, the expert needs to convince the fact finder that the delay had little or no impact on the examination/inspection, or if changes were made, that he accounted for them in his report.

Example 16.227: Scene visited one year post-accident
Cross-examination:
Q. As you didn't go to the scene until one year after the accident, your inspection, analysis, conclusions, and opinions are flawed, aren't they?
A. No. I reviewed the police reports, the reports of the accident reconstructionist, the photos, the witness statements, and the town hall for building permits. There were no changes to the scene between the time of the accident and the time I visited the scene. If you like, I can show you both sets of photos. They are identical.

Comment: The expert was able to explain why the one-year delay in the inspection did not affect the accuracy of her report, conclusions, and testimony.

Tactic 28: Changes from a draft report

Counsel can be expected to carefully compare the draft and final report to look for additions, modifications, alterations, and discrepancies. Counsel will try to show that the expert:

- was too hasty in her draft report,
- made a mistake initially, or
- was pressured by counsel or others.

To defeat this tactic, many experts do not issue draft reports. If time or circumstances make a draft report necessary, the experts leave themselves an out by adding a phrase anticipating these issues:

"This is a draft report. When more information becomes available, an additional report may be provided. Such information may or may not change the opinions contained in this draft report."

If trapped by counsel, the expert must be prepared to discuss why a draft report was issued and explain any discrepancies between the draft and the final report.

Example 16.228: Discrepancies between draft and final report
Cross-examination:
Q. In your draft report, you listed three findings for your suspicions that the claim was fraudulent, correct?
A. That's correct.
Q. In your final report, you listed six findings. Why the discrepancy?
A. Additional information was provided to me: identical claims were found, alterations were made to the document, and an address change was made to a post office box. These three additional findings were added to my initial three for the total of six in my final report.

Comment: The expert was able to explain the changes made to her draft report.

Tactic 29: Report mentions discussions with retaining counsel
Counsel will question any mention of discussions between the expert and the attorney who retained him. Here counsel will try to show that the attorney:

- unduly influenced the expert,
- pressured the expert, or
- had a substantial hand in drafting the report.

Proof of any one of these could destroy the credibility of the attorney and expert. To defeat this tactic, experts should not include statements about discussions with counsel in their reports.

If trapped by counsel, the expert needs to provide the innocent explanation for the discussion with counsel.

Example 16.229: Discussions with retaining counsel
Cross-examination:
Q. You mentioned in your report your discussions with counsel, correct?
A. Yes, that's correct.
Q. How many "discussions" did you have?
A. Three. He would call me and ask when I would get to the report. I would explain that I was busy and I would get to it as soon as I could.

Comment: Here the expert provided an innocent explanation for the discussions. Counsel might still try to pursue the matter by trying to show the expert was hurried or pressured due to time or being overworked with other high-paying forensic work.

Tactic 30: Expert asked to acknowledge a mistake

Counsel can be expected to review the expert's report for any kind of mistakes. Counsel will then confront the expert with the mistake in an attempt to:

- have the expert deny it,
- have the expert blame someone else for the mistake,
- rattle the expert,
- intimidate the expert, forcing other admissions out of her,
- show that the expert was sloppy,
- show the expert's indifference to the mistake, or
- show the expert is unaware of the mistake.

To defeat this tactic, the expert needs to carefully review her reports and have them reviewed by a knowledgeable third party before they are issued. If trapped by counsel, the expert should take a moment to see if the purported mistake is in fact an error. If it is, the expert should acknowledge it and force counsel to move on.

Example 16.230: Mistake made
Cross-examination:
Q. You stated in your report that the defendant had a paranoid personality disorder due to the three findings you made. This is a mistake, correct?
A. I did. That was an error. Under DSM IV Diagnostic Criteria 301.0 four findings are required. I failed to note that the defendant persistently bears grudges. That was the fourth finding.

Comment: The expert quickly recognized the tactic and his mistake. He acknowledged the error and corrected it.

Tactic 31: Comments on the veracity of another expert

The expert can expect to be confronted about any comments she makes in her report about the veracity of another expert. Here counsel will try to show that the expert is:

- acting as an advocate,
- not impartial,
- improperly denigrating another professional,
- acting unprofessionally herself, or
- complying with a request by retaining counsel to "tear down" the opposing expert.

To defeat this tactic, the expert should refrain from putting these types of remarks in her reports. If trapped by counsel, the expert will probably want to subtly back off the tone of the remarks while still maintaining their substance.

Example 16.231: Veracity of opposing expert questioned
Cross-examination:
Q. You state in your report that you question the findings and veracity of Mr. Dean, the expert retained by the defendant, correct?
A. I do not agree with his findings at all. The plaintiff here has had three back surgeries and has an implantable pain device. To conclude that there is nothing wrong with him medically and he is cleared to return to heavy lifting of 50-100 lbs. makes no sense to me at all.

Comment: Here the expert recognized the tactic and wisely did not comment directly on her veracity statement. She was able to do so while still standing behind her findings by explaining the factual basis for her conclusions.

Tactic 32: Challenge on estimation
Counsel can be expected to challenge the expert who, in his report, bases his opinion and conclusions on an estimation. Here counsel will attempt to show that the expert was:

- sloppy,
- lazy,
- eyeballing a measurement,
- incorrect, or
- untrustworthy.

To defeat this tactic, the expert should only rely on estimates in his reports when there are no reasonable alternatives. If trapped by counsel, the expert needs to be able to explain simply and convincingly why he made and relied on the estimate.

Example 16.232: Estimated value
Cross-examination:
Q. Your report is based on an estimate of the value of a 2.5-carat diamond which you never personally examined, correct?
A. That's correct. The diamond in question was stolen and not available. I based my estimate on the numerous excellent photographs of the diamond, the sales receipt, the insurance binder, and the jeweler who sold the piece. This was a hypothetical appraisal and I noted on page 1 of my report the reasons for my need to make certain estimates.

Comment: Here the expert explained the valid reasons why he was forced to use his estimate in reaching his opinions and conclusions set forth in his report.

Tactic 33: New developments, research, or information

Counsel can be expected to question the expert about new developments, research, or information that became available after the writing of the report. Here counsel is attempting to show that the expert:

- did not consider this information,
- has not recently updated his report,
- may not be interested in the truth,
- is not current, or
- may simply be wrong.

To defeat this tactic, the expert should update his report if there is a long lag time between the time the report was prepared and the trial. If this is not practicable, the expert should, at a minimum, be brought up to date immediately prior to his testimony. The expert should insist that retaining counsel be forthcoming with all the information. If trapped by opposing counsel, the expert should admit he has not had the benefit of the new information, but he should not be too quick to admit he would change his opinion based merely upon the characterization of counsel.

Example 16.233: Missing records

Cross-examination:

Q. Your finding of no psychiatric overlay was made without the benefit of the record of the plaintiff's three-week involuntary commitment after his suicide attempt. This additional information would change your opinion, correct?

A. I would consider it. I do not know how it would impact my opinion in this case.

Comment: Here the expert admitted he would consider it but did not immediately back off his opinion based upon a characterization by counsel of records he has never seen.

Tactic 34: Labeling the report confidential

Counsel can be expected to pounce on expert reports that are labeled "confidential." Here the attorney will try to show that the expert:

- is trying to hide something from the judge, fact finder, or opposing counsel,
- is following the instructions of retaining counsel, or
- is sneaky or dishonest.

To defeat this tactic, experts are well advised not to label their reports as confidential. As a practical matter, this label carries no weight. (See section 14.5 on confidentiality.) If trapped by counsel, experts need to explain simply and convincingly why they labeled their reports confidential.

Example 16.234: "Confidential"
Cross-examination:
Q. You labeled your report "confidential" in large red block letters to hide it from the jury, didn't you?
A. No. As I reviewed the personal, medical, and substance abuse records of the defendant, I wanted to make sure that only those persons authorized by the court would have access to the report. I was attempting to protect the confidentiality of your client, counselor.

Comment: The expert convincingly explained why he labeled his report confidential.

Tactic 35: Ethical violations
Counsel can be expected to closely question experts on any potential deviations from their ethical standards that are revealed in their reports. Here counsel is trying to show that the expert is:

- unethical,
- untrustworthy,
- unprofessional,
- cutting corners, or
- completely lacking in credibility.

To defeat this tactic, experts are advised to exercise great care in not engaging in unethical activities or even giving the appearance of impropriety in their reports. If trapped by counsel, the expert needs to deal with the charge head-on due to the potentially devastating impact on the jury or fact finder.

Example 16.235: Denial of ethical violation
Cross-examination:
Q. As a member of the Association of Certified Fraud Examiners, you agreed to be bound by the Association Code of Professional Standards, correct?
A. Yes.
Q. You violated ethical standards III C(4) when you permitted your assistant to work on the investigation and the report without adequate supervision, correct?
A. That's not true. Number 4 of the Code of Ethics states, and I quote, "Work performed by assistants on a fraud examination shall be adequately supervised. The extent of supervision required varies depending on the complexities of the work and the qualifications of the assistant."
My assistant has 32 years of forensic fraud experience. He is a former FBI agent specializing in white-collar crime. Despite his wide experience, I supervised his work closely. Counselor, I did not violate the Code of Ethics and I resent your question.

Comment: Here the expert recognized the seriousness of the tactic and the seriousness of the charges. He responded in an informed, powerful manner to rebut the charge.

Tactic 36: Taking a section of a report out of context

Counsel often will read a section of the expert's report as part of his cross-examination. Counsel may take the excerpt of the report out of context. To defeat this tactic, the expert should demand to review the complete report. This serves three important purposes. First, it breaks up the cross-examining attorney's rhythm and thus makes his cross-examination less effective. Second, this allows the expert time to prepare a thoughtful, considered response. Finally, this allows the expert time to review the document and verify that counsel is not taking the portion of the report out of context. If trapped by counsel, the expert should point out how the lawyer took his statement out of context.

Example 16.236: Section of report taken out of context
Cross-examination:
Q. You did say in your report, did you not, that the driver was not wearing his seat belt prior to the accident?
A. Where are you referring to?
Q. Page 3, first paragraph.
A. May I see that please?
Q. OK.
A. (Pauses and reviews.) You're taking that out of context, sir. What I went on to say was that in this particular case, had the plaintiff been wearing his seat belt, his injuries actually would have been more severe.

Comment: When questioned about an expert report, the expert should demand to see the report and affirmatively counter any instances of taking portions of the report out of context.

Tactic 37: Mischaracterizing the report

Counsel may often read a section of a report and intentionally or unintentionally mischaracterize it. To defeat this tactic, experts should ask to see the report if they suspect mischaracterization. If trapped by counsel, the expert should point out how counsel has mischaracterized the testimony.

Example 16.237: "History of mental illness"
Cross-examination:
Q. You stated in your report that the plaintiff was crazy, didn't you?
A. Where are you referring to?
Q. Page 7, third paragraph.
A. May I see that, please?
Q. OK.
A. (Pauses and reviews.) I never said that, counselor. You are mischaracterizing my report and misleading the jury. What I said was, quote,

"The plaintiff had a history of mental illness," unquote. There is a big difference between that and being crazy.

Comment: This expert's response was extremely effective. He reviewed the language in question and did not allow counsel to mischaracterize his report.

Tactic 38: Sarcasm
Counsel may employ sarcasm for one of three reasons when cross-examining the expert about her report. Counsel hopes to upset the expert so she cannot think clearly, wants to embarrass her before the jury or fact finder, or seeks to pressure her into making an admission or mistake. To defeat this tactic, the expert needs to remain calm, self-assured, and confident. If trapped by counsel, the expert should ignore the sarcasm, thus making the lawyer look foolish.

Example 16.238: Foreign medical school
Cross-examination:
Q. You obtained your medical degree from a foreign medical school because you could not get into one in the United States, correct, doctor?
A. Yes. My residency was at Johns Hopkins and I had additional training at Mass General Hospital.

Comment: Here the expert answered the question calmly, directly, and without embarrassment. He softened its impact with some additional pertinent details. Counsel is now forced to move on.

Tactic 39: Cheap shots
Counsel may use any one of a number of cheap shots to get a rise out of or distract an expert when he is testifying. The expert should recognize the tactic for what it is, remain calm, smile, and stay focused. If trapped, the expert may also, when appropriate, turn the tactic against the lawyer.

Example 16.239: Collusion with counsel
Cross-examination:
Q. You were strategizing with plaintiff's counsel immediately prior to your testimony, weren't you?
A. I said good morning to her, counselor, just like I said good morning to you, if that's what you mean by strategizing.

Comment: Here the expert remained calm, recognized the cheap shot, and turned it around on counsel.

Tactic 40: Typographical errors
Counsel may use typographical errors in an expert's report to show that the expert was sloppy or lazy. If counsel can get the expert to "blame" the typo on someone else, the expert can also look guilty for failing to accept

responsibility for the error. If trapped by counsel, experts should admit the error and accept responsibility for it, giving counsel nowhere to go and forcing him to move on.

Example 16.240: Date typed incorrectly
Cross-examination:
Q. You say that the plaintiff was born on 3/17/04? That would make her how old?
A. That's a typographical error I should have caught when I proofread the report. It should read 3/6/48—she is 53.

Comment: The expert admitted the mistake, accepted responsibility for it, and forced counsel to move on. Additional questioning about the typo by counsel would probably be counterproductive.

Appendix A Advice from the Trenches

This appendix contains advice regarding the drafting of expert reports from experts and attorneys across the country. The authors would like to express their profound thanks to those who provided their thoughts so that others could benefit.

Terrance L. Baker, MD
Columbia, SC

1. Always perform a complete review of all available facts before rendering a final report to your attorney client. If preliminary opinions are requested, clearly state the facts that have been reviewed to date and state clearly areas of review still open secondary to ongoing investigation and discovery.
2. Always tell the truth. Never exaggerate nor embellish as this will usually come out during deposition and or cross-examination.
3. Do what you say you are going to do. Be an expert of your word. Timeliness of communications and timeliness of preparation of reports is very important. Meet any and all deadlines established by the attorney or yourself for producing reports, i.e., interim reports and/or final reports.
4. Make sure counsel is aware that you will need access to all materials in the case. Guard very carefully against attorneys who selectively give you facts and data upon which they desire you to render an affidavit and/or a final report. During deposition and cross-examination, your reliance on only partial facts in the case will severely limit your ability to present the trier of facts with any meaningful opinions.
5. Make sure the attorney understands what you are saying. Communicate, communicate, communicate—both written and orally. It is your job as an expert to insure that your attorney client understands both the strengths and weaknesses of the defense or plaintiff position in your reports. Always communicate case strengths and case weaknesses with your attorney.
6. Make sure you clearly understand what questions the attorney is looking for answers to in your report. A report that answers many questions but does not address those specific areas and questions identified by the attorney client is of little or no benefit to that client, in fact, it may be harmful by addressing areas or

bringing areas to light that your attorney client did not desire to develop for reasons that perhaps you are not able to understand since the attorney as the "quarterback" has a broader picture of both the case facts, case law, and his ability to demonstrate to the trier of fact, specific points on behalf of his client. Therefore, be very careful in your reports to address only those areas identified by your attorney client.

7. Communicate regularly with your attorney prior to the preparation of your final report to discuss theories that are evolving as to the facts and the events that occurred.

8. An expert's report should be organized, easy to read, easy for virtually anyone to understand. Remember that the attorney client and the opposing counsel have little or no education in the area of your expertise and therefore, your report should be worded in such a way that lay individuals can understand what it is that you are attempting to say and report and the opinions that you are rendering.

9. Keep your billing charges current From time to time, if accounts are not kept current, an expert may find himself performing case evaluation and review and preparation of reports for which he will not be compensated.

10. Review your final report personally for grammar, spelling, and typographical errors.

11. Establish a format for your area of specialty and follow that format whenever preparing reports so that you don't forget any of the basic areas including when, why, where, what, who.

In conclusion, reports that are well-written, following a format that is easy to follow are clear to virtually anyone reading it and are easy to defend. Facts stated in the report which reflected truths are easy to present and resistant to cross-examination as the truth always stands strong no matter what the attack may be. My experience has been that the truth, time and time again, will prevail. Reports that are clear and easy to understand and follow a flowing sequence and clearly describe the events and questions being investigated, the resources and materials that have been studied in preparation for the opinions formed, a brief statement of your qualifications, and a clear and concise statement of each of your opinions, will weather any storm and any amount of cross-examination time and time and time again. Also, in years to come, when subsequent attorneys review your reports which undoubtedly will be attached to the deposition and court records, time and time and time again your reports will stand clear as to the quality of your investigation, the quality and clarity of your opinions, and will serve as an excellent advertisement for future attorney clients.

Richard Carman
Puyallup, WA

Why does report writing seem like such a drudgery to many of us? After all, it is a major portion of any investigator's job responsibility. I realize that we sometimes forget, report writing is as much a part of our job as examining, photographing and sketching the scene or interviewing witnesses and suspects. Having authored thousands of reports in my thirty-three years with the Puyallup Fire Department, I have had plenty of experience in this area. I have also experienced "writer's block" on many occasions. That is, I did, until I began using a specific format to develop my reports. This format may not be acceptable to, or, work for everyone. I can only say it works for me and my staff.

What is a supplementary report?
Funk and Wagnalls defines supplement as: "To make additions to; provide for what is lacking in. Something that supplements; especially, an addition to a publication."

This is not an article about completing "Washing Fire Incident Reporting System" forms or "Fire Fighter's Observation Reports" forms. The methodology presented here, however, can be used by company officers and others who are responsible for completing the supplemental portion of either of those reports.

I refer to our investigative reports as supplemental because we generally author them as a result of an initial response by a fire company or police patrol officer, or, both. If we respond to and investigate an incident that is not the result of another agency response, we call them simply, "Fire Investigation Report."

Why is it so essential to author a report?
Once you have left the scene and it has been physically altered, your report is the only representation of what you and others saw, thought and accomplished. Your report becomes a historical record.

Why is it so essential to author a report that is clear, concise, accurate, and complete?
It is my opinion there are myriad reasons to do this. However, in an effort to be clear and concise, I will discuss what I believe are the three most important reasons.

1. To ensure the reader is presented with the most factual information possible; in a manner that is easy to comprehend.
2. Your report is a representation of your personal intelligence and abilities. It is automatic for the reader, no matter what their

reason for reading a report, to judge the author through his ability to communicate.

3. Credibility. If you must discuss or refer to the incident at a later date, which may be a period of years, your report represents, not memory, but the facts as you presented them at the time the incident occurred.

<u>Who may read your report?</u>
1. Your supervisors (who are also your evaluators)
2. Law enforcement
3. Attorneys
4. Prosecutors
5. Judges and Jurors
6. Owners
7. Insurance Agents
8. Insurance Adjusters
9. Insurance Investigators
10. Plaintiffs/Defendants
11. Experts, such as:
     i. Electrical engineers
     ii. Mechanical engineers
     iii. Architects
     iv. Code enforcement agencies
     v. Contractors

To command respect and maintain credibility, your report must be well written with correct grammar, proper spelling and contain well-established factual information.

<u>What is the single most difficult problem associated with authoring a report?</u>
Getting started. Sometimes referred to as "writer's block." I have authored well over 4,000 reports during my career and for years suffered from "writer's block."

Over the years I have been introduced to many different types of formats that may be used to form the outline of a report. Since I began using this format, I have not experienced writer's block.

Paul Dorf, APD
Upper Saddle River, NJ

I have had the opportunity over the years to review, and in several cases, refute other experts' reports. A common theme is a proliferation of a mass of data or footnoted case studies, much of which are of dubious value.

In my estimation, the role of the expert is to conduct a thorough, systematic, and completely objective review and examination of all facts necessary to render an opinion. This process begins with a technique of conducting comprehensive research and examining all facts thoroughly. Only after undertaking this process can an unbiased, defensible conclusion be reached.

My experience, covering more than 20 years as a qualified expert in compensation matters in which I have researched and prepared expert reports, has supported the theory that one of the most important ingredients in developing a strong and defensible report is a systematic approach that is consistently applied. In order to accomplish this, a detailed workplan covering the scope of the assignment must be developed. This workplan would contain key dates relating to discovery, interrogatories, depositions and trial. It would identify all deliverables, including a report of preliminary findings and, finally, the actual Expert Report. Based on the workplan, the expert would be able to produce an Initial Request for Documentation, which identifies the initial line of research and the various documents that need to be reviewed by the expert in order to begin the case analysis.

As documentation is received by the expert, the process of accurately cataloging and carefully reviewing the data begins. This process must be a very disciplined endeavor in order to ensure that the information is secured and properly identified. One advantage of this process is that it focuses the expert on the data, thus avoiding a rush to judgment until all of the facts of the case have been clarified, sorted through, and sufficiently examined.

The next step in the process is to establish the key hypotheses that will be explored in the course of the study. It is possible that some of these hypotheses may prove to be inaccurate or inappropriate areas of exploration, but it is very important to identify all possible scenarios initially and then examine each one in an orderly, methodical fashion. Although every expert has undoubtedly taken at least one or more courses on report writing, it is critical to begin the report writing process by preparing a detailed outline of the primary areas of discussion and then expand each section as research develops. This in itself will not only keep the report on track, but will allow the expert to maintain the "theme" of the report so they don't miss any of the important elements that need to be included and that the focus of the report is clear. As the research is developed, the intention is to determine how to present the report in the most clear, articulate and systematic fashion that will present information in a way that will best clarify the issues. There is, unfortunately, a tendency for experts to sometimes become "overly impressed" with their own words and forget what they were intending to report. Occasionally, they actually create their own minefields. To that end, I believe it is always best to have an independent, but knowledgeable, individual review the report from the standpoint of identifying weak areas, as well as any areas that could potentially pose problems and loopholes in the report itself, (i.e., consistencies, advocacy, lack of objectivity, etc.). While it is important to identify all of the data that supports the conclusion, it is equally important to insure that the report and findings are properly documented, footnoted, and most of all, are consistent with other conclusions that the expert has reached in the body of the report, as well as in past reports and written material which the expert has prepared.

The key to writing and defending an expert report is for the expert to truly be an expert, to follow a very systematic and consistent methodology both in research and preparation of the report, and finally, to have the report reviewed not only for typographical errors, but for substance. Lastly, the expert must always maintain his or her integrity as an expert. Inconsistencies of data and an unsupported conclusion, all contribute to leaving an expert report open and indefensible.

Beatrice Engstrand, MD, FAAN
Huntington, NY

My advice to write and defend an IME report is as follows:

1. Always review all medical records.
2. Stick to and emphasize objective data.
3. Keep moral judgments out.
4. Dictate and send reports out as quickly as possible.
5. Discuss any confusing points with the company or lawyer that sought your opinion.
6. Try to extrapolate future problems of increased disability. For example, a head trauma patient who has not yet had a seizure might develop a seizure disorder in the future. Head trauma predisposes to seizures. "He also faces the strong risk of developing a seizure disorder years out from this trauma as a result of his cerebral scar tissue."

Vince Gallagher
Audubon, NJ

The advice I would give to colleagues would be to state your methodology of evaluation and then perform an evaluation based on that method.

My experience after having reviewed hundreds of expert reports is that it is very rare for an expert to be explicit in the body of their report relative to the method that they use. I think this is what *Daubert* and *Kumho* were trying to get at. The court looks for a consistent and reliable methodology of evaluation. That is, they look to see what the expert considers to be the "standard of care." You will see in my report in paragraph V, I state the methodology of evaluation, and in paragraphs VI and VII, I set forth what the authorities say relative to who is supposed to do what and why.

I also ask my attorney to be clear as to what specifically I am being asked to do. In plaintiff's cases, it seems to me that the report should be written based on an assignment to consider the conduct of the defendants relative to responsibility for the injury. In order to do that, the evaluator has to consider the conduct of the employee and others. But rather than writing a very broad report giving opinions about all possible entities that could share some responsibility, it is more efficient to limit the assignment to the evaluation only of the entities being sued. During the deposition, the expert must be prepared to answer questions about the responsibility of the plaintiff, the employer, and any other entities which appear to have some responsibility.

When questioned by the defense attorney why I did not consider the conduct of the plaintiff or others in my report, I simply state that I was not asked to do so. I further state that I could not help but consider the conduct of the plaintiff and other entities when I did my evaluation. I simply didn't comment on it in my report because I was not asked to. However, I say that I would be glad to answer any questions in that regard.

I think it is also important for the expert to make clear when he/she bases opinions on certain assumptions. It is not unusual that there is conflicting testimony by witnesses. The expert does not have expertise in determining the veracity of sworn statement by witnesses who testify to different things. However, the expert's opinion should vary depending upon which facts are assumed. I think the expert should make it clear as to what testimony is assumed to be true and what testimony is assumed to be incorrect. If the expert has good reason to accept one witness over another, that could be stated. However, the expert should be quite willing to change his/her opinions based upon assumption of different facts.

I think the expert should never comment on the other expert's report by making personal attacks.

WRITING AND DEFENDING YOUR EXPERT REPORT

Richard S. Goodman, MD, FAAOS
Smithtown, NY

To write and defend a report or testify, read the report back to yourself, listen objectively and discern any incongruities or ambivalent terms which are open to cross-examination.

One of the ways to avoid ambiguities is to use short sentences, whereas compound sentences tend to leave the question open to interpretation. Second of all, answer the questions in a truly denotative form for which the testimony, the report and the transcription by the court reporter, leaves nothing to the imagination with no ambiguities or conflicts. Be sure that Roget's Thesaurus has been entered as an authoritative book on the English language and the use of synonyms between the report, deposition and trial testimony does not affect the concept being carried across. Another example of the use of Roget's Thesaurus is when one is asked to make an estimate in reply to certain questions. Remember that the definition of an estimate is that of a "guess."

Andrew E. Greenberg, Esq.
Philadelphia, PA

The report should describe the information reviewed, the analysis applied, and the conclusions drawn from the review.

In contemplation of the foregoing, I believe that the following thoughts should be considered:

1. Do not simply regurgitate the information provided— that approach wastes time, suggests a lack of analysis, and translates into an unnecessarily long and dull court presentation;
2. On the other hand, it is important to describe—perhaps with bullets—all of the information considered in performing the analysis;
3. Set forth with specifics the nature of the analysis undertaken;
4. Address the question presented—do not attempt to impress with irrelevant, unrequested, or unnecessary opinions. Be efficient.

My clients find it particularly disturbing when it appears that the expert has prepared the report without knowing precisely what issue he or she is to address or without taking the time to contact me in order to determine precisely what issue he or she is being asked to address. When, in disregard for that consideration, the expert issues an initial report and requires a request for a supplemental report in order to address the specific issue in question, the client typically becomes disenchanted with the expert's inefficiency, lack of cooperation, and apparent desire to incur additional charges.

It is also important that the expert be candid by conceding where to conclude, otherwise it would suggest an unreasonable effort on the part of the expert to act as an advocate for the retaining party.

Tom Gutheil, MD
Brookline, MA

Here are some thoughts. Please also feel free to turn to Chapter 8, "Writing to and for the legal system" in "The Psychiatrist as Expert Witness," Wash., DC, APPL, 1998, where there is extensive discussion of some of these main points.

The written forensic report, like transcripts of trial or deposition testimony, is a durable expression of your views and opinion which is frozen in time, capable of being supplemented, but usually not of being modified. Hence, extremely careful thought, review, proofreading and critical assessment should go into this document.

There are three report contexts. First, the retaining attorney may wish you to write no report to protect discovery of your opinions as a legal strategy. Second, a brief summary report may be requested as an aid to mediation, settlement discussions, preliminary testing of the waters and so on. Finally, the full-fledged forensic report may be required. Note, that in federal cases, reports are expected to include all opinions that will be expressed, and experts may be barred from expressing any opinions at trial that are not in the report.

Particular care should be taken in identifying the sources of data, since this is a common focus of attempts at impeachment of the expert through the report. Witness reports, documents, clinically based inferences and conclusions should be carefully identified and distinguished from one another. The level of certainty should be stated, distinguishing between hard data, such as lab tests, data consistent with, but not probative of, a particular conclusion, and so on.

Finally, the report should be so constructed as to allow the reader to follow the process of reasoning leading to the expert opinion without the need to go to external sources; thus, important documentary data should be quoted or summarized in the report, the reader should not have to go to the secondary source to understand the points made.

WRITING AND DEFENDING YOUR EXPERT REPORT

Captain John Hardin
West Sacramento, California

I have the following thoughts on written reports:

1. Written reports must be treated as sworn testimony.
2. You should never rush a report, everything you say in it can and will be used against you.
3. It helps to have a professional editor to review the report for clarity, accuracy, grammar, spelling, and general readability.
4. Once submitted, the report is final and can't be changed unless additional information which was not available to you is made available. For this reason, when given the task of writing a report, you should make certain the attorney has provided you with all relevant information.

William G. Hime
Northbrook, IL

My experience has been that the greatest troubles one gets into are:

1. Writing and sending a report before discussing your findings with your client.
2. Writing *any* report in many states (including California).

Keith Kasper, Esq.
Burlington, VT

First, stay within your specialty. Second, do not speculate on information which has not been provided to you. If you need additional information, you are certainly welcome to inquire as to that additional information, but <u>never</u> take such leaps of faith as to issues which are not before you and facts which may not exist. Not only will your report be severely compromised but your reputation in the community may be adversely affected by just one such bad report.

As to other, more generalized, issues, be careful to avoid equivocating your report into meaninglessness. While it is fine to suggest areas of caution where you are not certain, I am paying for a report; I seek a conclusion. Again, if you need more information to come to a reasonable determination, then seek that additional information. Qualifying language has its place, but I need an unequivocal opinion at some juncture.

Also, pursuant to the materials presented at the Ninth Annual Expert Witness Conference, in writing their reports, the experts should keep in mind the possibility of a *Daubert* challenge. Is what they are saying "provable"? Are they the appropriate ones to be rendering this opinion or should they be deferring to another specialty? These *Daubert* challenges can come very late in the process and could foreclose the proponent from obtaining sufficient additional information and/or expert opinion to save the case. A brief reference to published materials supporting their position, while an easy and free education point for the other side, may be sufficient to foreclose the other side from attacking the admissibility of your opinion.

H. Boulter Kelsey, Jr., PE
St. Louis, MO

Enclosed, you will find two reports generated last year from cases that have closed. Both of these cases settled advantageously for the plaintiff and I was told that part of the reason for the successful conclusion was traced to my report. The first report, addressed to Tom Jones in San Antonio, Texas, is relative to the Smith case. This report was prepared under the Texas rules as it was venued in State Court in Texas. The second report to Scott Peters is the Reed v. Brady case was in Federal Court and was therefore prepared in compliance with Federal Rule of Civil Procedure 26(a)(2). In both cases, as a result of the influence of *Daubert*, the reports are highly detailed and include the significant references in the appendices. I think the key element is to assume nothing in the drafting of a report and support virtually all opinions and bases with published information or testing that is done in compliance with accepted technical methodology. Nothing less is acceptable today.

Recently, we have adopted a new format for drafting our reports. We did this so that we could be in compliance with the ASTM Designation E 620-85 "Standard Practice for Reporting Opinions of Technical Experts." I have enclosed a copy of this standard for your reference. We have gone to this format to accomplish uniform reporting technique for the various engineers on my staff. By following the standard practice, we can more readily defend the report when attacked by opposing council by stating that we are in compliance with the standard practice for reporting opinions. It may seem like a small thing but it has been my experience that opposing counsel when filing a *Daubert* motion will use any conceivable crack in your armor to attempt to persuade a judge that you should not be allowed to testify.

WRITING AND DEFENDING YOUR EXPERT REPORT

William C. Lanham, Esq.
Atlanta, GA
Johnson & Ward

The primary issue in Georgia regarding [expert] reports concerns how much assistance an attorney may give an expert witness in preparing the report, and whether such information is discoverable. The matter was squarely addressed by the Supreme Court of Georgia in *McKinnon vs. Smock*, 264 Ga. 375, 445 SE2d 526 (Georgia 1994), where one party sought to compel production of "all correspondence, common notes, or other writings directed" by opposing counsel to his expert witness. The Court, noting that determination of this issue requires an evaluation of the interplay between the law which protects attorney opinion work products from discovery and the law which permits discovery of facts known and opinions held by an expert, held that while one seeking discovery of the expert may do so without exhibiting a substantial need for the material or establishing that undue hardship would result should the seeker have to employ other means to develop the evidence, such discovery is subject to the provision against disclosure of mental impressions, conclusions, opinions or other legal theories of an attorney or other representative of a party concerning the litigation. Id. at 244 Ga. 376, 378. Accordingly, the Court held that:

> [C]orrespondence from an attorney to an expert is protected from disclosure to the extent that the correspondence contains the opinion work product of the attorney. Should a dispute arise over whether a particular document does contain protected work product material, the trial court must conduct an in camera review to insure that mental impressions, conclusions, opinions, or legal theories of a party's attorney or representative are not disclosed. {Cites omitted}. Id. at 264 Ga. 378.

Therefore, ordinary work product is discoverable only upon a showing of substantial need, while opinion work product is never discoverable. See generally *In re Murphy*, 560 F2d, 326, 336 (8th Cir., 1977); and *Duplan-Corp vs. Moulinhee et Retorderie de Chavanoz*, 509 F2d 730, 732 (4th Cir., 1974), *cert. den.*, 420 U.S. 997 (1975).

In other words, in Georgia, in assisting an expert in formulating his expert report, an attorney may provide the expert with his theory of the case, his opinion as to the manner in which the expert's field of expertise impacts his theory, etc., and his input is not discoverable. Obviously, the more guidance an attorney provides in this regard, the stronger and less vulnerable to destructive cross-examination the ultimate expert opinion will be. It is not as if the attorney is dictating the opinion for the expert, but simply insuring that he is aware of all relevant facts and factors which bear on his opinion, and that his ultimate opinion is couched in language appropriate to the Plaintiff's cause.

William Lewis, MD, PC
Bridgeport, CT

With respect to "advice" that I might share, and in no particular order:

1. Stay away from vague and imprecise terms.
2. Opinions are for the "summary" or "discussion" section—not the "history" or "examination" section.
3. If you can't learn how to write in clear, simple English, learn how to.
4. Make sure your stationery and printing look "airborne sharp."
5. Proofread and keep typos to a minimum.
6. Don't say anything that you can and will not defend in a deposition or open court.
7. Be 100% honest and do not ever lie. If you do not know something, admit it.
8. No matter how much you may not like a patient, do not let your feelings come across to the patient or a reader of your report.
9. Try to examine and/or evaluate for both defendants and plaintiffs lest you be branded as favorable to one side or the other (and believe me, the judges and compensation commissioners and attorneys around here know this). It is very important for your validity
10. Keep your CV updated and "looking sharp" and be honest!!

Kenneth MacKenzie, MCBA, FIBA
Boynton Beach, FL

Reports, of course, must be tailored to a particular function, e.g. medical, business valuation, etc.

Tone of the report, should match the statistics. (e.g., Company X has tremendous growth of 2%!)

Do not, for the most part, use superlatives; we are providing testimony not a market sales pitch.

Does the report present a cogent story of the assignment? Are the questions of what, when, where, how and why covered professionally?

My personal experience indicates that the expert witness has 3 to 5 minutes in order to make his case with the court. E.g., you never have a second chance to make a first impression. Report reading may even be shorter.

My personal style as an executive of Xerox, Pitney Bowes, etc. and as a business appraiser has taught me to write a one to one-and-one-half-page "executive summary". The remainder of the report, no matter how it is labeled, is just an appendix.

My "executive summaries" are always read and do not intimidate the reader.

Make sure the report is written to the reader, e.g. the court, IRS, etc. Probably not to the client if in litigation.

Spelling, punctuation and typos destroy your credibility. As a client reads the report and observes transposition errors, poor grammar, they intuitively they ask themselves, did the expert make errors in key areas I do not understand?

Is there a good table of contents? Are the pages numbered?

Should there be a bibliography and does it relate properly through footnotes to the appropriate pages and articles? The bibliography must not be boilerplate. Essentially the report facts should be replicable by the reader.

Is the description of the assignment clear?

Are key definitions defined in the body or as an appendix?

Are the principle sources of information stated and cross-referenced?

Is there a statement to the objectivity and independence of the witness or is this an advocate witness?

The content should be cross-supporting, not self-contradicting.

Does the witness have any certifications and are they true?

Is there a particular section of "Assumptions and Limiting Conditions"?

If there are several approaches or methods to demonstrate one's opinion are the various methods reconciled and supported as compared to "trust me, I'm good"?

Are there any particular standards to be stated and followed?

James Marsh
Galena, IL

1. Complete and detailed statements of all opinions and support them with documentation from: depositions, statements, reports, national standards, and cite case law.
2. List important points of information.
3. List reference material and cases cited to support opinions.
4. Read all the materials and documents available, interview the principle(s) involved and make site visitations if possible.

5. Use physical evidence, if available, to support your opinions or weaken opposing expert's opinion.
6. Reenact the incident to better understand the facts.
7. When possible, back up an opinion with diagrams or charts.

Robert Powitz, PhD, MPH
Old Saybrook, CT

My forensic practice is a bit out of the mainstream. I work in public health as a forensic sanitarian. Here are my brief comments.

1. I try not to write in a passive language... if I do, it is by direction of my attorney clients.
2. Every adjective or adverb that has a subjective connotation, is supported in my field notes by an objective measurement. Quantifiable and, to some degree, qualifiable terms and phrases are likewise supported by actual finds.
3. Whenever possible and practical, I use the ANSI/ASQC Z1.4 1993 sampling scheme (aka: MIL-STD-105E), and let my client determine, or rather set the "Acceptable Quality Level." By doing this, it is easy to defend my work under cross-examination.
4. Whenever practical, I try to use consensus standards to support my finds. If this is not possible, I will write an article on the subject prior to court or deposition. Since I author a regular column in the "Journal of Environmental Health" and in "Corrections Managers' Report" I can generally establish some standard where none exists. Opinions, particularly in the public health arena that are published (and may not necessarily be refereed), are seldom challenged. If they are, using citations or actual published papers usually diffuses the opponent's arguments.
5. I try to provide a real-world example if I have to present an abstract idea. However, avoidance is preferred.
6. I always provide 1.5 line spacing in my reports for liner notes in preparation of testimony and deposition. It helps my repartee. The notes are reviewed by my client.
7. I try to stay away from idiomatic language.

WRITING AND DEFENDING YOUR EXPERT REPORT

Martha Sorensen, Ph.D.
Longmont, CO

As far as advice goes, here's what I've found useful in defending my reports:

1. Speak English. If you use unfamiliar terms the reports lose usefulness to those involved in treatment. If you need to use unfamiliar terms, attempt to explain them so the reader has a clear picture of what you are suggesting.
2. Cover the information needed. Too often reports are too brief. While a brief report might be helpful to some (lawyers, insurance company), they may not be helpful to others (cognitive-rehabilitation specialists).
3. Back up your statements with examples. Provide a mental picture for the reader.
4. Prove scores and explanations of the scores.
5. Write for the client/patient. They should also be provided with a copy of their results, in addition to a face-to-face explanation of the results and what they can expect to happen as a result.
6. Make useful and complete recommendations. Possibly explain why that type of specialist or treatment is recommended.
7. Make sure to mark the report CONFIDENTIAL.
8. Provide pertinent information (e.g. medical case number, name, age, date of birth, etc.) so that those involved in the various aspects of care can locate their needed information. While it isn't always possible to cover all the bases, attempts at addressing many people versus the one who made the original referral helps in future response to the report.
9. Never make a hard and fast statement unless you can support it. Keep notes and information regarding the results easily accessible for court preparation and support during testimony. Sometimes it is helpful to include articles or quotes from textbook sources in the report, depending on the audience being addressed.
10. Short, succinct statements with complete coverage appear to work best in adding helpful information for client/patient care and keeping you out of court.
11. Clearly mark the sections of the report. This allows report readers to quickly find the information they seek.
12. Always have the client/patient sign a release of information form for anyone you include in your cc: list. This helps prevent misunderstandings as to who gets a copy of the report. This information is the client's unless determined prior to assessment and report.

Johann Szautner, PE, PLS
Quakertown, PA

Pitfalls:
Rule 702 of the Federal Rules of Evidence alone no longer assures a scientific or technical expert opinion's standing solely on the basis of his knowledge, skill, experience, or education. "Ipse Dixit" is no longer admissible and any scientific or technical expert better be prepared to be challenged by the opposing trial lawyer as a matter of course.

As the judge is the gatekeeper to screen an expert's opinion and to determine its admissibility, it is important for the expert to understand not only federal rules of evidence, but also the legal principles born out of the *Daubert* Supreme Court decisions.

It is, therefore, of cardinal importance for the expert and his report, weaving into his analysis, the five (5) *Daubert* principles:

1. whether the method can be tested;
2. whether the method is subject to peer review;
3. whether the method is in respect to a certain technique;
4. whether the method has a high rate of error; and
5. what level of acceptability it has within the scientific community.

These principles need to be reflected in the report's analysis and discussion of observations, statement of facts, and conclusions reached. Documentation of relevant research and/or experience in the expert's curriculum vitae, as well as citations of appropriate and state-of-the-art references, all need to demonstrate compliance with the *Daubert* principles.

In certain instances, not involving routine scientific or technical (but purely scientific) analysis for which standards and protocol may not be readily available, peer review by other experts in the field may be necessary. To withstand a *Daubert* challenge, by all means do not venture into areas where you do not have a solid track record.

In my opinion, all graduate and licensed engineers in this country have a sufficient theoretical background in scientific fundamentals to competently analyze most accidents and products liability injuries. However, you might be torn to pieces if you serve as an expert in your first boating accident case although you may have analyzed hundreds of the vehicular accidents, and the basic methodology of investigation, fact-finding, and technical analysis is the same.

Report Structure:
Acknowledging the necessity of an expert's report to be crafted so as to stand up to a *Daubert* challenge, the writer should use a format that is widely accepted and easily recognizable by the scientific and technical community

at-large. But, the report must also be written to be self teaching and easily understood by the general public. It is the expert's duty to analyze and evaluate complex scientific and technical issues, and to make his findings and conclusions understood by jurors, typically lay persons, often struggling to understand the scientific and technical facts.

To this end, I find it advisable to follow the "Standard Practice for Reporting Opinions of Technical Experts" (ASTM Designation E620-85), re-approved 1997. ASTM stands for the American Society of Testing Materials.

My experience taught me the following format is generally widely accepted and easily understood.

1. <u>Introduction:</u> This element of the report should indicate why this report is written, for whom it is prepared, a summary of facts, and chronology of events.

2. <u>Scope of Investigation:</u> Include a preamble to state the basis of the claim and a specific assignment. For technical experts, it would typically include:
   a. Technical review of field observations, documents (including complaint), and depositions.
   b. Discussion of the results of your technical review in terms of customary technical standards and practices.

3. <u>Data Available:</u> Include a listing of all data you reviewed; even if ultimately they were not used in reaching conclusions. This should also include records of direct observation made, either by photographic documentation or notes; preferably both.

4. <u>References:</u> Include all references you might find useful, not only for the report preparation but for later reference during direct and cross examination. The references used should be current technical handbooks, governmental regulations, and industry standards. References used to play crucial role in establishing a credible basis for observations made and conclusions reached.

5. <u>Review of Data:</u> Always review **all** data you listed in your report, albeit your review comments may be limited to the data you found pertinent to your fact-finding mission.

6. <u>Review of References:</u> Review all references cited in your report; eliminate the ones which appear outdated, stagnant or marginally relevant. If you include governmental regulations and/or industry standards, make sure you use the latest addition and are aware of relevant pending legislative proposals.

7. <u>Discussion:</u> Next to your conclusion, this is the most important element of your report. It is here where you must be keenly aware of a *Daubert* challenge and preemptively weave in the

Daubert principles in your analysis, laying the foundation for conclusions reached.

8. <u>Conclusion</u>: This is not only the most important, but also the most tricky, part of your report. Based on civil law doctrine, you must establish your conclusions "with a reasonable degree of scientific certainty," which essentially means you must be more sure that you are <u>right</u> than that you are <u>wrong</u>. You must then specifically marry your findings to existing standards of care established by laws, rules, regulations, industry standards, or what can be reasonably expected by the general public in protecting them from torts.

9. <u>Curriculum Vitae</u>: Your CV will represent the basis of establishing your experience and "expertise." Make sure you sufficiently cover all areas of your expertise or you'll be vulnerable when challenged. Your CV will be a keystone in the bulwark you must erect to withstand a *Daubert* challenge.

<u>Some Additional Thoughts</u>:
Make sure you discuss your findings and potential conclusions with the attorney who commissioned you before you start on a report. It is not unusual to have your attorney not prepare a report until he is sure your findings will not be helpful to the other side, or until already in the trial phase so as not to be vulnerable to premature disclosure, allowing the other side to prepare for a vigorous challenge.

Appendix B Model Reports

<u>Report #1: Toxic Tort</u>
This report is most notable for the following:

- An objective statement of the expert's impressive qualifications.
- A precise listing of and frequent citation to the literature relied upon.
- The explanation in layman's words of technical terminology.
- Its precision and detail.
- The time and thought that obviously went into the report's preparation.
- It is extremely well-written. The language is tight and precise.
- The absence of typographical errors.

Areas of possible improvement:

- An executive summary with conclusions at the beginning in place of current first two paragraphs.
- A renaming of the "introduction" section as "qualifications."
- The author should not use the term "continually" in his sentence "I continually read and update my knowledge of cancer causation, diagnosis, and treatment in connection with the writing of this book and its revisions."
- A much more precise listing of the pages, reports, and medical records reviewed by the witness.
- The author should not use the word "various" to describe the literature reviewed.

Max Daley, M.D., F.A.C.P.
Medical Oncology

1000 Maple St., #1A
Bayview, CA 90000

Clinical Professor of Medicine
State University

915 Pleasant Hill Place
Sierra, CA 91234

Office: (300) 555-1234
Fax: (310) 555-6789

Mailing address:
205 W. Via Royale
Sierra, CA 91235

William Klein, Attorney at Law
Law Offices of J. William Klein
1212 Legal Ln., #300   September 6, 2000
Lonestar, Texas 75000   Re: Terrance O. Murray,
                                        deceased

Dear Mr. Klein,

This report is prepared at your request, to review the medical history,
diagnosis, treatment, and clinical course of the above individual, Terrance O.
Murray ("subject"), specifically his development of myelodysplastic
syndrome and acute myeloid leukemia, and to discuss the potential
relationship between such illnesses and his history of prior exposure to
ionizing radiation in the form of x-rays. He was exposed to ionizing
radiation (x-rays) in the course of his employment, and subsequently
developed a bone marrow disorder, myelodysplastic syndrome, which was
followed by the development of acute myeloid leukemia. I will also review
and express my medical and scientific opinions regarding the biological
effects of ionizing radiation in general, and specifically with respect to
causation of his cancer-related illness, myelodysplastic syndrome changing
and transforming to acute myeloid leukemia (sometimes also called acute
myelogenous leukemia or acute granulocytic leukemia).

    I will discuss the causation of cancer by radiation, specifically the
nature of the specific disorders: myelodysplastic syndrome, as well as
malignancy (cancer): acute myelogenous leukemia which affected this
subject, as well as the medically probable relationship and causation of such
malignancy, as well as the antecedent myelodysplastic syndrome, to his
previous exposure to ionizing radiation in his workplace.

    I will review the exposure of this subject to ionizing radiation
produced as x-rays in his work environment. He worked for 15 years at
Acme Co., in close proximity to strong electron-producing machines used as
printing presses, and developed by 123 Technologies, and as a result was
exposed to a spectrum of x-rays. The scientifically probable spectrum,
intensity, character, and dose of such x-ray exposure has been determined by
Marvin Resnikoff. This work environment, and the ionizing radiation
produced there, is described and summarized in detail in the materials
reviewed, as documented below. The device that produced the x-ray
exposure is referred to as the 123 Processor.

Introduction:
I am currently Clinical Professor of Medicine at the State University School
of Medicine. After my undergraduate education at Whitcomb and medical
degree at Coolidge, I completed a residency in internal medicine at the State
University Hospital system in Sunnydale, and a three-year fellowship in

medical oncology [cancer] at the Shoreline Cancer Center in Metropolis. I was subsequently on the full-time staff at that institution, and then spent one year in the private practice of cancer medicine in Sunnydale, California at the Sunnydale Oncology Institute. I was then Director of Oncology at Memorial General Hospital in Bayview, CA. From 1971 to 1994 I was in the full-time private practice of cancer medicine in Bayview, CA, and from 1995-1998 was vice-president of medical affairs at the Cancer Institute in Terra, CA. I am currently in the private practice of medical oncology in Bayview and Sierra, CA.

During my training as a cancer specialist, as well as during my subsequent career as a practicing and teaching clinical oncologist, I have continued to read widely in the scientific and professional cancer literature, to be able to understand and draw valid conclusions regarding the causes of various cancers in patients, not only my own but those involved in the teaching program at the State University School of Medicine, where I teach physicians in training to be cancer specialists. I have been on the Medical School teaching faculty since 1980, and have taught the principles of cancer causation, diagnosis, and treatment to medical students, resident physicians, and fellows in training to be cancer specialists.

I have co-authored a book for the public, "A Guide to Cancer Treatment." This was first published in 1991, and is now in its 3rd US edition (1997). The 4th edition is now in preparation. There are two Canadian editions (endorsed by the Canadian Medical Association) and three other foreign editions. It is a widely read and sold comprehensive cancer book for the public in the United States (over 100,000 copies). I continually read and update my knowledge of cancer causation, diagnosis, and treatment in connection with the writing of this book and its revisions. I have written 95 publications, including scientific articles, book chapters, and books. My prior research activities have included basic research in biochemical pharmacology, clinical trials of new anticancer agents in man, investigations on new methods of diagnosing and treating cancer, as well as (most recently) evaluation of cancer detection programs and patterns of care for cancer patients.

In addition to my private practice (over 30 years) and teaching activities, from 1990 to 1993 I was the Director of the Golden State Clinic Cancer Risk Assessment Center, and thus am quite familiar with the various factors: hereditary, environmental, infectious, chemical, radiation, and others, involved as risk factors in the causation of cancer in man. I have had occasion to advise individual patients regarding these factors and risks.

In addition to being certified by the American Board of Internal Medicine and the subspecialty board of Medical Oncology, since 1993 I have served on the writing and review committee panels for the latter board examination. I am also certified by the American Board of Quality Assurance and Utilization Review Physicians, with subspecialty certification in risk management and managed care.

I am a member of the American Association for Cancer Research, the American Society of Clinical Oncology, the American College of Physicians (Fellow), and various other scientific and medical organizations, and have received a number of awards, including Visiting Scholar, Shoreline Cancer Center; and several American Cancer Society awards for various achievements in cancer treatment, education, and scholarship.

On the basis of my education, training, and experience, I am therefore familiar with the risk factors and causes, as well as the natural history, diagnosis, treatment, and prognosis for the various types of cancer in man, in particular those cancers caused by radiation.

I have been admitted in Federal Court (Denver, CO; San Diego, CA) as a medical expert in the specialties of Internal Medicine as well as Medical Oncology/Cancer. My hourly fee for review of documents and records, analysis, conferences, and preparation of reports is $300/hour. My fee for deposition testimony is $500/hr, and my fee for out-of-town trial testimony is $4500/day. A listing of medical/legal cases in which I have given deposition or trial testimony during the past five years is attached to this report.

Materials Reviewed and Examined

This review and report is based, in part, on my education, training, and experience in the field of cancer medicine. In addition, I have reviewed and consulted, and rely upon certain materials prepared or furnished by other individuals and sources, as noted below.

1. Copies of key and pertinent pages, reports, and portions of the extensive medical records of this subject, the cancer-related documents in particular, as well as additional medical information concerning this subject, provided by plaintiffs' counsel. Records reviewed were obtained from Western Memorial Hospital, Dr. Leonard Stracks, Gardenville Memorial Hospital, Dr. James S. Ford, and Dr. Chris Dell.

Such primary medical record documents consist of such materials as pathology reports, surgical and operative reports, clinical data and information, consultations, laboratory studies, and medical correspondence regarding the diagnosis of myelodysplastic syndrome as well as the cancer diagnosis (acute myeloid leukemia) in this individual. These documents furnish the usual and customary data required and necessary to document and understand the diagnosis of cancer, specifically the type of cancer that has been diagnosed in this subject, acute myelogenous leukemia, as well as the clinical, surgical, pathologic, and other medical aspects of such diagnosis. These documents also supply information regarding the diagnosis of the preceding illness, myelodysplastic syndrome. This review of submitted materials was for several purposes:

A. To familiarize myself with this subject's general health status, for example the presence of other related or unrelated illnesses and symptoms.

B. To determine the nature and type of this subject's malignancy, as well as any cancer-related symptoms, signs, and conditions that may have developed. It is useful and important to review clinical summaries, reports of bone marrow examination, genetic and chromosome analysis, and consultations by various specialists who participated in his care.

C. To determine if there were other potential causative or contributing factors which might exist, in relation to this subject's myelodysplastic syndrome and acute myelogenous leukemia. Examples might include various personal and/or environmental factors which might also be a cause or a substantial contributing factor of his cancer or cancer-related illness.

D. To study the events associated with his terminal illness, and to determine if the cancer or a related complication of the cancer or its treatment was the cause of death.

2. In addition, various documents, materials, and scientific/medical articles and references were consulted and reviewed:

1. Straume, T. High-energy gamma rays in Hiroshima and Nagasaki: Implications for risk and W_R. Health Phys. 69: 954-956, 1995.

2. Gundestrup, M., and Storm, H.H. Radiation-induced acute myeloid leukemia and other cancers in commercial jet cockpit crew: a population-based cohort study. Lancet: 354: 2029-2031, 1999.

3. Report of Marvin Resnikoff, Ph.D., Radiation exposure data document. Received (faxed) May 2, 2000.

4. Fairlie, I., and Resnikoff, M. No Dose Too Low. Bulletin Atomic Scientists. Nov.-Dec.1997, pages 52-56.

5. Schottenfeld, D., and Fraumeni, Jr., J.F. Cancer Epidemiology and Prevention, 2nd ed, Oxford University Press, New York, 1996.

6. Your covering letters of July 8, 1999, August 3, 1999, April 14, 2000

7. Dollinger, M.R., Rosenbaum, E.H., and Cable, G. Everyone's Guide to Cancer Therapy. Somerville House/Toronto and Andrews-McMeel/Kansas City, 1998.

8. Wilkinson, G.S., and Dreyer, N.A. Leukemia among nuclear workers with protracted exposure to low-dose ionizing radiation. Epidemiology 2: 305-309, 1991.

9. Band, P.R., et al. Cohort study of Air Canada pilots: mortality, cancer incidence,a dn leukemia risk. Am. J. Epid. 143: 137-143, 1996.

10. Stewart, A.M. Low-level radiation: the cancer controversy. Bull. Atomic Scientists. Sept. 1990, pp. 15-19.

11. UNSCEAR77, pages 412-413, faxed by M.Resnikoff, Dec. 2, 1999.

12. Ellenhorn, M.J. Medical Toxicology: Diagnosis and Treatment of Human Poisoning. Chapter 70: Radiation poisoning. 2nd Ed. Williams & Wilkins, Baltimore, 1997.

13. Hall, E.J. Risk of Cancer Causation by Diagnostic X-rays. Supplement to Cancer Prevention, eds. DeVita, V.T. Hellman, S., and Rosenberg, S.A. March 1990.

14. Flodin, U., et al. Acute myeloid leukemia and background radiation in an expanded case-referent study. Arch. Env. Health. 45: 364-366, 1990.

15. Wing, S., et al. Mortality among workers at Oak Ridge National Laboratory: Evidence of radiation effects in follow-up through 1984. J.Am. Med.Assn. 265: 1397-1402, 1991.

16. Bonin, S.R., et al. Treatment-related myelodysplastic syndrome following abdominopelvic radiotherapy for endometrial cancer. Gynec.Oncology. 57: 430-432, 1995

17. Upton, Arthur C. The Linear-Nonthreshold Dose-Response Model: A Critical Reappraisal. Proceedings of the Thirty-Fifth Annual Meeting of the National Council on Radiation Protection and Measurements. Bethesda, MD, National Council on Radiation Protection and Measurements, 1999, pp 9-31.

18. Resnikoff, M. "Preliminary calculations re T. Murray (rev. 1), faxed by William Klein, Esq. 10/29/99 [9 pages]

19. 123 Processor Presentation, Revision "D" Date: November 8, 1989.

20. ICN Dosimetry Service, Fountain Valley, CA. Radiation Exposure Report. Bates numbered TP 0001 to TP 00072

21. Letter from Mr. Klein to Western Memorial Hospital, June 24, 1999, requesting medical records, with attached medical records [pages un-numbered, about 3/16" thick]

22. Extensive medical/hospital records from Western Memorial Hospital [about 4" thick]

23. Deposition transcripts: Terrance Murray, Vols. I and II   [10/26/98 and 10/28/98]

24. Resnikoff, M. [Memo] Preliminary calculations re T. Murray (rev. 1) faxed October 29, 1999 [9 pages including cover page]

25. Pederson-Bjergaard J. Radiotherapy- and chemotherapy-induced myeloysplasia and acute myeloid leukemia. A review. Leuk Res. 16:61, 1992.

26. Little, J. B. Ionizing Radiation *in* Holland, et al, <u>Cancer Medicine,</u> Fourth Edition, Williams and Wilkins, Baltimore, 1997.

27. Portions of CFR: Department of Veterans Affairs, Ch.1 (7-1-97 Edition), pages 221-226 [alternatively sections 3.309 to 3.312], dealing with radiation exposure-related cancers in veterans exposed to radiation.Kouides, P.A., and Bennett, J. M., The Myelodysplastic syndromes, *in* Abeloff, M.D., et al Clinical Oncology Churchill Livingstone, New York. 2000

28. Stone, R.M., and Mayer, R.J., Acute Myeloid Leukemia in Adults, *in* Abeloff, M.D., et al Clinical Oncology Churchill Livingstone, New York. 2000

29. Upton, A.C. The linear-nonthreshold dose-response model: a critical reappraisal. Proc. of the thirty-fifth annual meeting of the National Council on Radiation Protection and Measurements. Bethesda, MD. National Council on Radiation Protection and Measurements, 1999, pp 9-31.

30. Gundestrup, M., Storm, H.H. Radiation-induced acute myeloid leukemia and other cancers in commercial jet cockpit crew: a population-based cohort study. Lancet: 354: 2029-2031, 1999.

31. Wallace, R.W., and Sondhaus, C.A. Cosmic radiation exposure in subsonic air transport. Aviat. Space Environ. Med. 49: 610-623, 1978.

32. Hall, E.J. Risk of Cancer Causation by Diagnostic X-rays. Cancer Prevention [DeVita, Hellman, and Rosenberg, eds], p 1-9, March 1990.

33. Fairlie, I. Risk of radiation-induced cancer at low doses and low dose rates for radiation protection purposes. National Radiological Protection Board. Vol. 6: No. 1, 1995.

34. Portions of CFR: Department of Veterans Affairs, Ch.1 (7-1-97 Edition), pages 221-226 [alternatively sections 3.309 to 3.312], dealing with radiation exposure-related cancers in veterans exposed to radiation.

35. Dreyer, N.A., and Friedlander, E. Identifying the health risks from very low-dose sparsely ionizing radiation. Am. J. Pub. Health. 72: 585-588, 1982.

36. Martland, H.S, et al. Some Unrecognized Dangers in the Use and Handling of Radioactive Substances: J. Am. Med. Assn. 85: 1769-1776, 1925.

37. Notice: United States District Court Eastern District of Texas April 11, 2000.

Medical/Clinical History of Terrance Murray:
[Reviewer's explanation of medical terms indicated thus in brackets.]

Mr. Murray [DOB 5/25/41] was admitted at the age of 57 (June 4, 1998) to a Gardenville Hospital with symptoms of fatigue, fever, night sweats, pallor, shortness of breath on exertion, and generalized weakness. His white blood cell count was noted to be 900 [normal 4000-10,500], hemoglobin of 5 [normal 12.5-17], and platelet count of 25,000 [normal 140,000-415,000]. Bone marrow examination revealed aplastic anemia [failure of bone marrow to make blood cells]. In the discharge summary prepared by Dr. Richard Mallory (6/25/98), he states, "...We also transfused him several units and began asking him about risk factors. He had apparently been around some electrical radiation at work for some time and we had actually warned him a couple of years ago, after he had been working there for 12 years, that it could cause problems similar to this." A progress note dated 6/10/98 states: "Spoke to Dr. Borrman – initial impression ? aplastic anemia ~ radiation exposure at work."

He had no known chemical (e.g. benzene) risk factors, but it was noted that in his work as an electrical technician he had been exposed to one of the electrical devices, but had not been aware that this was any health hazard. There was no apparent other identified cause of his blood problem, such as a viral infection or medication or an inherited condition. Review of his initial bone marrow examination showed some regeneration and no frank signs of leukemia at that time, and was consistent with either recovery from a previous "injury" or could represent a dysplastic marrow [abnormal appearance of marrow cells]. He was given antibiotics and supportive care and transferred to Western Memorial Hospital.

Subsequently he was seen by Dr. James Ford at the Marrow Transplant Services of Southwest Oncology, P.A., and he noted (9/4/98) that "We have been looking diligently in an expedited way for a marrow donor for Mr. Terrance Murray, a patient who has severe myelodysplasia, with marrow failure." Prior cytogenetic analysis of his bone marrow showed multiple genetic abnormalities, specifically monosomy 5, 11 and 18, trisomy 6 and 8, and various abnormalities [these terms refer to single and triple numbers of chromosomes, respectively, rather than the normal pair of each chromosome]. He wrote (6/30/98), "This constellation of abnormalities was felt to be most consistent with myelodysplasia or early acute myeloid leukemia." A repeat bone marrow examination (June 26) revealed a marrow consistent with myelodysplasia. At that time he had received a total of 11 red cell transfusions.

He was also seen by Dr. Chris Dell, who performed specialized studies on his bone marrow, called flow cytometry, and he reviewed the prior findings. A repeat bone marrow examination was performed on 10/21/98 and reviewed by the pathologist at Western Memorial Hospital. This showed a "dysplastic marrow with excess blasts consistent with conversion to acute leukemia" ["blasts" are the earliest blood cells in the bone marrow and may normally be up to 5% of the marrow cells. An excess of blasts is a sign of acute leukemia or a related disorder]. The genetic studies were reviewed, in particular the abnormal chromosome #5. The constellation of genetic abnormalities was felt to be most consistent with marrow involvement by a myelodysplastic syndrome or acute myelogenous leukemia. The karyotype [genetic pattern] was regarded as "an unfavorable prognostic sign." Dr. Dell noted in his initial office visit (6/12/98) that (subject) "…does work around a beta emitter that is used in the wiring business." He also developed (7/6/98) left hip pain, and MRI showed bilateral femoral avascular necrosis, left greater than right. There was also an abnormal marrow signal.

Mr. Murray developed sepsis and pneumonia, and was given antibiotics as well as a trial of chemotherapy for his leukemia. He continued to worsen, with severe fevers, recurring headaches and increasing shortness of breath, and he expired on November 6, 1998. The death certificate, signed by Dr. Dell, listed as the cause of death: "acute leukemia due to myelodysplasia." Pneumonia was listed as a contributing event.

What is "myelodysplastic syndrome" or "myelodysplasia"?
Blood cells are manufactured in the bone marrow, found inside most of our bones. There are three types of cells that are manufactured inside the bone marrow, which then leave to enter the systemic circulation. These are called red cells (carry oxygen), white cells (fight infection) and platelets (stop bleeding). White cells are also called leukocytes and the prefix "myelo" or "myeloid" refers to the white cells or to the marrow production of blood

cells. The cells in the bone marrow consist of earlier stages or forms of these three "peripheral" blood cells, as well as other types of cells, e.g. plasma cells, which seldom leave the bone marrow.

As a result of insults of various kinds, for example exposure to ionizing radiation or certain chemicals, the early bone marrow cells may acquire genetic mutations or abnormalities. As a result they may develop an abnormal appearance, compared with the fairly typical and well-recognized appearance of normal bone marrow cells, e.g. white cells or leukocytes. These genetic mutations can sometimes be identified and categorized. Causes of these mutations include ionizing radiation, various chemicals (e.g. drugs used in cancer treatment, benzene), genetic predisposition (several familial cases have been reported), as well as immunological (there is an associated defect in the immune system). In the case of radiation, it has been stated that low doses of ionizing radiation appear to be more leukemogenic than high doses.(Pederson-Bjergaard)

Once myelodysplastic syndrome develops, it is not curable. Additional genetic changes often lead to a transformation into acute myeloid leukemia, and there is an International Prognostic Scoring System that predicts how long it is likely to take for such a transformation to occur.

What Is Acute Myelogenous Leukemia?

This is a disorder that may arise "de novo" (without a pre-existing disease, such as myelodysplastic syndrome), secondary to various types of chemical and toxic exposures, as a result of exposure to ionizing radiation, or as a result of continuing genetic transformation of myelodysplastic syndrome. In the case of ionizing radiation as a cause, there may or may not be an intervening stage of myelodysplastic syndrome. Ionizing radiation has been implicated as a cause of acute leukemia. Many examples have been reported in the medical and scientific literature, for instance the atomic bombings in Japan [commonly acute leukemia developed 6 to 10 years after exposure]; leukemia developed in association with certain medical therapies [e.g. patients with a spinal disorder, ankylosing spondylitis, who received radiation therapy have a fivefold excess incidence of leukemia]; in fact leukemia was a more common event in radiologists in earlier years, where protective measures to minimize radiation exposure were not used. Thus, the association of exposure to ionizing radiation and the subsequent development of acute leukemia has been known since the 1920's. Various chemicals have been invoked as causes of acute leukemia ("chemical carcinogens"), including benzene (rubber and shoe-making industries), cigarette smoking, and cancer chemotherapy.

Acute myelogenous leukemia is fatal if untreated, and aggressive chemotherapy is often used to obtain a remission. Complete remission [bone marrow appears normal after intensive treatment] rates vary from 48% (over age 60) to 72% (under age 60) but a substantial proportion of such patients will subsequently relapse and die of this disease, despite the early remission which may be obtained. Therapy itself is complex, aggressive, and life-threatening. It is important to note that acute myelogenous leukemia that arises as a complication of other bone marrow diseases, e.g. myelodysplasia, has a lower chance of remission and control.

Source of Radiation/X-ray Exposure Involving This Subject

Subject was employed for 15 years at Acme Co., in close proximity to strong electron-producing machines used as printing presses, and developed by 123 Technologies, and as a result was exposed to a spectrum of x-rays. The scientifically probable spectrum, intensity, character, and dose of such x-ray exposure has been determined by Martin Rhodes. The total dose estimate states that his total dose of ionizing radiation was 2.8 rads per year, which over a period of 14 years of exposure, was 39 rads. It was noted that there were differing energy levels of x-rays, and that lower energy x-rays have a higher bone dose than do higher energies. Specific details of the source and character of the ionizing radiation, and the physical and biological details of exposure of this subject to such ionizing radiation have been documented and have been reviewed by this examiner.

These reports and conclusions appear to be conducted in a reasonable, sound, logical, and scientific manner, and I have assumed that these studies, measurements, and data furnish accurate and reliable information on ionizing radiation/x-ray exposure of this individual during the times specified. Excessive exposure to sources of ionizing radiation was demonstrated and documented. The findings and conclusions outlined appear to be and are considered accurate and valid.

Ionizing Radiation and Cancer

Ionizing radiation, for example that produced by x-ray exposure, produces damage in biological systems through ionization of molecules. The damage may occur directly, via damage to chromosomal DNA (the genetic material), or indirectly, via creation of free radicals resulting from ionization of ubiquitous water molecules. DNA is the genetic blueprint that directs the growth and development of the cells and organs in our bodies. Certain types of damage to DNA, termed cancer mutations, may lead to the production of cancer cells. Examples include deletion of a cancer-suppressing gene or activation of a cancer-causing gene. If these cancer cells, containing these mutations produced as a result of ionizing radiation exposure, are able to survive and grow, for example early blood-forming cells in the bone marrow, eventually a "clone" of genetically identical (and abnormal) early white blood cells is formed, and the "normal" bone marrow cells are replaced by these abnormal or leukemic white blood cells. They take up space that should be available for production of normal blood cells, and the resulting reduction in production of normal red cells results in anemia, reduction of normal white blood cells results in infection, and reduction in normal

261

platelets results in bleeding. These three symptoms are common in new and untreated acute myelogenous leukemia. There are various pathways and mechanisms for production of these genetic changes, including for example the activation of a cancer-causing gene, or the deletion of a cancer-protective gene.

The genetic material that is inside the center (nucleus) of the cells in our body is called DNA, the "genetic code." This genetic code determines all the characteristics of our body appearance, growth, metabolism, regulation, structure, and life. An important and revolutionary research effort now nearing completion, the "Human Genome Project" will define the approximately three billion "base pairs" [see below] that defines the human genetic code. DNA serves as a "template" for the production of RNA, which then serves as a template for the production of proteins. DNA is composed of two intertwined spirals of chemical "bases," and there are four different bases that make up the genetic "code." The pairings between the bases on the two spirals (helix) are known and specified, so that when the two strands of the DNA spiral separate, for example when one cell divides to form two and one strand goes to each new cell, each single strand can serve as a template to re-create another strand, so the genetic material of the new cell is "whole" again. A simple analogy would compare this pairing to the four playing card suits: the red ones: hearts and diamonds always pair up, as do the black ones, spades and clubs. The "cards," or in the case of the cell, chemical bases, are arranged in a long line, like a railroad train.

If a "spade" is deleted from one strand as a result of a mutation, the same location on the other strand can serve as a template, since it will contain a "club," and clubs and spades always "match." This common analogy substitutes playing card suits for the names of the actual bases, adenine, guanine, thymine, and cytosine [A G T C], but the pairing concept is easy to understand.

There are normally many accidents or mishaps that occur when a cell divides and the strand of DNA bases separates from its partner and creates a new "matching" strand. These errors of reproduction are usually repaired, and only when such a repair is incorrect or does not occur does a mutation occur. Some mutations are "lethal," meaning that the cell with the abnormal chromosome, or new mutation, dies, and is never discovered. Sometimes the mutation is trivial, and does not result in any detectable abnormality. Sometimes the mutation produces some type of disease, such as an illness other than cancer, or produces a form of cancer. These cancer cells seem to be "hardier" than other cells, and grow preferentially, to "take over" and invade normal cells and tissues, as well as being able to spread to other parts of the body.

Rapidly growing cancer cells in particular have the property of being able to ignore the usual controls on growth of cells, and such cancer cells "take over" the area where the cancer starts. The only *normal* rapidly growing cells are those that heal wounds and those following fertilization of an egg, that create a fetus and new baby.

Clearly, damage to a gene on one chromosome strand (but not the same gene on the other "paired chromosome": a "single strand" break), is much more likely to be repaired by natural repair processes, since there is still a normal "template" to work from: the other chromosome strand. However, if the same genetic area on both chromosome strands is damaged or broken, there is no longer a "normal" template to furnish a repair model. As an analogy, if my remaining playing card is a diamond (red), I know the pair card is a heart (also red). If no card is left (analogous to a double strand chromosome break), I have no idea which card to use, and the body, by analogy, cannot know which chemical "base" to insert in the genetic blueprint.

As to DNA damage, ionizing radiation is much more likely to produce double-strand breaks with impaired ability to repair, compared with single-strand breaks, *e.g.*, from chemical carcinogens. Free radicals produced by ionizing radiation are very unstable and combine with other molecules causing damage. Radiation may produce genetic damage and mutations (genotoxic), damage to the developing fetus (teratogenic) and genetic changes leading to cancer (carcinogenic). The latter subject is the principal focus of this review and opinion.

In the case of exposure to ionizing radiation, there is no lower threshold of exposure that is required to produce genetic mutations that may lead to abnormalities including cancer. The effects of ionizing radiation are "stochastic." This means that:

a. there is no threshold, even a very small dose can produce a key genetic mutation leading to cancer;

b. increasing doses of radiation produce a higher risk of genetic damage. At least two "hits" (points of genetic damage), and usually more, are required to produce a cancer mutation. Thus prolonged exposure would favor the occurrence of more than one "hit"; and

c. once the key genetic damage occurs, the effect that finally occurs is independent of the dose required to produce it.

Once the cancer mutation occurs, at whatever dose or time interval, it is permanent in that cell, and if the body does not control and destroy the cancer cell, it eventually produces clinical cancer. Fairlie has stated…"for the majority of tumor types, a single mutational event in a single target cell *in vivo* [in the body] can create the potential for neoplastic [cancer] development. On this basis, a single radiation track (the lowest dose and dose rate possible) traversing the nucleus [central point] of an appropriate target cell has a finite probability, albeit low, of generating the specific damage that results in a tumor initiating mutation. Thus, at the level of DNA damage there is no basis for the assumption that there is likely to be a dose threshold below which the risk of tumour induction will be zero."

Because even a single ionization event is capable of producing critical DNA damage leading to a cancer mutation, there is no threshold dose of ionizing radiation which is "safe." The existing industrial radiation-production standards and guidelines define legal or statutory permissible thresholds of maximum exposure. But there is no "safe" dose of radiation. These guidelines serve industry and society only as designated parameters. These maximum thresholds of exposure have been lowered over time as the scientific community progressed in discovery regarding the health effects of exposure to radioactive materials. The commonly used nuclear industry term, ALARA—as low as is reasonably achievable—has been used to guide radiation exposure. Unfortunately, what is "reasonably achievable" is still an amount of ionizing radiation capable of producing biological effects, specifically, genetic damage leading to cancer.

In addition, the health effects on humans of more than one toxic material or exposure may be additive or synergistic. It is quite likely, therefore, that the risk of chromosomal damage from ionizing radiation may be increased due to repeated exposures over time as well as the presence of multiple sources of ionizing radiation. Thus, the incidence of future health risks from exposure to ionizing radiation, cancer in particular, may be significantly greater than what would normally be expected based on a single exposure to a single source of radiation. For example, genetic damage via radiation is much more likely to produce cancers, as well as other genetically related diseases, after multiple exposures as compared to a single exposure. Specifically, exposures like those experienced by this subject, that is exposure to x-rays at various times, are more likely to produce genetic (DNA) mutations, with the resulting risk of cancer, than a single or a small number of exposures. According to the stochastic model, the risk of cancer is higher with increased exposure.

In addition, the genetic damage caused by ionizing radiation may take years to unfold and transform into clinical cancer. In the production of various types of cancer by ionizing radiation, this "latency" means that several to many years may be required after the radiation exposure before the development of clinical cancer. Thus the initial damage and the total damage done by radiation may not be apparent for a long time after it occurs. For example, in the data derived from the atomic bombings of Japan, the incidence of radiation-induced leukemia reached a peak at about five to seven years, and most were diagnosed by 10 years later. In the case of this subject's exposure to ionizing radiation as a result of the described x-ray exposure, the latency observed was consistent with periods of time commonly observed as latent intervals for this malignancy. Upton quoted studies indicating that the overall risk of solid cancers in Japanese atomic bomb survivors is significantly elevated at doses of only 5 to 50 mSv.

Regulators apply the linear non-threshold hypothesis. In other words, they assume the risk of cancer increases linearly with dose and that there is no dose too low to cause adverse effects. This model is widely accepted, for example a recent comprehensive report of The National Council on Radiation Protection and Measurement, chaired by Dr. Upton. It accurately reflects the mechanism by which ionizing radiation induces cancer and other damaging effects.

Dr. Little states: "...radiation induces a type of genetic instability in cells as a cellular response to the nonspecific DNA damage it produces. This genetic instability enhances the probability of the occurrence of malignant transformation or other cellular effects in progeny cells, sometimes after many generations of replication." Dr. Little agrees with the stochastic model of radiation carcinogenesis, which states that there is...."no threshold, but the severity of the effect is not influenced with dose." There is an extensive discussion of the risk models and epidemiology of radiation-induced cancers, including, for example, a table showing attributable risk in the atomic bomb data (percentage of all cancers observed that can be attributed to the radiation exposure). It is clear that this data, as well as many other sources of data, verify and document that there is documentation of radiation-induced cancers.

Various studies in the medical and scientific literature have studied the production of various cancers, acute leukemia in particular, as a result of exposure to ionizing radiation. The Japan atomic bomb studies and the ankylosing spondylitis studies have been mentioned.

Wilkinson compiled seven studies of nuclear workers, and found that the relative risk (RR) of leukemia was 1.5, for doses equal to or in excess of 10 mSv [1 rem] or greater, compared with less than 10 mSv. For workers exposed to 10 to 50 mSv [1 – 5 rem] the relative risk was 1.8. These combined data indicated an elevated risk of leukemia for doses of ionizing radiation under 50 mSv.

Dreyer and Friedlander, in an earlier study, reviewed the health risks from very low-dose ionizing radiation, and noted that leukemia has been observed repeatedly to occur at cumulative doses of equal to or greater than 30 rads.

Wing, in a study of workers at Oak Ridge National Laboratory, found that there was a 63% increase in leukemia. Median cumulative dose of external radiation was 1.4 mSv.

Band studied Air Canada Pilots, and referred to published estimates of in-flight radiation exposure. Acute myelogenous leukemia was significantly increased, with a standardized incidence ratio [SIR] of 4.72 [90% confidence intervals 2.05 to 9.31. Various estimates of radiation exposure were cited, for example a)1 rem/year, b)0.3 to 0.6 rem/year, and c) 0.1 to 0.18 rem/year in various reports.

Gundestrup and Storm reported that there was a significantly increased risk of developing acute myeloid leukemia in Danish male cockpit crew members flying more than 5000 hours. The SIR was 5.1 [CI 1.03 to 14.91]. The mean annual dose equivalent was in the range of 3 to 6 mSv/year

Wallace and Sondhause reported an FAA and NASA-sponsored study of cosmic radiation doses received by airline passengers and crewmembers. The latter dose was 160 mrem/year. This value is in general agreement with other reported values, as noted above.

Hall has estimated the risk of developing leukemia from the use of diagnostic x-rays. Certainly there are valid and essential uses for x-ray examinations, and modern medicine frequently uses such examinations as an essential part of diagnosis. However, there is also a risk of radiation exposure, and although the benefits are easily defined, there are also risks that have been quantified. Certainly the scientific community, including the medical profession, is aware that there are risks to radiation/x-ray exposure. Some of us have had the experience of a lead shield being placed over the pelvic area during x-ray examinations of other parts of the body. This shield protects the gonads and pelvic bone marrow and the x-ray technician asks every woman of childbearing age if she is pregnant, before any x-rays are taken. Many years ago there were x-ray machines in retail shoe stores, to aid in fitting shoes; this practice has long been outlawed.

Hall has calculated that each year there are 840 cases of leukemia generated by the practice of diagnostic radiology. The mean active bone marrow dose for diagnostic x-ray exposure was reported to be 746 to 1137 microGray (that is 1/1000 of a milliGray). This dose illustrates the stochastic model, including the absence of a threshold and the fact that the character of the defect/mutation, if it does happen, is independent of the dose of radiation which produced it. Although there are a great number of radiographic/x-ray procedures performed, these cases of leukemia represent real and potentially fatal complications of these diagnostic x-ray examinations, using relatively low doses of x-ray/radiation. The United States Government has identified a variety of cancers resulting from radiation, in particular referring to servicemen serving in or near Hiroshima or Nagasaki following the atomic bombings, or who participated in atomic bomb testing, who later developed cancers. Acute leukemia is included in this listing, which also relates to compensation of such individuals for their cancers induced by radiation exposure.

Fairlie and Resnikoff have discussed the latest mortality data (1996) from the continuing study of Japanese A-bomb survivors, showing a statistically significant upward trend of risk with doses in the region of 50 mSv. This has reinforced the validity of the no-threshold concept.

It should be noted that the dose to bone of this subject, Mr. Murray, 39 rads [39000 millirads] total, or 2.8 rads [2800 millirads] per year, is much higher than the average "background" dose of ionizing radiation, which is about 300 millirem/year to the whole body.

Straume points out that high energy gamma rays (e.g. the Japanese exposure) are expected to be substantially less effective in producing biological damage compared with lower energy radiation. Acute leukemia was clearly evident as a result of radiation exposure in those cities in Japan, and it would be expected that the lower energy x-rays produced in the present situation would be even more effective biologically than the high energy gamma rays in the Japanese exposure.

Historical Aspects of Ionizing Radiation, Including X-rays, As a Cause of Cancer, Including Leukemia

Ionizing radiation has the property of producing mutations in living cells, including cancer-causing mutations. The source of the ionizing radiation does not determine the damage; if the radiation produces ionization in living cells, which causes mutations, it has the ability to produce cancer, regardless of the particular source of the ionizing radiation, whether it be a particular isotope [e.g. naturally occurring Uranium, artificially produced Plutonium, irradiation from x-rays or gamma rays, or mixed sources of ionizing radiation (atomic bombings or industrial accidents, such as Chernobyl)]. Ionizing radiation produced by x-rays has the same harmful effects as ionizing radiation from any other source, assuming the radiation reaches vulnerable tissues in the body, and is thus capable of producing mutations.

The effects of ionizing radiation on living tissues follow the stochastic model. As defined earlier, this states that there is no threshold, and the higher the dose the more likely the adverse effect, and once the adverse effect (i.e. genetic mutation) occurs, the quality of that effect is independent of the dose. Thus even a limited radiation exposure has the risk of significant harm, of causing cancer in particular, and cancer of the blood especially.

As a simple illustration, when this reviewer was a child, it was common to have x-ray machines in retail shoe stores, to view the "fit" of a new pair of shoes. When the dangers of ionizing radiation, including x-ray irradiation, became known, especially after 1945, such machines were outlawed. Even such a "brief" exposure was known to be harmful.

The harmful effects of ionizing radiation on the blood and blood-forming organs (hematopoietic system) has been known for many decades. For example, as early as 1925 there was a report in the Journal of the American Medical Association by Martland, H.S, et al. entitled: "Some Unrecognized Dangers in the Use and Handling of Radioactive Substances" warning physicians that "…when long-lived radioactive substances are introduced into the body...death may follow a long time after, from the effects of constant irradiation on the blood-forming centers."

The standard exposure unit, the Roentgen, was proposed in 1928, by the International Committee on Radiation Protection. The modern unit, the rad [now renamed Gray], was proposed in 1953. These terms illustrate the intensive technical and scientific work then in progress, to define and limit the exposure of humans to ionizing radiation. As a matter of fact, an early demonstration that x-rays could cause mutations in fruit flies (*Drosophila*) by Muller, in 1927, formed the basis for world-wide research on the effect on x-rays/ionizing radiation in causing mutations.

Beginning in 1945, with the explosion of the atomic bombs at Hiroshima and Nagasaki, the effects of ionizing radiation on humans has been intensively studied. At first the Atomic Bomb Casualty Commission published reports regarding early and late effects, and subsequently the Radiation Effects Research Foundation has continued this dissemination of information. One of the effects of ionizing radiation noted early was the production of leukemia. Various medical uses of radiation, e.g. irradiation of the spine for ankylosing spondylitis, use of radioactive isotopes for diagnosis and treatment, and occupational exposures, as well as industrial accidents have all been carefully studied to determine the increased risk of cancers resulting from such exposures, especially excess cancers of the blood-forming organs, such as leukemia.

The first described cases of cancer from radiation were in fact reported in 1902, in the skin of scientists who were studying radioactivity. Leukemia was initially suspected as being increased in incidence by exposure to radiation as early as 1911. The role of radiation in causing leukemia in humans was first reported in 1944 in physicians and radiologists. Although leukemia, cancer of the blood-forming organs, was described early as a result of exposure to ionizing radiation, various other forms of cancer arising from exposure to ionizing radiation have also been described many years ago. Lung cancer was described in pitchblende and uranium miners, due to breathing radon gas, and bone tumors were observed in radium dial painters, who swallowed radioactive materials. Other examples include liver cancer from the use of Thorotrast, and various other forms of cancer, e.g. thyroid, breast, salivary gland have been described in subjects exposed to ionizing radiation.

In 1956 authoritative reports were published by the U.S. National Academy of Sciences- National Research Council on the adverse effects of ionizing radiation. As noted above, leukemia in atomic bomb survivors was reported as early as 1952. It is clear, therefore, that the adverse effects of ionizing radiation on humans, such as that produced by exposure to x-rays, in causing leukemia in particular, have been known in the scientific community for many, many years, certainly prior to the exposure of this subject to ionizing radiation in his workplace. This knowledge is illustrated by the use of radiation detection devices/monitoring badges/radiation counters/monitoring equipment used and/or worn by workers/personnel/inspectors at the facility, as well as by the creation and maintenance of written records of such radiation exposure.

Conclusions and Expert Medical Opinions:

It is therefore medically probable that ionizing radiation, produced in the work environment of this individual, and which contaminated that general and his personal environment, was a substantial contributing factor and was a cause of the myelodysplastic syndrome and the acute myeloid leukemia that occurred in this subject, and of his death that was a result of these diagnoses. Based on the various reports and materials cited, this exposure at least doubled his risk of developing these diseases, myelodysplastic syndrome and acute myeloid leukemia.

The initial myelodysplastic syndrome was a precursor to the subsequent development of acute myeloid leukemia, and in this case both disorders may be considered to have a unified cause, exposure to ionizing radiation. This is in agreement with generally accepted medical science, which states that acute myeloid leukemia is a common result of having myelodysplastic syndrome.

The diagnosis of these conditions required extensive diagnostic testing and procedures, including invasive procedures such bone marrow examination. Treatment included chemotherapy and extensive supportive and other treatment measures. He sustained various forms of disability and inability to perform normal life functions and activities, impaired bodily functions, as well as specific symptoms and side effects of this particular form of cancer and its required treatment. There also resulted shortened and limited life expectancy, and his ultimate demise. In addition there were likely various social, financial, marital, and familial implications and correlates associated with the development of this malignancy, that will not be further commented upon here.

The nature, location, timing, and dose of such exposures to ionizing radiation has been well documented. Within reasonable medical probability, this ionizing radiation acted as a carcinogen (a cause of cancer), and such exposure to ionizing radiation was a cause and a substantial contributing factor in the development of his malignancy, and the signs and symptoms, required treatment, and outcome that did result.

Max Daley, M.D.

Report #2: Medical Negligence

This report is most notable for the following:

- The specification and quoting of the precise standards allegedly violated by the defendant.
- The easy-to-read chronology of events.
- The easy-to-read risk for fall assessment.
- The numerical listing of the specific reasons the defendant failed to meet the standard of care.
- Objective, confident, and precise language.
- Absence of typographical errors.

Areas of possible improvement:

- A more precise listing of the documents reviewed.
- The listing of the documents reviewed could be made at the beginning of the report, not the end.
- The deletion of the apparently boilerplate language at the end of the report.
- The use of head notes to break up the report.

Florence Lundgren, 80 years old, was admitted to Memorial Nursing Home in Mountainview, KY on September 10, 1997 after having lived independently in an apartment with home health assistance. She reported she was unable to care for herself, often forgetting to eat and take her medications. Admission documentation shows that she was alert though with periods of confusion, which continued to be reported throughout her record. She had a history of cardiovascular disease, stroke, dementia, arthritis, and diabetes mellitus, Type II, and was taking several medications. On admission she required the assistance of one for activities of daily living for dressing, grooming, bathing, ambulating, and transferring. Her vision was adequate with glasses. She discharged and readmitted herself twice. During her stay at Memorial Nursing Home, she suffered five falls, the last of which resulted in head injuries from which she did not recover.

A summary of events after her admission to Memorial Nursing Home is as follows:

Date	Event
9/10/97	Admitted to Memorial Nursing Home.
9/19/97	Discharged home to live with niece.

11/18/97		Readmitted to ICF level of care, periods of confusion.
11/19/97	11:45 a.m.	Rolled off bed, no apparent injuries.
12/7/97		Fall documented in untitled report; no further information.
2/16/98		Referenced on 2/24: Medication error. No further notes.
2/19/98	7:40 p.m.	Found sitting in floor, slid out of bed. No apparent injuries.
2/27/98	3:30 p.m.	Found sitting on floor beside recliner, states "slid down."
3/6/98		Signed out of facility AMA.
3/9/98		Returned to Memorial Nursing Home for admission.
3/11/98	12:55 a.m.	Found lying on floor, groaning, large knot on head. Diagnosis: multiple head injuries/closed head injury.
3/17/98		Readmitted to SNF (Skilled Nursing Facility)
3/23/98		Fall risk assessed.
04/01/98 – 04/24/98		Condition deteriorates, patient expires.

In my opinion, the nursing home failed to meet the minimal regulations and nursing standards of care with regard to OBRA and the Nursing Process as described below:

Federal OBRA Regulations:
§483.20 Resident Assessment: The facility must conduct a comprehensive, accurate
assessment of the resident's status initially and periodically, providing information necessary to develop a plan of care.

§483.20 (k) Resident Assessment, Comprehensive Care Plans: The facility must develop a comprehensive care plan for each resident that includes measurable objectives and timetables to meet a resident's medical, nursing, mental, and psychological needs, identified from the comprehensive assessment. The care plan is prepared by an interdisciplinary team and is evaluated and revised as the resident's status changes.

§483.10(b)(11) Resident Rights, Notification of Changes: The facility must immediately inform the resident, consult with the resident's physician, and if known, notify the resident's legal representative or an interested family member when there is an accident, clinical complications or a transfer or discharge from the facility.

271

§483.25 Quality of Care: Each resident shall receive, and the facility shall provide, care and services to enable the resident to attain or maintain her highest practicable physical, mental, and psychosocial well-being in accordance with the comprehensive assessment and plan of care.

§483.25 (a) Quality of Care, Activities of Daily Living: A resident's abilities in activities of daily living, including ambulation, do not diminish unless circumstances are unavoidable.

§483.25(h) Quality of Care, Accidents: Each resident receives adequate supervision and assistance devices to prevent accidents. The facility identifies each resident at risk for accidents and falls and plans care and implements procedures to prevent accidents.

§483.75 Clinical Records: The record must be complete, accurate, and reflect the nursing process. Staff interventions and resident's response to treatment shall be documented. The nursing process, as a standard of nursing care, requires continuous assessment, identification of patient needs and problems, interventions to meet those needs, and evaluation of the patient's response. The nursing process dictates that the care plan is evaluated for effectiveness of the plan and revised as indicated to meet the patient's needs.

§483.25 Quality of Care, Nutrition: The facility must ensure that each resident maintains acceptable parameters of nutritional status.

§483.60 (c) Drug Regiment Review: The drug regimen of each resident must be reviewed at least once a month by a licensed pharmacist.

Ms. Lundgren should not have experienced the falls that occurred. The fifth fall that caused the injuries that proved to be fatal could likely have been prevented had the proper precautions been implemented on the patient's initial and subsequent admission assessments and included of the plan of care. It was clear that the staff was aware of the patient's unsteady gait and that she required assistance when ambulating, using an assistive device (walker/cane) "when she remembered it." The fact that the Ms. Lundgren had painful arthritis that potentially further limited her mobility nor the fact that she experienced long-term use of a narcotic pain reliever and an antihistamine for nausea were integrated into the plan of care as risk factors for potential injury. Further, the fact that she was intermittently confused to the point of not being able to find her way back to her room was noted on aspects of the care plan other than prevention of injury. Episodes of diarrhea added further fall risk to a patient with an unsteady gait.

All of the aspects noted above are categories scored on the Falls Risk Assessment used at Memorial Nursing Home on 3/23 and should have alerted the staff to the fact that a risk assessment was in order on each of Ms. Lundgren's admissions. Had the assessments been performed, the scores would have dictated that the Fall Alert be implemented for safety, a score of 15 points required for the high risk Fall Alert. The one assessment that was done was not documented until 3/23/98, 12 days after the injurious fall occurred. Ms. Lundgren's score was 60 of a possible 65. When each fall occurred, documentation did not reflect the circumstances of the fall, i.e., call light in reach, reminders to patient, glasses available, side rails up, etc.

Using documentation in the medical record, the following fall risk assessments for each admission was simulated. In all cases, a Fall Alert protocol would have been indicated. The assessment on 3/23 was found in the record, documented by staff (unsigned).

RISK FOR FALL ASSESSMENT

I. To place a patient on FALL ALERT (high risk), 15 or more points must be scored.
II. To place a patient on FALL PRECAUTIONS (risk for fall), 5-14 points must be scored

CATEGORY	Points	9/10	11/18	3/9	3/23
1. History of Previous Falls	15		15	15	15
2. Confusion	15	15	15	15	15
3. Age over 70	5	5	5	5	5
4. Impaired Mobility (i.e. unsteady gait, ambulatory devices…)	5	5	5	5	5
5. Impaired Neurological Status (i.e. dizziness, seizures, paresthesias)	5			5	5
6. Sensory Limitations	5	5	5	5	5
7. Impaired Nutrition	5				5
8. Impaired Cardiovascular Status	5				
9. Medications i.e. laxatives, diuretics, sedatives, narcotics, antihypertensives	5	5	5	5	5
TOTAL		35	50	55	60

After only two of the five falls were attempts made to notify the family/contact person and the physician, ignoring the standard of care. The family/contact person and the physician were inconsistently notified of patient transfers out of Memorial Nursing Home for tests and hospitalizations as well.

Basic to the nursing process is assessment of a patient's nursing care needs and evaluation of any interventions that were done to meet that need. Documentation by this nursing home does not reflect the nursing process as evidenced by the fact that the care plans were rarely updated, even after the falls occurred. Of particular note is the fact there is no record that the plan of care was not completed or revised on Ms. Lundgren's return to the nursing home after her severe injuries when her care needs had changed dramatically.

As result of inadequate nursing care and supervision, Ms. Lundgren's abilities diminished greatly. She was an independence-loving woman with many friends and family, discharging herself on two occasions. One discharge was Against Medical Advice (AMA) because the staff felt she could not take care of herself living alone due to her confusion and condition. Further, a wound was noted on the patient's wrist after a hospital discharge. The wound was described as Stage IV, covered with eschar (black, hard cover). While the treatment of the wound may have been appropriate given the patient's condition, a wound care specialist should have been consulted for proper staging and care. Further, once the resident became bed-bound, the facility failed in not completing a pressure ulcer risk assessment in a debilitated, at-risk patient.

Staff failed to recognize the possible effects of at least two of Ms. Lundgren's medications. Darvocet is known to cause dizziness, sedation, nausea and vomiting. She began receiving Phenergan for complaints of nausea on 11/20/97. Side effects of Phenergan include sedation, sleepiness, dizziness, increased or decreased blood pressure, and nausea and vomiting. (PDR, 2000). The cause of the patient's continued complaints of nausea were not investigated and the medication was continued. Since any of these symptoms would increase one's fall risk, measures should have been taken to ensure the patient's safety if the medications were deemed needed and appropriate for the patient's comfort. Both are potentially inappropriate in the elderly and should be given for as short a time as possible (OBRA Regulations and Survey Procedures for the Long Term Care Facility, pp 163.1-163.8). The drug regimen was reviewed for 12/97-4/98 (none found for 9/97-11/97), violating the standard of once a month review. On those reviews that are present, the continued use of Darvocet and Phenergan is not questioned nor is their use mentioned in the physician progress notes.

The facility did not meet standards with regard to Ms. Lundgren's needs related to her Type II Diabetes Mellitus. The plan of care does not reflect a goal for her blood sugar level until 4/17. Consequently, her blood sugars remained well over recommended levels. Blood sugars were assessed regularly by the staff and reported to the physician with a rare change in orders. Once again, a failure to follow the nursing process.

The facility failed to ensure adequate nutrition for Ms. Lundgren as evidenced by a gradual loss of 17# over a six month period, a severe weight loss of 12% (OBRA Regulations and Survey Procedures for the Long Term Care Facility, pp. 106). Had the nursing process been followed, reassessment of the patient's nutrition goal of maintaining a weight of 155-160# would have resulted in revising the care plan to prevent further loss, finding the therapeutic diet was ineffective in maintaining goal weight and in stabilizing blood sugars. By the patient's own admission, she often forgot to eat. The need for supervision was not included on the care plan. A calorie count, monitoring of albumin levels, and supplements could have lessened her nutritional risk early on. After her 3/11 fall, Ms. Lundgren's weight continued to decrease and her nutritional status became even more perilous when she became unable to swallow.

The nursing home failed to maintain accurate and complete medical records. There are large gaps of time in which there is no nursing documentation. The nursing aid records that are included cover only the month of April and are not complete. There are no records of activities of daily living, reflecting a disregard for the patient's health and well-being. In addition, the record of next of kin/contact person is inconsistent with the documentation of notification of next of kin/contact person/powers of attorney. Medication administration records are incomplete and often not dated.

Ms. Lundgren's condition deteriorated dramatically after the 3/11 fall. She suffered severe head injuries and was returned for supportive therapy. She returned to the hospital for treatment of Deep Vein Thrombosis and a heart attack. She progressively became more confused, able to swallow only honey-thickened liquids, she was oriented to her name only, and required total assistance with all her activities. She expired 4/24/98 after losing the independence and dignity she craved.

In summary, Memorial Nursing Home failed to meet the standards in at least, but not limited to, the following ways:

1.   Failure to provide adequate assessment of patient risk for injury/falls at the time of each admission and ongoing shift to shift assessments.

2.   Failure to provide and follow an individualized plan of care that is appropriate to meet this resident's needs.

3.   Failure to notify the physician when the falls occurred.

4.   Failure to notify the next of kin/contact person when the falls occurred and when transfers occurred.

5.   Failure to provide adequate supervision and assistance to prevent falls.

6.   Failure to meet this resident's nutritional needs and properly monitor her nutritional state.

7.   Failure to provide an accurate and complete clinical record and failing to document the nursing process.

8.   Failure to monitor safe medication distribution and administration.

Memorial Nursing Home failed to meet the standards of care for Ms. Lundgren. In my professional opinion, the fall and subsequent injuries that lead to Ms. Lundgren's suffering and death would not have occurred if her care had been based on the nursing process and if even minimal assessments and precautions had been taken to prevent the falls she experienced. Her family was not allowed the opportunity to participate in the patient's plan of care. The above deficiencies lead to the death of this resident.

The preceding report provides my nursing opinions based on the information I have reviewed in the case of Ms. Lundgren while she was a resident at Memorial Nursing Home. This report does not necessarily embody the details of all my opinions. I reserve the right to amend and add to my opinions upon further review of records.

The records reviewed by me to this date (1/17/2001) include:

A.   Medical Records from Memorial Nursing Home, Mountainview, KY 9/10/97-04/24/98 for Ms. Lundgren
B.   Specific portions of the medical records from
       1. Northside Medical Center, Stone's Throw, KY
       2. Bluegrass Hospital, Cantor, KY
       3. General Hospital, Grantsburg KY
C.   Several pages were copied blank

Report #3: Correctional Facility Safety Evaluation

This report is most notable for the following:

- Good cover page.
- Well-written.
- Easy to read, with effective use of bullet-points and headnotes.
- Exhaustive factual justification for conclusions.
- Absence of typographical errors.

Areas of possible improvement:

- A more precise and complete listing of documents reviewed.
- The use of photographs to buttress the report.
- Citations to the specific standards violated.

To:	Gale Young, Esquire Sally Simms, Esquire Southern Center for Human Rights
From:	Robert W. Paulson, PhD, MPH, RS Forensic Registered Sanitarian
Subject:	Environmental Health and Safety Evaluation of the Carson County Jail Facilities, Smalltown, Alabama
Re:	Johnny Smithe, et al., vs. Kent Lewis, et al.
Date:	March 14, 2000

INTRODUCTION

On July 6 and 7, 2000, I conducted an environmental health and safety evaluation of the Carson County, Smalltown, Alabama main jail and jail annex facilities. Notice of these inspections was given to the Sheriff's Department prior to this inspection tour.

The purposes of these inspections were fourfold. First, to assess the degree of compliance with the Agreement of Settlement Subject to Court Approval, and Proposed Notice under Rule 23, Federal Rules of Civil Procedure, dated May, 1982. Second, to determine what effect administrative policies, practices and procedures have upon the environmental health and safety of the prison population. Third, to determine a level of compliance with current health and industry consensus standards, and, finally, to learn if any existing environmental conditions may affect the public health of the prisoners and subsequently, the general public health of the community.

The inspections covered each jail's program, service and storage areas of environmental health and safety significance. All housing and prisoner holding units in both facilities were likewise evaluated. We did not enter any cell where a prisoner was asleep, or where members of the plaintiff's inspection team precluded reasonable and safe entry. In these instances, a visual inspection from outside of the cell was conducted.

Whenever practical, nondestructive representative environmental measurements were taken with precalibrated portable instruments to assess the facility conditions and verify findings.

A lawyer from the Southern Center for Human Rights accompanied me throughout this inspection. One or more representatives of the Sheriff's Department, as well as an attorney for the Defendant also accompanied me. I was freely able to inspect all areas of the facilities, and to speak with prisoners as the situation warranted; facility staff were always available to answer questions.

In preparing this report, I relied on my knowledge and experience as an institutional Sanitarian, established and recognized case law and several documents. These documents included voluntary correctional industry standards, published public health and epidemiological research and literature reviews relating to institutional public health and safety. These documents included, but were not limited to those published by:

- American Public Health Association (APHA),
- American Correctional Association (ACA),
- Illuminating Engineering Society of North America (IESNA),
- National Fire Prevention Association (NFPA),
- USDHHS – Centers for Disease Control and Prevention (CDC), and,
- USDHHS – Public Health Service / Food and Drug Administration (PHS/FDA)

SUMMARY OF FINDINGS

The Carson County Jail and the Carson County Jail Annex, fail to provide a habitable environment for a significant number of inmates. I observed numerous serious violations of accepted public health standards and failures in the systems designed to maintain adequate environmental conditions. These deficiencies have a direct impact on the risk for contracting a communicable disease and/or sustaining an unintentional injury. They include, among others:

RISK OF ILLNESS AND INJURY
- Severe crowding in several facilities, particularly Annex 2 and the Kitchen Trustee dormitory.
- Inadequate ventilation was provided in the Annex dormitories, and the main jail ventilation system is in need of cleaning, maintenance and rebalancing.
- Annex temperatures in the living area exceeded 90° F.
- Openings to the outside in the Annex complex are unscreened against flying insects.
- Inmates and prisoners are not provided with sheets, pillows and pillow cases.
- The shower stalls in the main jail are uncleanable, and several shower heads were not functional.
- Hot water is not provided to several areas in the main jail.
- An inadequate number of sinks are provided in Annex 2.
- There is no sanitary barbering.
- Kitchen facilities are too small for the number of meals being prepared.
- No HACCP plan is provided for raw chicken.
- Transportation and service of prepared food exceeds two hours at the Annex.
- Medically prepared diets are not served at safe temperatures.
- Serving utensils at the Annex are not properly washed and sanitized.
- Good and accepted environmental infection control practices are not followed in the clinics.
- Vermin infestations were seen in the Annex complex.
- Suicide prevention policies and practices are inconsistent with acceptable industry standards.
- Lighting in most areas in the main jail is below 20 foot-candles.
- Emergency egress lighting from the main jail cell block areas appears to be below 5 foot-candles.

INJURY PREVENTION
- Evacuation drills are not performed in the main jail complex.
- Several defective electrical outlets and wiring were found throughout the facilities.
- Noise standards are exceeded in living areas because of air moving devices and toilets.

The following sections detail the summary and conclusions of this inspection.

COMMUNICABLE DISEASE CONTROL
CROWDING

Overcrowding is responsible for the greatest risk of communicable disease spread in an institutional setting; more so than any other single factor. Institutional overcrowding is also responsible for compromising the public health and potentially being the point source of an epidemic. Some of the facilities at the main jail and jail annex greatly exceed the safe housing capacity and are therefore a serious risk to the public health. This risk from overcrowding is made more acute by the lack of a medical examination and particularly the absence of any screening for tuberculosis, of the newly admitted prisoners. In fact, neither are the CDC recommended guidelines for the detection of tuberculosis among incarcerated individuals followed, nor is any mention of such a policy in the operations manual.

In virtually every overcrowded situation, the bed arrangement does not allow for at least a six-foot separation between the heads of adjoining bunks. In most instances, only 2½ feet separated bunks. In the most crowded area, only 4 ft² of unencumbered space was available per inmate. These minimum space requirements were originally established through epidemiological surveillance of catastrophic pandemics, and subsequently verified through other incident investigations. The minimum space requirements for multiple occupancy areas are 60 ft² and 35 ft² of unencumbered space per individual. The following table lists the space available per prisoner/inmate in selected areas. These calculations are based on measurements taken during the inspection; all linear measurements were rounded up to the nearest foot.

MAIN JAIL

Room Number	Total space per inmate (ft²)	Unencumbered space per inmate (ft²)
3 (trustee)	36	25
7 (trustee)	33	24
A1	33	20
A3 (cells)	17	10
C1 (infirmary)	51	23
D1 and D2	38	31
D4	40	29
Kitchen Trustees Dorm	13	4

ANNEX

Area designation	Total space per inmate (ft²)	Unencumbered space per inmate (ft²)
Annex 1 (North and South)	44	35
Annex 2	24	16

The crowding in both facilities becomes more critical in the absence of regular recreation. The inmates and prisoners in the main jail told us that they were given no opportunity for recreation, although a multipurpose room, which at one time had been used, was available. This room is being used for the storage of dry and canned goods. Inmates in Annex 2 informed us that the opportunity for outdoor recreation is sporadic, and when it is offered, the time allotted is usually considerably less than one hour.

AIR QUALITY AND VENTILATION

An adequate and effective ventilation system is the most significant environmental measure to reduce airborne contagion and minimize odors.

The main jail is a completely closed building that relies entirely on mechanical ventilation; airflow, humidity and temperature were not uniform. Some areas had ample ventilation; others did not and were malodorous and stuffy. Most of the air-return vents are partially or completely occluded with dust and dirt, thereby preventing adequate air turnover as originally designed and installed. In addition, in the one pipe chase we inspected, the ductwork integrity had been breached, thereby allowing air exchanges to occur in the chase-way instead of the prisoner/inmate occupied areas. It appears that the system requires some repairs, cleaning and balancing. It is my opinion, that the ventilation system in the main jail can be restored to optimal operation.

At the time of this inspection, a new air conditioning system was being installed in Annex 2, but had not been completed and was not operational. Upon our initial inspection, the ventilation system a Annex 2 consisted of a single 3' x 3' belt-driven exhaust fan and two 3' x 3' wall openings for fresh air supply. The supply and exhaust openings were at opposite sides of the room, located approximately at 12-foot height. There was no perceptible air movement, the temperature within the room was particularly oppressive (91°F, with a relative humidity of 68%). The malodor resulting from the crowded conditions and lack of ventilation was overwhelming. The toilet area had no exhaust ventilation, the temperature and relative humidity respectively approached 100 degrees. Temperatures exceeding 80 to 85° F are extremely detrimental to individuals on psychotropic medication.

Although the ambient temperature and humidity levels in Annex 1 were similar to those in Annex 2, the air exchange rate seemed to be greater, although actual air volume measurements were not possible.

Room 1 of Annex 3 was similar in air makeup and turnover rate as Annex 2, however, the 28 bunks located in the garage bay were open to the outside. The toilet area had no exhaust ventilation.

The annex building is that a simple shell consisting of metal and cinder block with no appreciable insulating qualities. Radiant heat exacerbates the excessively high temperature in the dormitories. During the height of the afternoon sun, radiant temperatures in excess of 100° F were measured on the ceiling and exposed wall.

LAUNDRY AND LINENS

No inmate or prisoner, other than those individuals who reside in Annex 3 have bed linen. Sheets are not available and pillows are not distributed in all areas; of those that are available, none have pillow covers. From a public health standpoint, clean bedding, issued regularly, provides for health maintenance and minimizes acquisition of illness or infection. The excuse given for not providing bed linens is that sheets are a fire hazard. Although this is not true, the fact that these facilities are now smoke-free and inmates are no longer permitted matches, makes this argument moot.

The laundry facilities in the main jail and Annex 1 are adequate, although those in Annex 1 were poorly maintained and unclean. Whereas, Annex 2 has only a household washer and dryer to serve 122 prisoners and inmates. We were told by an inmate in that area that although everyone has the opportunity to get their clothes cleaned, it is necessary to pay a gratuity to the inmate worker to assure the safe return of one's clothing.

PERSONAL HYGIENE

The ability of prisoners and inmates to maintain an adequate level of personal hygiene is vital to good health. Although all residents are able to shower on demand (within time limitations, count, etc.), the facilities are either crowded, minimally functioning or not functioning properly. Examples of this are as follows:

- The finish in the shower stalls in the main jail is poor and no longer cleanable without excessive friction and caustic cleaners. The spray nozzles on numerous shower spray heads had become encrusted with lime scale and no longer functioned as designed. To minimize the erratic spray pattern, the facility residents have tied towels around these heads to minimize splash. The towels had become septic and aerosolization of the organisms growing on and in them is probable.
- The women's facilities do not receive adequate hot water, except in the shower. Hot water was not available for handwashing and oral hygiene.
- The inmate to sink ratio in Annex 2 exceeds recommended

standards. The facility has seven toilets and five urinals, eleven showers, and ten sinks; of which one shower and three sinks are not operational. The ratio of individuals to sinks is 17:1; exceeding the standard by 9.

- Annex 3 toilet has only one, three spigot gang sink to serve its entire population of working trustee inmates.
- Numerous plastic or metal-surface mirrors used for personal grooming were badly scored and no longer reflective.
- Prisoner/inmate volunteers serve as the jail's barbers. There is no area specific for barbering that includes a handwashing sink and an area to clean and sanitize barbering utensils. We found no evidence that neck papers are used, or that clipper heads and combs are routinely sanitized between cuttings; Barbicide® or a similar sanitizing agent was not available.

FOOD SERVICE

All meals are prepared at a central kitchen located in the main jail. This facility was originally designed to serve no more than approximately 800 meals per day, it now is used for the preparation of 1,800 and 2,100 meals per day. These facilities are however maintained in a sanitary manner and the inmate workers practice good personal hygiene. Although the kitchen management is competent, the risk of food borne infection from potentially hazardous foods cannot be minimized because of space and facility limitations. This is particularly critical in the preparation of raw chicken, which we were told is frequently on the menu, and subsequent time delays encountered in the delivery of prepared bulk foods to the annex. The following are the public health concerns with the food service operation:

- No Hazard Analysis Critical Control Point (HACCP) plans exists for the preparation and service of potentially hazardous foods, particularly with the use of raw chicken. This issue is critical because neither a temporal, nor is an adequate spatial separation possible in handling the raw and cooked product. Additional limitations with preparation area and cooking equipment such as ovens and tilt fryers further exacerbate this problem. Although the facility shortcomings cannot be overcome except with new construction, a HACCP plan, when followed will minimize the risk of cross-contamination of pathogenic organisms and subsequent development of an infectious dose in the cooked foods.
- Dried mashed potatoes are reconstituted with water at near boiling temperature, but are not subjected to further heating. The temperature of the potatoes taken before delivery was 136°F. Cooked potatoes are also considered "potentially hazardous" and must be maintained at a temperature greater than 140°F at all

times before serving.

- During this inspection, we witnessed a two-hour delay from finished preparation of the food to feeding at the annex. An acceptable time delay in the absence of any temperature-maintaining equipment (hot holding and cold holding; not insulated carriers) is a maximum of one hour. If pathogenic bacteria are present in the cooked foods, the hour limit will not permit the growth of more than three generations of organisms. However, in transport containers without heating elements, these foods cool to a temperature of less than 140°F.

- Special and medically prescribed diets for the annex and all trays for the main jail are served on a Styrofoam plate and covered with plastic film. These trays were placed in an insulated carrier and taken to the site for distribution. Surface temperatures of the food at the point of delivery were ±104°F. The trays and plastic film will not maintain safe temperatures, and start losing heat immediately.

- Plastic trays delivered to the annex are not air-dried, but are placed wet in lined 35-gallon covered containers. Desiccation is an effective means of disinfecting. Wet trays can carry over pathogenic organisms, particularly those trays which are chipped, cracked and/or scored.

- The serving utensils used at the annex are not returned to the main kitchen for washing and sanitizing. Rather, they are cleaned by an inmate in the common toilet sinks and subsequently stored in the C/O cube until the next meal. This practice is highly unsanitary. Since no three-compartment sink or dishwasher is available at the annex, the utensils must be returned for proper cleaning and sanitizing.

- Some of the fluorescent bulb luminaries, particularly those along the main route of travel, were not protected against breakage. If a bulb is inadvertently shattered, shards of glass may contaminate food that is being prepared or transported in the immediate area.

- Traffic through the kitchen area by other than kitchen help wearing clean outer garments and hair covering, is not controlled.

MEDICAL FACILITIES

The storage of medical supplies and pharmaceuticals in the main jail and jail annex clinics were inconsistent with established infection control practices. Specific examples include the following:

- Pharmaceuticals and personal food were not separated in the refrigerator.
- Sterile supplies were not protected during storage and use. The inner-wrap of single-use disposable items was not protected against multiple handling and crimping of the packaging material to maintain sterile integrity. Inner packs of single-use disposable items were not protected against the deposition of biological aerosols.
- Sterile, clean and contaminated items were not separated to prevent cross-contamination on the examination supply stands.
- Opened containers of saline solutions were not dated and subject to adulteration by the growth of contaminants.
- I did not observe any specially marked biohazard containers for the disposal of contaminated gloves, and other medical supplies. Proper sharps disposal containers were available.
- Blood pressure cuffs were soiled and not protected against contamination during storage.
- Absorbent towels were used as shelf liners.
- The two exhaust grills that would provide room air exchange and subsequent dilution of any contagion, were almost completely occluded with dust and dirt.

No crash-cart or emergency tray was seen at either clinic location.

PEST CONTROL

Potential disease-carrying cockroach and housefly infestations were seen in the jail annex. The roach infestation was confined to the janitor's closet and laundry-room located below the observation tower in Annex 1. Houseflies were present in large numbers in Annex 2, particularly around the toilet and communal feeding areas. None of the annex outer openings were screened against flying insects. No active or passive control measures for either infestation were evident.

Fresh mouse feces, an indicator of an infestation, were observed along the wall/floor junction on the interior perimeter of the commissary. Only one, old and non-activated mousetrap was in the area; its placement was not in the mouse run. The facilities were not broom-clean and storage of food was not off the floor and away from the walls to allow for cleaning and prevention of mouse harborage and nesting sites.

SAFETY
SUICIDE PREVENTION

During our inspection, we came upon a prisoner who was housed in cell number 01 in the A3 area. The prisoner was in an unlighted cell without a mattress or blanket. When I asked of the correctional staff whether this prisoner was on suicide watch, no one could provide me with an answer. The door to the cell was unmarked. I also learned that the jail had no formal policy on housing and observing a suicidal prisoner. While several explanations were proffered, none could explain the prisoner's status. If the prisoner was being held under a suicide watch, the cell was not within the line of sight of the correctional officer. In addition, the shower stall within the room provided a sight barrier; the lack of any room illumination precluded observation, and, periodic rounds were not conducted.

However, if the prisoner were confined for punitive reasons, he was not provided with any basic necessities such as a mattress, towel and toiletries.

LIGHTING

We routinely found less than 10 foot-candles of illumination throughout the main jail and annex, except in hallways and major routes of egress. However, egress routes from the suite of cells in the Main Jail were also below 10 foot-candles. Specific examples of lighting deficiencies are detailed below:

- The Main Jail illumination in the living areas is through a grated opening in the ceiling, above which is an incandescent light. According to both the inmates and correctional staff, these lights are never turned-off. To compensate for the continual light, the inmates have covered these openings to provide them with a darkened room for sleeping. Even in those instances where the openings were not covered, the level of illumination did not reach 20 foot-candles.
- The luminaries in the Annex 2 are kept off except for the area of tables and benches around the observation cube.
- However, I measured the level of illumination in the MDC clinic pharmaceutical dispensaries at less than 10 foot-candles. All standards that reference pharmaceutical dispensing areas require a level of direct illumination of 100 foot-candles to prevent medication errors.
- Inmates and prisoners housed in some of the solitary confinement cells in A2 of the main jail and Annex 2 have no daylight orientation.
- There is no task lighting in the clinic dispensary. Task illumination in this area should be at least 100 foot-candles.

FIRE SAFETY

Neither the main jail nor the Annex has a fire suppression system. The Annex is located at grade, evacuation is hampered only by the positioning of the bunks and lack of adequate aisle space. However, the main jail occupies the 9th and 10th floors of the courthouse building, and is served by a single, secured elevator. The correctional staff conduct and document a monthly silent fire drill on all three shifts; there are no full evacuation drills. Since the main jail serves newly admitted prisoners, even those who may be handicapped, as well as those requiring the services of an infirmary, full evacuation drills are essential to ensure safety. The policy manual does not include any reference to the emergency evacuation of prisoners and inmates who are motor impaired or infirm. Other obvious fire safety issues included the following:

- The fire extinguishers located in the main jail janitorial supply closet and kitchen were inaccessible.
- The dryer exhaust duct in Annex 1 was occluded with lint and presented an immediate fire hazard.
- Inmates in D4 had fashioned a cooker, using an outlet as an ignition source. The room had a strong odor of burnt paper.

ELECTRICAL SAFETY
Several outlets and outlet covers located in the main jail were damaged from using them for "stingers". Electrical outlets were also found badly worn and with open ground. Frayed and exposed wires and damaged plugs were likewise found in several occupied areas.

NOISE
Noise from the toilet in the "drunk tank" intake area was measured at 90 dBA (3- feet from the unit, at a height of 4-feet). This sound power level exceeds the daytime and nighttime acceptable standard by almost two- and four-orders of magnitude respectively. Additionally, the toilet runs in excess of 30 seconds with each flush activation.

A sustained noise level of 80 dBA / 84 dBC was measured in Annex 1 North. The fans that provide air movement in both North and South dormitory, emit a constant sound power level of 75 dBA. There is no sound attenuation in either Annex areas.

Respectfully submitted,

Richard W. Paulson, PhD, MPH, RS
DLAAS, ACD, DABFET
Forensic Registered Sanitarian

Report #4: Products Liability, Rule 26

This report is most notable for the following:

- Conciseness.
- Lack of typographical errors.
- Easy to read.
- Clearly written.
- Substantial and credible reasons for opinion provided.

Areas of possible improvement:

- Better language prefacing opinions and reasons. "The subject miter saw was unsafe and unreasonably dangerous when it was designed and manufactured for *one or more* of the following reasons:" Better if words "one or more" were not included.
- Avoiding use of the passive voice ("as the time between releasing the trigger switch and contacting the saw blade is not known...")
- More specificity in the descriptions of information considered; for example, the dates of the reports and depositions reviewed.
- A documentation of more literature reviewed and relied upon. This report is heavily based on the expert's experience. Citation to literature would bolster the opinion.

The following represents my Rule 26 Report in the matter of Hurt v. Brown & Drecker. It is based on review of materials submitted to me by your office (enumerated later), my involvement in cases involving accidents while using Brown & Drecker and other brands of miter saws, my education and experience as a mechanical engineer and my experience designing and using miter saws and other power tools as well as my knowledge of Brown & Drecker'' policies and procedures during and subsequent to my employment there. I reserve the right to amend this report if other evidence becomes available.

Summary of Accident:
Mr. Hurt was operating a Brown & Drecker Model 100 power miter saw at the time of the accident. He was cutting an approximately six inch length off the right end of a long piece of shoe molding. With his left hand Mr. Hurt was holding the molding against the saw's table and fence while his right hand operated the saw's trigger and brought the saw blade downward to cut the wood.

Mr. Hurt was using the saw in an expected manner to cut wood molding that the saw was designed to cut. Nothing that Mr. Hurt was doing during or immediately prior to the accident was unusual or unexpected to a qualified design engineer designing a power miter saw.

Shoe molding is a standard wood molding which approximates an unequal one-fourth of a circle. It is approximately three-quarters of an inch high, three-eighths of an inch thick and the other side is a smooth curve. Normally it is made of a soft wood such as white pine.

Professional Opinions and Basis for these Opinions:
In my professional opinion the subject miter saw was unsafe and unreasonably dangerous when it was designed and manufactured for one or more of the following reasons: It should be noted that contact of a hand or other body part with a spinning saw blade has been recognized for many years in the industry as a hazard which can result in serious injury, amputation or death. Therefore, safe design of a miter saw requires that the operator be protected from that spinning blade during all foreseeable uses and misuses of the saw. Obviously, part of the blade must be exposed to the workpiece in order to cut wood, but exposing additional blade to accidental contact with the operator is an unsafe practice.

1. Because the lower blade guard is retained in its guarding position only by the force of gravity the lower blade guard is easily and readily moved from its guarding position by a small force imparted from the workpiece and/or hand. The spinning saw blade is thereby exposed to the operator allowing them to be injured. Prior to the date of manufacture of this saw and prior to the date of the accident, Brown & Drecker and other manufacturers have made miter saws using a lower blade guard which is moved by a linkage assembly. This type of guard will not move from its guarding position when hit by the workpiece or a hand. If the link-driven guard had been installed on this saw Mr. Hurt would not have been injured.

2. The lower blade guard, as provided on this saw, rests of the top of the fence when small cross-section pieces of wood are being cut. This raised the lower blade guard higher than required to cut the wood and thereby exposes saw blade teeth to accidental contact by the operator's hand. If the miter saw had a larger opening in the fence, or the lower guard were of the linkage-driven design, no extra blade would have been exposed.

3. It is most likely that prior to being injured Mr. Hurt released the trigger switch that controls power to the saw's motor. Had the saw been equipped with an automatic blade brake which is actuated by releasing the trigger switch, the blade would have stopped or slowed prior to Mr. Hurt's contacting the blade. Brown & Drecker made miter saws with

such an automatic blade brake as early as 1976. These would stop a saw blade typically in less than two seconds. As the time between releasing the trigger switch and contacting the saw blade is not known, the speed of the saw blade at the moment of hand contact cannot be determined but any decrease in blade speed would have resulted in a less-serious accident.

4. One of the requirements of proper safety engineering is to evaluate the adequacy of the safety systems during actual consumer usage. Specifically, the adequacy of the blade guarding to prevent accidental contact with the spinning saw blade. To do this properly a company must collect and analyze accident information to determine how an accident happened, detect trends in accidents, evaluate alternative designs including those used by other manufacturers, determine whether an alternative design would provide superior safety and, if so, rapidly incorporate this change into production saws. Brown & Drecker failed to do this because their Records Retention Policy required then to destroy all information on an accident immediately after a lawsuit was settled or otherwise closed thereby denying them the ability to detect long-term trends in accidents. Further, as evidenced by Brown & Drecker failing to produce any record of analysis of miter saw accidents or discussions of alternate guard designs and their effectiveness, clearly reveals that the required feedback and evaluation step was lacking at Brown & Drecker.

    It was recognized by some miter saw manufacturers in the early to mid-1970's that one of the more common accidents was caused by the operator's arm, hand or finger(s) moving the lower blade guard out of its guarding position and allowing contact with the spinning saw blade. Analysis of the method of injury of the lawsuits filed against Brown & Drecker as early as early to mid-1970's would have come to the conclusion that a gravity-actuated guard was inadequate since it can readily be deflected from its guarding position and was therefore unsafe and that a link-actuated lower guard was a much safer type of guard for all miter saws. However, no evidence has been forthcoming that this analysis was ever performed and, therefore, Brown & Drecker still sold miter saws with the gravity actuated guard as late as 1996 when other miter saw manufacturers had all but abandoned that type of guard.

Information considered in Formulating the Above Opinions:

1. Video deposition of Mr. Hurt, volume 2.
2. Report of Dr. Lance Sherwood
3. Report of Dr. Margie Mullins
4. Deer Park Hospital Emergency Department triage Record, Operative Report, Post-operative Report and Consultation.

5. Inspection and testing of miter saws made by Brown & Drecker and other manufacturers including the B&D model 100 miter saw.

6. Knowledge, training and experience as a Mechanical Engineer including fourteen years experience in designing power tools including the first B&D miter saw.

7. Training and experience as a safety engineer and applying that to power tool design.

8. Knowledge of Brown & Drecker's policies and procedures during and subsequent to my employment there.

Attachments:

Attached and made a part of this report are my Curriculum Vitae (Exhibit A) and a list of cases I have testified, by deposition and/or during trial, in the past four years (Exhibit B). Also attached is a copy of Brown & Drecker's Records Retention Policy (Exhibit C) and selected pages from "Fundamentals of Industrial Hygiene" (Exhibit D).

Compensation:

My fee schedule is $200.00 per hour plus expenses. To review all materials to date and prepare this report, I have been compensated approximately $1,300.00.

Report #5: Biomechanics

This report is most notable for the following:

- Frequent and specific citation to authority to bolster the opinion.
- Conciseness.
- Specificity of summary.

Areas of possible improvement:

- More confidence in stating opinion. (Delete preface's "I believe.")
- More completeness in description of records reviewed. (Delete "These include.")

I acknowledge with thanks the records you have sent me regarding Charlie Jenks' birth injuries. These include:

1. The labor and delivery records of Colette Jenks surrounding the birth of her son, Charlie, in December 1995 from Northstar Medical Center.

2. Charlie Jenks' newborn records from Northstar Medical Center, December 1995 through January 1996;

3. Office records Wendell Storm, MD and Ped. Doctors of America;

4. Charlie's records from Children's Hospital in Mapleton, including the operative reports from September 1996 and July 1998; and

5. Deposition transcripts of Steven Jenks, Colette Jenks, Bad Guy, MD and Good Guy, MD.

Per your request, I have formulated my opinions regarding Charlie Jenks' birth injuries from a bioengineering perspective as a result of my review of these records and depositions beyond reviewing these documents, I base my opinions on more that a dozen years of research on shoulder dystocia and its related birth injuries.

Summary:
Colette Jenks' labor and delivery records indicate that her second child, Charlie Jenks, was born via a cephalic, spontaneous vaginal delivery complicated by severe shoulder dystocia. Charlie presented in an OA

presentation. After extending a second-degree episiotomy, and having a nurse apply suprapubic pressure, Dr. Bad Guy was unable to deliver Charlie's left anterior shoulder. He made a second attempt using McRoberts positioning and more traction. After this second attempt failed to deliver the left shoulder, Dr. Good Guy entered the room to perform the Woods screw maneuver. This was successful at delivering Charlie (a 4167 gm. newborn) at 12:58 p.m. on 4 December 1995. The records indicate that it took about three minutes to resolve the shoulder dystocia. Charlie's Apgar scores were four and eight; he was diagnosed at birth with a left upper extremity paresis.

Charlie's newborn evaluations confirmed the left upper extremity paresis and also noted decreased tone in the right arm, which improved. Charlie was diagnosed with a left brachial plexus injury with involvement of the neural roots to the diaphragm. As a result, he had respiratory distress that kept him hospitalized for more than a month.

Although Charlie regained some movement in his left upper extremity during his initial months, he reached a plateau, and was operated on initially in August 1996. The brachial plexus surgery revealed that there were significant injuries to nerves at levels C4 through C8 and T1. Specifically, there was a large neuroma that was entered by all of the nerve roots. The operative report diagram revealed ruptures through the neuroma affecting nerves connected to C4 through C7. The nerve root, CS, was found to be intact and supplied most of the intrinsic hand muscles and the triceps muscles. Because of the rupture, stimulation of the nerve roots, C5, C6 and C7 did not elicit any distal activity. In August 1998, Charlie underwent a second surgery to address the secondary deformity in his left upper extremity.

In his deposition, Dr. Bad Guy confirms the medical records by indicating that he recalls using McRoberts maneuver and suprapubic pressure along with downward traction in his unsuccessful attempt to deliver Charlie. He also recalls extending the episiotomy. Because he was unable to place his hands in position to perform Woods screw maneuver. he recalls asking Dr. Good Guy for assistance. Dr. Good Guy was able to perform the maneuver and Charlie was successfully delivered. He believes that the injury occurred during the birth process, during labor or delivery or both.

Under oath, Dr. Good Guy recalls helping upon request. He recalls performing the Woods maneuver, which took about 30 seconds, by putting one hand behind the posterior shoulder and rotating the shoulders to facilitate delivery. Once the anterior shoulder was disimpacted, he recalls that Dr. Bad Guy delivered the rest of the baby. Because Dr. Good Guy had no knowledge of what transpired before he came in the delivery room to help, he left shortly after the delivery, expecting nothing to be wrong with Charlie.

In his deposition, Steven Jenks recalls seeing Dr. Bad Guy pulling on Charlie's head. He also recalls the strain on the face of Dr. Bad Guy, which indicated to him that Dr. Bad Guy was exerting himself. He also remembered that the nurse who was standing on the left side of the bed was exerting pressure on Mrs. Jenks' upper stomach. He does recall that Dr. Good Guy assisted in the delivery at some point. Mrs. Jenks does not recall many specific events concerning events the birth of Charlie. She does indicate that she has given birth one more child, a boy. His was an uneventful delivery, and he was a healthy newborn.

Findings:

To within reasonable bioengineering certainty, my opinions are as follows:

Charlie's medical records indicate that he has a permanent and severe brachial plexus and phrenic nerve injury, which include traumatic ruptures and neuromas to four of the nerve roots on his left side. These injuries are indicative of a brachial plexus and phrenic nerve stretch injury. Health care providers first diagnosed these injuries immediately following Charlie's birth.

While there are a number of reported causes of obstetric brachial plexus impairment (1) the overwhelming majority of these are iatrogenic traction injures. (2) (3) This is true for cephalic, breech and cesarean deliveries. (3) This is especially true for shoulder dystocia deliveries resulting in bilateral injuries, ruptured nerves, injuries involving both the upper and lower brachial plexus, and injuries involving the phrenic nerve. In studies designed specifically to hypothesize alternative causes of obstetric brachial plexus impairments, an injury as extensive as Charlie's has never been reported in a delivery not complicated by reported shoulder dystocia. (4) (5) or via a cesarean section delivery. (6)

In a delivery where no injury occurs, uterine contractions typically average .50 mm Hg and typically peak at 100 mm Hg. and doctors generally apply gentle downward traction to the fetal head to effectuate deliver. (2) (7) This traction is equivalent to about 45 N (newtons), or about 10 lb on average. (8) (9) In contrast, clinicians apply about 100 N (22 lb.) of force for some shoulder dystocia deliveries. (8) (9) At this load level, some injuries – fractured clavicles and temporary Erb's palsies – may occur. (8) (9) (10) Some clinicians apply significantly more traction than 100 N; some more than double this force level. (11) (12) (13) To induce a brachial plexus stretch severe enough to cause a mild residual Erb's palsy, at least 140 N (-30 lb.) of force must be applied to the fetal head. (14) This is three times the force doctors normally apply during routine deliveries.

For Charlie to have the brachial plexus injuries that he sustained at birth, Dr. Bad Guy must have applied more than 180 N (-40 lb.) of force to Charlie's head at the time of his birth. This clinician-applied force was mostly directed toward Charlie's right shoulder because the permanent injuries affect the nerves on his left side. This is consistent with Mr. Jenks' deposition, where he indicates Dr. Bad Guy straining and with the medical records, which indicate that Charlie presented with his left shoulder anterior. In this position, clinician-applied downward traction would be directed toward right shoulder. Dr. Bad Guy probably employed upward traction as well, resulting in Charlie's reduction in tone on his right side at birth. (11) Beyond this, the two maneuvers that Dr. Bad Guy used – McRobert's maneuver and suprapubic pressure, both also rely on traction. The maneuver that Dr. Good Guy reportedly performed to successfully deliver Charlie, the Woods screw maneuver, would not have contributed to the injury because it not a traction based method.

Due to the nature and severity of his brachial plexus injuries, and the specific circumstances surrounding Charlie Jenks' birth, I believe that Dr. Bad Guy exerted at least four times the normal amount of force to deliver a newborn. Applied to Charlie's head at the time of his shoulder dystocia birth, it was this traction that caused his permanent brachial plexus injuries. Had this traction not been applied, Charlie Jenks would have been born neurologically intact.

Ronald Del Santo, PhD

References
1. Al-Qattan M, El-Sayed AA, Al-Kharfy TM, Al-Jurayyan NA. Obstetrical brachial plexus injury in newborn babies delivered by cesarean section. Journal of Hand Surgery 1996; 21-B; 2:263-5.

2. Cunningham PG, MacDonald PC, Gant NF, Leveno KJ, Gilstrap LC III, Hankins GDV, Clark, SL. Williams Obstetrics.20th ed. Norwalk, CT: Appleton & Lange, 1997.

3. American College of Obstetricians and Gynecologists. Precis, obstetrics: an update in obstetrics gynecology. Washington DC: American College of Obstetricians and Gynecologists, 1998.

4. Gherman RB, Ouzounian JG, Miller D, Kwok L, Goodwin T. Spontaneous vaginal delivery- A risk factor for Erb's palsy? Am J Obstet Gynecol 1998;178: 423-7.

5. Ouzourian JG, Korst LM, Phelan JP. Permanent Erb palsy: A traction related injury. Obstet Gynecol 1997;89:139-141.

6. Gherman RB, Goodwin T Ouzounian JG, Miller D, Paul R. Brachial plexus palsy associated with cesarean section- An in utero injury? Am J Obstet Gynecol 1997; 177: 1162-4.

7. Pearse WH. Forceps versus spontaneous delivery. Clin Obstet Gynecol 1965;8:813-21.

8. Allen R. Sorab J, Gonik B. Risk factors for shoulder dystocia: An engineering study of clinician-applied forces. Obstet Gynecol 1991;77:352-5.

9. Gonik B, Allen R. Sorab J. Objective evaluation of the shoulder dystocia phenomenon: Effect of pelvic orientation on force reduction. Obstet Gynecol 1989;74:44-8.

10. Meghdari A, Dovoodi R. Mesbah F. Engineering analysis of shoulder dystocia in the human birth process by the finite element method. J Eng and Med 1992;206:243-50.

11. Allen RH, Bankoski BR, Butzin CA, Nagey DA. Comparing clinician-applied loads for routine, difficult and shoulder dystocia deliveries. Am J Obstet Gynecol 1994;171:1621-7.

12. Allen RH, Bankoski BR, Nagey DA. Simulating birth to investigate clinician-applied loads on newborns. Med Engin & Physics 1995;17:380-384.

13. Gonik B, Allen RH. Establishing an engineering model to define shoulder dystocia: A preliminary report on applied forces. In: Seventh Annual Clinical, Scientific and Business Meeting for the Society of Perinatal Obstetricians (B. Young, Program Chair), 1987: Abstract No. 151.

14. Caulfield, JN, Allen RH, Miller F.A. finite element idealization of the newborn spine and brachial plexus nerves. In: A.I. duPont Orthopedic Research Symposium (F.Miller, Editor), Wilmington, DE 1995:58-59.

Report #6: Vocational Evaluation

This report is most notable for the following:

- Well-organized.
- Pinpoint citations to specific pages in deposition testimony.
- Citations to literature in the report.

Areas of possible improvement:

- Numerical listing of the documents reviewed.
- Avoidance of emphasis such as italics and underlining.

Introduction:
Case file materials concerning Ms. Melanie Cullen v. Best Group Tours (BGT) were sent to this Independent Vocational Evaluator (State of California) and forensic economic consultant on October 10, 2000 by Connie Williams of Eagle Consultants at 8000 E. Oakton, Suite 201A, Hillsdale, CA 90000. The specific case assignment was for this expert to evaluate mitigation earning capacity, pre v post incident actual/demonstrated as well as expected earnings, past wage loss and if appropriate, future impairment to income stream if in fact the defendant was found liable for wrongful discharge.

Data included the plaintiff's 186-page deposition dated 9/20/00; the 17 exhibits attached to said deposition; payroll records from BGT, including biweekly earnings statements dated 3/17/99 through 6/16/00; Defendants' responses to interrogatories; portions of the personnel file from Stewart Theatre regarding Melanie Cullen; and the personnel file from BGT. It should be noted that discovery is ongoing and that this report is a preliminary document only that is subject to change given supplemental data. For example, this expert has not seen any reports from plaintiff expert witnesses in the fields of vocational rehabilitation or forensic economics.

Pursuant to the Federal Rules of Civil Procedure, this office, includes as addenda to this written report the following supplemental data: (1) a current curriculum vitae detailing formal education, work experience, written papers, teaching experience, conference presentations, other relevant work activities, and a listing of six defense and six plaintiff attorneys who have written letters of recommendation on this examiner's behalf; (2) a listing of cases in which either trial or deposition testimony was given over the last four years (Rule 26 Disclosure); and (3) a written fee schedule detailing a professional hourly rate of $225, and a testimony rate of $375 per hour.

Vital Statistics:

Plaintiff:	Melanie Cullen
DOB:	April 23, 1976
Age:	24.75 years
Term Date:	June 16, 2000
Age at Term:	24.15 years

Employer:	Best Group Tours
Job Title:	Program Coordinator
Earnings:	$11.26/hour base pay or $23,420 per annum, and sales commissions
Fringe Ben's:	Medical and pension, total estimated at 20% of gross wages
Total Comp:	$33,118 plus $6,624, total equals $39,742

Education:	College graduate, voice performance major, Halley College (Fallon, GA)
Job Title:	Ticket seller and administrative assistant
Current Job:	Stewart Theatre

Earnings:	$10.50/hour or $21,840 per annum, no commissions
Fringe Ben's:	Unknown, estimated at 16% of gross wages
Total Comp:	Estimated at $21,840 plus $3,494, total equals $25,334

Life Exp:	56.05 years (to age 80.80)*
Worklife Exp:	31.16 years (to age 55.91)*

*   *"U.S. Life Tables,"* U.S. Department of Health Statistics, 1999.
**   *"Worklife Expectancy for the Civilian U.S. Population,"* Hunt, et.al., Journal of Forensic Economics, Vol. X, #2.

Vocational Analysis:
The plaintiff, Ms. Melanie Cullen, is a 24-year-old Caucasian female who was born on April 23, 1976. Deposition testimony and her resume indicate that she has lived in the states of Tennessee, Georgia, Florida and California, and that her work history and interests have been music, arts and sales professions. At the time of the disputed wrongful termination, the plaintiff was apparently pregnant with the child due in early December of 2,000. Of note, she transferred from the Orlando, Florida office to Los Angeles in August of 1999, and the plaintiff's mother is a long term employee of BGT.

Educationally, Ms. Cullen completed her Bachelor of Arts degree in May of 1998 from Halley College at Fallon, Georgia. Her major was Voice Performance. She also studies languages, including Spanish, Japanese and

German. Her resume states that she received at least three scholarship awards in voice performance.

In terms of *employment history,* the plaintiff had two summer jobs and worked for Halley College prior to her full time stint with Educational Field Services. Specifically, at Halley, she worked in the Advancement Office all four years (1994 – 1998) soliciting donations and compiling alumnus' data. In 1996, she also worked in the Music Department at Halley planning tours and reorganizing the music library.

Summer jobs included working as an intern for Smithson Management in 1997 at Nashville, TN. As a personal assistant to a country music solo artist, Sonny Sixstring. Secondly, Ms. Cullen indicates she worked at BGT (Orlando, FL. Office) primarily as a receptionist from 1994 through 1998. Presumably, this did not include 1997 when she was at Nashville, TN.

Post termination, the plaintiff was employed within two weeks of her dismissal by Stewart Theatre. However, her job search activities were sparse and unsophisticated. She merely used the phone book per deposition testimony and either admits or suggests she did not utilize the Internet, Sunday paper, a friends and family network of potential employers, or employment agencies. Her job consists of being a ticket seller and front desk administrative assistant. She remained thus employed as of her deposition on 9/20/00. Earnings are at a fraction of her pay at BGT as Ms. Cullen was expecting a raise to $10.50 per hour from $9.75 at 35 to 40 hours per week. She does not receive commissions per her deposition testimony (page 164).

Her productivity statistics were available as a part of the 17 exhibits to the deposition. She started her employment on 2/16/99 with BGT in Florida. Sales were apparently positive for 1999 when selling BGT science products yet declined substantially in late 1999 and 2000 following her transfer to Los Angeles where she subsequently sold tours to Washington, D.C. to private parochial schools. Specifically, as bottom line figures she reached a productivity level of 117% of quota in 1999 yet was only at 4% of annualized quota when dismissed in June of 2000. A sales report dated 6/16/00 depicts sales of 65 camp days for the plaintiff in 2000 compared to 78, 177 and 393 for her three sales associates (See plaintiff deposition, exhibit 13).

Two other sales individuals were listed in this report that the plaintiff did not identify in her deposition as colleagues (perhaps they worked in a different sales department). Their number of camp days were 282 and 1,111. Moreover, Ms. Cullen had the lowest quota rate of the six sales associates at 1,800 per annum. The median and mode were 2,500 camp days. It should be noted that camp days are simply the number of students times the number of days such as 15 students over five days would translate to 75 camp days.

This contrasted significantly with 1999 wherein she exceeded the quota by 17% and had the greatest percentage of feasible (sold) camp days at 37% as of June 9, 1999 while at the Orlando office. The next highest ranking sales associate was at 32% of quota (See plaintiff's deposition, exhibit 14). Finally, for the 1999 year when her quota was only 800, 850 emanated from Florida and only 69 of the 917 total came from Los Angeles despite her transfer in August. She worked approximately six months in Orlando, and five months in Los Angeles. Nonetheless, 93% of her sales emanated from the plaintiff's work in Florida.

Consequently, despite the plaintiff's insistence that her performance was at least average for the Los Angeles office and allegations that she was never confronted by management about her low productivity, the sales statistics clearly evidence that she was far more productive selling science tours while at Orlando compared to selling tours to private parochial schools while at Los Angeles. The results were significantly different. The plaintiff's contention that she was unaware of her job being in jeopardy does not seem plausible given all of the preceding sales figures, and the fact that she did not sell one tour during the first three months of 2000.

Despite the preceding, annualized wages for 1999 ($23,195) equals $27,834 inclusive of commissions while 2000 wages ($17,601) equal $38,402 for the entire year. The compensation package at BGT is quite complicated with certain commissions earned in one year paid partially during the next year. Ms. Cullen also received draws against commissions which were substantially higher in 2000 compared to 1999. Finally, she received two weeks of severance pay. Each of these factors in combination may explain this anomaly.

Vocationally, it is evident that Ms. Cullen took the first job offered to her yet one that was well below her level of education and previous remunerative achievement. Rather than engage in a more thorough job search, the plaintiff took a transferable job involving voice performance, administrative duties and sales thus meeting her varied interests yet sacrificing pay. Again, she reports receiving no commissions for the sales component.

The job at Stewart Theatre is well below expected earnings. As a female college graduate, the weighted average for all age groups is $42,444 with those in the 18-24 grouping earning $25,994 on average. However, the 25-34 age grouping is a more appropriate comparison given her position of program coordinator and age at termination (24.17 years of age). This group earns $37,988 on average (See U.S. Department of Commerce, Bureau of the Census, *Money Income of Households, Families and Persons in the United States*). She is now turning age 25 and earns only $21,840 per annum.

It is conceivable that Ms. Cullen did not wish to pursue higher level employment positions because of her pregnant status at the time of her dismissal from BGT. This state may have been perceived as a barrier to employment whereas working as a noncommissioned ticket seller/receptionist was sufficiently below her work and educational status so as not to be a substantial barrier. However, she was only three months pregnant at the time of her dismissal and would not be showing at that time.

The California unemployment rate in December 2000 when the child was due to be born was 5.1%. This is a significantly low figure, and the figures for college graduates are minuscule. The *median duration of unemployment nationwide was only 5.2 weeks at that time.* (See U.S. Department of Labor, *Monthly Labor Review*, November 2000, Vol. 123, #11). Finally, it is a placement axiom that for every $10,000 in earnings it will take approximately one month of diligent job search to recoup prior earnings. In Ms. Cullen situation, this would range from three to four months.

Utilizing these figures and the latter contention that a commensurate position (full mitigation) should have been delayed until after the birth of the child, wage loss is partial from June 16, 2000 through December 2000. Subsequently, there would be a 3.5 month period of no offset income. Afterward, complete mitigation would be expected given her educational and work history coupled with only moderate earnings at BGT. She would essentially be expected to match her earnings by education at such time, and this exceeds her remuneration at BGT. All in all, this presumes full mitigation after a *loss period of 8.5 months* (back and front pay).

Alternatively, one might forecast a wage loss period ranging from only 5.2 weeks to 3.5 months. Ms. Cullen could have and should have attempted to secure commensurate employment in the general commissioned sales field. She may have negotiated and arranged to start work after the birth of her child in December of 2000 or early in 2001. It is also this examiner's understanding that the plaintiff is on maternity leave from Stewart Theatre at this juncture. *Sales positions are easy to come by, especially for college graduates with previous sales experience.* Moreover, her group sales experience translates too many related industries including the vast hotel and resort industry.

Economic Analysis:
Two supplemental generic and non-narrative economic reports are included as addenda to this vocational economic report. These detail the estimated losses as framed above in the last two paragraphs. The **minimum wage loss at 3.5 months of back pay without offset income equals $12,287.** This is based on a pre-incident compensation package of $39,742, and does not include interest.

The **maximum wage loss at 8.5 months of back and front pay with partial mitigation equals $25,271.** Future wage loss incorporates a net present value discount rate of 2.0% where real interest exceeds real wage growth by this amount after subtracting out inflation. This figure has been advocated by the Doca and Pfeifer federal court decisions. The latter is the only time the U.S. Supreme Court has concerned itself with economic discounting methods to this expert's knowledge (see *Jones & Laughlin Steel Corporation v. Howard E. Pfeifer*, 103 S. Ct. 2541 (1983) at 2550).

Respectfully Submitted,

_____

Samuel Joynson, M.A., I.V.E., MFCC

Addenda: 1) Curriculum Vitae
                2) Rule 26 Disclosure List
                3) Fee Schedule
                4) Two economic reports

Report #7: Legal Malpractice Affidavit

This report is most notable for the following:

- Objective statement of expert's impressive qualifications.
- Conciseness.
- Lack of typographical errors.

Areas of possible improvement:

- Specific listing of the material reviewed.
- More reasons provided to support the opinions.

AFFIDAVIT OF EDWARD A. CARLSON

BEFORE ME, the undersigned authority, on this day personally appeared Edward A. Carlson, known to me, who, being by me first duly sworn, on his oath deposed and stated:

1. My name is Edward A. Carlson. I am 58 years of age. I am an attorney licensed to practice law in the State of X. I was licensed to practice in X in 1966. I am a Senior Partner with the law firm of Perry & Mason. I received my J.D. degree from the University of the Southwest and my L.L.M. from the University of Lincoln.

2. I am a former Justice of the Supreme Court of X, having served in such capacity from September 1, 1988 to January 1, 1993. I was a member of the Supreme Court when the Court adopted the X Disciplinary Rules of Professional Conduct. I served as Chairman of the Committee on Professionalism of the Supreme Court of X. I have served three years on a Grievance Committee for the State Bar of X, including one year as Chairman of the Grievance Committee. I have taught ethics as an adjunct assistant professor at the University of Southwest Law Center.

3. I have spoken at over 40 programs on the topic of ethics and professionalism. I have authored law review articles and a chapter in a book with respect to ethics and professionalism. I am currently serving on five committees at the local, state and national level dealing with the subject of ethics and professionalism.

4. I have received the Harlan Stevenson Award from the American Inns of Court for exemplary service to the profession throughout the United States in the areas of legal excellence, professionalism,

civility and ethics. I was the national recipient in 1992. I received the Lola Wright Award from the X Bar Foundation for outstanding public service in advancing legal ethics. I have also received from the X Law Center for Legal Ethics and Professionalism the Distinguished Professionalism Award.

5. I am a Fellow of the American College of Trial Lawyers. I am board certified by the State Bar of X in both civil law and family law. I am a former President of the Southwest Bar Association. In 1989 I was the recipient of the President's Award form the State Bar of X as the Outstanding Lawyer in the State.

6. I have served as Chairman of the Consumer Law Section of the Southwest Bar Association and Chairman of the Consumer Law Section of the State Bar of X.

7. Attached hereto and incorporated herein by reference is a true, correct and complete copy of my Biographical Information. The statements made therein about my education, professional career, board certifications, societal memberships, bar activities, awards, publications, teaching experience, and civic activities are true and correct.

8. I have retained as an expert witness in this case. In forming my opinions in this case I have reviewed pleadings, correspondence, documents, discovery, depositions, and have conducted independent research. Based on my knowledge, skill, experience, training, and education, it is my opinion that:

> A. Dewey, Cheatem, & Howe, (hereinafter collectively referred to as "the Law Firm Defendants") each and all owed Judy Smith; a duty of care and a fiduciary duty.
> B. Judy Smith was a consumer of the Law Firm Defendants' services within the meaning of the Deceptive Trade Practices Act.
> C. The Law Firm Defendants' representation of Judy Smith in claims against Acme Co. created an insoluble conflict of interest which could not be waived.
> D. The Law Firm Defendants failed to properly disclose to Judy Smith the conflict of interest.
> E. The Law Firm Defendants failed to disclose to Judy Smith their financial interest in representing Acme Co. and in execution of the purported waiver of conflicts of interest.
> F. The Law Firm Defendants failed to advise Judy Smith to

seek independent counsel with respect to the purported waiver or the release of liability.

G. The Law Firm Defendants failed to follow their client instructions.

H. The Law Firm Defendants attempted to procure a release of liability form their client.

I. The Law Firm Defendants breached the duty of care and fiduciary duty owed by them to Judy Smith.

J. The Law Firm Defendants are guilty of negligence and gross negligence.

K. The Law Firm Defendants violated the Deceptive Trade Practices Act.

L. The Law Firm Defendants are guilty of misrepresentation.

M. Judy Smith was entitled to recover $80,000 in actual damages; and pre-judgment interest on such actual damages $22,000 in exemplary damages; pre-judgment interest on such exemplary damages; and attorneys' fees.

N. The Law Firm Defendants' negligence, gross negligence, breaches of duties of care, and breaches of fiduciary duties were a proximate cause of damages to Judy Smith.

O. The Law Firm Defendants' deceptive trade practices were a producing cause of damages to Judy Smith.

P. The Law Firm Defendants profited from their breaches of fiduciary duties and were unjustly enriched.

Q. Acme Co. profited from the Law Firm Defendant's breaches of fiduciary duties and were unjustly enriched.

FURTHER AFFIANT SAYETH NOT.

_____

Edward A. Carlson

SUBSCRIBED AND SWORN TO BEFORE ME, the undersigned authority, this 18th day of March 1997, to certify which witness my hand and official seal of office.

_____

NOTARY PUBLIC

Report #8: Independent Medical Evaluation

This report is most notable for the following:

- Cover page, summary, and table of contents.
- Great formatting.
- Exhaustive summarizing of medical records. This shows that the expert really did his homework.
- Photos and X-rays attached to report. A picture says a thousand words.
- Good use of tables.
- Citation to and quoting of authority from the literature.
- Numbered list of diagnoses.

The authors would have liked to have seen in this report:

- Numbered listing and specific description of documents reviewed.
- Less commentary and emphasis. These make the expert appear biased.
- Less use of boilerplate language.

Examinee:	Martha Vane
Identification Number:	123-45-6789
Date of Examination:	May 15, 2001
Examining Physician:	Collin Eddington, MD, FACOEM, FAADEP, CIME
Examination Location:	Eddington and Associates, Inc., 27 W. Seminary Ave., Suite 100, Bellview, Maine 04111
Date of Injury:	May 7, 1997
Client Organization:	Bellview Law Firm
Referral Source:	Todd Gia, Esquire

MODEL REPORTS

Summary

Diagnosis:
1. Symptom magnification behavior, marked
2. Arm pain, with no evidence of physical pathology, including no evidence of reflex sympathetic disorder (e.g., no evidence of Complex Regional Pain Syndrome, Type I.)

Impairment: 0% whole person permanent impairment

Work Capacity: No restrictions

Introduction

This 36 year-old, right-handed woman was referred for a Section 207 independent medical and impairment evaluation (IME) by the above client. This evaluation focused on case evaluation and impairment evaluation, according to the AMA *Guides to the Evaluation of Permanent Impairment*, Fourth Edition. She had been previously scheduled for an evaluation on December 19, 2000, however failed to show for that appointment. I have previously issued a report based on my medical file review on the date of that previous evaluation.

The independent medical examination process was explained to the examinee, and she understands that no patient/treating physician relationship was established. Ms. Vane was advised that the information provided will not be confidential and a report will be sent to the requesting client. Informed consent was obtained with the examinee providing written permission to proceed with the evaluation, including the physical examination. She also agreed to obtaining digital photographs, including those attached to this report.

Ms. Vane arrived at 1:00 pm. She was advised of the evaluation process, provided consent to proceed, and then completed a questionnaire and a series of pain inventories. The interview commenced at 1:35 pm followed by the physical examination and this phase was completed by 2:50 pm. She completed further inventories, the BHI and MMPI, following the clinical evaluation, and departed at approximately 4:10 pm. Ms. Vane was cooperative. History was provided by the examinee who was a vague historian. The information she provided was, however, consistent with the medical records provided. The entire process, inclusive of the review of my prior report and briefly these medical records, interview, physical examination, reviewing x-rays, case analysis, and preparation of the report, took nearly eight hours, as itemized, with additional time involved in the scoring of the inventories completed.

A questionnaire and pain inventories were completed by my assistant Stephanie Demich, on the basis of information provided by the examinee. She reported she was unable to write. Ms. Vane did however, complete a Battery for Health Improvement (BHI) and a Minnesota Multiphasic Personality Inventory (MMPI) using a large marker. To ensure accuracy, the examinee's clinical history was dictated in her presence.

A staff member, Stephanie Demich was present throughout the physical examination. Ms. Vane reported no new difficulties occurring during the examination, only her usual pain with activity.

You provided and I reviewed the records of: Francis Boul, M.D., John Cole, M.D., Matthew Wallace, D.C., Randy Falk, M.D., Colleen Shore, Psy.D., Victor Hough, D.O., Jon McCord, M.D., S. T. Williams, M.D., Justin Perry, M.D., Howard Fabbiano, M.D., Richard Miller, M.D., Jordan Vance, M.D., and Ben Cortland, Jr., M.D. The provided medical records will be returned to the client upon request, otherwise they will be purged from this file in approximately one year. The report, questionnaires, pain inventories, and other material specific to this evaluation will be retained.

Medical Record Review

(The following is a summary of this information)

Date	Provider	Type[1]	Summary
5/23/97	Williams	M	…the **right flexor aspect of her wrist is extremely painful** and bothering her all the time.
6/2/97	Williams	M	…still having problems with her right wrist…still is tender at the flexor carpi ulnaris area at the end of her hamate region. Manipulation of her hand in the

---

[1] Type of Encounter: C = Consult, H = Hospital, I = IME, M = Medical Visit, O = Operation, R = Report/Letter, P = PT/OT Visit, S = Diagnostic Study, X = X-ray, * = Other

range of motion does cause a clicking in that region but she does have full range of motion.

6/10/97	Williams	M	…isn't a whole lot better

6/24/97	Williams	M	…she is really not doing all that well. The problem has gone up her arm towards her medial elbow and she has tingling in her fifth digit.

…compression of the ulnar nerve at the medial elbow does cause paresthesias in her fifth digit only. She does have full range of motion in her wrist and elbow.

6/27/97	Williams	M	…she is in terrible pain, her elbow is really sore

Today on exam she's quite tender and swollen over the lateral epicondyle and at the triceps insertion on the right.

7/1/97	Williams	M	…right arm is no better.

7/15/97	Hough	M	Follow up physical examination finds her complaining bitterly of pain primarily at the volar wrist on the ulnar side. Negative impingement. Negative Spurling's maneuver. 1+ edema at the right arm and also some apparent pallor after examination at the palm.

Impression:
Right arm RSD
Pain generator not clear at wrist.
Chronic right arm overuse syndrome with myofascial pain, epicondylitis, tendonitis, proximal symptoms improved.
Vocational dysfunction currently out of work.

Note: Inadequate objective criteria to support the diagnosis of RSD; a diagnosis label that has been used since that time, despite lack of supporting data.

7/25/97	Williams	M	...had a problem with a sprain to her right wrist, ulnar flexor aspect

...does have some nagging **aching** in the palmar aspect of the ulnar region, and on palpation specifically over the pisiform and hamate bones. I do not feel any crepitation. She has **full range of motion.** Palpating long tendons emanating from that area show that there's really not any tendinitis that I can appreciate at this time.

10/6/97	Williams	M	...comes in saying that her right wrist really has never gotten better.

11/12/97	Falk	C	...seeing Martha today, a 33-year-old lady, for evaluation of significant discomfort around the right lateral epicondylar area in the elbow and the volar ulnar aspect of the right wrist near the insertion of the flexor carpi ulnaris.

Specifically she notes pain in the proximal palm on the right side, ulnar wrist pisiform area, near the insertion of the flexor carpi ulnaris. She notes some lateral epicondylar discomfort as well with some radiation up to the humerus. The left side is pretty much minimally symptomatic. She has occasional sensory symptoms there.

Strength measurements show a significant reduction in strengths in the right compared to the left side. She has 23 lb of grasp strength on the right, 64 lb in the left. Lateral pinch strength is 6 ½ lb right, 15 lb left. 3-jaw pinch is 2 ½ lb right, 19 lb left. She has normal 2-point discrimination in the fingertips, negative Tinel test in the carpal tunnel region and a mildly positive Tinel test over Gunyon's tunnel on the right side in the right, positive Tinel test in the cubital tunnels on both sides, negative Phalen tests on both sides.

I feel that Martha has an **overuse tendonitis condition involving the flexor carpi ulnaris and the lateral epicondylar area,** both right side.

Note: Subjective complaints more marked than objective findings. Diagnosis of reflex sympathetic dystrophy not made.

12/1/97	Williams	M	…says that she is feeling somewhat better. She is not having any paresthesias.

Overall she is **doing much better.**

12/31/97	Williams	M	**…comes in for a flareup of her right lateral elbow…feels that her wrist is doing better**

3/17/98	Cortland	C	33-year-old right handed female…here for evaluation of her right arm symptoms

She works as a Certified Nurses Aid at Woodson Gardens and apparently two years ago while lifting a patient at the facility she noted a "snap" at the wrist and subsequent pain.

She describes a persistent right wrist pain that radiates to the elbow as well as a right lateral elbow pain that radiates distalward. She also notes paresthesias into digit five of the right hand.

On exam, a Tinel's sign is evident at the right medial wrist as well as over the right condylar groove. There is tenderness to palpation volar wrist as well as over the right lateral epicondyle. Strength in the upper extremities 5/5 with no atrophy. DTR's are 2+ and symmetric. There are no physiologic sensory deficits to pinprick.

Impression: **Suspected multifocal tendinitis, including right flexor carpi ulnaris as well as lateral epicondylitis. The chronicity of her symptoms,**

however, is striking and I would have to wonder whether some other unsuspected pathology such as ligamentous tear at the wrist might be at play, perpetuating her symptoms. There is, however, **no suggestion of any nerve compression syndrome.**

Note: Subjective complaints more marked than objective findings. Diagnosis of reflex sympathetic dystrophy not made.

4/29/98	Boul	M	…condition has worsened again.
5/4/98	Williams	M	…comes in noting that she is really just the same.
5/13/98	Hough	C	Chief Complaint: Chronic severe right arm discomfort.

…33-year-old, right-handed female referred today for an evaluation

…states that her problem started approximately May 7, 1997, at which time she was working on the Alzheimer's unit at Woodson Gardens and had a large number of clients grab, pull and twist on her arm. She states that this has been going on for over a year now and she has had literally hundreds of injuries of that right arm in a cumulative fashion.

She specifically denies neurologic symptoms such as numbness, tingling, weakness or radicular pain but, rather, has rather diffuse and severe discomfort from the right elbow down through the forearm into the wrist.

Today she demonstrates full and normal range of motion at upper extremities, shoulders, elbows, wrists and cervical spine. Negative Spurling's maneuver. No radicular symptoms. Negative impingement at shoulder.

She has thoracic kyphosis, drooping shoulders and the left shoulder is significantly elevated compared to the right.

Right side normal reflexes, touch and pinprick. Strength is 4/5 throughout.

Palpatory exam reveals exquisite tenderness at the right lateral epicondyle, to a lesser extent the medial epicondyle, the flexor forearm. She has several trigger points. Phalen's maneuver causes digits 4 and 5 to go numb. She has a positive Tinel's at the elbow at the ulnar nerve.

Impression:
1. Chronic severe right upper extremity overuse syndrome, component of lateral greater than medial epicondylitis, ulnar nerve neurapraxia, flexor tendonitis, right wrist strain and severe myofascial pain at right shoulder girdle with active trigger points.
2. Possible early RSD.
3. Obesity, deconditioning and poor posture.
4. Asthma.
5. Migraine headaches.

To some degree I think her posturing is playing into this. She also has somatic dysfunction accompanying her myofascial pain.

Note: Subjective complaints are again more marked than objective findings. He reintroduces the possibility of reflex sympathetic dystrophy, despite inadequate criteria to support this diagnosis.

5/26/98	Williams	M	...tells me that her right arm, although it is still bothering her, is doing better with the acupuncture treatments...In particular she feels that the elbow and forearm have calmed down a bit and it is now mostly

focusing in the wrist. She does not have any thermal changes, diffuse swelling or color changes today. Her deep tendon reflexes are normal. I can fully mobilize the wrist in all directions as well as her elbow but she is quite tender at the lateral epicondyle, the extensor tendons emanating from that and also towards the pisiform and hamate area on the ulnar portion of her ventral wrist.

My feeling is at this time that **I don't see any clear-cut evidence of RSD occurring.**

(Author's Note: The remaining summary of medical records has been deleted.)

History (per Examinee)

Pre-Existing Status
Ms. Vane reports that in 1996 she did have a right wrist injury which was sudden in onset but that occurred when she was lifting a resident. She reported it to the "first responder" at the work place, however did not have ongoing care. She states that she was told that CNAs "don't get wrist injuries" and were "not allowed to go to doctors". She reports that this problem with her wrist resolved in approximately one week.

Injury
The onset of her wrist pain itself was more insidious early in 1997, and reflected by an injury date of May 7, 1997. She reports that this was gradual in onset and attributes this to repeated grasping of her wrist by patients with Alzheimer's disease. This became increasingly bothersome to the extent that she then sought medical care with Dr. Williams, who continues to be her primary treating physician.

Clinical Chronology
She reports to me that she has seen "14 doctors" and has been involved in a variety of treatments since that time. She has had ongoing problems with right arm pain and also at some point developed left arm pain, which essentially has been unresponsive to therapeutic interventions. These interventions are as reflected in the above medical records review, and according to her has involved pain clinic, diaphoresis, cortisone shots, TENS unit (which made this more bothersome), pisiform injection of the right wrist, stellate ganglion blocks, and acupuncture. Despite this, she has had ongoing

problems with her right arm and to a lesser extent and more of an onset subsequently of problems with the left arm.

Ms. Vane states that she has seen a "slew of doctors" and the medical records as noted above were reviewed in a summary fashion with her and verified that this represents the individuals that she has been seen by in evaluation treatment. She also reports having a previous Independent Medical Evaluation by Justin Perry, MD but did not like him, because he made statements that she appeared to be exaggerating or embellishing in her pain.

She continues to be followed by Dr. Williams, treated with a variety of medications as reflected below and restrictions. She saw him recently and he has made a referral for her to be seen within the next week by Dr. Cortland for nerve conduction studies. Her follow up appointment with Dr. Williams will be on May 29th.

Current Status
She reports that her greatest concern is "wants to work and to be able to enjoy her kids". It is also noted that at the completion of the questionnaire, which was performed in conjunction with my assistant, Stephanie Demich, who wrote the responses, she states in terms of other comments to understand her situation of "in pain, pain, pain."

She has problems with pain involving both extremities although much more marked on the right than on the left. On the right, she has pain from her wrist up to almost her shoulder and on the left has pain from her wrist up to her elbow.

The pain is constant. On a scale of 0 (no pain) to 10 (excruciating pain so severe she could not live with this pain), she reports her pain at this time as a 7 to 8, during the past month averaging a 7, with a high of 9 to 10 and a low of 7.

She is not able to identify particularly precipitating factors, more relieving factors. The pain is constant.

She has also had problems with numbness involving the tip of her right index finger. She has significant weakness of her arms bilaterally. She has attempted to maintain motion to avoid contractures.

Functional Status
She reports marked interference with activities of daily living as reflected in the inventories noted subsequently in this report. This includes simple tasks

such as showering, brushing teeth, etc. She reports that her maximum ability to lift is five pounds.

Occupational History
She was employed since 1995 at Woodson Gardens Nursing Center as a R.C.N.A. She reports this work involved intense lifting, moving, feeding, etc. She previously worked at Burger King and does have a high school education.

For the past two years she has been working up to 20 hours per week baby sitting for a five-year-old. She states that she can't sit for younger children because she is not able to lift them. She reports that she has restrictions of no lifting and no repetitive movements.

Social History
She lives in Cambridge, Maine with her children ages 15 and 7, and her fiancé. She has been through a divorce recently; this became finalized this past February. She reports that one of the problems with the divorce was her husband coping with the problems that she has experienced with her arm pain.

She reports in a typical day she will get up, get her daughter ready for school, walk to the bus stop, watch TV, trys to do things around the house, goes for walks, and does a lot of sitting. Periodically she will go dancing. She denies involvement in any other significant recreational activities.

She smokes approximately a half of pack per day, and has perhaps one alcoholic beverage per week.

Past Medical History
Medical: Asthma

Surgery: S/p tubal ligation, cesarean section, tubes in ears, and tonsillectomy

Medications: Effexor, Accolate, Prempro, Prilosec, Inhaler (Flovent, albuterol)

Allergies: She reports that she is allergic to multiple medications, "too many (for her) to write down"

Review of Systems
Denies other problems in a general fashion. Reference inventories performed.

Family History
Positive for bladder cancer, heart disease, and diabetes.

Observations
The examinee is an obese female. She appears in no acute distress during the interview. Examination of the hands reveals no unusual callus; her hands largely remain at her sides. No assistive devices were used.

Weight was reported as 206 pounds and height was reported as 5 feet 3 1/2 inches.

(Note: A women with a "large" frame and a height of 5' 4", according to data from the Metropolitan Life Insurance Company, 1999, would have a desirable weight in the range of 134 – 151 pounds, e.g. she is a minimum of 55 pounds overweight and her weight is 136% of the maximum desirable weight.)

She demonstrates poor posture with drooping shoulders.

Behavioral Observations
The examinee was pleasant and cooperative. Affect was flat, and at times, she would avoid eye to eye contact. During the interview she appeared quite comfortable, this being inconsistent with a reported pain level of 7. She sat continuously for up to 7 minutes during the interview.

Pain behavior during the physical examination included grimacing, rubbing and verbalization. She was very inconsistent in moving her upper extremities, at time being very dramatic and guarded, and at other times appeared to have no difficulties. Numerous nonphysiologic findings were present, as documented in this report. These findings suggesting a major behavioral overlay.

Upper Extremity Examination
There was antalgic posturing, with her arms at her side, however there were no findings of swelling (other than excess adipose issue due to her weight), scars, discoloration, deformity, atrophy, hair loss, nail changes, thermal abnormality, nor hyperpathia.

Surface temperatures measured digitally of her forearms were symmetric, 88.9 degrees F on the right and 88.6 degrees F on the left.

Shoulders
Measurements of the shoulders were performed in accordance with the methodology described in Section 3.1j (41–45) of the AMA *Guides to the Evaluation of Permanent Impairment,* Fourth Edition.

Right Shoulder

	Measurement	Reference (4th ed.)	Normal	Upper Extremity Impairment
Flexion	180	Figure 38. (43)	180	0
Extension	50	Figure 38. (43)	50	0
Adduction	40	Figure 41. (43)	40	0
Abduction	160	Figure 41. (43)	170	1
Internal Rotation	80	Figure 44. (43)	80	0
External Rotation	60	Figure 44. (45)	60	0
Total				1

Left Shoulder

	Measurement	Reference (4th ed.)	Normal	Upper Extremity Impairment
Flexion	180	Figure 38. (43)	180	0
Extension	50	Figure 38. (43)	50	0
Adduction	40	Figure 41. (43)	40	0
Abduction	180	Figure 41. (43)	170	0
Internal Rotation	80	Figure 44. (43)	80	0
External Rotation	60	Figure 44. (45)	60	0
Total				0

Inspection of the shoulders was normal. Arc, resisted motions, and passive motions were all reportedly uncomfortable, and were cautious. It appeared her motions were controlled, either consciously or by her pain complaints. There was no discrete focal tenderness. Impingement tests were negative.

In summary, there no objective abnormal findings of the shoulders, except slight, questionable, deficit of abduction motion on the right.

Elbows
Measurements of the wrists were performed in accordance with the methodology described in 3.1i Elbow (38–41) of the AMA *Guides to the Evaluation of Permanent Impairment,* Fourth Edition.

318

MODEL REPORTS

Right Elbow

	Measurement	Reference (4th ed.)	Normal	Upper Extremity Impairment
Flexion	140	Figure 32. (40)	140	0
Extension	0	Figure 32. (40)	0	0
Supination	70	Figure 35. (41)	70	0
Pronation	80	Figure 35. (41)	80	0
Total				0

Left Elbow

	Measurement	Reference (4th ed.)	Normal	Upper Extremity Impairment
Flexion	140	Figure 32. (40)	140	0
Extension	0	Figure 32. (40)	0	0
Supination	70	Figure 35. (41)	70	0
Pronation	80	Figure 35. (41)	80	0
Total				0

Inspection of the elbows was normal. Resisted and passive motions were diffusely uncomfortable and cautious. It appeared her motions were controlled, either consciously or by her pain complaints. She reported significant discomfort over her lateral epicondyles bilaterally. There were no abnormal findings. In summary, there were no objective abnormal findings of the elbows, only the subjective complaint of pain.

Wrists
Measurements of the wrists were performed in accordance with the methodology described in Section 3.1h Wrist (35–38) of the AMA *Guides to the Evaluation of Permanent Impairment,* Fourth Edition.

Right Wrist

	Measurement	Reference (4th ed.)	Normal	Upper Extremity Impairment
Flexion	50	Figure 26. (36)	60	2
Extension	40	Figure 26. (36)	60	4
Radial Deviation	20	Figure 29. (38)	20	0
Ulnar Deviation	30	Figure 29. (38)	30	0
Total				6

The reliability of her flexion and extension of her right wrist is questionable, since it appears she was controlling her extent of motion, and these measurements did not appear to be the same movements noted casually during the examination.

Left Wrist

	Measurement	Reference (4th ed.)	Normal	Upper Extremity Impairment
Flexion	60	Figure 26. (36)	60	0
Extension	60	Figure 26. (36)	60	0
Radial Deviation	20	Figure 29. (38)	20	0
Ulnar Deviation	30	Figure 29. (38)	30	0
Total				0

Inspection was normal. Resisted and passive motions were, as with the shoulders and elbows, diffusely uncomfortable and cautious. It appeared her motions were controlled, either consciously or by her pain complaints. There were no abnormal objective findings. Finkelstein's was negative. In summary, there were no objective abnormal findings of the wrists, other than questionable motion findings on the right.

Palpatory Examination
She subjectively reported tenderness diffusely over her entire right arm and distal to her left elbow, with greatest tenderness over the ulnar flexor aspect of her right wrist and over her lateral epicondyles bilaterally. There were no confirmatory objective findings, such as trigger points, spasm, or inflammatory changes. Her objective examination was entirely unremarkable. The areas of greatest tenderness are noted by the marks in the enclosed images.

Neurological Examination of Upper Extremity

Motor Examination
Motor examination revealed diffuse give-away weakness, particularly on the right. This is inconsistent with an organic basis, rather consistent with symptom magnification.

Grip strength measurements resulted in complaints of pain, with 0 to 1 kg of grip bilaterally. She would not complete five position testing, nor rapid alternating grip, because of complaints of pain.

It is noted that these "findings" are inconsistent with the ability to do simple tasks of daily living, such as opening a door or driving a car as she did so today to travel to this appointment.

		Right	Left
Upper arm circumference (cm.)	10 cm. above the elbow	38.5 cm.	37.0 cm.
Forearm circumference (cm.)	10 cm. below the elbow	27.2 cm.	26.8 cm.

The lack of atrophy on the right is inconsistent with her report that she is unable to make any significant use of that arm.

Sensory Examination
Sensory examination was normal to soft touch and pinprick.

Non-Organic Findings

Test	Negative	Positive	Result
Superficial Touch Painful		x	Diffuse, non-anatomic
Range of Motion Inconsistent		x	Motion measurements appear controlled
Sensory Deficits Non-Organic		x	Dysesthesia, unsupported by findings
Muscle Weakness Giveaway		x	Diffuse, and no demonstrable grip strength.

The presence of multiple non-organic findings, particularly in the context of no objective findings, strongly supports the conclusion of illness behavior.

Diagnostic Studies

Right wrist, August 5, 1998. Normal. No evidence of bony abnormality. No evidence of osteoporosis. (Please see enclosed X-rays.)

Right elbow, August 5, 1998. Normal. No evidence of bony abnormality. No evidence of osteoporosis. (Please see enclosed X-rays.)

Pain Status Inventories

Pain Drawing

Ms. Demich, my assistant, completed under Ms. Vane's direction, a pain drawing using symbols to describe sensations.

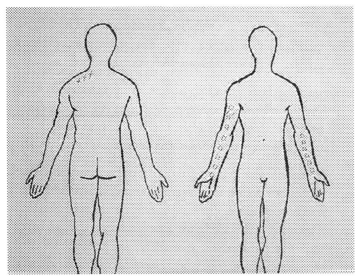

Pain Drawing

Pain Disability Index

The Pain Disability Index uses rating scales to measure the extent of perceived disability in seven areas of life. The results are as follows:

Area	Perceived Disability
Family/home responsibilities	90%
Recreation	100%
Social activity	70%
Occupation	70%
Sexual activity	90%
Self-care	100%
Life-support activities	80%

The total score is 60 out of a possible 70, for a total index of 86%, an extremely elevated level, consistent with a perception of being crippled.

Short-Form McGill Pain Questionnaire

The McGill Pain Questionnaire specifies fifteen potential pain descriptors. The examinee rates the intensity of each descriptor on a scale of 0 to 3. The total of all descriptors was 24, the total of the eleven somatic descriptors was 20, averaging 1.8, and the total of the four affective descriptors was 4, averaging 1.0. This was consistent with a significant behavioral overlay.

CES-D

The Center for Epidemiologic Studies Depressed Mood Scale was administered. The examinee scored 23, which is consistent with a depressed mood.

Battery for Health Improvement - BHI

The Battery for Health Improvement was administered, and a copy of this analysis is appended. It is noted that she has a high score on the Depression scale, there is a marked elevation for symptom dependency, elevations for doctor dissatisfaction, and elevation for pain complaints. She endorsed an item that may indicate a history of physical or sexual abuse. She also endorsed a critical item indicating that she has recently wished she were dead. (With her written consent, I have contacted her primary care provider, Dr. Williams, by phone, re this issue. I have advised him and her this report is available through the requesting client.)

Minnesota Multiphasic Personality Inventory - MMPI

The Minnesota Multiphasic Personality Inventory was administered, and a copy of this analysis is appended. The results of this inventory confirmed other findings noted on the examination. The profile was valid. The following observations are made:

1. Very high profile definition characterizes the MMPI-2 profile code that includes Scales Hs and Hy. This suggests that she is reporting a number of vague physical complaints and has a tendency to develop physical problems when she is under stress. The medical history is likely to be characterized by excessive and vague physical complaints, weakness, and pain.
2. She may not be greatly incapacitated by her physical symptoms. She tends to rely on hysterical defenses of denial and regression in the face of conflict.
3. Her high-point clinical scale core (Hs) occurs infrequently in a normative sample of women and is consistent with chronic pain manifestations.
4. Individuals with her profile tend to use physical complaints to influence or manipulate other people.

5. Her personality make-up is consistent with a psychological basis to her symptoms.
6. Her MMPI-2 profile most closely matches the "A" type pattern found in cluster analytic studies of chronic pain patient profiles. The "A" type pattern is thought to characterize one of the most frustrating groups of pain patients to work with because of their initial defensiveness and denial of psychological problems. Patients with this pattern typically show low psychological-mindedness and a seeming lack of awareness of psychological mechanisms involved in their pain behavior. Individuals with this pattern are frequently diagnosed as having conversion symptoms.

Conclusions

Diagnoses
1. **Symptom magnification behavior, marked, suggestive of malingering**
   1.1. Somatoform pain disorder
   1.2. Iatrogenic component, related to inappropriate diagnostic labeling (e.g. "RSD") and excessive medical interventions
   1.3. **Chronic upper extremity pain – no evidence of physical pathology**
       1.3.1. Reflex sympathetic dystrophy, questionable history of, no objective evidence at this time
       1.3.2. "Cumulative trauma disorder", possible history of; no evidence of significant pathology at this time
2. Personality disorder, possible, Cluster B
3. Depression
4. Obesity
5. Deconditioning
6. Postural dysfunction
7. Asthma, with ongoing tobacco usage
8. Migraine headaches
9. s/p unrelated surgeries
   9.1. s/p tubal ligation
   9.2. s/p C-section
   9.3. s/p myringotomy
   9.4. s/p tonsillectomy

Ms. Vane demonstrates marked illness behavior with marked subjective complaints of pain, without any verifiable objective findings to support these complaints. The extent of this inconsistency suggests that this is more significant than that of symptom magnification behavior of an unconscious origin, rather this may be purposeful.

In my prior report dated December 19, 2000, I noted:

> Reflex sympathetic dystrophy (RSD) is a diagnosis currently in
> wide use and particularly popular among orthopaedic surgeons,
> pain medicine physicians and physiatrists. The term RSD is
> currently used to refer to subjective complaints of pain associated
> with soft-tissue changes, which many not be due to sympathetic
> nervous system dysfunction and for which no reflex has been
> demonstrated. The indiscriminate use of the term RSD has
> rendered it vacuous and not useful as a clinical designation;
> nonetheless, the term is widely used. One of the primary
> differentials as in this case, is whether she actually has RSD or
> whether her problems are more reflective of a somatoform pain
> disorder.

Since the writing of the *Guides,* 4th Edition, a consensus statement has been
published proposing a redefinition of RSD which led to the description of
"complex regional pain syndrome" (CRPS), which is replacing the terms
"reflex sympathetic dystrophy" (now CRPS type I) and causalgia (now
CRPS type II).[6] CRPS differs somewhat from earlier views of RSD and
causalgia. First, CRPS is diagnosed by history and clinical findings.
Second, regional sympathetic blockade has no role in the diagnosis of CRPS.
Third, sympathetic dysfunction is not assumed to be the basic
pathophysiologic mechanism; rather, sympathetic dysfunction is associated
with a group of pain disorders that responds positively to sympathetic block
but that may be independent of CRPS. Fourth, sympathetically maintained
pain (SMP) may be present in a variety of painful conditions including or
independent of CRPS.

Since the subjective complaint of pain is the hallmark of these conditions,
and since all of the associated physical signs and radiological findings can be
the result of disuse, the differential diagnosis is extensive and includes in this
case: conversion disorder, factitious disorder, DSM-IV pain disorder and
malingering.

This in-person evaluation clearly supports the conclusion that although she
has been labeled in the past as having reflex sympathetic dystrophy, at this
time there is no objective basis, whatsoever, to support this diagnosis.
Complex regional pain syndrome and its associated complexities were
addressed by Ensalada in the November 1997 and January 1998 issues of the
Guides Newsletter. [2]

---

[2] Ensalada LH. The Challenge of Evaluating RSD Impairment and Disability.
Guides Newsletter. November 1997, January 1998.
http://www.impairment.com/ref/ue-rsd-11-97.pdf

Objective diagnostic criteria for CRPS have provided and are also incorporated in the Fifth Edition of the AMA *Guides to the Evaluation of Permanent Impairment*. Although the Fifth Edition is not the basis for rating impairment in this state, the clinical information does reflect our understanding of our clinical problems. Objective diagnostic criteria for CRPS are provided in Table 16-16 and reflect local clinical signs (vasomotor changes, pseudomotor changes, and trophic changes) and radiographic signs.

As noted, she fails to have any clinical signs of complex regional pain syndrome, e.g. reflex sympathetic dystrophy, although I am unable to exclude the possibility of this in the past. Her "findings" have been inconsistent, primarily subjective complaints of pain and tenderness, and others have also doubted this diagnosis.

There are several factors that simply cannot be explained on an anatomic basis in this case. If she had reflex sympathetic dystrophy, which she self-reports, then I would expect to find at least some clinical evidence of this disorder and I would expect to find evidence of "dystrophy" e.g. evidence of atrophy. In fact, her right upper extremity, her dominant arm, is not atrophied, rather it is larger than her left arm, without any evidence that this is due to a problem with swelling. Her inability to demonstrate any significant grip strength is inconsistent with her ability to drive a car, as she did so today to come to the appointment or even to open a door.

It is useful to contrast this case against another case which I saw last year, that of an unfortunate 48 year old women actually had Complex Regional Pain Syndrome – Type 1 (Reflex Sympathetic Dystrophy). This other case had multiple criteria supporting the diagnosis, and her associated impairment was 60% whole person permanent impairment, which contrasts to no ratable impairment for Ms. Vane, as discussed below.

Issues pertinent to this case were examined in a recent article by Ochoa published in the Journal of Neurology and entitled "Truth, errors, and lies around 'reflex sympathetic dystrophy' and 'complex regional pain syndrome.'"[3]

> The shifting paradigm of reflex sympathetic dystrophy-sympathetically maintained pains-complex regional pain syndrome is characterized by vestigial truths and understandable errors, but also unjustifiable lies. It is true that patients with organically based neuropathic pain harbor unquestionable and physiologically demonstrable evidence of nerve fiber dysfunction leading to a predictable clinical profile with stereotyped temporal evolution. In turn, patients with psychogenic pseudoneuropathy, sustained by conversion-somatization-malingering, not only lack

---

[3] Ochoa JL, *J Neurol*. 1999 Oct; 246(10): 875-9.

physiological evidence of structural nerve fiber disease but display a characteristically atypical, half-subjective, psychophysical sensory-motor profile. The objective vasomotor signs may have any variety of neurogenic, vasogenic, and psychogenic origins. Neurological differential diagnosis of "neuropathic pain" versus pseudoneuropathy is straight forward provided that stringent requirements of neurological semeiology are not bypassed....Errors include historical misinterpretation of vasomotor signs in symptomatic body parts, and misconstruing symptomatic relief after "diagnostic" sympathetic blocks, due to lack of consideration of the placebo effect which explains the outcome. It is a lie that sympatholysis may specifically cure patients with unqualified "reflex sympathetic dystrophy." This was already stated by the father of sympathectomy, Rene Leriche, more than half a century ago. As extrapolated from observations in animals with gross experimental nerve injury, adducing hypothetical, untestable, secondary central neuron sensitization to explain psychophysical sensory-motor complaints displayed by patients with blatantly absent nerve fiber injury, is not an error, but a lie. While conceptual errors are not only forgivable, but natural to inexact medical science, lies particularly when entrepreneurially inspired are condemnable and call for peer intervention.

Although it is tempting as a clinician to label a problem with an anatomic diagnosis, in this case such labeling is inappropriate and is likely to reinforce dysfunctional illness behavior. Therefore, it is probable that this incorrect diagnostic labeling the performance of unnecessary treatment interventions (including unjustified and excessive stellate ganglion blocks), and unsupportable work restrictions have contributed to "iatrogenic disability." The intents may have been well intentioned by her providers, however the result of failing to identify the behavioral issues and treating her for a diagnosis she does not have is most unfortunate, and clearly contrary to directions provided by Hippocrates of "first do no harm."

Her history reveals marked subjective complaints consistent with illness behavior. Her physical examination revealed no significant objective findings and many inconsistencies, as referenced above. Her pain, psychological, and disability inventories were enlightening. Her MMPI was particularly revealing in terms of her manifestation of physical complaints due to underlying psychological difficulties. These reveal evidence of a high level of perceived disability, depression, and evidence to support the conclusion of marked illness behavior and somatization.[4]

The term "malingering" should be used cautiously, and, based on my extensive experience in the occupational medicine field, this disorder is rarely encountered. In this case, however, this should be considered within

---

[4] Ensalada LH, Brigham CR. Somatization. *Guides Newsletter*. July-August 2000. http://www.impairment.com/ref/psych-somatization-07-00.pdf

the differential. The DSM-IV, Diagnostic Statistical Manual of Mental Disorders – Fourth Edition, states on page 683 that "the essential feature of malingering is the intentional production of false or grossly exaggerated physical or psychological symptoms, motivated by external incentives…"

The array of the very evident behavioral and psychological issues suggests and underlying personality disorder, Cluster B or C.[5] This would certainly have predated the work related injury and be an unrelated process, however would explain some of her behavioral dysfunction.

She does report being depressed, and has been through significant stressors beyond that of her perception that she had a work related injury. She recently went through a divorce, this being completed in February.

Ms. Vane is obese, deconditioned, and has significant problems with postural dysfunction. She also has asthma, however continues to smoke. It does not demonstrate the characteristics of an individual who assumes responsibility for personal physical fitness and well-being.

In summary, based on my thorough review of the medical records and assessment, I find no evidence of any objective work related injury nor any evidence of complex regional pain syndrome. She demonstrates marked behavioral dysfunction which appears to be a purposeful misrepresentation, suggestive of malingering.

Causation
Based on the available information, to a reasonable degree of medical certainty, there is no evidence at this time of any sequelae from a work-related injury in May of 1997.

Prognosis
I am concerned about her prognosis from a behavioral and psychological perspective and her unneeded reliance on [the] medical care system.

Maximum Medical Improvement
The examinee has achieved maximum medical improvement. If there was a soft tissue injury associated with the May 7, 1997 event, it is probable that resolved no later than the end of 1997.

MMI is defined as the date after which further recovery and restoration of function can no longer be anticipated, based upon a reasonable degree of medical probability.

---

[5] Bourne D. Personality Disorders in Disability Arena. *Guides Newsletter*. November 1999. http://impairment.com/ref/psych-personality-disorder-11-99.pdf

Permanent Impairment Evaluation
Permanent impairment evaluation was performed in accordance with the AMA *Guides to the Evaluation of Permanent Impairment,* Fourth Edition. Other than very questionable deficits of motion, there is no evidence of any physical loss e.g. any physical ratable impairment. An impairment is defined as "the loss of, the loss of use, or derangement of any body part, system or function." There is no objective evidence that this has occurred for her upper extremities.

The only possible ratable impairment at this time would be for motion deficits however it is probable that these findings were controlled by pain behavior, and therefore not valid for rating impairment. If, hypothetically, her mild deficits were true then there would be minimal impairment associated with them. In terms of her right shoulder, she portrayed a lack of 10 degrees of abduction which according to Figure 41 (4th ed., 44) would result in a 1% upper extremity impairment. For her right wrist she could have a lack of flexion of 10 degrees resulting in 2% upper extremity impairment according to Figure 26 (4th ed., 36) and lack of 20 degrees of extension according to Figure 26 (4th ed., 36) would result in a 4% upper extremity impairment. Therefore, if hypothetically these measurements were valid and reliable, her total impairment would 7% upper extremity, which converts via Table 3 to a 4% whole person permanent impairment. With the questionable nature of these findings, e.g. not being consistent with other observations, I find no ratable impairment.

Work Capacity
There is no objective basis, whatsoever, to impose any restrictions due to the referenced injury date of May 7, 1997.

Appropriateness of Care
It is probable that excessive medical attention, in terms of unnecessary treatments, has reinforced dysfunctional illness behavior, and therefore contributed to her dysfunctional presentation and her portrayal of a high level of perceived disability.

Recommendations
There is no evidence that she requires any ongoing treatment for the alleged injury date of May 7, 1997. It is probable that continuing to treat her for a medical disorder, e.g. reflex sympathetic dystrophy, will be detrimental and reinforce dysfunctional behavior.

Qualifications
My comments are based upon the specifics of this case and my knowledge, skills and abilities in this domain. I serve as Editor-in-Chief of the AMA

Guides Newsletter, Editor of *The Guides Casebook* (the AMA companion textbook to the *Guides*, Fourth Edition) and have trained thousands of physicians in the US, Canada and Australia on how to use the AMA *Guides to the Evaluation of Permanent Impairment*. I have published and spoken extensively in this field, and am featured in several videotape and audiotape productions on this and related topics. I am the author of two of the primary texts in the field of independent medical examinations: *Independent Medical Evaluation Report* and the *Comprehensive IME System*. During the past fifteen years I have analyzed and performed several thousands of impairments evaluations using the AMA *Guides to the Evaluation of Permanent Impairment,* Fourth Edition.

I am Board-Certified in Occupational Medicine, Founding Director of the American Board of Independent Medical Examiners, a Certified Independent Medical Examiner, a Fellow of the American Academy of Disability Evaluating Physicians, and a Fellow of the American College of Occupational Environmental Medicine. My curriculum vitae is available upon request.

Disclosure Statements
The above analysis is based upon the available information at this time, including the history given by the examinee, the medical records and tests provided, the results of pain status inventories, and the physical findings. It is assumed that the information provided to me is correct. If more information becomes available at a later date, an additional report may be requested. Such information may or may not change the opinions rendered in this evaluation.

My opinions are based upon reasonable medical certainty. Medicine is both an art and a science, and although an individual may appear to be fit for work activity, there is no guarantee that the person will not be reinjured or suffer additional injury. If applicable, employers should follow the processes established in the Americans with Disabilities Act, Title I. The opinions on work capacity are to facilitate job placement and do not necessarily reflect an in-depth direct threat analysis. Comments on appropriateness of care are professional opinions based upon the specifics of the case and should not be generalized, nor necessarily be considered supportive or critical of, the involved providers or disciplines.

Any medical recommendations offered are provided as guidance and not as medical orders. The opinions expressed do not constitute a recommendation that specific claims or administrative action be made or enforced.

I declare under penalty of perjury that the information contained in this report and its attachments is true and correct, to the best of my knowledge and belief, except as to information that I have received from others. As to that information, I declare under penalty of perjury that the information accurately describes the information provided to me, and except as noted in this report, that I believe to be true. I further declare under penalty of perjury that to the best of my knowledge and belief, the contents of this report and bill are true and correct. The foregoing was signed in the County of Nolan, State of Maine, on the date of this report.

Thank you for asking me to see this examinee in consultation. If you have any further questions, please do not hesitate to contact me.

Sincerely,

Collin Eddington, MD, FAADEP, FACOEM, CIME

Enclosures: *Guides Newsletter* articles: Somatization and Complex
               regional pain syndrome
               Battery for Health Improvement Report
               Minnesota Multiphasic Personality Inventory Report
               Curriculum Vitae
               Invoice

CE:dn/sd

Report #9: Products Liability

This report is most notable for the following:

- Excellent, specific list of documents reviewed.
- Good documentation of supporting literature.
- Pinpoint citations to depositions in text.
- Well-supported opinions.
- Tight and objective language.

Peter Reese, P.E.
Lawrence, IL

INTRODUCTION

At your request, ABC Consultants, Inc., has undertaken an engineering and safety analysis of certain causes of a high-voltage electrical contact accident which occurred on January 17, 1996 and which resulted in serious injury to Mr. Frederick Jefferson. What follows is our initial report of findings and conclusions to date. As additional work may be done in this matter, any conclusions and opinions expressed herein will be amended or supplemented as required.

MATERIALS REVIEWED

In the course of this analysis, reference was made to the following materials supplied by your office:

1. Depositions (with exhibits) of:
Walter Bailey	1-28-99
Alexander F. Kornelly	1-28-99
Kyle L. Kuhlmann	8-30-00
Joshua D. Lynch	8-17-99
Peter Mitchell	11-16-98
Frederick Jefferson	8-17-99
2. Recorded Statement of Peter Mitchell 3-13-98.
3. Photographs of post-accident scene, product involved, and competitive products.
4. Videotape of fire scene.
5. Patent, DES. 226, 559, (The Ornamental Design for a Platform and Support Yoke for an Aerial Tower).
6. Answers to Plaintiffs' Request for Production of Documents, Set II.
7. Answers to Request for Product of Documents, Set IV.

8. Defendant's Acme Corporation's Response to Request for Production of Documents of Plaintiffs, Frederick Jefferson and Jean Jefferson.
9. Answers to Plaintiffs' Interrogatories Propounded Upon the Defendant, Acme Corporation, Set One.
10. Answers to Plaintiff's Interrogatories Propounded Upon The Defendant, Acme Corporation, Set Two.
11. Defendant Acme Corporation's Response to Plaintiffs' Interrogatories Propounded Upon The Defendant, Acme Corporation, Set Three.
12. Answers to Defendant, Utility's Interrogatories, Set I, Directed to Plaintiffs'.
13. Acme Literature – Raising the Aerial Standards for Over 35 Years Acme Model 95 and 100 FT Aerial Platforms.
14. Truck information and damage reports.
15. Operator's Manual for The City of Littleton, Pa Fire Department Models 110, 210 by Best AlarmCo. as well as other Best AlarmCo. documents.
16. DOE OSH Technical Reference Chapter 7 – Mobile Work Platforms – Part 3 – Protective Devices.
17. NIOSH Alert "Preventing Electrocutions of Crane Operators and Crew Members Working Near Overhead Power Lines".
18. OSHA 1926.550 Cranes and Derricks.
19. Contracts, Proposals, and Purchase Documents.
20. City of Granville Specifications for Fire Apparatus Vehicle and Related Equipment.
21. American Test Center Test Report for Renegade Fire Apparatus, Inc. dated 11-30-96.
22. Police Report dated 1-17-96.
23. Incident report of Jason Lynch, Jr. dated 1-16-96

Additional materials related to applicable standards, reference materials, and principles of product safety engineering and design were also reviewed and considered as follows:

1. NFPA Standard 1901 – 1979, "Automotive Fire Apparatus".
2. NFPA Standard 1901 – 1985, "Automotive Fire Apparatus".
3. NFPA Standard 1904 – 1991, "Aerial Ladder and Elevating Platform Fire Apparatus".
4. CFR 29 1910.333.
5. The Fire Chief's Handbook, 3rd Edition, J.F. Casey, R.H. Donnelly Corp., 1967. (Excerpts from Chapters 4 and 14).

6.   A Fire Officer's Guide to Operation Aerial Ladders, 3rd Edition, National Fire Protection Association, 1974. (Excerpt page 37).

7.   Fire Apparatus Purchasing Handbook, W.C. Peters, Fire Engineering Books and Videos, 1994. (Excerpts from Chapter 2).

8.   The complete Book of Fire Engines, P.C. Ditzel, Bekman House, 1982. (Excerpts pages 95 and 96).

9.   Safety Engineering, Marshall, Wadsworth, Inc., 1982, pages 40-47.

10.   Product Safety Management and Engineering, Hammer, Prentice-Hall, 1980, pages 51-57 and 111-130.

SUMMARY OF ACCIDENT

Mr. Frederick Jefferson was a firefighter employed for almost six years by the City of Granville, and was assigned as part of the crew to Truck No. 2, a 1986 Acme Aerial Elevating Platform Truck. In the early hours of January 17, 1996, the truck was called by a second alarm to a suspected arson fire at 700 E. Forest Avenue in Granville, Pennsylvania. The fire was fully involved and numerous equipment was already at the scene when the truck arrived and set up near the center of the street, with parked cars and snowbanks on either side.

Two firefighters, Captain Tim Hansen and Private Jason Lynch entered the bucket of the truck and prepared for possible rescue as there were reports of entrapment and fire was showing through the roof. As the aerial was raised, the self-leveling feature of the platform failed to function, and the two firefighters had to monitor and control the movement of the apparatus while hanging on to the severely tilted platform

Mr. Jefferson was on the ground, and after setting the outriggers to allow the boom to be raised, was assigned to attach a 2 ½ inch water hose line to the pump control panel of the truck. As Mr. Jefferson was making this hook up, the elevated tower made inadvertent contact with one phase of a three phase 13.2k utility wire which had not yet been disconnected. Mr. Jefferson was severely injured as a result of this inadvertent contact, as he was standing on the ground while in contact with the energized truck.

DISCUSSION

1. RELEVANT TRUCK HISTORY & DESIGN FEATURES

The fire apparatus involved in this accident was a Model A1, Serial Number 0123 which was manufactured by Acme Corporation and delivered to the City of Granville on January 31, 1986 for a price of $344,866.00. The elevating portion of the apparatus is comprised of a 4-section telescopic boom mounted to a rotating turntable and elevatable to a platform height of approximately 100 feet. Water, air, and electrical lines are routed through the boom to the platform.

There are two control stations for operating the tower, one mounted on the turntable at the base of the boom, and another in the platform. These controls are labeled and back lit in accordance with NFPA requirements. The platform controls are electrical, operating solenoid-controlled hydraulic valves located at the base of the tower.

The platform itself is suspended in a yoke attached to the top of the boom, and anchored on each side of the platform with self-aligning bearings. Leveling of the platform is accomplished by a self-contained hydraulic system mounted in the end of the fourth-section boom. Two mercury switches are mounted in the platform, and when an out-of-level condition of the platform is sensed by the switches, an electrical signal is sent to the hydraulic system which actuates a bi-directional hydraulic pump sending hydraulic oil to leveling cylinders attached between the platform and the boom, which move to bring the platform back to a level condition. This system failed to operate properly during the time preceding the power line contact incident. According to Mr. Kyle Kuhlmann, Acme Corporate Designee, Acme realized that there could be failures in any part of the leveling system (Kuhlmann, page 141).

Two manual over-ride valves were provided mounted to the side of the tip of the boom which would need to be operated by a person in the platform reaching back to turn the two over-ride valve control knobs. When these valves are opened, hydraulic oil is allowed to flow freely between the rod-end and tail-end of the leveling cylinders, allowing the platform to swing freely in the yoke, much like a Ferris wheel chair being leveled by gravity. The two over-ride control knobs were unlabeled as to their function, and neither of the occupants of the platform at the time preceding the accident even knew of their existence. After this accident, and in response to this litigation, Acme incorporated an instruction plate on their units describing the operation of the over-ride system (Kuhlmann, pages 103-104).

In spite of the fact that Acme knew that mercury switches do fail from time-to-time (Kuhlmann, page 134), or that wiring or other malfunctions could occur in the leveling system (Kuhlmann, page 139), Acme failed to group the safety-critical over-ride controls with the rest of the controls in the bucket and failed to label these controls as to their function and operation. The only reason provided by Acme for not grouping the over-ride controls with other controls in the platform was that hydraulic lines would have to be run into the bucket and would be subject to continual flexing and exposure to heat (Kuhlmann, page 151). The issue of exposure to heat does not seem a valid concern, since Acme uses Dexron II hydraulic fluid in this hydraulic system, which is flammable. Non-flammable hydraulic fluids, such as water-glycol solutions, were available for such systems since the early 1970's.

2. ELECTRICAL CONTACT HAZARDS

The severe hazard of contact with overhead electrical wires by elevating boom equipment has been recognized for decades prior to the manufacture of the subject apparatus. The fire service in particular, was cognizant of these hazards which are addressed in the references cited. Members of the Granville Fire Department were properly trained to treat all overhead electric wires as live unless power was confirmed to have been cut. If overhead electrical contact is made, the entire metal structure of the unit will become energized, and any person providing a path from the energized structure to ground could be severely or fatally injured.

On the subject truck, the pump controls are located on the side of the truck, completely accessible and operable by a person standing on the ground. In this case, Mr. Jefferson was attaching a water line to the pump inlet at the pump control station on the driver's side of the truck, and his body provided the path-to-ground when electrical contact was made. Acme knew of the electrical contact hazard involved with the operation of his truck (Kuhlmann, page 166) but failed to equip the truck with any safety features whatsoever to reduce the risk of contact or the hazard to persons who might be in contact with the truck (Kuhlmann, page 167).

The NFPA also recognized the hazard, and in its 1901-1979 and 1985 Safety Standard for Water Tower Apparatus, required that a platform be provided for the operator to stand on while operating the tower to help avoid possible electric shock in case of apparatus contact with live electrical lines. In 1991, the NFPA issued Standard 1904 specifically dealing with aerial ladders and elevated platforms, and included a requirement that the pump operator's position incorporate provisions so that the pump operator is not in contact with the ground as well as requiring signs to warm the pump operator of electrocution hazard (NFPA 1904-1991, paragraph 7-9.2). Mr. Kuhlmann, Acme's Corporate Designee, was a member of the NFPA Committee and acted as its Secretary when these Standards were promulgated.

DISCUSSION OF HARZARD COUNTER-MEASURES AND DESIGN ALTERNATIVES

1. Hazard Identification and Control

The basic principles of the methods to be used in the safe design of a product are designated in the referenced texts. Essentially, the methodology is to first conduct a hazard analysis to identify hazards based on the product's foreseeable uses and misuses and its environments of use. Second, to evaluate the risks posed by those hazards in terms of their probability and severity. Third, to control exposure to the assessed risk by the following means, listed in order of precedence:

A. Designing Out The Hazard.
B. Incorporating Safety Devices.

C. Providing Warning Devices.
D. Mitigating the Hazard by Means of Operating Procedures &
Training.

These are the methods which should be used by a manufacturer in
designing a product which is safe for its intended use, and these are the same
methods which are used in analyzing accidents and reaching conclusions
about the causes and prevention of accidents as has been done in this report.
Practical, feasible, and cost-effective alternative designs were
available to Acme to address the hazards related to the foreseeable and
expected use of this product.

2. Elevated Platform Design Alternatives
An out-of-level condition of the platform creates a serious hazard to the
occupants of the platform in that (1) the occupants may become disoriented,
(2) the occupants may not be able to properly view or control the movement
of the boom, (3) the occupants are at risk of falling from the platform, (4) the
occupants may not be easily and quickly able to identify and reach the over-
ride control knobs.
Feasible means of correcting the hazards produced by a malfunction
of the platform leveling system have been assessed. These include the
following:

A. Electrically controlled over-ride system: Such a system would
replace the two hand-operated over-ride valves with electric
solenoid-operated valves (readily available, reliable, and used
elsewhere on this product) operated by a switch located on the
platform control panel connected by wiring to the solenoid valves.
The platform operator would only need to actuate the over-ride
switch on the control panel in the platform to open the solenoid
valves and permit the platform to self-level. A reasonable estimate
for the cost of this system would be under $300.00, less than .01% of
the price of the apparatus.

B. A redundant leveling systems: This would incorporate an
additional set of mercury leveling switches and associated housing
and wiring. Such a redundant system operating in parallel to the
existing leveling system in the platform would substantially increase
the reliability. For example, if the current leveling system (mercury
switches and wiring) were 95% reliable, a redundant system would
raise the reliability to 99.75%. Such a system would use existing
hardware and a reasonable estimated cost would be well under
$300.00, again less than .01% of the cost of the unit.

C. An all-hydraulic leveling system: A majority of aerial products which incorporate elevated platforms use a fully hydraulic platform leveling system comprising a master cylinder to sense elevation of the boom, sending hydraulic fluid through hydraulic lines in the boom to leveling cylinders at the elevated platform. Such a system is completely self-contained, requires no power source, and the components are readily available. Hydraulic fluid supply from the base of the boom at the master cylinder would be provided via hoses on take-up reels mounted in the telescopic boom. This hose arrangement would be the same as that which already exists on the subject unit to provide life-support air from the base of the tower to the platform.

It is likely that such a system could be incorporated in this unit at no net increase in cost, since it would utilize the existing leveling cylinders at the platform and would completely eliminate the self-contained hydraulic unit mounted at the tip of the boom and its associated control devices.

3. Electrical Contact Design Alternatives

The well-recognized hazard of high-voltage electrical contact could have been mitigated in two feasible ways, (1) providing an isolated platform for the pump operator to stand on, and (2) providing a proximity warning system for the elevated boom.

Provision for an insulated, isolated platform on which the pump operator would stand would prevent the operator from providing a ground path for the electrically-charged structure. Such a platform, according to Mr. Kuhlmann is "easy to do" (Kuhlmann, page 117). In fact, at the time the 1991 NFPA Standard 1904 came into effect, Acme added such steps to its products. Mr. Kuhlmann also indicated that if a purchaser specified an anti-electrocution step, Acme would be able to build one (Kuhlmann, page 117). Thus, in spite of the existence of the known hazard, and the feasible and reasonable counter measure of adding an anti-electrocution step for the pump operator, Acme failed to address this hazard.

Proximity warning devices sense the electromagnetic field produced by electrical conductors, and can be set to sound a warning to alert the aerial platform operator that the boom is approaching high voltage wires. Such systems have been available for many years prior to the manufacture of the subject apparatus, and in fact were supplied by Acme at special customer request since the early 1970's (Kuhlmann, page 168).

CONCLUSIONS AND OPINIONS

Based on my review of the materials referenced, as well as my experience and training as a mechanical engineer, I have reached the following conclusions and opinions to date with regard to relevant design aspects of the subject Acme Model A1 aerial platform fire apparatus:

1. Acme failed to utilize proper safety engineering methodology to assess the risks associated with the use of its product and provide a product design to mitigate or eliminate the hazards associated with the foreseeable and expected use of the product.

2. Acme failed to adequately warn and instruct users of the foreseeable and expected hazards to be encountered in the use of the product.

3. Acme failed to utilize technically and economically feasible design alternatives to reduce or eliminate risks to users of its product, with specific regard to the platform leveling system and electrical contact hazards as discussed above.

4. The foregoing failings resulted in a defective, unreasonably dangerous, and negligently designed product, not fit for its intended and foreseeable uses.

5. The defective conditions of the product by design were causes of Mr. Frederick Jefferson's accident and injury.

Report #10: Trade Secret Declaration

This report is most notable for:

- Easy to read.
- Well-organized.
- Use of examples to help explain opinion.
- Multiple reasons given to support conclusion that data in question was a trade secret.
- Objective language is used, even when refuting opposing expert's declaration.
- No superfluous information included.

Areas of possible improvement:

- Include materials reviewed.
- Include list of authorities.

DECLARATION OF RICHARD A. KRYSTI

I. BACKGROUND AND EXPERIENCE

1. My name is Richard A. Krysti. I am the cofounder of Klein Marketing Services, a marketing consulting firm located in Wintersburg, Massachusetts. A complete copy of my curriculum vitae is attached as Exhibit 1.

2. I have held a variety of positions over the past 30 years in the field of marketing and marketing science. Many of these activities have involved the collection and analysis of data for marketing and sales-related purposes. Examples of these activities include:

- Analysis of geographic trends in consumer goods sales data, including cookies, crackers, snack foods, beer, autos, and energy.
- Analysis of trends in purchasing behavior of various demographic groups determined by relating individual item sales in supermarkets to the demographic makeup of each store's trading area.
- Selection of representative markets for test marketing and experimentation based on U.S. Census data.
- Adjustment and weighting of consumer survey sample results to correspond with U.S. Census data.

- Projection of national and regional industry sales volumes and share based on sales data collected from supermarket scanners.

II. ASSIGNMENT AND SUMMARY OF OPINIONS

3. I have been asked by Huske and Allen ("Husk") on behalf of ABC Mutual Automobile Insurance Company, ABC Fire and Casualty Company and ABC General Insurance Company ("ABC") to provide this declaration in the above-captioned litigation between ABC and the California Department of insurance ("CDI"). As I understand the litigation, ABC has provided certain zip code level information, referred to as the Record A information, to the CDI as required by law. This zip code level information contains information on the type of insurance, the number of total exposures earned during the year, the number of new exposures acquired during the year, the number of exposures cancelled during the year, the number of exposures not renewed during the year, and the total earned premium for the year.

4. Husk has asked me to opine as to whether the zip code level information submitted to the CDI has significant value and whether firms would typically consider this sort of customer information to be a trade secret. My expertise is in the fields of marketing and marketing science, and I was asked to address this question generally based on my experience with companies in various industries, rather than as an issue somehow specific to insurance. I have analyzed markets for competitive purposes in many industries and the same knowledge, experience and expertise is applicable to each of the various industries. If asked to provide competitive advice and analysis to an insurance company, I would use the same knowledge, experience, and expertise that I have developed over 30 years of studying markets in numerous industries.

I apply that same knowledge, experience, and expertise here. Addressing the question with that understanding, in my opinion, the zip code level information contained in Record A would have significant value both to ABC and to competitors. Because of its strategic importance for internal decision-making and its value to competitors, it is the sort of information firms tend to consider a trade secret and would take steps to prevent its discovery by competitors.

5. In my experience, zip code level information on customers and sales is widely used within companies and by competitors to determine patterns of behavior, identify market segments, develop and refine marketing and advertising strategies, and make other important marketing and business decisions. Indeed, the CDI's own use of the Record A data to analyze penetration of regional markets demonstrates the importance and the value of using this zip code level data. In a similar manner, competitors can use this

342

zip code level data to understand patterns of behavior and market segmentation, to target any vulnerabilities may have, and to avoid competing in areas where ABC is strong.

6. In the remainder of my declaration, I review some of the potential uses and sources of value of zip code level information such as the Record A data. These include:

- Using zip code level data for market share and market position analysis;
- Using zip code level data to develop regional advertising and marketing strategies;
- Using zip code level data to develop other targeted advertising and marketing strategies;
- Using zip code level data to assist in agent recruiting efforts;
- Using zip code level data to evaluate the success of advertising efforts; and
- Using zip code level data to measure the impact of price changes.

7. I conclude by commenting on some of the arguments being raised that seek to deny the value and trade secret status of the Record A data. These include:

- Arguments that the data are not detailed enough to have any value;
- Arguments that Record A data provide no additional value since rate data is already available at the zip code level; and
- Arguments that if the data were released for all companies, all companies would be on equal footing.

III. SOURCES OF VALUE FROM ZIP CODE LEVEL DATA

8. As I understand it, earned premium and earned exposure data are currently available in the annual statements filed by ABC and other insurers at the state-wide level for California. The relevant question is what additional value may result from the data being available at the zip code level, and whether this value may be great enough that the data should be considered to be a trade secret. In my experience, zip code level information such as this is commonly used for a wide variety of marketing and other business purposes. It is also information that many companies consider confidential and would not want to fall into competitors' hands. In this section, I will discuss several of these uses in more detail.

A. Value of the Record A Data for Market Share and Relative Market Position Analysis

9. One of the most important uses of ABC's Record A data would be as part of either a market share analysis or a relative market position analysis at the zip code level. Market share analysis is the comparison of the share of the market of one company relative to all of its competitors and relative to the market as a whole. Relative market position involves a comparison of one company's position relative to another. Both of these are key elements of market intelligence and are useful for measuring and evaluating the performance of a product or service.

10. Currently market share information is available annually by line of insurance for the entire state of California. However, given the tremendous size (over 34 million people) and geographic diversity of the population in California, this statewide market share provides only a limited picture of the market and is much less information than a company would want to have in order to understand a competitor's actions.

11. Were ABC's Record A data to be available, other companies would be able to develop relative market position analyses at the zip code level by line of insurance, comparing their business to ABC. This type of analysis is of particular importance when the lines of personal insurance, including automobile and homeowner's insurance. Thus while most carriers would perhaps not care very much about how they were performing relative to a small insurer, they are likely to care very much about how they were performing relative to the largest company in the market.

12. Manufacturers and marketers routinely spend hundreds of thousands of dollars to buy market share and competitor market information. Indeed, there are a number of companies that specialize in collecting and selling these data, including Information Resources, A. C. Nielsen, NPD, and others. In each case, however, the information is collected from a sample of stores, customers, etc. rather than a complete enumeration of all the sales of all the competitors in all the outlets. The Record A data at the zip code level are much more precise, and thus even more valuable, than the best data available in most other industries. The Record A data represents a census, and the resulting market shares can be calculated exactly with zero sampling error.

13. If a competitor wanted to approximate the information available in the Record A data, it would be necessary to interview respondents in every zip code and ask them details about each type of insurance they own. Due to normal sampling variation, a very large number of respondents would be needed to provide usable measures of market share at the zip code level. For example, 400 respondents would be required from each of the over 1,800 zip

codes in California to be able to estimate the market share in a zip code plus or minus 4% (20% plus or minus 4% = 16% to 24%). The cost of such a data collection effort would exceed $20 million per year and yield information that is significantly inferior to the Record A data due to factors such as normal sampling error, respondent bias due to potential language issues, and the reluctance of respondents to answer questions about potentially sensitive insurance-related issues.

14. I have reviewed the declaration of J. Robert Hult, dated May 1, 2000. In his declaration, he states that the insurer, "knows where it is gaining or losing market share to other competitors because agents and others selling the insurance know such information through their on-the-ground sales activities." Based on my experience in marketing and analysis of marketing data, such on-the-ground, anecdotal information is often inaccurate and inadequate for use in marketing activities. While there may be some value to such information, it is certainly not a substitute for the sort of reliable, detailed information found in the Record A data.

B. Value of the Record A Data for Developing Regional Marketing and Advertising Programs

15. In addition to being valuable simply as market intelligence, the zip code level information available in ABC's Record A data has additional uses that are of equal or even greater value. For example, using Record A data, competitors would be able to analyze their position relative to ABC's and develop marketing and advertising strategies to exploit this information in distinct local markets. ABC is obviously a formidable competitor, but the zip code level information available in the Record A data can be used to determine if there are any weaknesses that might be exploited at the regional level.

16. As an example of how this might be done, consider the following example. If a competitor insurance company sought to target ABC, it might begin by using the Record A data of ABC and its own Record A data to identify those zip codes or groups of zip codes where it had experienced some success over time at the expense of ABC. It could then use this information to target its media advertising in those areas where it had already shown that is was most likely to attract customers away from ABC.

17. California consists of twelve distinct broadcast media markets ranging in size from Los Angeles (number 2, nationally) to Eureka (number 189). By focusing advertising dollars on those media markets where they would have the greatest impact, a competitor could spend

hundreds of thousands or even millions of dollars less than it might otherwise have to in order to obtain a given number of former ABC customers from a major advertising effort.

18. Based on my review of the reports of the insurance industry over the past few years, I do not believe that this is simply a theoretical possibility. The information contained in Record A data would be of particular use to a company specifically targeting ABC. An example of such a company would be BestBuy Insurance Company. The CEO of BestBuy Insurance has publicly stated that the company's goal is to surpass ABC in auto insurance premiums written by 2010. He has further stated that his company is "using specifically designed strategies to gain market share."3 The Record A data provides the type of information BestBuy could use to both target its efforts and evaluate the success of those efforts. With this information BestBuy could precisely target the exact zip codes where ABC is most vulnerable.

19. One strategy being used by BestBuy is to "expand its direct business sales via direct mail, the Internet, the telephone and to affinity groups. BestBuy claims that its direct business comes from taking business away from the captive agents of its competitors. These are the type of agents used by ABC, and the Record A data would be extremely valuable in determining the areas where this direct marketing effort should be focused. More evidence of this tightly focused strategy is the use of television commercials "specifically designed for rollout on local cable outlets."5 By using the Record A data, BestBuy could choose the specific media alternatives and specific areas that would best meet their stated needs.

C. Value of the Record A Data for Developing Other Targeted Marketing and Advertising Programs

20. Zip code level data can also be combined with other data to develop targeted marketing and advertising programs. The U.S. Census Bureau publishes detailed information on age, income, employment, ethnicity, family size, education, housing characteristics, pets, and other information. This is collected by the Census Bureau at what is known as the "block group/enumeration district" level, an even finer level of geographic detail than zip code. Independent companies will aggregate this data for a fee to match any geography of interest, including zip code.

21. Analyzing market share and changes in market share in relation to the demographic make up of the customers in a zip code or group of zip codes allows a company to see where and why its competitors succeed and fail with

different customer groups. This can provide critical competitive intelligence concerning their marketing strategy and the relative success of that strategy. It can also allow competitors to design strategies to target those population groups where ABC or other competitors may be vulnerable, as identified by the patterns of customers entering and leaving ABC's customer base. This would be particularly true if the Record A data were released for a number of years, thus allowing competitors to identify trends of customers entering and leaving ABC's customer base in each zip code and each line of insurance.

22. As an example of how this might be done, consider the following. If a competitor insurance company sought to target ABC's most vulnerable customer groups, it could use the Record A data spanning several years and combine this with the Census Bureau data. The results of this analysis might show that ABC was losing customers in the markets with higher concentrations of young families. This information could then be used to develop direct mail marketing and advertising campaigns specifically focused towards young families. By targeting only those groups with the largest potential impact, a competitor could use its marketing resources to the maximum advantage.

D. Value of the Record A Data for Agent Recruiting Purposes

23. Another possible use of the Record A data, and thus another source of its trade secret value, is as a tool for recruiting new sales agents. ABC, the largest insurer in California, has offices throughout the state of California staffed with agents under exclusive agency contracts. Inevitably, some of these agents and their employees are going to be more successful than others. By using the Record A data strategically, competitors could significantly improve their own agency force at the expense of ABC by raiding ABC's best offices.

24. Currently information on where ABC's agents are located is available from the yellow pages or other public sources, and is not considered by ABC to be a trade secret. This information includes the zip codes of these agents and the agent names. Combining this information with ABC's and a company's own Record A data would provide opportunities to improve a company's sales force through the targeted recruiting of ABC agents.

25. For example, a competitor could use the Record A data to identify zip codes where ABC was experiencing the greatest sales growth. It could then attempt to recruit either the primary ABC agents or the employees of those agents in those zip codes. While the data do not provide details as to exactly which agent or employee of the agent would be the cause of the success, this sort of information would nonetheless be of value in any effort to recruit new agents.

E. *Value of the Record A Data for Advertising Evaluation and Strategy*

26. If zip code level data such as the Record A data were available for all competitors, it could also be used by a competitor in the measurement and evaluation of advertising media. Insurance companies such as ABC currently spend tens of millions of dollars a year on a wide variety of media in order to promote brand awareness and deliver their unique marketing messages.

27. Because the Record A data measures market share and customer activities exactly and without error, evaluation of advertising is feasible even if the effect is small relative to the other factors affecting market share. The advertising weight of each company will naturally vary because every television station, radio station, and newspaper has a different pattern of coverage. Each of these media alternatives reports its reach and penetration by geography, and syndicated information services track advertising spending by company and media outlet. Thus it is possible to calculate the broadcast advertising weight each company is applying against each geographic area. This information can then be used to determine the impact of advertising on the market share achieved and to evaluate the payoff for increases or decreases in advertising. It will also indicate which geographic areas are most responsive to different types of advertising so that these funds can be allocated in the most efficient way possible.

28. Any properly advised company wishing to target ABC would see this data as being uniquely valuable. This information can be particularly important for companies that are aggressively seeking to grow their insurance business in California. Because ABC is the largest insurer in California in the major lines of personal insurance, it would be the obvious target for smaller companies wishing to grow their business. By using the Record A data to determine where advertising is most effective, competitors can target their advertising efforts to maximum advantage.

29. In addition to its value in evaluating the success of overall advertising efforts, the effectiveness of particular advertising themes can also be identified using zip code level information. Companies spend a great deal of time and effort developing advertising messages that "position" the company and its products in the minds of potential customers. Particular advertising themes are well established, but others are much more short-lived or may be focused on a particular demographic group or geographic area. When campaigns do change, an evaluation of this impact on the market is almost impossible without very precise market share information. By analyzing the year-to-year changes in market share coinciding with changes in advertising message, the overall effectiveness of the message can be measured. In addition to measuring the effectiveness of one's own advertising messages in increasing market share, the Record A data could also be used to measure of

the effect on retention, turnover, and market shares of advertising efforts by competitors.

30. The Record A data, the advertising weight data, and the Census Bureau data previously discussed can be combined to analyze the demographic makeup of the zip codes with the largest and smallest response to advertising messages. These changes will allow competitors to develop their advertising to counter competitive gains or exploit competitive losses. This analysis is only possible because the Record A data is a complete census, not a sample. Market share information derived from surveys is typically too imprecise due to sampling error to be used for this purpose.

F. Value of the Record A Data for Measuring the Impact of Price Changes
31. Measurement of price elasticity—the change in business resulting from a change in price is also possible by using the Record A data in conjunction with publicly available pricing data. Here the result is not only the loss of competitive advantage to ABC, but the potential for some consumers to see the cost of their insurance increase. The prices insurance companies charge are based on cost and risk, which can vary by location. Every insurance company is likely to have a unique cost structure and risk experience in each location where it operates. Thus prices can vary by zip code.

32. The result of all of this is that a customer in a particular location may be exposed to different prices from each company, with prices typically changing every year. When these year-to-year price changes are correlated with the changes in market share measured by the Record A data, the relative price sensitivity of the customers in every zip code can be measured for each insurance company. These measured price elasticities can be used to determine the potential profit impact of any price changes.

33. The following example illustrates how this might work. A competitor could use the publicly available insurance rate information along with the zip code level Record A data to identify zip codes or demographic groups that are relatively more or less sensitive to price changes. Assuming it was profitable to do so, the insurer could then undercut ABC's prices in the markets with the largest potential benefit and maintain or possibly even raise the rates in those zip codes where price changes appeared to have little effect. This is an analogous strategy to the price discrimination strategy used by the airlines to identify business travelers and charge them more.

G. Summary
34. In summary, the nature of the zip code level Record A data makes it particularly valuable as a competitive tool. There is no feasible or affordable means available to competitors to develop comparable information using surveys or other means. Because this information is valuable and has

multiple uses, it is logical and reasonable that an insurance company with a substantial presence would consider this information to be a trade secret and do everything possible to prevent it from falling into a competitor or future competitor's hands. This is particularly true for ABC, which is the largest insurer in California, and is therefore an obvious target for many of its competitors.

IV. ANALYSIS OF STATEMENTS CLAIMING THE RECORD A DATA IS NOT A TRADE SECRET

35. It is my understanding that various arguments have been raised in this litigation concerning the issue of the value of the Record A data, and thus by extension its status as a trade secret. In particular, I have read the Declaration of Andrew Hult, FCAS, MAAA, In Support of Intervenors' Motion For Summary Judgement, dated May 1, 2000 and filed July 28, 2000.
In this section, I will comment on certain of these arguments.

A. The Data Is Not Detailed Enough to Have Any Value

36. According to this argument, zip code level data has little or no value since the names, addresses, and telephone numbers of policyholders are not included. While it is true as a general rule that the more detailed the data, the more value it provides, it certainly does not follow that anything less than a complete list of customers and their history has no value. The existence of much more important data does not bear on whether a particular class of information has value.

37. As discussed earlier, analysis of zip-code level aggregate sales information is routinely performed in the marketing and market research departments of most large companies. Specialized computer software to facilitate such analyses has been in wide use for over 20 years, and companies pay large sums of money to obtain and analyze zip code level data.

38. A variant of this argument states that only if actual loss or profitability data were available at the zip code level would the Record A data actually have value. Again, while it is true that having more detailed data or additional fields would increase the value of the Record A data, it is still very valuable information even without these additional fields.

B. The Record A Data is of No Value Since the Premium Rate Data is Already Publicly Available

39. Insurance companies such as ABC currently file their rate information at the zip code level, and thus these data are already available to competitors and the general public. The rate data provides information on the price per

unit of insurance but does not provide the zip code level data set forth in Record A.

40. Undoubtedly, price is an important driver of customer choice, but if it were the only factor, the company with the lowest rates would have all the business. Consumers choose many things on the basis of more than just price. Issues of trust, brand loyalty, reputation, customer service, company and brand image, advertising, personal interaction with the agent, prior positive or negative experience with the company, word-of-mouth recommendation of friends and neighbors, and other factors all play a role in the consumer decision process.

41. Zip code level market data such as the Record A data can be used to develop models to estimate the importance of these non-price factors in different areas. This can then provide strategic intelligence for competitors for targeting ABC's customers for their new business. Any firm that does not consider customer data such as the Record A data as trade secrets puts itself at risk in the marketplace. While "reverse engineering" may not be an actuarial concept, it is a common marketing science notion, and is used in practice by many large, sophisticated companies.

42. A variant of this argument has been made that the anecdotal "on-the-ground intelligence" of agents could provide most, if not all, of the value provided by the Record A data. While this on-the-ground intelligence may have some value, in a state as large and as important as California, doing any systematic analysis of markets would require the sort of information that is included in the Record A data. To consider that anecdotal impressions of the market can provide anything approaching the precision of the Record A data is significantly overstated.

43. In fact, many of the studies described in this declaration are only enabled by the precision of the Record A data. These same studies would not be nearly as accurate—and therefore as valuable—if the only available data was anecdotal feedback from agents. Among other problems, differences in the perception of agents as to the changes in the market would result in inconsistent data across regions, thus resulting in biased data and analysis.

C. If the Data Were Released for All Companies, All Companies Would be on Equal Footing

44. This argument states that if the data is released for all companies and all years, then it would no longer be a trade secret for anyone. This argument has two problems. First, it amounts to an argument that says that by destroying everyone's trade secrets, everything will be fine. This does not change the fact that by releasing the information, the trade secret is being damaged or destroyed.

45. The second problem with the argument is that it fails to recognize that the value of the information can vary among companies, and that the release of such information could harm some companies more than others. For example, since ABC is the largest insurer, it would be a logical insurer for many smaller companies to target for sales growth. In those circumstances, the small companies would derive tremendous value from ABC's information, which causes ABC to place a high value on its confidentiality. It is unlikely to be true that ABC would derive the same amount of value from obtaining the Record A data from most smaller insurers.

46. Given this potentially large difference in the valuation of the Record A data, it is not surprising that ABC might have a stronger interest than some smaller companies in protecting the Record A data. It is likely that several smaller companies would actually benefit from across the board release because they would obtain access to ABC's Record A data and the Record A data of other historically successful insurers, which is of greater value than the confidentiality of their own data. To ABC and other historically successful insurers, on the other hand, the confidentiality of their data is likely to have more value than does access to other insurers' data.

D. Summary

47. It is certainly true that ABC likely has data in its possession that it considers even more valuable than the Record A data. Zip code level data on loss experience, specific customer behavior, specific agent sales, and other data would be extraordinarily valuable to competitors. However, it is also the case that the zip code data contained in Record A would also be very valuable to competitors, and would typically be considered to be a trade secret.

Using modern marketing technology, this sort of data can prove extremely useful to competitors. As an expert in the use of data in marketing, I can attest to the fact that this sort of information is both very useful and very valuable, and should thus be considered to be a trade secret when claimed by the firm and treated as confidential.

I declare under penalty of perjury under the laws of the State of California that the foregoing is a true and correct statement of my opinions and the supporting facts and that this declaration was executed on August 9, 2000 at Wintersburg, Massachusetts.

Report #11: Accident Reconstruction
This report is most notable for:

- Easy-to-read formatting.

Areas of possible improvement:

- Avoid passive voice and writing in third person.
- More specific listing of documents reviewed, avoiding "various documents from...."
- Include an illustration of accident scene.
- More specific citation to the literature.

1.0   INTRODUCTION

On 13, 1998 Top-Flight Consulting, Inc. was requested to review and reconstruct a motor vehicle accident involving a passenger car and three pedestrians which occurred in the City of Broad Hollow, Pennsylvania on February 19, 1997.

2.0   MATERIALS REVIEWED

2.1   City of Broad Hollow Police Department Accident Report #12-1212 dated February 19, 1997.

2.2   Deposition of George Porter.

2.3   Smithson Investigators, Inc. reports, including witness statements.

2.4   Defendant, Archdiocese of Broad Hollow, responses to interrogatories.

2.5   Various documents from residents and City of Broad Hollow officials.

2.6   Times newspaper article dated February 26, 1997.

2.7   Morley Adjustment, Inc. report dated October 4, 1999.

3.0   REVIEW OF POLICE INVESTIGATION

Date of Accident:	February 19, 1997.
Day of Week:	Wednesday
Time:	2:40 P.M.
Location:	Dryden Road, approximately 150 feet south of Oak Road, City of Broad Hollow, Pennsylvania.
Weather Conditions:	Clear, no adverse weather conditions present. Roadway surface was dry.
Speed Limit:	Dryden Road posted at 35 miles per hour. Dryden Road posted at 15 miles per hour during School opening, closing and dismissal.

Lighting: Daylight.
Traffic Control: No parking signs located along both sides of
                        Dryden Road at or near the locations of Saint
                        Victor's parish school and Archbishop Lewis High
                        School. School crossing signs located at the
                        Pedestrian crossings before and in the school zone.
                        Standard school speed limit signs located in the
                        school zone.

The police report that was filed by Officer Myer of the Broad
Hollow Police Department Accident Investigation Division was reviewed.

The police report indentifies unit #1 as a 1995 Taurus four door
sedan, burgundy in color, bearing Pennsylvania Registration #XXX-333,
which was being driven by George Porter.

The police report also identifies the pedestrians involved in this
accident as Patrick Donald, Linnea Jacobs, and Maureen Dooley.

According to the police report, the pedestrians were students at Saint
Victor's elementary school and Archbishop Lewis High School. Both
schools are located adjoining each other on the east side of Dryden Road
south of the impact zone. The pedestrians were all positioned on the
sidewalk adjacent to the northbound lane of Dryden Road approximately 150
feet south of the intersection of Dryden Road and Oak Road. The pedestrian
Patrick Donald was operating a bicycle just prior to being struck by the Ford
Taurus (vehicle #1).

According to the police accident report the Ford Taurus (vehicle #1)
that was being driven by George Porter (driver #1) had been traveling north
on Dryden Road in the right lane, when a school bus stopped in the right lane
north bound to discharge passengers. George Porter (driver #1) abruptly
changed lanes from the right lane to the left lane on Dryden Road at which
point George Porter (driver #1) applied his vehicle's brakes due to a backup
of traffic in the left lane on Dryden Road at Oak Road. George Porter (driver
#1) lost control of his vehicle traveling across the right northbound lane up
on the sidewalk and coming into contact with the pedestrians.

4.0   SITE INSPECTION
Dryden Road was found to be basically a north/south roadway
located within the limits of the City of Broad Hollow. Dryden Road has a
posted speed limit of 35 miles per hour. The 11500 block of Dryden Road is
primarily the location of a high school, elementary school and parish church
located on the East Side of Dryden Road. The area surrounding the 11500
block of Dryden Road was found to be a combination of commercial
establishments and highly populated residential area.

Dryden Road has two lanes of travel in both the north and
southbound directions. A ten-foot wide combination grass and concrete

median delineates the north and south lanes. The two travel lanes are delineated by standard broken white lane lines, which delineate the right and left lanes. Standard concrete curbing and sidewalks are installed on both the east and west sides of Dryden Road.

The travel lanes are composed of asphalt in good condition and free of defects. The right lane in the northbound direction is approximately 20 feet wide and the left northbound lane is approximately 12 feet in width. Visibility from Belmont Drive northward to Oak road past Archbishop Lewis High School and Saint Victor's Parish School was found to be good and free of sight line obstructions.

There are traffic control signs, which indicate a speed limit of 15 miles per hour during opening, closing and recess. The first sign located at the south end of the school zone was found located on the center median facing south controlling northbound traffic. The second similar sign was found posted on the East Side of the right northbound lane also facing south approximately 33 feet north of the first sign. A third similar sign was found posted in the center median approximately 625 feet north of the first sign. A fourth sign was found posted on the center median approximately 790 north of sign number three. A fifth similar sign was found posted on the center median approximately 440 feet north of sign number 4.

Traffic signals and additional 35 mile per hour traffic control signs are present through the school zone. The standard flashing school zone beacons were not located at this school zone nor where they any standard begin and end school signs posted at the start and the end of the school zone. This school zone extends for approximately 2115 feet along Dryden Road.

5.0   PERSONNEL

The driver of the Taurus (vehicle #1) was identified as George Porter (driver #1) 19-year-old male at the time of this accident. Mr. Porter (driver #1) was driving under a current Pennsylvania Drivers License. Mr. Porter (driver #1) was the sole occupant of his vehicle at the time of this accident. While the police report does not indicate what type of safety equipment was available to Mr. Porter (driver #1) at the time of this accident, the vehicle specifications for a 1995 Ford Taurus (vehicle #1) indicates that this vehicle was equipped with three point front and rear seat belt combination and the vehicle is also equipped with front seat airbags, which according to the police report did not deploy.

Pedestrian #1 was identified as Patrick Donald a 9 year old male at the time of this accident. Patrick Donald was operating a bicycle along the sidewalk adjacent to the northbound lane of Dryden Road. Patrick Donald was a student at Saint Victor's school and was enroute to his home after being dismissed for the day from school. Upon being struck by the Ford Taurus (vehicle #1), Patrick Donald disengaged from his bicycle and he sustained severe injuries to his legs, he was transported from the accident scene by a Broad Hollow Fire Medic vehicle to University Hospital for treatment of his injuries.

Pedestrian #2 was identified as Linnea Jacobs a 16 year old female at the time of this accident. Ms. Linnea Jacobs was a student at Archbishop Lewis High School and she was enroute to her home after being dismissed from school for the day, when she was struck by the Ford Taurus (vehicle #1) as she walked north bound on the sidewalk adjacent to the north bound lane of Dryden Road. Ms. Linnea Jacobs sustained injuries to her back and she was transported from the accident scene by a Broad Hollow Fire Medic vehicle to General Hospital for treatment of her injuries.

Pedestrian #3 was identified as Maureen Dooley a 16-year old female at the time of this accident. Ms. Maureen Dooley was a student at Archbishop Lewis High School and she to was enroute to her home after being dismissed from school for the day, when she was struck by the Ford Taurus (vehicle #1) as she walked north bound on the sidewalk adjacent to the north bound lane of Dryden Road. Ms. Maureen Dooley sustained injuries to her head and she was transported from the accident scene by a Broad Hollow Fire Medic vehicle to the General Hospital for treatment of her injuries.

6.0   RECONSTRUCTION

This section of the report will address the various stages and elements of this accident, prior to the vehicle coming to their final positions of rest.

6.1   PRE-CRASH

On Wednesday, February 19, 1997 Patrick Donald, Linnea Jacobs, and Maureen Dooley were traveling north on the sidewalk located on the east side of Dryden Road, on their way home from school. Mr. George Porter (driver #1) in his mother's 1995 Ford Taurus (vehicle #1) had been traveling north on Dryden Road and he had turned right into the driveway of the Archbishop Lewis High School parking lot to pick up his girlfriend. Mr Porter (driver #1) exited the Archbishop Lewis School parking area turning right onto Dryden Road traveling north.

6.2   CRASH

As Mr. Porter (driver #1) continued traveling north on Dryden Road in the right lane, according to the police accident report, he encountered a yellow school bus that had stopped abruptly in the right lane which forced him to swerve into the left lane and he applied his brakes firmly and he lost control of his vehicle striking the three pedestrians who were walking along the sidewalk adjacent to the right north bound lane on Dryden Road.

6.3   POST CRASH
During the accident scenario Mr Porter (driver #1) came into contact with the guardrail, fire hydrant, and a steel and concrete pole. Mr Porter's (driver #1) vehicle was towed from the accident scene. The pedestrians sustained moderate to severe injuries and they were transported to hospitals for treatment of their injuries.

7.0   ANALYSIS
This section of the report will address the various elements and factors involved in this accident.

7.1   WEATHER
At the time of this accident, the Police Report indicates that there were no adverse weather conditions present at the time of this accident. The weather was clear and the roadway surface was dry.

7.2   HUMAN FACTORS
There was no evidence found in the police investigation that Mr. Porter (driver #1) was suffering from any medical or mental conditions that would have impaired his ability to safely operate a motor vehicle before this accident.

7.3   VEHICLES
The vehicle that was involved in this accident was identified as a 1995 Ford Taurus (vehicle #1). The vehicle was not available for examination. Mr. Porter (driver #1) stated to the investigating officers that his vehicle had been serviced on February 18, 1997 for a problem with tire rods and an engine stalling problem (police statement page 4). It is assumed that Mr. Porter (driver #1) meant tie rods and "tire rods" was a typing error.
The Broad Hollow Police Department on February 21, 1997 inspected the Ford Taurus (vehicle #1) and their records indicate that this vehicle was in good condition for safe operation upon the roadway.
Their was no information contained in the police report or any records produced that would indicate that the mechanical condition of the Ford Taurus (vehicle #1) Mr. Porter (driver #1) was operating at the time of this accident was a factor in this accident.

7.4   ENVIRONMENT
Dryden Road from Chalfront Drive northbound is a combination of a densely populated area composed of businesses, homes, a church, high school and elementary school. Dryden Road in both the north- and south-bound directions is a high vehicular traffic volume roadway.
The posting of traffic control signs at the beginning and through the school zones was found too inadequate for the amount of pedestrian and

vehicular traffic through this area. This issue will be discussed in detail later in this report.

8.0   DISCUSSION

In reviewing the report that was filed by Officer Myer of the Broad Hollow Police Department, it was noted that she never conducted formal interviews of Patrick Donald, witnesses Richard Mulder, Suzanne Dorling, Tyler Olsen, and Lucas Moran.

Mr. Joseph A. Bunter, Jr., who conducted a follow investigation to this accident in April and July 1997, was able to obtain statements from the following witnesses:

Witness #1 Lucas Moran who stated he was a 10th grade student at Archbishop Lewis High School when this accident occurred. Mr Moran stated he heard tire screeching and when he turned around he observed the Ford Taurus (vehicle #1) spinning and he observed the Ford Taurus (vehicle #1) mount the sidewalk and the strike the boy on the bicycle with the left rear of the vehicle and then continue northbound traveling backwards where it struck the two girls before striking the fire hydrant and a green pole.

Witness #2 Tyler Olsen was a 12-grade student at Archbishop Lewis High School at the time of this accident. Mr. Olsen was standing on the grass median in the center of Dryden Road, when he heard a car accelerating behind him. Mr. Olsen observed the Ford Taurus (vehicle #1) in the left lane approaching stopped traffic or moving very slowly in the left lane.

Mr. Olsen observed the Ford Taurus (vehicle #1) suddenly change lanes and it started spinning mounting the curb and sidewalk striking the boy on the bicycle with the driver's side of the car. The Ford Taurus (vehicle #1) continued into the two girls, then the car struck the fire hydrant before coming to rest against the guardrail.

Witness #3 Richard Mulder a retired Broad Hollow Police Officer. Mr. Mulder stated he had been traveling northbound on Dryden Road and that the traffic in the left turn lane on Oak Road had backed up into the left northbound lane. Mr. Mulder came to a stop and he was checking for traffic behind his vehicle in his rearview mirror. Mr. Mulder observed a SEPTA transit bus also in the left northbound lane on Dryden Road. Mr. Mulder decided not to continue to turn left onto Oak Road and he was looking for a break in traffic to continue traveling north using his rearview and right side-view mirrors.

According to Mr. Mulder the Ford Taurus (vehicle #1) came up behind the SEPTA transit bus and the driver of the Ford Taurus (vehicle #1) made a sudden turn from behind the SEPTA transit bus into the right lane. Mr. Mulder observed the driver of the Ford Taurus (vehicle #1) lose control of the vehicle; spinning in a clockwise direction two or three times mounting the curb were the kids were standing. The car then went through the fire hydrant and he observed one child fly up into the air.

Based on the above statements, it is apparent that Mr. Porter (driver #1) was not traveling north on Dryden Road in the right lane, he was in the left lane prior to impact and there was no yellow school bus, it was a SEPTA transit bus located in the left lane.

In the investigation and reconstruction of serious traffic accidents, such as this accident, especially where a criminal prosecution was contemplated, the investigating officer failed to record the witness statements and conduct a full investigation, which should have included environmental issues, such as highway design, highway markings and traffic control devices.

Dryden Road in the area of this accident has been established as a heavily traveled roadway. The school zone, which is located north of Belmont Drive, is unusual in that we have a parish school located at Saint Victor's Church, which is located adjacent to the Archbishop Lewis High School. A newspaper article in the February 26, 1997 edition of the Times estimates that the combined enrollment of Saint Victor's Parish School and Archbishop Lewis High School.

Dryden Road has a posted speed limit of 35 miles per hour. The City of Broad Hollow has posted additional traffic control signs indicating a school speed limit of "15 during opening, closing and recess." The first sign in the northbound direction on Dryden Road was located to the left of the northbound travel lanes on the concrete/grass median. A second sign was found located on the right side of the northbound lanes of Dryden Road approximately 33 feet north of the first sign. Both signs were found located at the south end of the Archbishop Lewis property. Two additional traffic signs indicating the same message were located on the median at or near St. Victor's Parish School.

The function of traffic control devices such as signage and traffic signals is to provide the drivers of motor vehicles with information. The traffic signs posted along Dryden Road at Archbishop Lewis High School and Saint Victor's Parish School provided information as to a reduced speed limit during Opening, Closing and Recess. What was not provided on these signs was the hours of operation the schools to drivers.

Saint Victor's Parish School would have standard and fixed times of operation, but Archbishop Lewis with a larger enrollment of students would have staggered hours operation.

Historically this area has been a high volume traffic area, with high pedestrian traffic. Area residents have complained to the City of Broad Hollow Mayors Office who in turn referred resident complaints to the city traffic department. The complaints are documented back to 1991.

The students of Saint Victor's Parish School, after their classmate Patrick Donald was severely injured, wrote to City of Broad Hollow Councilman Mr. Stephen Davies who addressed the students of Saint Victor's Parish School. Mr. Davies stated in his address to the students that it's a safety issue and not an educational issue and he felt the city should bear the lions share of the costs of the School Flashing Lights.

The City of Broad Hollow on December 4, 1996 forwarded to the Archdiocese of Broad Hollow a list of the disocesion schools that were approved for the installation of school lights. Included in this letter was an agreement for the installation of the school lights and for the diocese to obtain insurance for the school lights and maintenance costs. As of the date of this accident, no action was taken on this agreement by the Archdiocese of Broad Hollow.

The parish and disocesion high schools in the four surrounding counties have official school lights installed for the protection of their students. An area parish, Saint Johns, which is located approximately one mile from this accident site, has School-flashing lights installed. It appears that these lights were installed after a member of the clergy was struck and killed crossing the street in front of the parish facilities.

The general motoring public expects to see flashing school signals at the beginning and end of a school zone. Traffic control devices are designed to alert drivers and it is assumed that 85 per cent of drivers will comply with traffic control devices. Enforcement of school zone speed limits is an important element, but in this situation, police presence around this school zone would be enhanced due to the fact that the City of Broad Hollow Eighth Police District Head Quarters is located a half mile south of the schools. Police traffic through this area would be increased due to the location of there head quarters. However, a patrol officer traveling through this school zone would not be aware of the times that the speed limit would be reduced to 15 miles per hour due to the inadequate information provided by the signage. If flashing school lights were installed with timers, the flashing signals would provide the police and the motoring public with the information as to the hours of operation of the school zone and the proper speed limit.

Student traffic at an estimated combined enrollment of both schools of 3000, certainly would make the Archdiocese Broad Hollow and the City of Broad Hollow aware that the protection of this high number of students warrants protection by the installation of standard flashing school lights, which indicate a reduced speed of 15 miles per hour.

Driver expectancy is that when a school bus is in operation, it is yellow in color, with yellow flashing lights as it prepares to stop and red flashing lights when it is discharging passengers, thus controlling the movement of vehicles around a school bus. Driver expectancy was violated at this site, due to the lack of school flashing lights. Drivers expect to see school-flashing lights when they enter a school zone during hours of school operation. The lack of school flashing lights violates the principles of driver expectancy, as does the placement of the three school signs to the left of the northbound travel lanes on Dryden Road on the center median. Drivers expect signs to be located overhead or the right.

An article in the Institute of Traffic Engineers Journal of November 1999 indicated that "School-zone speed limit signs with flashing lights were effective in slowing vehicles." The use of flashing light signs should be considered for all schools located on roads with higher approach speeds. Dryden Road with a posted speed limit would be in my opinion has a higher approach speed to a highly populated school zone.

The Institute of Traffic Engineers Journal of June 1993 indicated that flashing beacons give the motorists positive information as to when they must slow down. This is in contrast to static signs that list several speed times and are much more difficult to view. This would also allow enforcement to be much more effective in reducing speeds even further. The people in this study from the police, parents and motorist in general all felt that the use of flashing beacons had more effect on reducing speeds in school zones.

The City of Broad Hollow and the Archdiocese of Broad Hollow were negligent in that they failed to post the school times and the beginning and end of the school zones. The Archdiocese of Broad Hollow failed to properly ensure the safety of their students by continuing in negotiations with the City of Broad Hollow to properly post Dryden Road for the safety of their students and more effective enforcement of the reduced school speed limit.

From personal experience as a policeman, people react to flashing lights on school buses and flashing lights at school zones, as the penalties for violating school bus and school zone speed limits are severe under the provisions of the Pennsylvania Motor Vehicle Code.

While Mr. Porter (driver #1) would have entered the south driveway of Archbishop Lewis High School he would have exited the north driveway turning right onto Dryden Road, this would have placed him beyond two of the three school traffic signs. Mr. Porter (driver #1) testified that he only observed one school sign located in front of Archbishop Lewis High School after the accident (page 13 line 21). Mr. Porter (driver #1) testified that there had been a blinking light where the accident happened, he would have obeyed the rules (page 31 line 23).

Even if Mr. Porter (driver #1) had not obeyed a flashing school light, it is assumed that other drivers (85th percentile) would have observed a flashing school signal at the south end of the school zone and they would have been traveling at a reduced speed through the school zone in Front of Archbishop Lewis High School and Saint Victor's Parish School, thus slowing vehicular traffic down and other drivers who may have traveling in excess of the 15 mile per hour zone.

The known facts of this accident are as follows:

(A)   Mr. Porter (driver #1) was traveling north on Dryden Road after exiting the parking area of Archbishop Lewis High School.

(B)   Mr. Porter (driver #1) while traveling at a speed, which he estimates at 40 to 45 miles per hour, he observed a school bus or SEPTA transit bus stopped in front of him and he had to brake suddenly and executed a lane change which caused him to lose control.

(C)   Mr. Porter (driver #1) upon losing control of his vehicle, mounted a curb/sidewalk and struck three pedestrians, injuring them.

(D)   The school zone located on Dryden Road in front of the Archbishop Lewis High School and Saint Victor's Parish School was poorly posted with traffic control signs, which provided insufficient information to the motoring public as they traveled through the school zone.

(E)   The location of the pedestrians on the sidewalk was proper and their location was not a factor in this accident.

9.0   OPINION

From the information available to me now at the present time, the following conclusions have been reached within a reasonable degree of professional certainty.

9.1   Mr. Porter had exceeded the posted speed limit of 35 miles per hour and the 15-mile per hour speed limit during dismissal time from Saint Victor's Parish School and Archbishop Ryahn High School

9.2   Mr. Porter failed to maintain a proper lookout for other vehicles in front of his vehicle on Dryden Road in the northbound direction. Mr. Porter upon observing vehicles stopped in front of his vehicle, braked and changed lanes abruptly losing control of his vehicle and striking three pedestrians.

9.3   The City of Broad Hollow and the Archdiocese of Broad Hollow had been aware of complaints regarding this school zone since 1991 and only in December 1996, did the City of Broad Hollow passed an ordinance for the installation of school flashing lights at eight Diocesan of Broad Hollow Schools including Archbishop Lewis High School and Saint Victor's Parish School.

9.4   The Archdiocese of Broad Hollow failed to properly ensure the safety of their of approximately 3000 students attending both Saint Victor's Parish School and Archbishop Lewis High School, by not promptly responding and negotiations an agreement with the City of Broad Hollow for the installation and maintenance of school flashing lights at this school zone.

9.5   The City of Broad Hollow and the Archdiocese of Broad Hollow have failed on numerous occasions to respond to parent and area resident concerns for the safety of the students by not agreeing on the installation of standard school flashing lights.

In conclusion, the lack of standard flashing school lights at Archdiocese of Broad Hollow Schools places their students at risk and violates driver expectancy when entering a school zone. The location and information of the traffic control signs along the 11500 block of Dryden Road were found to deficient in the information they provide to drivers traveling in both the north and south bound directions on Dryden Road.

The comments of Ms. Kathy Lorenz a spokesperson for the Archdiocese of Broad Hollow in which she stated "we are not in the traffic light business" and "parochial schools can not accept what the city is asking for". The Archdiocese of Broad Hollow as part of the education process would also include the safety of their students while enroute to and from school. As of June 13, 2000, over four years after this accident, flashing school lights still have not been installed. The Archdiocese of Broad Hollow has failed to reach an agreement with the City of Broad Hollow since December 4, 1996 over two and half months before this accident.

Mr. Porter in his sworn testimony indicated that if he had observed flashing lights, he would have obeyed the rules, as most of the motoring public would have. The pupils of the Broad Hollow Schools in the Archdiocese of Broad Hollow deserve the same protection as the students in the other counties composing the Archdiocese of Broad Hollow.

The lack of standard school flashing beacons, which would indicate a reduced speed limit during programmed hours, was a substantial factor in the cause of this accident. If the standard school flashing beacons had been in operation at the time of this accident, they would have provided information to drivers to reduce their speed and even if Mr. Porter (driver #1) choose not to comply, the other motorists who would have been traveling at a reduced speed would have caused Mr. Pieck (driver #1) and other drivers who did not choose to travel at the reduced speed through the school to slow down. Any driver traveling at a reduced speed would have had a longer period of time to perceive and react to student movements in the school zone.

The actions of the pedestrians did not contribute to the cause of this accident in any way.

If any additional information has become available, please forward it to my office so that it may be reviewed and my report updated accordingly.

Report #12: Custody/Visitation Evaluation

This report is notable for:

- Details and specific list of documents reviewed.
- Meticulous documentation of dates of contact.
- Recommendations contained in beginning of report, essentially an executive summary.
- Documentation of detailed research and investigation.

Areas of possible improvement:

- Long paragraphs with single spacing are tedious and difficult to read. Break up long paragraphs and use more heads.
- Better if some of the information or opinions, such as test results, were expressed in numbered fashion.
- Citation to authority would have bolstered the opinion.

**Custody/Visitation Evaluation
The Marriage of XX**

Names: J. XX, P. XX

Children's Names: A. XX

Dates of Birth: 6-22-97

Documents Reviewed: Petition for Dissolution of Marriage, 07-21-00

Response to Petition for Dissolution of Marriage, 08-16-00

Notice of Motion for Custody Evaluation Pursuant to Section 604(b), 10-03-00

Motion for Custody Evaluation Pursuant to Section 604(b), 10-03-00

Journal maintained by J. XX, 10-10-00 to 10-29-00

Letter to Evaluator from Mr. Steven Solano, Esq., 10-18-00, enclosing copy of order of appointment as 604(b) evaluator

Authorization for Release of Confidential Information regarding A. XX from Elletsville Healthcare, 10-22-00

Emergency Department Report for A. XX, 10-22-00

Emergency Room Report, 10-22-00

Consultation Report of possible child abuse, 10-22-00

Letter to Evaluator from Ms. F, 10-25-00

Facsimile to Evaluator from Ms. F enclosing copy of correspondence to Ms. S, 11-07-00

Facsimile to Evaluator from Ms. S enclosing copies of correspondence sent to Counsel, 11-07-00

Facsimile to Evaluator of correspondence sent by Ms. F to Counsel, 11-07-00

Collateral Contacts:

Facsimile to Evaluator of correspondence sent by Ms. F to Counsel, 11-14-00 Dr. B., Psychiatric Intern, Ellettsville Hospital, 10-??-00

Dr. L., Ellettsville Hospital Pediatrician, 11-7-00

K. XX, paternal grandmother, 1-26-01

Mr. & Mrs. S., maternal grandparents, 1-27-01

Dr. P., Mrs. XX's therapist, 1-30-01

Dr. M.F., XX's marriage counselor, 1-30-01

Dr. T. F., A.'s pediatrician, 1-31-01

C.C., teacher at parent-tot program, 2-5-01

Dates of Contact:

A. XX	Office interview-mother	10-30-00
	Office interview-mother	11-1-00
	Home visit-mother	01-25-01
	Home visit-father	01-26-01
	Office visit-father	01-30-01
J. XX	Office interview with A.	10-30-00
	Office interview with A.	11-1-00
	Interview & Testing	11-21-01
	Interview	12-9-00
	Interview & testing	1-6-01
	Home visit	01-24-01
	Testing	02-01-01
P. XX	Interview	10-30-00
	Interview	11-2-00
	Interview & testing	11-6-00
	Testing	11-13-00
	Home visit	01-26-01
	Office visit-A.	01-30-01

Reason for Referral: On October 13, 2000 the Honorable L.R.M. appointed this evaluator to conduct a 604(b) examination for the above named parties.

Recommendations: Both parents love A. and provide a proper home environment, appropriate toys, books, games and activities, and attempt to give him a structured routine so that he can feel safe, comfortable and happy. The parents' customs and ways of life differ radically from one another with considerable distress resulting in this clash of values. However, A. does not seem to suffer from the difference, and may benefit from being the recipient of both points of view. Mr. XX seems amenable to adhering to his wife's dietary restrictions for the child, and A. appears to be a healthy and happy youngster. By design, necessity or choice, Mrs. XX has been his primary care provider since his birth.

While Mr. XX told this examiner that he wanted to be considered for sole custody, to this examiner's knowledge, he has not filed a Petition in that regard.

What this examiner has on hand from him is a Petition for Dissolution of Marriage wherein Mr. XX requests joint custody. This examiner does not view this couple as good candidates for joint custody because they are unable to work with one another in a civil, businesslike manner. At least once, and probably twice during transitions, the police were summoned to mediate disputes between the parties.

Both parents view one another as in some ways dangerous or peculiar to the detriment of the child.

These feelings probably stem from as yet unresolved issues from their marriage; nevertheless, their attitudes regarding one another, and their resulting behaviors do not allow them to co-parent in any reasonable manner. Therefore, this examiner respectfully recommends to the Court that Mrs. XX be considered as the sole custodian and primary residential parent of the minor child, A.

With respect to visitation, A. is at an age where regular visitation with his father could occur. As a result, this examiner respectfully recommends that the Court award Mr. XX overnight, unsupervised visitation with A. every other weekend and one weekday visit each week from after work until 6:30 PM. In the summer, Mr. XX should enjoy two non-consecutive weeks of vacation with A. Mr. XX should have visitation with A. on Father's Day, his birthday and A.'s birthday from 10:00 AM on a weekend or from after work on a workday until 6:30 PM, unless these days fall on his regularly scheduled weekend. Mrs. XX should have visitation with A on Mother's Day, her birthday and A.'s birthday for a four to six hour period when these dates occur during Mr. XX's scheduled visitation. Other holidays should be equally divided between the parents on a yearly rotating schedule. Mr. XX should enjoy Christmas eve, Christmas day and Easter Sunday with A., and Mrs. XX should enjoy Rosh Hashana and Yom Kippur with A., regardless of other visitation schedules. When A. reaches school age, longer vacation periods in winter and spring should be divided equally between the parents.

Despite awarding of sold custody to Mrs. XX, the parents should consult with one another regarding medical and educational decisions for the child, and they should work with their chosen pediatrician to insure that they make appropriate health care decisions for him.

Both parents should inform the other if they intend to take A. away from their home for any overnight period during their times with him, giving an itinerary and telephone numbers so that daily telephone contact can occur. Summer visitation should be negotiated each year prior to June 1st.

The parents should each respect one another's lifestyle and values, allowing A. to learn what is necessary from the viewpoint each parent has to offer. Irrespective of their own feelings, they will need to work together to make transitions comfortable and stress-free for the child.

A. XX

Observations

A. is a well-developed, Caucasian three year old child with brown, wavy hair and blue eyes. On each occasion the examiner met with him he was relatively engaging. He appeared to be developing appropriately as observations of his gross and fine motor skills and language and social skills development were all within reasonable expectations. This examiner saw A. twice in the office at the initiation of the evaluation as the result of claims of sexual abuse of A. by his father. A. was first seen in a play session with his mother. They interacted well with one another. Mrs. XX sat on the floor to play with A. and engaged in appropriate conversations and play with him. He responded well to her. At one point while playing with a doll house, A. intentionally broke one of the plastic pieces. Mrs. XX intervened in a reasonable manner and then diverted his attention to less aggressive behavior. When left alone with the examiner, A. was able to separate from his mother without undo, negative reaction and he sustained play with the examiner for some time. The destructive behavior toward objects was again noted, appearing as A.'s testing the limits with the examiner. He was easily distracted from this behavior.

During the interview, A. had difficulty sustaining attention, being distracted by toys and other objects in the room. The examiner was able to give A. instructions as to telling the truth, saying, "I don't know" when he did not know and other preliminary instructions. He demonstrated his understanding of these instructions, but then responded, "I don't know" to the questions of substance the examiner asked him.

He was able to engage in extended play with the examiner, but resisted other discussion, preferring instead to play with the examiner. Appropriate to his age, he did not discuss abuse when asked open ended questions. When the examiner asked more directive questions, A. ignored the examiner and then asked about his mother instead. He was not able or willing to discuss any events relative to the allegations of abuse.

This examiner saw A. at the home of his mother on 01-24-01. Mrs. XX lives in a three-story, single-family home in a residential area of Ellettsville, Illinois. Mrs. XX answered the door, mentioning that A. always went away from the door when it was opened. He was seated in a chair in the living room. The home is tastefully furnished. The first floor has a foyer, living and dining room, bathroom and kitchen. On the second floor are the bedrooms. Mrs. XX showed the examiner A.'s room which has a double bed, dresser and other children's toys. There was a humidifier in the room as well. Mrs. XX's room is across the hall. A. was eager to show the examiner the third floor which contained a computer work station and table with a wooden train set. Throughout the home were children's toys and books appropriate for A.'s age.

The visit began in the kitchen. A. applied stickers to a piece of paper and demonstrated a very good knowledge of the names of animals and colors. He then asked his mother for cereal which she gave to him, but he did not eat. He pasted various stamps of dinosaurs onto his mother's finger, and she took time to look at each of the stickers with him, commenting upon the characteristics of the animals. This seems to be a very child-centered environment, and Mrs. XX was very skilled at supplementing topics A. brought up for discussion with other information. She spoke to A. in a conversational way, using words he could understand, but also saying things in a manner that would promote language development.

Mrs. XX suggested a tour of the house which A. agreed would be a good idea. He rushed the party through the tour of the second floor bedrooms, eager to take the examiner to the third floor. There he asked his mother to help him work on the computer. A. was patient as his mother set up the program, giving her instructions to make the print on the screen very large. He then typed in various letters and punctuation marks, asking his mother to print out his work when finished. He next turned his attention to his train set. He and his mother played with the set. Some of the tracks were not attached together, and she asked him to suggest ways they could accomplish this. When the examiner had to leave, A. had some difficulty disengaging from his train set, but did eventually agree to walk the examiner to the door.

The examiner also visited Mr. XX's home when A. was there. Mr. XX resides in his studio apartment in the VVV area of YYY. His home is tastefully, though somewhat sparsely furnished with a double bed, a chair, television and several of A.'s larger toys. There is a small, galley kitchen and bathroom. At this visit, A. was quite excited and running around the apartment. He told his father he wanted to kick the ball, and began kicking various balls that were in the living room. At times he kicked the balls into the blinds covering the window which seemed to amuse his father. Mr. XX encouraged A. to play in this manner, and then helped him to accomplish bounding the ball off of his head in a soccer-like fashion, instructing him to "butt" the ball with his forehead. He praised A. when he did this correctly.

On the side of the bed A. had lined up several plastic toys in the Power Ranger mode. He said he wanted to play with these, and he took one of them with a pincher-like appendage over to a wooden train set that was assembled on the floor in front of the window. Mr. XX said he wanted to repair a part of the train set that had come apart, but instead, A. began disassembling the train set using the pincher-like appendage. A. was intent on demolishing the train set.

Then A. said he wanted to bat the ball. He took the bat and told the examiner that he might hit her when he was batting. The examiner elected to be the catcher and stood behind A. and in front of the television screen. Mr. XX pitched a small, hollow rubber ball to A., telling him to keep his eye on the ball, praising him when he made a "hit." Then he told the examiner that she should sit in the chair while he batted the ball. He took the cushion off of the footrest, telling the examiner to hold it in front of her so that she would not be hit. He also brought over his sleeping bag and piled it on top of the cushion for extra protection. A. and his father explained that at times they play in this manner with his grandfather. A. then batted the ball, squealing in delight when it hit the cushion.

Next he told his father he wanted to play with a large plastic tower which was for the plastic figures previously described. He gave each person one figure, and he again chose the figure with the pincher-like appendage. Mr. XX found some batteries for the contraption which allowed the control panel to work, turning on and off lights and emitting buzzing and beeping sounds. A. enjoyed pushing the control buttons for various sounds and lights. After some play in this area, the examiner said her goodbyes.

On 1-30-01, Mr. XX brought A. to the office, bringing his plastic action figures and *Candyland*. Mr. XX offered A. some soy milk and cookies. A. went into another room of the office and took a stuffed alligator, placing it near him. They then set up the *Candyland* game and began the play. In the beginning of the play, when A. moved his piece, he knocked his father's piece off of the board, remarking that it was just an accident. This delighted A., and his father teased him about it in a good-natured manner. A. asked, "Why" to most things his father said, and Mr. XX patiently explained reasons for his statements. Throughout the game, Mr. XX kept up a running commentary about the colors chosen, the fact that A. always won the game, and that this time he was going to try to win himself. A. chose cards for himself and his father, and both moved their pieces around the board. Although A. was squeezing his genitals, he denied having to go to the bathroom. Mr. XX asked him several times, but A. refused. A. asked to sit in his father's lap where the view was better. A. seemed to recognize colors very well. A. won the first game, then said, "Dad, how about if you go fast and you be in the front this time?" They played another game, seeming to thoroughly enjoy the interaction together. Both father and son frequently laughed and smiled at one another.

The examiner suggested this would be a good time for all to have a bathroom break. Although A. did not want to leave, he agreed when both adults said they were going to. He wanted to know why the examiner went into a different bathroom than he and his father. When everyone returned, A. invited the examiner to play with him and his father. She suggested they go into another room with there was more floor space. A. watched as the examiner moved a small toy trunk, inquiring what was in it. The examiner opened it, and A. asked to play with the toys in the trunk. First he chose *Let's Go Fishing*, but this game was too difficult. He then said he wanted to play *Hungry, Hungry Hippo* which he and his father played while the examiner looked on. A. has a larger version of this game at his father's house, and he soon tired of it. *Chinese Checkers*, telling the examiner again that she had to play. Everyone set up the game, and Mr. XX told A. how to make basic moves. Once the game began and A. understood the object of the game was to get your pieces to the opposite side, he would often "jump" his opponents, with one large jump from his side of the board to the other. Not surprisingly, A. won this game.

Next he pulled out a *Magic Sketch* board, drew on it and erased his drawings. The examiner told A. that it would be time to go very soon. He then left the board and looked into the trunk again, selecting some crayons. Mr. XX told him he had crayons at home, but he said he wanted to color. The examiner told him there were coloring books in the trunk. A. chose a Lion King coloring book, but then asked the examiner to tell him the story. The examiner read the captions under the pictures as A. turned the pages. He looked intently at each picture and questioned the examiner about what was happening in the story as she read. A. sustained his attention to this story surprisingly well, leading the examiner to believe that he has been read to often. Although A. wanted to stay longer and exhaust the toy trunk, he was persuaded to leave after the story.

J. XX

Observations

Mrs. XX is an attractive, Caucasian woman with long dark hair and dark eyes. She dressed in casual clothing that was appropriate to the varying weather conditions and her hygiene and grooming were good. This examiner discussed the nature and purposes of the evaluation, including possible negative outcomes, the on–therapeutic and non–confidential nature of the process. Mrs. XX read, said she understood and signed an agreement to participate in the process. She was well-oriented to time, person and place, and gave no indications of bizarre thinking or behavior. After each of the first two office visits with A., Mrs. XX told the examiner that she and A. would take a while to collect themselves before leaving. On 11-1-00, the examiner walked into the waiting room to find Mrs. XX nursing A.

When A. saw the examiner coming, he pulled his mother's shirt down over his face. It was at times difficult making timely appointments with Mrs. XX to finish necessary tasks in the office, but she was otherwise cooperative during the evaluation.

Synopsis of Mrs. XX's Statements

Mrs. XX is the oldest of two children born to Mr. and Mrs. S. in Ellettsville, Illinois. Mrs. XX reported that in her family, rules and structure were quite lax. She recalled going to Michigan with the family every summer, as her family has done for generations. There was laughing around the dining room table, folk music, beer and marijuana which she shared in with her parents. Few if any restrictions were placed on Mrs. XX as a child, and neither parent took the role of disciplinarian in the family. She said her father was probably depressed, and her mother experienced severe clinical depression for three months a few years ago. Mrs. XX was diagnosed with Tourette Syndrome in the 5th grade and offered medication because of physical tics, constriction of her throat and difficulty breathing. She did not exhibit the vocalizations which often accompany this disorder. Mr. S. insisted that she'd take antipsychotic drugs beginning in her adolescence to combat the symptoms of this disease. Mrs. XX said these drugs froze part of her brain and she could not function well. She became progressively worse and could barely keep her eyes open. She was then diagnosed with narcolepsy and given Ritalin in addition to her other medications.

Mrs. XX was an outgoing tomboy, playful and fresh. She did well in school and enjoyed the company of many friends. While not wishing to go into great detail, Mrs. XX said she knows she is the survivor of varying degrees of emotional and verbal abuse from her father. In her sophomore year of high school, she began drinking and smoking marijuana and doing poorly in school. She did graduate and attend Washington University in St. Louis, majoring in drama. Later she ran a not-for-profit children's theater company which was beginning to receive positive attention from granting agencies after three years. However, she closed the company at her husband's insistence after three years. She then worked retail and worked as a nanny. At this point she decided to wean herself off of medication. She had gone off medications once before. At that time she experienced continuous seizures of neurological activity which made her decide to resume her medication regimen. This time she reduced the medications gradually, over a period of many months. This worked well until there was a period of "huge release where whatever the medications suppressed came out for a month or couple of months." She was seizuring, expending incredible energy. She stopped working full time in order to detox and get healthy. She found an 82 year old holistic naprapath who treated her for one year and helped her clean her body and heal herself with herbal medicines. Mrs. XX became a vegan.

Dating for Mrs. XX began in grade school. She said she could recall few periods in her life when she did not have a boyfriend. While she was in college, she was thrown out of her sorority because they could not "get her to think like the other girls." At the time she smoked and drank a lot and experienced hallucinations which her father said was a drug-induced psychosis. She met P., who on one occasion, sat by her bed all night to help her. She was floored by his attentiveness, and they became inseparable. This was in 1988. She needed him, and he needed to own her, take care of her and make her dependent upon him. He reinforced the idea that it was them against the world. He even convinced her that she could not write and he began doing her school work for her. As their relationship progressed, she had few other friends. She only wanted and needed to be with P. When he was not there, she waited for him. She did not even shower without him.

On his part, Mr. XX continued in both subtle and overt subjugation of her through cutting remarks, tantrums, withholding, berating and belittling. These abusive behaviors continued until A. was born in 1997. Then he began to withhold himself to the point that she begged him on her knees to talk to her, that she could see he was unhappy. He would experience huge mood swings. Occasionally Mr. XX would hold A., but when he would cry, Mr. XX would scream at her that the baby needed to nurse. She never did the dishes or laundry because Mr. XX would not care for the child, and would stand near her so she could take over if the boy cried. They began seeing a counselor after Mrs. XX found out there had been sexual acts performed by women at a bachelor's party. The relationship continued to deteriorate, and the couple separated in the fall of 1999.

Initially she had difficulty getting him to visit A. He would babysit occasionally. They went to treatment a few times. Mrs. XX still sees Dr. P. Dr. F saw her a few times. Mrs. XX discontinued reaching for her parents because it was unhealthy for her. They continued a relationship with Mr. XX because they borrowed money from him for some land. Through mediation she and her husband arranged a visitation agreement where she could go to Karate and Mr. XX could visit A.. But he complained that A. would only go to sleep if he was nursing. Then Mr. XX wanted to visit at his house, but the visiting times were right in the middle of A.'s nap time and she could not get him to sleep earlier.

A. slept over at his father's home on 10-20-00. When Mr. XX returned A. on 10-21-00, Mrs. XX noted that at the first touch of toilet paper to his bottom, A. said, "Ow," and moved away. Mrs. XX asked him if his butt got hurt at his father's house, and A. said it did. When she asked how, he said with the part of a candle where the fire was. He told her his father was holding the candle to his butt, but he wiggled, rolled and got away. This, A. said, occurred during a game where A. runs and his father chases him with a candle. He told his mother this story was real and not pretend. When his mother questioned him further, A. said it was just an accident.

Later Mrs. XX again questioned A., telling him it was not OK for anyone to hurt him. A. again told her it was an accident. Mrs. XX questioned him a third time, and A. told her this occurred just before the Halloween walk at the Ellettsville Art Center. The next morning she got someone else's opinion who told her that A. was in pain, and she needed to be "freaking out." This friend had seen Mr. XX meet her with a baseball bat. Then during a play date with this friend, A. was clinging to her, saying, "Help me, help me, " seemingly terrified. This friend had previously advised her to call DCFS based on what Mrs. XX told her about things A. did or said. When the candle incident came up, Mrs. XX felt she had to make a report and called the DCFS hotline. They suggested she take A. to the emergency room immediately because any tears in his anus would immediately heal up, and she needed to go immediately. So she did.

A. told the triage nurse, the doctor and the psych intern the same story consistently. The doctor told her there was no physical evidence of abuse and found the story strange. The psych intern asked her if she thought the father would do this to A., and she said she did not know. Mrs. XX took A.'s story seriously. She felt that he was in trouble and she had to help and protect him. She felt A. was being hurt, but she did not know how to protect him. The hospital did not call DCFS. They gave her a number to call to get information about her rights. She called DCFS because she felt she would be failing to protect A. if she did not, and she worried that Mr. XX might be trying to set her up in some way.

Mr. XX's visits were curtailed and then supervised by the maternal grandmother for a time, but then were reinstated. On 11-21-00, Mrs. XX told this examiner that A. has been waking up in the middle of the night since just before the first unsupervised visit with his father. He has had several nightmares about insects. He told his mother they had to go and hide. She tried to comfort him, but he insisted that they sleep under the dining room table. They did go there, but then returned to bed. He awakened several times after that, insisting they go under the table, and when she would not go, all he wanted to do was nurse. Several nights later he again awakened, telling her his feet were bad on the inside. Mrs. XX reassured him and he fell back to sleep.

Mrs. XX said she is a survivor of abuse and is extremely sensitive to A. and what he expresses and the way he expresses himself. She is positive something is going on with his father. A. is feeling alone and neglected. On 11-14-00, A. was extremely sorrowful when returning from a visit with his father, reaching for her immediately. She asked him how his night was, and he said he had eaten seasoned chips that hurt his lips. Then he put his head back and began wailing. At the next visit, A. had a good time. Since then A. has made a complete turn around, calling his father and requesting to see him.

Mrs. XX continues to expand her support group, going to Karate and other women's groups where she meets other mothers and sets up play dates. She has reached out to her Karate teachers and peers. At present the attorneys are waiting her financial disclosure. She has only had her own credit card a few months and she wants to see what she spends on things. This is a big job to figure out and she is working on her budget.

A. is a bright, interested, funny, smart, good caring boy. He loves to eat, play with other children and read stories. He helps around the house and can now dress himself and cut with a butter knife. He enjoys listening to music, singing, and building things. Mr. XX has an ability to see what might be good for A. in the long run. When A. is doing everything right, his father is fun and likes to play with the child. The father does disrespect her in A.'s present, calling her names and engaging in belittling, disgusting and disdainful looks. In situations where A. may misbehave, he tends to agitate the child, and he seems unable to control his anger. She on the other hand, is empathic, respectful, considerate and a good communicator. She has the ability to do an incredible job of single parenting. Her support system may be weak. Her greatest fear is that A. is not OK at his father's house.

Mrs. XX takes A. to a parent-tot program at WWW School. This is the only program where they could be together since neither is ready to be apart. It took A. 3 to 4 months to be in a room apart from his mother, but now he loves his school. She believes A. needs to be with other children. WWW school is a small school with a holistic mind-set. They offer a K-12 program, with a early childhood program of mixed ages. They encourage less television and more imaginative play, stressing self-development.

At present, she is able to manage civil communication with the father, but this takes great strength on her part because he is no less disgusting. A. sees only business-like communication. Mr. XX will say she is psychotic, that she abandoned him and she is not a good mother. She believes she should be the sole custodian because she is the better parent and joint custody is not an option because they cannot agree on anything. There should be plenty of visitation as long as A. is safe. Two or three evenings a week would be alright with split holidays. In the summer, she should have 2 weeks of vacation and the father could have three or four days. The older A. is, the longer he can be away from her.

Right now she is weaning A.. The LaLeche League says the average age for weaning is 4. She talked to A. recently, telling him he could put himself to sleep without nursing. The first night it was difficult for him. They have slept in the same bed for 3½ years, but recently she feels she needs some space. She lies down with him at night, and he usually wants to nurse. She now only allows 10 seconds of nursing.

If she were named as the custodial parent, Mrs. XX would continue doing what she is now doing-that is to talk with her husband about the paternal extended family and also talk with A.. When A. hits or does hostile things because he watches cartoons with his father where this behavior is depicted, she will say, "Your Daddy thinks it is OK to watch cartoons, but it is not OK to hit." She almost never brings up his father with him except to put up a calendar so A. can see when he will visit. She encourages him to call his father and see what his plans for the day are. When A. discusses activities with his father, she responds in an excited way so that he is supported.

Test Results

The results of the MMPI-2 revealed a statistically significant elevation on the L, Lie, Scale (T=66), suggesting that she attempted to present herself in an overly favorable light. This "impression management" stance, which seemed to be the result of a naive attempt to deny human frailties or failures and present a picture of high moral value and virtue. Consequently, the results of the MMPI-2 may not fully reveal current problems. None of the Clinical Scales were elevated to a point of significance, but one Supplementary Scale, O-H, Overcontrolled Hostility, was elevated at T=66. Such a scale elevation suggests that the individual does not have the skills to express strong feelings, particularly anger, at the time of the irritating event; however, often angry feelings are later displayed impulsively, in response to some minor irritation. The MCMI-III revealed a "low" score on the Disclosure Scale (BR=12), suggesting a disinclination to disclose problematic behavior. As a result, test results may under-represent current problems to some extent. Three Personality Scales were elevated to significant anchor points. The Compulsive Scale was elevated to a point suggesting a possible disorder in this area (BR=91), two Scales were elevated past the anchor point suggesting personality traits, namely, Histrionic (BR=81) and Narcissistic (BR=77).

The reader should be aware that under non-disclosure situations where the person attempts to present him or herself as conscientious or self-reliant, the Compulsive and Narcissistic Scales may be elevated. The CAP was within normal limits, suggesting that A. would not be at risk for physical abuse at the hands of his mother. The PSI results did reveal defensive responding, suggesting these test results should be considered to represent an "impression management" stance. As such, none of the Child Domain scores were significantly elevated. Only one of the Parent Domain scores was significantly elevated (i.e. Spouse at the 85th percentile), suggesting that Mrs. XX does not view Mr. XX as providing her with sufficient support and assistance in the parenting role.

Rorschach results suggest that Mrs. XX is vulnerable to experiences of depression or other affective disturbance. She seems to be an emotionally immature individual who allows dramatic and intense expression of transient feelings, resulting in mood swings. She is the type of individual who avoids processing strong emotions, using intellectualization to keep emotions at a distance and minimize their impact. This results in a limited ability to deal with feelings in a genuine and forthright fashion. Such aversion to emotionally-charged situations also leads to isolation and social withdrawal. She is ordinarily a complex individual so that the type of person she is will be difficult to determine. Current stressors impact upon her to a great degree, affecting self-control, clear thinking and realistic perceptions. However, imbuing otherwise pleasurable experiences with unpleasant affect and viewing others in at once positive and negative ways seems to be a more pervasive, chronic difficulty she exhibits.

As mentioned, she is a complex individual and one who becomes over involved in contemplating the underlying significance of events, sometimes making big productions or small matters. While in the main she shows good intellectual abilities and sophisticated processing, she is quite individualistic in her view of the world, resulting in a non-conformist presentation, even when social conventions are well-defined. Others may view her as odd or eccentric. Once she has made up her mind about a matter, she is unable to look at new information and change her opinion.

While she is quite self-focused, this self-absorption is not the source of satisfaction for her, but rather contributes to emotional pain and depression. Her focus is not the introspective kind in that she does not give the impression of being able to examine herself critically and subsequently modify her behavior. Her identity, although it may not be satisfying one, is nevertheless stable. While she has the capacity to form relations and is interested in others, she nevertheless avoids interpersonal relationships. Thus there are few who play an important role in her life at present.

P. XX

Observations

Mr. XX is a medium and athletically built, Caucasian man with brown eyes, red hair and a Van Dyke beard. He dressed in weather-appropriate clothing on each occasion the examiner met with him, and his hygiene and grooming were good. This examiner explained the nature and purposes of testing, including possible negative outcomes and the non-therapeutic, non-confidential nature of the evaluation. Mr. XX read, said he understood and signed an agreement to participate in the process. Mr. XX was well-oriented to time, person and place. He gave no indications of bizarre thinking or behavior.

Synopsis of Mr. XX's Statements

Mr. XX is the oldest of two children born to C and K XX. The XXs lived in six different locations during Mr. XX's childhood through early adulthood owing to C XX's employment at J. C. Penny Company. Mr. XX recalled a close, extended family and many friends despite the frequent moves. His family history was otherwise unremarkable. Mr. XX did well in school and enjoyed athletics. After high school he attended Washington University in St. Louis, Missouri, majoring first in business and later in English. He held various jobs until January 1992 when he became employed as a runner on the floor of the CBE. In May 1992 he became employed as a stock options trader with S Investment Group where he has been employed since.

Mr. XX dated occasionally in high school. During his first semester of college he met J. S. who he considered beautiful, a lot of fun and having a great personality. She was always a bit eccentric, but also always acceptable. They dated throughout college and had a good courtship. They were married on August 6, 1994, and, at least initially, married life was wonderful. His wife worked various jobs and then started a not for profit theater company, performing children's theater for hospitals. While all of the hospitals loved the productions, they would not contribute any money, and Mr. XX did not make enough at the time to support her theater group. Although they agreed to shut down the company, later, she would accuse him of insisting on this even though their finances were fine.

Mrs. XX had been diagnosed with Tourette's Syndrome as an adolescent. To combat the effects of this disorder, she took Ritalin in the morning and sleeping pills at night in addition to Orap. Sometime in 1996 she wanted to get off these medications. Her withdrawal was brutal, and the outcome was that his wife became vegan and went on a "crazed health kick." One day he came home and all scented things from their home were removed. Another day she packed up all the family pictures and took them to her mother's home based on her premonition there would be a fire. She changed her diet radically to fit the vegan lifestyle. This occurred about the time their son, A., was born (x-xx-97), and he felt that her behavior might be due to having a first child. They had a home birth, and Mr. XX felt at the time that his wife was taking positive steps. Now he does not understand why cotton cushions can protect one from "off gases" emitted from other kinds of cushions.

After A. was born, Mrs. XX took to the bed with A. She had him on no schedule, nursing on demand. She spent her day nursing or sleeping with the child. Mr. XX rarely saw or interacted with either of him. Instead, he took over the household functions in toto. On some days he might request that his wife do a load of laundry; however, when he arrived home from work she would tell him it was "too hectic," and could not complete the task. She would not allow anyone to touch the child, even the grandparents, saying she wanted no bad germs coming close to him. He became very depressed about the situation. His wife told him he had problems and should see a counselor. The counselor wanted to know what Mrs. XX did all day. Mr. XX attempted to reason with her, and she agreed to take on the laundry as a chore; however, the laundry was never done. Instead she told him, "I have to do this on my terms." The couple had no intimate life together.

She wanted a big birthday party for A.'s first birthday and invited more than 70 people. However, she did not lift a finger to help with preparations or cleanup. When A.'s second birthday came around, Mr. XX begged her to have people over for cake and coffee only, but she again insisted on inviting 50 or more people. Again, Mr. XX and his family did all of the work for the party. In the summer of 1999, Mrs. XX took A. to Michigan to spend the summer at her parent's summer home. This turned out to be a tremendous break for Mr. XX He visited on weekends and loved seeing A.. At home during the week, he did not have to clean and cook for or wait on his wife. During this time he realized they did not have much of a marriage, and he offered to move out before they came home. His wife became angry and told him to move out immediately which he did; however, 90% of his belongings are still in the marital home. They saw a therapist, Dr. P., in late fall of 1999, but this did not lead to reconciliation. They attended mediation in early March of 2000, but nothing was resolved in these sessions.

Initially, he saw A. twice each week at the marital home, on Wednesdays and Fridays. There were no overnights, because Mrs. XX sleeps with A. and nurses him to sleep. The pediatrician told Mr. XX that A. gets no heath benefits any longer from nursing, so this must be a comfort issue. Mrs. XX said she wanted a natural weaning process to occur. Now visitation is set up for Tuesdays and Fridays and alternating Fridays overnight. Since he has been having visitation with A. at his home, often Mrs. XX will nurse A. in the car in front of his home for an hour or more when she picks the child up from his house. Sometime when Mr. XX drops off A. after a visit, he will come in the house and say, "Let's nurse," and she will sit on the stairs and nurse him on the spot.

A. is a wonderful child with great understanding and memory. He loves to play and laugh. Many times Mr. XX must stop himself from laughing when A. misbehaves, but instead he talks to the child. At his age, A. only remains interested in things for a short time, but everything interests him. A. is very bright, loves books, animals, going to the zoo and kicking a ball. He has always believed Mrs. XX to be a good mother who would never hurt A.; however, she appears to be isolating him from the world. He is not allowed to explore his own independence without her being around. He worries about what she might be saying to him. In the past, Mr. XX used to become angry and yell, but now that he is separated, these behaviors no longer occur. He loves his son above all else and is completely responsible as a parent. He listens to A. and gives him credit as a person. He is patient; he listens and he loves to play with him.

He believes his wife views the divorce as being his fault. He has seen her turn the responsibility to others when they do not agree with her decisions and ideas. The world must move around her at her pace or she has problems. She is quite absent minded and does not pay bills. Since the separation, Mrs. XX has called him at night, saying that she did not trust him. In the past she told him she felt unsafe and threatened, feeling his visits with A. needed to be supervised. The first incident when she called the police involved them arguing during a transition. She told him to leave, and he said he wanted to get A. first. Mrs. XX then called the police, claiming he threatened her. This allegation was patently untrue, but the police made him leave her home anyway.

His visits begin at her whim, and she is often not on time. Often when Mr. XX goes to pick up A., he is not ready, but rather is asleep. During Mr. XX's overnight visit on the October 20-21, 2000 weekend, he and A. went to the zoo at Lincoln Park. They then had dinner with a friend, returning alone to Mr. XX's apartment where they played games. A. slept peacefully all night. In the morning they had breakfast and played at home before trying to find A. a Halloween costume. Later they went to Ellettsville Art Center for a Halloween walk. He dropped A. off at his mother's home at about 6:30 PM. For the next several days, Mr. XX called to speak to A. but got no response. As this is a common occurrence, he did not think much about it until his attorney's office called him to come in so they could tell him there had been an allegation of sexual abuse of A. by Mr. XX made to DCFS. Mr. XX was shocked. He talked to his wife's parents, who told him that Mrs. XX will not allow the maternal grandfather to be around A. either. As a result of these allegations, Mr. XX did not see A. for over one week. For a time his visits were supervised by the maternal grandmother until the Child's Representative could determine A. was not in danger in his father's care.

Since the abuse allegations were made, Mr. XX has rethought his original position of joint custody. He wants to be considered for sole custody. He believes a good visitation schedule would be for A. to see his mother two days each week and every other weekend Saturday to Sunday. If the court awarded him sole custody, he would take a three to six month leave of absence and buy a home so they could each have their own rooms. In the fall, A. could go to preschool. At present Mr. XX finishes work at 3:00 PM and has a flexible schedule.

Test Results

Mr. XX's responses on self-report instruments do reveal some avoidance of self-disclosure on the MCMI-III (Disclosure Scale low at BR=14) and testing defensiveness on the MMPI-2, K, Defensiveness Scale at T=68. The reader should be aware that individuals undergoing litigation are likely to produce such results. Only one Clinical Scale of the MMPI-2, Scale 6, Paranoia was elevated to a point of statistical significance (T=68). Individuals with this scale elevation are often described as overly sensitive and easily hurt, remaining aloof from others for fear of being taken advantage of. He may be moralistic or touchy and rigid in his approach to life. The subscales underling Scale 6 reveal one elevation on Pa3, Naivete, suggesting that he presents himself as extremely naive and trusting, denying hostility. The MCMI-III revealed one scale elevation past the anchor point suggestive of a personality trait on the Narcissism Scale (BR=77). The CAP was within normal limits suggesting that A. would not be at risk for physical abuse while in his father's care. Only one Parent Scale of the PSI was significantly elevated, Spouse, at the 92nd percentile. This elevation suggests he views his spouse as lacking in emotional or actual support of his parenting role. His Life Stress Scale indicated a high degree of current life stress (85th percentile).

Rorschach results also point toward a very high level of stress, probably related to a recent loss which exacerbates his need for closeness and contributes to a distressing state of emotional deprivation. In order to abate this discomforting stress level, he seems to have restricted his involvement to familiar actions undertaken in the presence of individuals who know and will not challenge him. Resolution of these stressors should result in better functioning.

Mr. XX seems more a thinker than a doer. He is able to grasp complex concepts, and his processing of ideas is sophisticated and well developed, usually indicative of a good intellect and educational accomplishment. He views things in a logical, coherent manner and his reality testing is good. He is able to recognize conventional modes of response, and he neither oversimplifies nor over complicates his experiences. However, his thinking seems somewhat rigid and inflexible. Once he has determined a course of action, he is highly resistant to any reconsideration of his beliefs.

He tends to over-value his own worth, and shows a narcissistic bent which may lead him to shift blame to others or harbor feelings of entitlement. Not all of this self-focus is positive. It appears that current circumstances have led him to a self-critical view which generates emotional pain and possible depression. These contradictory findings also suggest some identity diffusion or instability of self-image.

He seems averse to processing feelings. Therefore, while he has the capacity to form close relationships and is interested in others, he feels uneasy dealing with people on an intimate basis and lacks confidence in the social arena. As a result he may become defensive or show aversion when interactions with others are close and personal, leading to social isolation and withdrawal.

Discussion

Wishes of the Parents

Mrs. XX would like to be the sole custodian of A. because she is a better parent, and because she has been the primary parent since A.'s birth. Under these conditions, there should be plenty of visitation as long as A. is safe. Two or three evenings a week would be alright with split holidays. In the summer, she should have two weeks of vacation and the father could have three or four days. The older A. is, the longer he can be away from her. She almost never brings up his father with him except to put up a calendar so A. can see when he will visit. She encourages him to call his father and see what his plans for the day are. When A. discusses activities with his father, she responds in an excited way so that he is supported.

Since the abuse allegations were made, Mr. XX has rethought his original position of joint custody. He wants to be considered for sole custody because his wife appears to be on a path to eliminate him from his son's life. He believes a good visitation schedule would be for A. to see his mother two days each week and every other weekend Saturday to Sunday. If the court awarded him sole custody, he would take a three to six month leave of absence and buy a home so they could each have their own rooms. In the fall, A. could go to preschool. At present Mr. XX finishes work at 3:00 PM and has a flexible schedule.

Wishes of the Child

A. is too young to express a reasoned preference for one parent or another. A. seemed comfortable and secure in either parent's care.

Interactions and Interrelationships of All Parties

A.'s relationship with his mother is a close one. As the result of her decision to nurse him for an extended time, he seeks her out for this comfort apparently whenever they have been separated from one another. This examiner observed A. nursing in the waiting room after having been in session on 11-1-00 with the examiner for about 45 minutes. While the examiner did not observe the behavior directly on 10-30-00 when they were in the office, Mrs. XX and A. were in the waiting room for about 30 minutes after their appointment was over. Ostensibly Mrs. XX nursed A. at that time as well. Mr. XX reports that A. will nurse immediately after visits with him, at times Mrs. XX will remain in the car in front of his home nursing for as long as one hour. During the course of this evaluation, Mrs. XX told this examiner that she has begun weaning A. and the most he will nurse at present is for ten seconds just before bed.

While her behavior vis-a-vis nursing the child is somewhat outside of the norm for an American mother, there is nothing intrinsically wrong with it. However, some questions do arise as to the need to immediately nurse after a short separation, and to A.'s reaction at having been "discovered" nursing-that is to pull his mother's shirt over his face. When discussing her marital history, Mrs. XX suggested that it was her husband who constantly insisted that she nurse the child. With regard to her more recent nursing practices, Mrs. XX suggests that A. will demand to nurse after having been separated from her. Although from this examiner's point of view, Mrs. XX is in control of the nursing, in her conversations about the practice, she deflected responsibility to the son and father. According to Mrs. XX she has begun weaning the child, and they now sleep in separate bedrooms instead of "co-sleeping" as had been their habit. The examiner observed that A. had his own room and bed. Mrs. XX said she lies down with the child at night to help him get to sleep, but that they now sleep in separate beds.

Outside of the nursing question, Mrs. XX relates to A. in a caring, child-centered, positive manner. Her communication with him is quite good, helping him to understand his world and develop excellent language skills and good concepts. She organizes her day around the boy, arranging for both fun and educational activities for him. She has enrolled him in a parent-tot program so that socialization can occur, and her home is filled with many toys, books and children's activities which are appropriate for the child. A. seems to feel free to explore his world with her guidance, and he easily separated from her for a relatively long period of time to talk with the examiner in the office. In sum, their relationship appears to be positive, nurturing, child-centered and appropriate.

This examiner also observed A. with his father. Mr. XX's parenting style is quite different from that of his wife. Mr. XX provides A. with opportunities to exercise gross motor skill development, even in his home where such play would ordinarily be discouraged. A. is allowed to kick and bat a ball, and Mr. XX is quite relaxed about possible damage resulting from such activities. During an office visit, Mr. XX was equally skilled at playing more quietly with A., taking opportunities to teach him colors and counting. They enjoy their time with one another, and the interactions were characterized by joy, laughter and closeness.

A. is comfortable with either parent, seeking proximity to them both. He seems to be developing appropriately, and no undue anxiety at short separations was noticed, nor did A. express discomfort with either parent.

While the parents seem equally skilled in relating to the child, their ability to communicate and cooperate with one another is much less positive. Mr. XX views his wife as relating to him in a passive-aggressive style, interfering with his parenting time by not having the child ready on time, and he is quite concerned as a result of her recent allegation of sexual abuse of the child. Mrs. XX sees her husband as control oriented and hot tempered. She cited recent examples of his coming to her house and screaming at her because A. was not ready. Her view was that A. had been ill, and she allowed him to sleep until his father came not in an attempt to frustrate the father's visits, but for the comfort of the child. Because Mr. XX was unable to calm down and talk rationally to her regarding the care of A. during his illness, she summoned the police to mediate. She felt this was very unfortunate for A., but necessary because Mr. XX must understand he cannot scream and yell at her in the child's presence either. Regarding this situation, Mr. XX maintained that his wife exaggerated or fabricated events in order to summon the police.

Child's Adjustment to the Home, School and Community

A. appears to be well-adjusted in the parents' homes. As observed, each has appropriate toys, and books, and each involves A. in fun and educational activities which promote his happiness and development. A. is too young to be in the community without his parents or another responsible adult. The teacher from his day care reports that when A. began attending the program in the Fall of 2000, he was very wary of joining the group, staying close to his mother and wanting to remain on the periphery. Gradually A. gained confidence and blossomed. He now readily enters into play with other children. He and several other children in the program will sometimes attempt to control the makeup of the group, saying who can play and who cannot, so the group leaders are working with the group to understand inclusiveness. A. still wants his mother close by when he first enters the group, and he sits near her when snacks are served. But he will sit with other children at story time and will play independently of her. A. has come along beautifully and seems happy when he is at the WWW School. Ms. C has never had any contact with Mr. XX.

Mental and Physical Health of All Parties

A. appears free from mental health problems at this time. He is neither overly fearful nor overly aggressive. He can separate from either parent without undue anxiety or distress. His language and concept development seem slightly above average, and gross and fine motor skills were unremarkable for his age. A.'s pediatrician reported that she first saw A. in November of 1997. At that time both parents came to the office. They were in agreement that A. not be inoculated as this was viewed as unnatural." While Dr. F honored their decision, she has suggested inoculations almost every time A. has come in for appointments since. At present, A. has had no immunization shots. After the separation, Mr. XX called to inquire if his wife's nursing a 3 year old child was all right. Dr. F said this was all right. A. has had no unusual illnesses or injuries, although he was treated for a head injury in December of 1999, and a laceration on his toe in June of 1999. These were not serious injuries. A. appears to be healthy and doing well.

Mr. XX is in robust physical health. He has previously seen a therapist, Dr. M F, from January to March of 1999. Dr. F reports that she originally saw Mrs. XX years before the couple married. In late 1998, Mrs. XX called asking for help in dealing with Mr. XX. Dr. F. saw her several times. He was not as committed to making the marriage work as would have been realistic to keep the couple together. He did not want to work with Mrs. XX After that she saw Mrs. XX a few times who wanted to know if she was "fixing" Mr. XX. Dr. F said she was not. She then referred them for couples work.

Test results for Mr. XX reveal a somewhat defensive presentation. He appears to be an individual who may feel he is getting a raw deal from life. He tends to blame others for his problems, and may be suspicious, guarded and resentful. There are also certain narcissistic features to his personality including a sense of entitlement and self-focus. Underlying this self-aggrandizement are feelings of poor self-worth which may either be an indication that he is undergoing a critical review of his personality style, or may indicate some problems in his identity. Social skills may be lacking. On a more positive note, he seems to be a logical thinker with good reality testing. He is easily able to grasp complex concepts and probably has high educational achievement.

Mrs. XX has been previously diagnosed with Tourette Syndrome as the result of bodily tics experienced in childhood. While she took medication for this illness in the past, she has currently weaned herself from these medications and does not experience problems with tics. She reports her current health as very good. Test results for Mrs. XX suggest she may be experiencing depression or some other affective disorder. This results in her imbuing otherwise pleasant events as ambiguous or negative. In the main her thinking is sophisticated, but overly complex in that she may make big productions of small matters. She seems to be a highly individualistic, non-conforming individual who is socially isolated and has difficulties with feelings.

This examiner spoke to Mrs. XX's therapist, Dr. P. He said that Mrs. XX viewed her husband as controlling and domineering throughout the marriage. She remained dependent and adapted to his style until A. was born and she began refusing to comply with his demands. This made him furious and this is when the trouble began. At present Dr. P sees Mrs. XX weekly helping her to establish her identity in the world. He views her as having a "submerged personality," and there work together is helping her to take an assertive stance regarding what she wants. At present Mrs. XX is somewhat socially isolated, and this is another issue being addressed in treatment. Dr. P also saw Mr. XX in marriage therapy. Mr. XX was verbally abusive, complaining that he had to adjust to his wife's lifestyle in order to work out the marriage. Dr. P tried to help them work out preferences, but by the time he saw them, Mr. XX had stopped working on the marriage.

Violence or the Threat of Violence

Mrs. XX believes that her husband is an abusive individual, citing verbal and psychological abuse toward her while they were married. She has made one allegation of sexual abuse of a physically harmful nature during the course of this evaluation, and she has summoned the police on several occasions during transitions. This examiner could only corroborate Mrs. XX's claims that her husband is verbally abusive through Dr. P, her personal therapist. As a result, this examiner cannot determine the veracity of her claims.

With reference to the sexual abuse allegation, this examiner spoke to the attending physician and the psychiatric intern. The physician, Dr. L, said that there was no physical evidence of any type of abuse of A., and certainly no evidence of sexual abuse. Dr. B, the psychiatric intern, said that Mrs. XX left the emergency room with A. prior to being discharged. He said that he only had minimal conversation with A. who said that his bottom had been touched by a candle with no other elaboration. The child would not answer questions as to whether his pants were on or off. Because Mrs. XX left the emergency room, Dr. B was unable to complete the usual protocol used in such cases.

Allegations of sexual abuse are quite potent, often, as in this case, curtailing visitation between the child and the accused. In this case, this examiner is inclined to believe that Mrs. XX's negative view and perhaps personal experiences with the father colored her perspective of what A. told her. She questioned the boy several times, probably "alerting" him that something was wrong. She said that "friends" persuaded her to call DCFS, pointing out to her that she had to protect A.. This was apparently bad advice. Instead of listening to friends, in the future it would be to her advantage to check out her concerns with her therapist or some other, more objective and knowledgeable party before taking drastic measures.

Willingness and Ability of Each Parent to Promote a Positive Relationship Between the Child and the Other Parent

Mrs. XX seems to be a person of extremes. When she and Mr. XX first met, she became completely absorbed in this relationship, refusing even to shower without Mr. XX. As she attempted to change her life, she embraced an alternate life style with the same fervor. When A. was born, her whole world became the child. But in any case, she seems to have been isolated from others for various reasons, depending upon what consumed her at the moment. During the years of their marriage, Mr. XX admits to having been completely apprised of his wife's selected change of lifestyle, and fully supportive of it, even though it may not have been his preference. The paternal grandparents report that when they attempted to question their son about his wife's choices, he supported her and told them it was between his wife and him.

Her chosen lifestyle is mother and child-centered. This has not changed since prior to A.'s birth, and is no "news" to Mr. XX. However, the way in which this played out has caused him to re-evaluate what this means for him as A.'s father. Where he once supported her and defended her decisions to others, he now looks at her choices in a different light and is critical of what she does vis-a-vis the child. While this is certainly understandable, this lifestyle was a decision they originally both made and to which they both agreed.

While it is quite clear both of these parents love their child, their parenting practices are now at times at odds with one another. This does not seem to be a source of confusion for A., as Mr. XX still adheres to the dietary restrictions Mrs. XX imposed. The child seems to have adjusted to his parents' different way of handling situations, and he seems to be developing properly. Mrs. XX remains very protective of A., and may be inclined to misinterpret what is different about Mr. XX's parenting in a negative light. She further seems to overlay things related to A. with her own, somewhat negative feelings about Mr. XX. Mr. XX, on the other hand, views the results of her lifestyle decisions as particularly directed at him and at interfering with his relationship to his son. Although his view may be accurate, the impetus for following this lifestyle probably was not as a means to eliminate his input or involvement.

As a result of their varying points of view, problems in communication with one another arise with some regularity. Mrs. XX has summoned the police during transfers. This is probably quite distressing for A.. She claims that it is important for Mr. XX to learn that he can no longer berate her in her own home or in front of the child. Mr. XX views her actions as "trumped up" and frivolous. There is probably some element of truth in either point of view, but this examiner has no means to discern which parent, if either, is giving a more reasonable account.

The allegation of sexual abuse was probably the most extreme example of Mrs. XX's zealous adherence to a set of attitudes about herself, her son and their relationship. It does not appear that A. was sexually abused by his father, according to medical and psychological examination. Mrs. XX maintains that because of the closeness she has to A., she is exquisitely sensitive to his communication and expression, and she has concluded that A. is in some danger with his father. There is no objective evidence to support this claim. An equally plausible explanation is that Mrs. XX's boundaries with A. have been blurred in her mind, so that she attributes to him feelings of apprehension, threat and danger that come from her own experiences and interpretations of events. While her therapist says that they are working on Mrs. XX's assertiveness in treatment, it may be that what is also required is some balance between self-reliance/self-sufficiency and actions that are well reasoned and reasonable, at least when these actions have consequences for A. and his father. As the primary parent in a divorce situation, such balance will be essential. Mrs. XX should be aware that any other allegations rashly made may cause the Court to reconsider the advisability of her being the primary parent.

Recommendations

Both parents love A. and provide a proper home environment, appropriate toys, books, games and activities, and attempt to give him a structured routine so that he can feel safe, comfortable and happy.

The parents' customs and ways of life differ radically from one another with considerable distress resulting in this clash of values. However, A. does not seem to suffer from the difference, and may benefit from being the recipient of both points of view. Mr. XX seems amenable to adhering to his wife's dietary restrictions for the child, and A. appears to be a healthy and happy youngster. By design, necessity or choice, Mrs. XX has been his primary care provider since his birth. While Mr. XX told this examiner that he wanted to be considered for sole custody, to this examiner's knowledge, he has not filed a Petition in that regard.

What this examiner has on hand from him is a Petition for Dissolution of Marriage wherein Mr. XX requests joint custody. This examiner does not view this couple as good candidates for joint custody because they are unable to work with one another in a civil, businesslike manner. At least once, and probably twice during transitions, the police were summoned to mediate disputes between the parties. Both parents view one another as in some ways dangerous or peculiar to the detriment of the child. These feelings probably stem from as yet unresolved issues from their marriage; nevertheless, their attitudes regarding one another, and their resulting behaviors do not allow them to coparent in any reasonable manner. Therefore, this examiner respectfully recommends to the Court that Mrs. XX be considered as the sole custodian and primary residential parent of the minor child, A.

With respect to visitation, A. is at an age where regular visitation with his father could occur. As a result, this examiner respectfully recommends that the Court award Mr. XX overnight, unsupervised visitation with A. every other weekend and one weekday visit each week from after work until 6:30 PM. In the summer, Mr. XX should enjoy two non-consecutive weeks of vacation with A.. Mr. XX should have visitation with A. on Father's Day, his birthday and A.'s birthday from 10:00 AM on a weekend or from after work on a workday until 6:30 PM, unless these days fall on his regularly scheduled weekend. Mrs. XX should have visitation with A. on Mother's Day, her birthday and A.'s birthday for a four to six hour period when these dates occur during Mr. XX's scheduled visitation. Other holidays should be equally divided between the parents on a yearly rotating schedule. Mr. XX should enjoy Christmas eve, Christmas day and Easter Sunday with A., and Mrs. XX should enjoy Rosh Hashana and Yom Kippur with A., regardless of other visitation schedules. When A. reaches school age, longer vacation periods in winter and spring should be divided equally between the parents.

Despite the awarding of sole custody to Mrs. XX, the parents should consult with one another regarding medical and educational decisions for the child, and they should work with their chosen pediatrician to insure that they make appropriate health care decisions for him.

Both parents should inform the other if they intend to take A. away from their home for any overnight period during their times with him, giving an itinerary and telephone numbers so that daily telephone contact can occur. Summer visitation should be negotiated each year prior to June 1st.

The parents should each respect one another's lifestyle and values, allowing A. to learn what is necessary from the viewpoint each parent has to offer. Irrespective of their own feelings, they will need to work together to make transitions comfortable and stress-free for the child.

Submitted by:

Terry K. Stevenson, Ph.D.
2-5-01

Index

INDEX